D1613023

A TWENTIETH-CENTURY CRUSADE

Library of Congress Cataloging-in-Publication Data

Names: Chamedes, Giuliana, author.
Title: A twentieth-century crusade : the Vatican's battle to remake
Christian Europe / Giuliana Chamedes.
Description: Cambridge, Massachusetts : Harvard University Press, 2019. |
Includes bibliographical references and index.
Identifiers: LCCN 2018044176 | ISBN 9780674983427 (hardcover : alk. paper)
Subjects: LCSH: Papacy—Political aspects—History—20th century. | Catholic
Church—Political activity—Europe—History—20th century. | Catholic
Church—Foreign relations—Europe. | Christianity and politics—Catholic
Church—History—20th century. | Europe—Politics and government—20th
century. | Europe—Foreign relations—Catholic Church. | Vatican
City—Politics and government—20th century.
Classification: LCC BX957 .C43 2019 | DDC 327.456/3404—dc23
LC record available at https://lccn.loc.gov/2018044176

A TWENTIETH-CENTURY CRUSADE

THE VATICAN'S BATTLE TO REMAKE CHRISTIAN EUROPE

GIULIANA CHAMEDES

 Harvard University Press

Cambridge, Massachusetts · London, England   2019

The well-known is such because

it is well-known, not known

—G. W. F. HEGEL

Contents

Introduction

On the Brink of a New Era

IT WAS LATE May when an elegant Roman cleric stepped into a specially outfitted car of the Italian state railway. He was embarking on his first major diplomatic assignment. As the train rattled through northern Italy, the Swiss Alps, and southern Germany, the official prayed to the Virgin Mary and rehearsed his planned first speech (he abhorred speaking from written notes). On May 25, 1917, the train ground to a halt in Munich. A crowd was jostling at the station, eager to welcome Bavaria's new papal ambassador, Eugenio Pacelli. For a few hours on this springtime day, the mood in the heart of Catholic Germany was jubilant. But the festive atmosphere did little to mask the fact that the ambassador had arrived in dark times. More than a million and a half German soldiers had already been killed in the ongoing Great War, and the streets of Munich were crowded with widows, fatherless children, and injured veterans.

Eugenio Pacelli (later to become Pope Pius XII) wasted no time in explaining to the city's residents and rulers why he was there. Since the late nineteenth century, the fate of the Catholic Church lay in the balance. The unification of Italy had challenged the pope's status as a sovereign ruler and torn apart the Papal States, the vast swath of land in central Italy that had been controlled by the pope for centuries.

1

Next came the pan-European culture wars, spearheaded by liberals and socialists who professed false gods or no gods at all. Through the letter of the law and the spawning of mass social movements, liberals and socialists had sought to transform the continent. They had challenged the notion that Church and state must work together to guarantee the spiritual flourishing of individuals, on earth and as a means to guarantee their salvation after death. They had passed new legislation separating Church and state and decreasing the Church's rights to intervene in public life. Taking advantage of new communication and transportation technologies, they had built transnational links, gathering their followers regularly in international party conferences, legal institutes, and underground secret societies.

When in July 1914 the Great War exploded, Pacelli saw the event as a warning of what might happen when populations turn away from divine teachings and stop respecting the mission of the Roman Catholic Church. Pacelli and other papal officials were not sure that Europeans would heed the warning. For although the Great War had started as a European affair, in April 1917 the United States had joined the fray. As papal diplomats saw things, this decision was part of a plan to further diminish the power of the Catholic Church in Europe, and to buoy secular, liberal, and Freemason movements instead. When Wilson formally announced his plan to join the Great War so as to make the world "safe for democracy," officials like Pacelli expressed their unease.[1] The catchphrase, they feared, betrayed the American president's true aim: preparing the ground for an anticlerical upsurge. As Pacelli saw it, the Americans were following a carefully scripted plan based on "meddling in matters European" and transforming the identity of the continent for good.[2] Their real goal was to seize the opportunity to capture Europe and "Americanize the whole world, making it Freemason so as to liberate it from its servitude to the Kaiser, the pope, and the priesthood."[3]

World War I was a moment of great awakening for the papacy. The United States' entry into the war, and the concern that a fully secular Europe was in the making, motivated the pope to shift from defense to offense. In the nineteenth century, the pope had focused on combating liberalism and socialism through strong admonitions, condemning the ideologies as two sides of the same coin. During the Great War, the reigning pope, Benedict XV, changed tack, casting the Vatican as a statelike institution capable of providing a real-world solution to the European crisis. The Holy See, the pope announced at the height of the conflict, had a peace settlement of its own—one that would reorder European international society and permanently keep in check both liberals and socialists. This peace plan called for the overturning of secular visions of world order, and rested on the re-Christianization of European states via the embrace of national self-determination and international law.

As the pope adopted this novel approach, he asked his papal ambassadors to foreign states (known as nuncios) to lead the charge. Like Pacelli, they traveled by train and ship at the height of one of the most murderous wars in European history. Their task was to promote the papacy and provide Europe's rulers with concrete ways to oppose liberal and socialist movements. To advance these aims, the diplomats were asked to put an old piece of papal diplomacy to new uses. That old-and-new tool was the concordat, a bilateral treaty that would bind the Church and the nation-state together under international law. Concordats would provide legitimacy to emerging political leaders and help newly constituted nation-states firm up their claims to territorial sovereignty, by making diocesan lines coincide with desired national boundaries. The legal agreements would also provide new leaders with a way to oppose the influence of liberalism and the rise of left-wing revolution. In exchange, these treaties would greatly expand the Vatican's control over everything from education to family law, from press freedom to the organization of local churches. By making religious instruction in public schools mandatory, giving the Church jurisdiction over a range of civil-law matters, and increasing monies funneled from the state to the Church, the treaties spelled out relationships of tight Church–state collaboration. The papal use of law thus aimed to be, borrowing from Clifford Geertz's phrasing, "constructive of social realities rather than merely reflective of them."[4]

Though the pope's treaty diplomacy enjoyed a great deal of success, first in Eastern Europe and then in Central and Western Europe, the pope soon realized that he could not win back Europe through legal arrangements alone. Signing treaties was a top-down affair—something diplomats were in the business of doing over the heads of everyday citizens, and without consulting them for approval. Simply compelling Europe's citizens to follow a new set of legal constraints would not be sufficient shelter from the tidal wave of liberal and socialist internationalism that was mobilizing the masses. Thus, immediately after World War I, the Vatican decided to invest, as never before, in civil society's institutions and practices. In ways few scholars have noted, it created, expanded, and centralized youth organizations. It invented new groups and communication networks for Catholic factory workers and farmhands. And it ensured that lay activism would be regularly monitored and surveilled by parish priests, bishops, and the Holy See itself.

But despite the Vatican's best efforts, secular movements continued to gain ground. In November 1917, a few months after Eugenio Pacelli's arrival in Munich, the Bolsheviks seized power in Russia, inaugurating a new stage of the Russian Revolution. In a matter of weeks, left-wing radicals farther west led uprisings of their own—in Vienna, Budapest, Milan, and Munich. On the European continent, the short-lived insurrections were violently suppressed. But in 1919, Russian revolutionaries and their European comrades founded the Communist International, or Comintern, announcing that a new and more powerful wave of uprisings was imminent. An ambitious experiment in border-crossing mobilization, the International lifted Moscow's profile, making the Bolshevik capital the reference point for transnational revolutionary movements. By the 1920s the Comintern was widely recognized as an important hub for consciousness formation and leadership development. Gradually it became a true internationalist force, starting activities not only in Eastern and Western Europe, but in non-Western countries struggling to free themselves from imperial rule. As a cultural and diplomatic project, the International was bent on both increasing interpersonal connections among communist sympathizers and forging a shared praxis of struggle against communism's manifold enemies. Its existence constituted an assault on traditional pathways to political power, sending the message that anyone, anywhere, could capture the state, so long as they had ideological commitment and a bit of international training. It also posed a direct challenge to Catholic transnational activism, precisely in those years when the papacy was engaging in its own civil society revolution.

The papacy began to see communism as a real threat, and read its success as a direct result of the shortcomings and mistakes of the Paris peace settlement that had brought World War I to a close. A new generation of right-wing ethno-nationalists—active in Poland, Germany, Austria, Italy, and Spain—agreed. They condemned the League of Nations and the Comintern in the same breath, leaning on repurposed anti-liberal and anti-Semitic motifs. In the 1930s the papacy, in dialogue with these groups and terrified by the Comintern, launched a far-reaching anticommunist campaign. The little-studied campaign was a historic first for the Church. The Vatican's response to liberalism was primarily legal and diplomatic in nature, but its response to communism, which emerged from the battle against liberalism, was an ambitious cultural crusade carried forward by newly formed Catholic grassroots organizations, mass media instruments, and specially dedicated papal institutions. Its aim was to enlist the masses and send the message that communism was the earthly face of Satan himself.[5]

The pope called the new movement a Catholic International to underscore his confrontation with the Comintern. The Catholic International would become the largest and most ambitious experiment in cross-border anticommunist mobilization prior to the Cold War. By embracing new media, the pope's anticommunist movement helped globalize and normalize new communication technologies. It also created new transnational communities of belonging, forging a shared vision of what it meant to be Catholic in the twentieth century. However, the pope's International also erected boundaries between and within European states. By calling for the expulsion of communists from the body politic, the papal crusade sanctioned discrimination and violence, even as it freely referenced a range of racist credos (including the anti-Semitic myth of Judeo-Bolshevism) and did little to curb the rise of right-wing extremism. The new movement defined a common internationalist identity for European Christians living in uncertain times, but it also bound that identity to a rigid distinction between anticommunist Christian friend and communist atheistic foe.

Through its legal and cultural activism, the papacy invented a new form of internationalism in twentieth-century Europe—one that aimed to rival liberal and socialist competitors. "Catholic internationalism," in this book, is defined at once as a set of practices (crossing borders, forging connections), as a way of seeing the world, and as a vision for the future. Its claims dovetailed well with the Church's longtime espousal of universalism, though Catholic internationalism was, it bears emphasizing, a distinctly modern creation. Born at the height of World War I, its purpose was to use new and technologically advanced means to centralize power and glue members to Rome, even as it provided an infrastructure for increased sociability within national bounds. As one of the pope's flagship journals announced, the pope was the heart of the undertaking—"If Moscow's Comintern is at the head of the Communist International, [then] Rome is the center of the Catholic International!"[6] Participant observers concurred that the Catholic Church had "achieved an internationality beyond the wildest dreams of socialists or cosmopolitan theorists," and that Rome had become "the seat of the mightiest *Internationale* the world has ever seen."[7]

The Catholic International was active in a booming age of border-crossing internationalism—the age not just of the Comintern, but of the Anarchist International, the Labor and Socialist International, the International Labor Organization, the International Secretariat of Christian-Inspired Democratic Parties, and the League of Nations. Anticolonial internationalism was a significant force as well. So were a variety of non-Catholic forms of religious internationalism, insofar as European Protestants, Muslims, and Jews were also experimenting with new forms of transnational exchange after World War I. Indeed, internationalism as an ideal and a practice was an essential—not accidental—feature of Europe's short twentieth century. The years after World War I were characterized by an accelerating dialectic of warring international movements, each hoping to gain followers and attention in an increasingly crowded public sphere. Through the use of new media, new forms of grassroots activism, and new legal practices and institutions, these movements were able to create like-minded communities that extended across national borders. They directly informed European peace and war-making practices. They shaped interpersonal relations and state-to-state diplomacy.

We now know more than ever before about the liberal dreamers and hardened imperialists who built the League of Nations and its successor, the United Nations; about the pathways that connected anarchists from Madrid to Montevideo and Buenos Aires; about the successes (and failures) of the Communist International and the Communist Information Bureau (Cominform) in building international solidarity; and about the blinkered limits of European internationalism compared to its pan-Asian and pan-African counterparts. However, these well-studied manifestations of internationalism risk distorting our understanding of the past century. In the 1920s and subsequently, as internationalisms of various stripes vied for attention, the story was not just one of Wilson versus Lenin, imperialism versus anticolonialism, and liberal democracy versus Fascism. The papacy was an extremely important player as well, and was regarded as such by contemporaries. In ways that few scholars have studied, the Vatican's work helped foreground a new comprehensive understanding of the international order, even as it consolidated the ideal and reality of the nation-state—one people, one land, one culture—as a central component of that order.

The Catholic International did not lose the battle with "modernity." Instead, in ways that shake up textbook understandings of the rise of secularism in the nineteenth and twentieth centuries, Catholic internationalists actively militated against the separation between public and private spheres and successfully de-privatized religion.[8] Additionally, Catholic internationalism far outlasted many rival movements of the interwar years. It played a crucial role in the Christian Democratic revolution after World War II and in the launching of the early Cold War. It helped popularize new enemy discourses and bolster insurgent political forces. And though Catholic internationalism was largely repudiated in the 1960s, it found new defenders in the last quarter of the twentieth century. In fact, even as the papacy begrudgingly and belatedly accepted the separation of Church and state, it continued to call for the de-privatization of religion. During a recent period stretching from the papacy of John Paul II through that of Benedict XVI, Catholic internationalism returned to the fore, as did the Church's crusade to influence European policy, law, and society.

✦

The time has come for scholars to bring the Vatican from the margins to the center of the history of the twentieth century. In the wake of

9 / 11 and the glaring eruption of religious politics on the world scene, growing numbers of scholars have taken the "religious turn." They have challenged the idea that the experience of Europe's twentieth century was defined by the rise of secularism and the decline of religion.[9] They have investigated how religious organizations shaped everyday practices and norms pertaining to everything from birth control to disease prevention, and from relations between metropole and colony to relations between parents and children. Early pioneering work looked at the role of religious forces in helping to consolidate European party politics in the late nineteenth century and at the survival and expansion of "antimodern" practices like pilgrimage and saint veneration.[10] More recently, a flurry of new scholarship has begun investigating how Catholic intellectuals in countries like Poland, France, Austria, and Germany forged transnational connections in the years following the Great War. Scholars in this mold have highlighted how Catholic networks of information and exchange helped consolidate Christian Democratic parties and push forward plans for European integration. They have looked at how Catholics participated in (and resisted) anti-imperialist mobilizations in Asia and Africa. They have attended to the role played by Catholic youth and civil society organizations in transforming norms pertaining to gender, love, and sexuality. They have scrutinized the contributions of Catholic individuals to new discourses like human rights and intellectual movements like humanism.[11] Important research has also recast our understanding of how Protestant, Muslim, and Jewish religious communities shaped major political movements and intellectual trends in the twentieth century.[12] However, the study of the central government of the Roman Catholic Church remains isolated from broader trends. To date, few scholars have sought to bring the Vatican fully within the study of European history, showing how the papacy was not locked in monastic isolation but instead was responding to (and in some cases, anticipating) Europe-wide trends. Few have probed how the Vatican advanced a surprisingly successful international agenda after World War I, or shown how Fascism, communism, socialism, and liberalism engaged with the Vatican's vision for international society, as these movements clashed, jockeyed for influence, and defined themselves against the papacy and in dialogue with it.[13]

☼

The focus of this book is on the Vatican: how it saw the world, and how it shaped the world around it. The term "Vatican" demands some definition. Originally used as an adjective in classical Latin to refer to a hill in Rome across from the Tiber river, the term picked up usage in the ninth century when Pope Leo IV included Vatican hill within the limits of the city of Rome. Starting from the fourteenth century, the Holy See moved its headquarters to this hill. However, it was not until after the 1870s that the word "Vatican" started being used as a synonym for the papacy itself. This change was inaugurated by the papacy's decision to withdraw almost entirely to the Vatican palaces atop the hill as a result of the Italian wars of unification. Ironically, Pius IX's famous announcement that Italy had rendered the pope a "prisoner of the Vatican"—a phrase he used to emphasize the papacy's weakness—helped consolidate the term "Vatican" as a synonym for papal power and authority.

In keeping with standard current usage, the terms "Vatican," "Holy See," and "papacy" are used interchangeably in this book, to reference the central government of the Roman Catholic Church, composed of the body of congregations, tribunals, and offices through which the pope governs. In the period under exploration, the key decision-making bodies within the Vatican included the Secretariat of State, the leading governing bureaucracy of the Catholic Church, which was charged with performing all political and diplomatic functions of the Holy See; the Congregation for Extraordinary Ecclesiastical Affairs, comparable to the pope's Foreign Ministry; and the Holy Office, responsible for policing doctrine and issuing statements on matters of the faith. Though legally the pope was at the head of this vast decision-making body, he was neither alone in making decisions nor, in many cases, the ultimate authority on any given matter. Furthermore, because popes occupy their office for life, it was customary that as the leader's health diminished, matters were delegated to his Secretary of State. It was often the case that even though the pope was still nominally the head of the Roman Catholic Church, true power lay elsewhere.

The terms "Vatican," "Holy See," and "papacy" are not shorthand for Catholicism writ large. To be sure, the papacy sought to represent global Catholicism and, particularly from the late nineteenth century on, hoped that whenever individuals thought of the faith, they thought of the pope and his dictates. The centralization of ecclesiastical power in the person of the pope was part of this story; from the First Vatican Council of 1870, the pope claimed infallibility, and starting with the 1917 Code of Canon Law, the pope alone was vested with the authority to appoint or remove bishops anywhere in the Roman Catholic Church. This vastly expanded the pope's powers, while also increasing frictions with members of the upper hierarchy across the Catholic world who had traditionally seen themselves as rather independent from papal influence and oversight.

But despite the papacy's multiform attempts to centralize and police Catholic lay activism, Catholics in the nineteenth and twentieth centuries were not exclusively beholden to the institutional Church. After all, to count as "Catholics," individuals only needed to agree to a limited number of theological dogmas and participate in the sacraments. Most Catholics experienced Catholicism as a devotional and deeply personal practice, one that grounded them in cultural and family traditions and connected them to other members of their local community. It was not the case that all roads necessarily led to Rome, or passed, perforce, through it. Indeed, everyday Catholics were often drawn to leave their towns as pilgrims for any number of devotional sites across Europe, including Einsiedeln in Switzerland, Fatima in Portugal, Lourdes in France, and Jasna Góra in the Polish town of Częstochowa. National Church hierarchies also resisted papal control and, in certain contexts, exercised authority and raised funds without seeking the pope's preapproval. Neither did Catholic intellectuals see themselves as exclusively bound to Rome. For as growing numbers of highly literate Catholics founded literary and political journals and traveled outside their native towns and cities, they tightened their connections across boundaries and created webs of belonging that often bypassed Rome, stretching instead from Warsaw to Paris, Vienna to Berlin, Brussels to Toronto.

Nonetheless, one theme remained constant in the Catholic experience, up through at least the mid 1950s: the pope mattered. To be sure, Catholics did not always agree with what the Bishop of Rome had to say, but they were well-informed of the pope's key positions on a range of different political, social, and theological issues. Thanks to the rise of literacy, the expansion of centralized forms of Catholic associational culture, and the birth of media like Vatican Radio, lay Catholics were kept in the loop about the pope's view of the world. With the 1920s founding of institutions expressly dedicated to boosting internationalism, policing the faith's boundaries, and silencing dissidents within, the papacy's capacity to control a global Catholic message increased. There were always rebels and freethinkers, but even they worked out what Catholicism meant by dialoguing and arguing with the messages the Vatican was disseminating. They did not elaborate their opposition to papal hegemony in a vacuum.

The need to dialogue with the papacy was underscored by the fact that throughout the period under analysis, the papacy was professing not just a set of beliefs about the "world beyond," but a way of viewing and understanding the present. Popes of these years regularly referenced Augustine of Hippo, who had famously theorized that the city of man was intimately connected to the city of God. As a result, papal teachings were not exclusively about transcendent matters but also instructed on how to be citizens-in-the-world. For the pope, everything from how to treat one's spouse to the legal right to private property was a matter of concern. Theologically and historically, the link between religion and governance, or religion and politics, was well entrenched, as was the idea that the pope had a special role to play in addressing world crises and offering solutions.

This book charts the little-known story of how a novel mode of papal activism took shape with the First World War, when the Vatican invented an aggressive new diplomatic strategy to protect itself and promote Catholicism in the modern era. The changes inaugurated by World War I are essential to understanding the papacy's marriage of convenience with authoritarian and Fascist forces in the interwar years. Attention to the 1920s and 1930s also illuminates the 1940s and 1950s, insofar as the postwar ideas, practices, and beliefs of many Christian Democratic politicians in these decades were of interwar vintage, and heavily influenced both by the papacy's anticommunist crusade and its anti-liberal revolution. As Christian Democratic parties swept the polls, they demonstrated that a brand of Catholic politics that actively militated against secularism had not only survived the war but would become a shaping element of postwar political culture. Catholic anti-Americanism also returned as a feature of European political life. In this way, this book shows that any deep understanding of the shape of the European order after 1945 depends on an analysis of the survival of interwar ideas and practices. These trans-war continuities have been noted by many scholars in recent years, who have argued that 1945 was not a "year zero" and that it may be more appropriate to apply new periodizations to this stretch of European history. I advance a similar argument, and underscore a point made by the historian Charles Maier, who noted that the interwar years were years "of morning as well as dusk," in that its innovations carried Western European societies "through a half-century transit."[14]

The 1960s are my endpoint because this decade marked a decisive caesura in papal diplomacy. The changes introduced by the Second Vatican Council began the work of upending the interwar papal crusade against communism and liberalism, while the sweeping social and cultural changes of these years did the rest of the work. For the first time in decades, the central government of the Catholic Church renounced the concordat project and began to question its investment in the nation-state as the linchpin of international order. At the same time, the pope tentatively apologized for the ethno-nationalism, anti-Semitism, and racism that its internationalist crusade had helped unleash. But this reorientation—important as it was—proved incomplete. Despite all the innovations of the 1960s, the Church struggled to provide a convincing answer to the burning question of what *should* constitute the proper relationship between Church and state. It eschewed the project of robustly defining a new vision for the international order. And it did not clearly delineate who, or what, were the Church's core enemies (if liberalism and communism no longer were). As a result of these shortcomings and the companion success of competing internationalist movements in mobilizing millions of Catholics in Europe, Church membership hemorrhaged. By the 1970s the number of practicing Catholics in Europe had dipped dramatically, and although papal activity certainly did not disappear, it had taken stock of this profound shift by jettisoning its interwar praxis and shifting its emphasis to other parts of the globe.

In geographic terms this book focuses on the European continent, for a simple reason: until the 1960s, the pope saw the European continent as the key to any sort of global Catholic transformation. For the first six decades of the twentieth century, Europe was the key locus of the papacy's work. The papacy's Eurocentrism in these years was similar to that of the vast majority of European political leaders, who first blindly accepted the idea of Western hegemony, and then, once that hegemony started coming under threat, defended it with their teeth. By looking at how the central government of the Roman Catholic Church—with all its praise of universalism—was narrowly interested in Europe, this book charts how midcentury Eurocentrism was buoyed by internationalist discourses, and how, despite the shockwaves of postwar decolonization, that Eurocentrism lived on well beyond its shelf life. Internationalism was thus a tool Europeans used to impose their vision on the world, while simultaneously bolstering and "saving" Western and European nation-states, propping them up at a moment when their fate seemed very much in question.[15]

The pope's foreign policy establishment was committed to Europe as a whole, but it was also convinced that some European countries were more important than others. In ways that scholars have failed to recognize, newly unified Poland played a critical role in the papal mindset, insofar as this Catholic-majority country was seen as a cultural and economic hub, and an important testing ground for new forms of diplomacy and legal activism. I also give Latvia and Lithuania more attention than they typically receive, for these two countries were laboratories for the new papal internationalism. Other places, like Bavaria and Italy, figure prominently because history and culture bound them so closely to the papal diplomatic corps that a story of how the Vatican set its priorities in the interwar years would be incomplete without some discussion of how individuals in these particular locales exercised influence and helped foster Bavarian-centric and Italo-centric understandings of world affairs. Spain demands our attention because of how it crystallized the tensions of papal diplomacy, in that the Spanish Civil War marked the first clear episode in which a minority of lay Catholics began openly contesting the implications of the papal anticommunist crusade—a challenge that would ultimately help undermine the bases of papal authority in the long term. The French Catholic Church—which, thanks to its strong independent tradition of Gallicanism, was more impermeable to papal influence—figures somewhat less prominently, although I do explore in detail French Catholic intellectuals, and their connections to Catholics both in Europe and in European imperial territories, for these figures pioneered an alternative form of Catholic internationalism that was critical of papal actions. Other European countries—such as Austria, Czechoslovakia, Yugoslavia, Portugal, Belgium, and Estonia—are brought in as a way to provide further exemplification of broader trends under way, such as the successes and failures of concordat diplomacy and the dénouement of the papal anticommunist campaign.

Historiographical concerns also shape the arguments found in the pages that follow. Though bookstores are exploding with polemical works on the relationship between Pius XII and the Holocaust, or Pius XI and Nazi Germany, few scholars have sought to situate the knotty question of the papacy's relationship to Fascism and Nazism within a broader context.[16] By taking a transnational perspective and attending to the complexity of the multiple governance organs of the Holy See, rather than focusing narrowly on the person of the pope or on Vatican-Italian or Vatican-German relations, this book provides some answers to enduring puzzles. It shows, for instance, that papal diplomacy first grew wings in Eastern Europe—not Western Europe. If we are to understand what precisely took shape in Germany or Italy, we must look to Eastern Europe first, to the Vatican's work in countries like Poland, Latvia, Lithuania, and Estonia. By showing the guiding importance of papal anti-liberalism and anticommunism, we see that the connections forged by the pope in the interwar years with Fascist and authoritarian rulers were not simply crafted out of necessity, to keep a dying Church alive, or as a result of some abstract preference for "authority" and "order."[17] Rather, these ties emerged because authoritarian and Fascist leaders promised to respect and implement both the papacy's legal revolution and its cultural anticommunist crusade—that is, to make common cause against the Church's two leading enemies.[18]

This book also aims to correct certain misconceptions about the broader aims and means of papal diplomacy. Papal internationalism, until the contested 1960s and 1970s, was about celebrating and promoting an alternative and uniquely Catholic international European order—one that was neither liberal nor communist (nor Protestant nor Jewish), and indeed that actively resisted alternative ways of seeing and of being. Against Wilson and Lenin, the papacy moved to establish friendships with nation-states that similarly sought to overturn the Paris peace settlement and eliminate the threat of communist revolution. After World War II, the papacy again lent its services to the project of erecting a wall of separation between imagined believers and presumed atheists, between Christianity's defenders and its enemies. Through the renewed legal internationalism of concordat diplomacy and the cultural reach of anticommunist mobilization, the Church sought to make its own vision for Europe an integral part of the post-1945 order. The divided Cold War Europe may have offended papal dreams of a united continent, but it also neatly embodied a separation of peoples and ideologies that the Vatican did little to challenge. Indeed, through the passage of a 1949 decree excommunicating not only all communists, but all those who dared dialogue with communism, the Church helped build a religious Iron Curtain even more impermeable than the political one. After World War I and after World War II, the Vatican's twentieth-century internationalism buttressed not-quite-inclusive European nation-states, as a means to protect Catholicism and stamp out its enemies.

In May 1917, as Bavarians flocked to hear Eugenio Pacelli's first speech in Munich, the papal diplomat was keenly aware that he stood on the brink of a new era. As he and the pope saw it, the Vatican's task in this new moment was to renounce a narrowly conceived spiritual mission and offer a detailed blueprint for rebuilding Europe along Catholic lines. Pacelli told Bavarians that they faced a stark decision. Would they join hands with the central government of the Roman Catholic Church and help "reconstruct human society on the solid ground of Christian justice [and] Christian law"? Or would they step aside and participate in the continent's capture by the Church's enemies?[19] Enmeshed as Bavaria's residents were in a solid cultural context of Catholicism as a way of life, we can imagine how poignant it must have been for them to hear Pacelli's words, knowing that he was speaking under the guidance of a figure whose mandate to rule came (they believed) from Christ himself. Children who had just completed their First Communion likely stood in awe of the gaunt and unsmiling nuncio, as did their devoted mothers, who rarely, if ever, had the opportunity to stand within arm's reach of a figure endowed with such otherworldly *gravitas*.

Pacelli was in action from the first day of his arrival in southern Germany. He was one of dozens of papal diplomats carrying the new gospel of concordat diplomacy across Europe, East and West. Would he and his fellow diplomats succeed? Over and against the real and imagined threat of competing internationalist ideologies, would they successfully shore up Catholicism and the Holy See? The following chapters investigate the papal response to the Paris peace process and how the papacy fared as it attempted to build its own postwar order and Catholicize European nation-states from within.

1

The Threat of a Secular Order

> The war of 1870 marked the disappearance of the Papal States and led
> the pope to the current disgraceful situation. But the vast majority of
> people throughout the world agree that the 1914/1915 Great War offers
> the opportunity for the pope to reclaim full freedom and independence.
>
> —MATTHIAS ERZBERGER, 1920

"THE INTERNATIONALISM OF THE pope is a constant menace for the
existence and the prosperity of the nation," an Italian Freemason announced in 1916, soon after his country's entry into the Great War. His
concern was with the papacy's close dealings with the German and
Habsburg empires—dealings that, he feared, would "sow trouble in the
conscience of the faithful."[1] Little did he know that the papacy would
soon embrace the invective "papal internationalism" as a term of honor.
In response to concerns of a secular peace settlement, the papacy would
spearhead a legal revolution that would foreground a new form of internationalism, as a way to advance Church interests and combat the
threat of liberalism and socialism through the letter of the law.

The pope's new strategy was defined in dialogue with the Central
Powers. As the Austro-Hungarian Empire came undone, the relationship with the German Empire came to assume an ever-growing importance for the Holy See. This was not least because of Germany's own
efforts, and its success in winning over the "wartime pope," Benedict
XV, who had been elected to the Throne of Saint Peter's just after the
start of hostilities. Born Giacomo Battista Della Chiesa, the Genoese

cleric had developed relationships with German politicians in the nine-teenth century when he helped negotiate a dispute between Germany and Spain over the Caroline islands.

Starting in 1915, a group of German Catholic politicians began to lean on this precedent and insistently court the Holy See. Germany was just one of a large number of powers that sought to win the pope's favor during the war. But while the pope responded to French, Italian, and British outreach efforts with suspicion, he welcomed German efforts. This was unsurprising. The Germans had a large number of diplomatic representatives at the Vatican and a close-knit relationship to the Jesuit headquarters in Rome. Additionally, German theologians had long been held in high regard in papal circles, and at this histor-ical juncture they were at the cutting edge of Vatican-approved intel-lectual work. Finally, the papacy was dominated by Italian clerics, and Germany had been Italy's ally for thirty years. It was regarded as a po-litical and cultural leader. Clergy were particularly impressed by the success of the German Church in facing its liberal and socialist chal-lengers through an explosion of lay activism and print journalism in the late nineteenth century. The success of the German Christian Democratic Center Party in curtailing the expansion of liberalism and socialism in the Reichstag was also hailed as an example of how Cath-olic politicians might band together to resist anticlericals who sought to separate Church and state.[2]

For these reasons, Pope Benedict XV and papal officials gave a warm reception to the German Catholic Center Party's leading politician, Matthias Erzberger, when he arrived in Rome. As the twentieth century's "most prominent Catholic German statesman before [Konrad] Adenauer," Erzberger had entered politics after a successful career in journalism and as a leader of Catholic lay institutions; in the 1890s he had been one of the founders of the Christian Trade Union movement, which had flourished despite the initial ridicule to which it was sub-jected by the Socialist Party. In 1903 Erzberger entered the Reichstag as its youngest member and helped buoy the party's success. Over-coming opposition from Socialists and Liberals, the Center Party held the presidency of the Reichstag from 1895 to 1906 and demonstrated to the papacy—and to the continent as a whole—that it was quite possible for a Catholic political movement to keep both socialism and liberalism in check.[3] Benedict XV was impressed; as he had noted during his time as archbishop of Bologna, socialists and liberals together forged a "tyranny of antireligious parties" that advanced a toxic strain of anticlericalism and exercised what, from the Church's point of view, was a "disastrous form of rule."[4] (In June and July of 1914, much to Della Chiesa's displeasure, the Socialist Party had captured the majority of seats in the administrative elections in the province of Bologna.)

During the Great War, Matthias Erzberger took advantage of his good reputation in Italy and made it a priority to strengthen ties with the Holy See. He maintained an active correspondence not just with the Apostolic Nunciature in Catholic-majority Bavaria, but also with high-ranking officials in Rome, including Rudolf Gerlach, the secret chamberlain and close confidant of Benedict XV. Erzberger was treated as an insider. When in February 1915 he made his first visit to Rome, he received the unusual grant of an audience by the pope within two days of his arrival. It would be the first of Erzberger's three visits to Rome in 1915 alone.[5]

The German diplomat used money and flattery to win over the pope. Within the year, he had successfully pushed the Deutsche Bank to begin regularly transferring funds intended for the Vatican to the Roman branch of a German bank (Nast-Kolb-Schumacher), and called upon European countries to follow Germany's example and provide the Holy See with a "starting fund" to the tune of 300 million Swiss francs. Erzberger loudly campaigned to restore the pope's territorial sovereignty. The politician became more adamant about this goal following Italy's decision to overturn its historic allegiance to the Triple Alliance and enter the war against Germany on May 24, 1915—a decision that was surprising and traumatic both for the pope and for the German Empire. From this point on, Erzberger asserted that the Roman Question was urgently in need of solution because Italy, in a situation of war, was unable to guarantee the Holy See's autonomy. Evidently the claim redounded in Germany's favor, neatly making the point that the Central Powers were Catholicism's best protector—an idea that Erzberger and fellow German Catholics had publicized since the start of the conflict.[6]

Erzberger ingratiated himself with the pope by working to internationalize the Roman Question. He did so via a large press campaign,

and through a German-sponsored "International Committee," dedicated to keeping alive the papacy's continued demand for territorial
sovereignty. He founded an international association for Christian international law with similar aims. These organizations announced that
should Italy fail to restore the territory it had seized from the pope in
1870, Germany would help broker the pope's transfer outside of Italy.
The locales proposed included Einsiedeln, a pilgrimage destination in
northeastern Switzerland; the medieval principality of Liechtenstein,
nestled between Austria and Switzerland; and, per the urgings of a
well-known German professor of international law, the sunny isles of
Mallorca and Menorca, off the coast of Spain.[7]

German and papal pressure on Italy was soon followed up by
German and papal pressure on the United States. Starting in the autumn of 1915, the Holy See agreed to work with Germany to press the
United States to stop providing arms and assistance to the Entente and
to promise to not join the war. As the Vatican Secretary of State Gasparri instructed the Apostolic Delegate in the United States, it was imperative to force the American president to embrace neutrality. "This
war is a crime against mankind, and it will last as long as the United
States sends arms, ammunition, and money" and continues to show
its "lack of neutrality" in supporting France, Russia, and Great Britain,
he noted.[8] A good two years prior to the United States' official entry
into the conflict, the Holy See saw the United States as a crucial factor
in the European war—and it called upon the United States to stay out
of European affairs. Papal concern about American foreign policy
moves was intertwined with a larger concern about the sort of international order the United States hoped to bring to Europe—an order
that, he feared, would be secular, democratic, and anti-Catholic. The
fact that Wilson was a devout Protestant only made things worse. Indeed, for the Vatican, any ideology that conflicted with its vision of
state Catholicism was problematic.[9]

Despite German and papal lobbying efforts, the United States' economic contribution to the Allied powers continued to increase, and in
April 1917 the American president formally announced that the time
had come for the United States to enter the European conflict. In an
eloquent speech before Congress, Wilson asked for a declaration of
war against Germany. Claiming that the German Empire directly

threatened the United States' core political values, Wilson asserted that "neutrality is no longer feasible or desirable." So as to stress that Germany's autocratic style of rule was out of step with the times, Wilson announced that "the world must be made safe for democracy."[10]

To our modern-day ears, promising to make the world safe for democracy might sound like innocent sloganeering. But to Eugenio Pacelli, papal officials, and Catholic conservatives, Wilson's phrase signaled that the American president was raising a revolutionary flag. They heard the phrase as proof that the president was entering the war in order to export American political values to the European continent.

By this historical juncture, the Holy See and many of its defenders had come to see the United States as an important source of the rise of anticlericalism and liberalism in late nineteenth-century Europe. Rome saw American-style liberalism as dangerous for its commitment to the separation of Church and state, liberty of conscience, and the idea of the social contract, which lodged sovereignty in "the people."[11] Fears were heightened because of the popularity in European circles of American Catholics who sought to marry liberalism and Catholicism. A key figure here was the priest and founder of the Paulist Fathers, Isaac Thomas Hecker, who famously argued that the time had come for Catholics to accept modernity, liberty, and Republicanism.[12] In 1885 the reigning pope, Leo XIII fired back. He called upon American clerics to work to build a closer relationship between the American Catholic Church and the state. "It would be very erroneous to draw the conclusion," the pope affirmed, "that . . . it would be universally lawful or expedient for State and Church to be, as in America, dissevered and divorced."[13] "Americanism," the pope noted in a subsequent document, was nothing less than a heresy "injurious to the Church and the spirit of God."[14] Though this condemnation was officially an attempt to bring back into line certain American clerics who were proposing nonstandard readings of the New Testament, Leo was also launching a far-reaching attack on American political culture. This culture, he believed, was cannibalizing the Roman Catholic Church in a bid to replace spiritualism with materialism and impose destabilizing American democratic norms on the hierarchical organization of the Roman Catholic Church.

When Woodrow Wilson announced that the United States was entering the Great War against the German and Austro-Hungarian

Empires, papal officials and mainstream Catholic newspapers and journals closely bound to the pope ratcheted up their attacks against the United States.[15] Eugenio Pacelli asserted that Wilson was engaged in "a tendentious attempt to mislead public opinion."[16] The official Vatican daily, the *Osservatore Romano*, ironically commented that "the man who preached peace now carries the mantle of war, and leads the world to take part in the horrors of the largest human carnage that old Europe has ever seen."[17]

Once the United States had joined the war, papal diplomats began meticulously compiling massive photography binders depicting Allied bombings of churches, which were presented as proof of the fundamentally antireligious and "profanatory" aims of the "liberal powers" under the United States' sway.[18] Regular consumers of Vatican publications in the Italian Chamber of Deputies argued that it was Italian liberals, buoyed by the United States' entry into the war, who had formally requested the papacy's absence from the peace conference at the end of the Great War, in the 1915 Treaty of London.[19] German Catholic politicians asserted that all should "look with skepticism upon the Wilsonian proposal" for a democratic Europe, "and judge its pacifying powers to be scant indeed." As Matthias Erzberger saw it, Wilson's plans for postwar Europe gave the lie to the American president's previous promise that the United States "has no desire to get mixed up in European matters."[20]

The fact that Wilson caught Catholics' attention in 1917–1918 was no accident. Starting in April 1917, Wilson's personal qualities were unceasingly praised by the Committee on Public Information, a U.S. government propaganda agency of the president's own making, which constituted the U.S. government's first serious initiative in the field of propaganda.[21] Additionally, President Wilson would embark on an 8,000-mile speaking tour around the United States in support of his vision for how to bring permanent peace to Europe. Wilson also hired a man who would soon be known as the father of public relations, Edward L. Bernays, to accompany him to the Paris Peace Conference and disseminate an image of Wilson as the emissary of American political values. In particular, Bernays paid a great deal of attention to the reception of Wilson in Italy—a country to which the papacy was, for evident reasons, well attuned.[22] Small wonder that the papacy came to judge Wilson as a larger-than-life presence in Europe. After all, that was precisely the aim of the propaganda campaigns that both preceded and followed the American president's visit to Paris.

The pope was not just concerned about the specter of a Wilsonian postwar order; he was also troubled by the fact that the socialists were until this point the leading movement identified with the cause of peace and disarmament. Thus, the pope decided that the time was right to move from a defensive to an offensive diplomatic strategy. No longer should the Holy See limit itself to protesting the dissolution of the Papal States or the rise of enemy ideologies: it should begin presenting itself as the maker of an alternative European order. Two manifestations of this shift were the release of an ambitious papal peace plan and the decision to turn an old instrument of papal diplomacy to new uses.

The Papal Peace Plan

In August 1917, the pope issued a seven-point papal peace plan. Its purpose was to present the Vatican as an international actor equipped with its own detailed solution to the European crisis. With the plan, the pope hoped to respond to the specter of a Wilsonian postwar settlement and to steal the fire of the socialists. The plan was developed in dialogue with German politicians. Even Emperor Kaiser Wilhelm II was brought in on the project prior to its release; he applauded and encouraged the papacy's work, noting that the initiative was a great idea, not least because it would help break the socialists' monopoly on the peace movement.[23]

The papal peace plan asserted that the time had come "for more concrete and practical proposals," and that the pope, as "the common father of the faithful," was ready to rise to the challenge, mediate peace negotiations, and bring the war to an end. Further, the pontiff's note proclaimed itself to be the basis "for a just and lasting peace."[24] The plan called for disarmament, freedom of the seas, and the renunciation of reparations. Occupied territories—including Belgium—must be restored to the status quo ante, and European powers must seek to settle rival territorial claims through international arbitration. The papal plan also protected the German Empire's integrity. It asserted that the

German Empire, including its colonies, must be preserved. However, in line with an emerging German consensus regarding national self-determination as a strategy for continued German influence in Eastern Europe (about which, more in Chapter 2), the plan accepted the idea that some territories might change hands in the new postwar Europe. In particular, the pope highlighted the need to assess the right to sovereignty and independence of the Balkan states and Catholic-majority Poland. He also urged a thorough examination of the status of Christian Armenia, in light of the mass violence suffered by the Armenian people during the war. Throughout, the papal peace plan and papal encyclicals hammered on one key point: it was neither "prudent" nor "safe," it said, for "governments or states to separate themselves from the holy religion of Jesus Christ, from which their authority receives such strength and support."[25] The postwar peace settlement, in other words, would not bring peace if it strengthened secular movements and failed to protect and promote the Catholic Church.

Soon after its release, the papal peace plan became a reference point in a lively debate on the conditions for permanent peace in Europe. "Just as the Dome of St. Peter dominates its surroundings," a Vatican representative boasted, the pope's message "overshadows [other] confused peace efforts."[26] By late August, the peace plan had been endorsed by all of the leaders of the Central Powers. In particular, the following figures had spoken out strongly in favor of Benedict's peace plan: the Chancellor of the German empire, Theobald von Bethmann-Hollweg; the German Kaiser, Wilhelm II; the king of Bavaria, Ludwig II; and the German Catholic politician and leader of the Center Party, Matthias Erzberger, who introduced Benedict's proposals for discussion in the Reichstag. The emperor of Austria, Karl I, also celebrated the plan. Even the German Socialist Party noted effusively that it would give a "new, powerful impulse to the movement for peace."[27] Neutral countries like Spain and Belgium praised the proposal, as did Christian Democrats in other countries, including Italy. The official newspaper of the German Center Party hailed the peace note as "the first great move of the pope as a neutral sovereign."[28] The celebratory statements were translated with extreme speed by the local papal nuncio, Eugenio Pacelli, and sent to Rome. Not all applauded the papacy's move, however; the Italian and French governments flatly dismissed the papal proposal.[29]

Wilson's secretary of state watched the unfolding chorus of assenters and dissenters with some concern. He decided to ask American ambassadors abroad to gather opinions on the pope's recent communiqué, not least because some commentators in the United States were affirming that the Allied cause would "depend on [Woodrow Wilson's] answer" to the pope.[30] Key Wilson advisers agreed, urging the American president to seize the "opportunity to take the peace negotiations out of the hands of the pope and hold them in [his] own."[31] It was important to distract the world from Benedict's proposal, which was already garnering so much attention.

On August 27, 1917, Wilson issued his reply to Benedict. The letter applauded the papacy's commitment to peace but advised Benedict to abandon naive hope in the goodwill of the Central Powers and in the advisability of allowing the German Empire to preserve its old boundaries. Peace would come, Wilson abjured, only when "the great peoples of the Central Empires" forged their own nation-states.[32] The letter was widely disseminated to the international press. In London and Paris, it was hailed as Wilson's most lucid enunciation of core principles since his speech before Congress urging the United States' entry into the war.[33] German Catholic politicians reacted predictably, emphasizing the "everlasting glory" of the papal peace plan and contrasting it to Wilson's letter, "which united us all the more strongly in our unshakable will to oppose any foreign intervention." Others affirmed that "on the one hand, we have the Holy Father's word, inspired by the most noble of sentiments, while on the other hand, we have a poisonous, mendacious accusation against the German people, delivered by a masked hypocrite."[34]

A few months later—in January 1918—Wilson issued his first concrete set of peace aims in his Fourteen Points address. The timing, many noted, seemed to indicate that this was Wilson's attempt to respond to the pope's peace statement.[35] Like Benedict's, Wilson's address called for disarmament and celebrated the principle of self-determination. But in place of endorsing an international order that took its cues from the Vatican, Wilson called for the spread of democracy, particularly in the former lands of the Russian and German Empires. Taking stock of the emerging struggle between the pope and the American president, a flippant contemporary observer noted, "Now it's Wilson who is becoming pope by drawing moral lessons for the belligerent powers. . . . Long live Pope Wilson!"[36] Papal observers were more acerbic, accusing Wilson of copying and "diluting" the papal peace plan, while trying to appear more authoritative by doubling the number of key points (the pope had seven, the American president fourteen).[37] As the Jesuit journal whose articles were all vetted by the papal Secretariat of State informed its readers, acts of intellectual theft of this sort were to be expected of *soi-disant* "honest liberals" like Woodrow Wilson, whose rhetorical niceties were directly supplied by an American clique of "Masons and anticlericals."[38]

Beginning in January 2018, Benedict's encyclicals and apostolic exhortations became more sharply worded and more numerous. In the crucial arc between 1918 and 1920, the pope issued twenty-three apostolic letters, along with seven encyclicals. These numbers begin to the tell the story of the shift that Benedict XV both brought about and enabled as World War I drew to a close. The shift was one from a papacy dominated by a fortress mentality to one that presented the pope as a pragmatist who would oppose the imagined possibility of either a liberal peace settlement or a socialist postwar order. Benedict alone was not responsible for the papacy's transformation in these years: he was aided and supported throughout by a new generation of papal diplomats and lawyers, who suggested a new way for Benedict to oppose the Church's enemies: international law.

A Legal Revolution

Starting from the 1910s, a new generation of papal lawyers had come to see the Catholic capture of international law as a privileged site for Europe's re-Christianization and as the best way to oppose the secularization of Europe. These functionaries had come of age right after the traumatic Italian wars of unification and the dissolution of the Papal States. Nearly all had been trained at the same place: the prestigious Pontifical Academy of Ecclesiastical Nobles. During the 1870s this Academy had carried out an important curricular reform, which brought about a gradual shift in emphasis away from the art of defensive *apologia* and toward fields like civil law and international law.[39] In the course of their studies, papal functionaries had been exposed to a series of brand-new texts penned by Catholic theologians and legal scholars about the nascent field of international law. These texts presented international law as a Catholic invention whose historical roots lay in medieval Christendom and in the Christian idea of the brotherhood of mankind. Modern international law would flounder if it did anything but try to "bring into the affairs of life the eternal principles of right at all times taught by the Christian Church," these writers noted.[40] Therefore, international law was and should be the preserve of the Catholic Church.

But the nascent field of international law had been captured, not by Catholics, but by their enemies—by secularizing liberals who aimed to use international law to eliminate the Church from public life. The nineteenth-century founding fathers of the field in fact believed that it was not possible for relations between states and the pope to fall under international law. Within their planned European order, the Church had no place: "Roman Catholicism is moribund," they said, adding that the new field of international law must be a fully secular undertaking.[41] Given the fact that the same European fathers of international law had stood at the forefront of battles to establish nonconfessional primary and secondary schools and to break diplomatic relations with the Vatican, their arguments regarding the necessarily secular character of international law were unsurprising. Nonetheless, they helped define the self-appointed task of Catholic jurists: to steal the fire back from the liberals and turn the field of international law into what they thought it should have been all along: a field dominated by Catholic individuals and Catholic prerogatives.[42]

Bringing together a few of these arguments, the influential German theologian and scholar Joseph Adam Gustav Hergenröther (made cardinal by Leo XIII and appointed first prefect of the newly opened Vatican archives in Rome) put it thusly:

The perfection of international law depends upon two conditions: (1) the degree to which the notion of a common humanity is developed

among nations; (2) the closeness of the connection by which they feel
themselves united. Christendom and the Church have had a powerful
influence upon both conditions. After the fall of the Roman Empire,
Christendom created amongst new States common interests and an
international law, which, founded upon the principles and laws of the
Church, was administered by her and her Head as an international
tribunal under the protection of the penalty of the Church's ban.[43]

For Hergenröther and many young papal jurists influenced by him, international law was the product of Christian civilization in a binding
sense. The idea was that not only had Christendom originally enabled
human beings to feel a sense of "common humanity"; historically,
popes had bound disparate European communities together through
their diplomatic and legal activities, "creat[ing] amongst new States
common interests and an international law." This usable past suggested that international law in the present could attain "perfection"
only if it recognized Christian principles of shared humanity and took
its cues from "the principles and laws of the Church."[44]

These texts gave papal legal scholars a way to think about how international law could be the continent's new unifier. Not only could
international law be a useful tool; additionally, it was an appropriate
one, insofar as the pope, as Christ's Vicar on Earth, was the true ani-
mator of international law, and its guardian. Therefore, it was not only
necessary for the pope to take hold of the reins of the new field; it was
written into the divine plan that he do so. Via international law, a
Christian Europe, led by the pope, could be attained once again.

The legal revolution under way in Rome in the late nineteenth and
early twentieth centuries was spurred on by the pan-European culture
wars. When in 1903–1904, Liberal France announced its intention to
separate church and state and send most religious orders into exile, the
pope was so incensed by what he called the *evento nefasto* that he asked
many papal lawyers to draw up a legal response, which argued for the
illegality, and hence illegitimacy, of the French attack on the Church.[45]
Soon thereafter, many of these same lawyers were enlisted in a new
project: the rewriting of the papacy's Code of Canon Law, which began
in 1904 and was completed in 1917. As an answer both to France and
to liberalism in general, the projected Code defended, in great detail, a
model of the Church and a model of the state that ran counter to that
articulated in the 1905 law.

The new Code simplified the papacy's legal architecture and significantly expanded the pope's powers. It gave him the exclusive right to nominate bishops, and affirmed that the pope alone had "the most complete and supreme jurisdiction in the Church as a whole, both in matters of faith and morals, and in matters concerning the discipline and the governance of the Church throughout the world."[46] As Pius X had announced in 1904, the new Code of Canon Law would take European nineteenth-century civil codes as its model, in a bid to make the Holy See appear "statelike," even as its territorial sovereignty lay in the balance. The Code, the pope noted, should be written *ex novo*, and its laws, referred to as "codes," should be stated in analytical and abstract terms, rather than fleshed out through case studies. Like its nineteenth-century European models, the Code should be arranged by subject rather than chronologically, and it should borrow its overarching organizational categories ("persons," "things," and "actions" or "procedures") from Justinian's sixth-century codification of Roman law, the Corpus Juris Civilis. All of this, it was hoped, would help put the Vatican back on firm footing as a state among states—despite the fact that its territorial sovereignty had been taken away in the course of Italy's wars of unification. The Code would be an exercise in self-legitimation.

On May 27, 1917, the Code was complete, and presented to the public. It entered into force on May 19, 1918. Though its 2,414 laws filled five volumes in place of the single volume Pius X had originally mandated, the new Code was an impressive synthesis of centuries of ecclesiastical law. The feat was significant, in that the codification of a formal legal structure guiding the Church and its faithful had begun in the thirteenth century and been poorly organized since. Legal materials were scattered across dozens of volumes, and these volumes were arranged chronologically, rather than by subject. In place of an abstract articulation of a set of rules, the laws in these volumes were explained through long and detailed case studies. As a contemporary American jurist noted, for these reasons and more, the 1917 Code was "certainly one of the greatest literary juridical achievements of the twentieth century."[47]

Each of the five volumes of the Code drove home the point that the Vatican, led by the pope, stood at the head of the Catholic world when it came to both temporal and spiritual matters. The first volume, Book I (codes 1–86), enshrined general norms—explaining, for instance, that where religious law conflicts with secular law, the former should be heeded. Book II, "On Persons" (codes 87–725), posited the ability of the papacy to regulate the conduct of clerics, monastics, and laypersons. Book III, "On Things," explained what it meant to be a practicing Catholic before the law, by focusing on the administration of Sacraments (codes 731–1153) and the duty to worship God in a particular, centrally mandated, way—for instance, via the veneration of what the Roman Church declared to be sacred times and places (codes 1154–1321). Book III of the Code also defended the primacy of the ecclesiastical magisterium within the Catholic world—that is, the historical-legal right of the pope and the Roman Curia to legislate on behalf of Catholics at large. It urged Catholics to recognize the central Church, led by the Supreme Pontiff, as an institution created by Christ and entitled to both territorial and political sovereignty (codes 1322–1551). Book IV, "On Processes," concerned the judicial system internal to the Church to which lay Catholics must also answer—for instance, in matters pertaining to family law. This book also laid out rules preventing local churches from superseding the central Church, discussing at length matters like the beatification and canonization of saints (codes 1552–2141). Finally, Book V, "On Crimes and Penalties," promised internal accountability by outlining the penal law of the central Church itself (codes 2195–2414).[48]

The monopoly of jurisdiction the Code created was a first in Church history. It had the effect of universalizing the Holy See's law, and reinforcing disciplinary and administrative uniformity. It powerfully linked Catholic laypeople and clergy members more closely to the institution of the Holy See, and helped the Holy See extend its influence across national boundaries. As such, the new Code of Canon Law was not only part of the Vatican's response to the burgeoning of secular nation-states. It was also part of the Vatican's offensive on liberalism as an emergent competing paradigm on the continent.[49]

As the Code of Canon Law was reaching completion, one of its drafters, Eugenio Pacelli, decided to go a step further. Convinced that law could be a game-changer in global affairs and a way to restore the papacy to primacy in its "bitter struggles to defend the rights of God and his church," the Roman cleric put together a tract arguing that it was necessary to radically modify the legal meaning of an old tool of papal diplomacy. It was time, he said, to use this tool to embed large chunks of the new Code of Canon Law into the fabric of Europe's new and newly emerging nation-states. The core claim was in keeping with official teachings: after all, until Vatican II, the Vatican officially demanded that wherever possible, church law should become state law. At the same time, however, the decision to turn the new Code into a mandate for Europe's new and newly reconstituted nation-states was entirely unprecedented.[50]

Concordats had been used by the papacy since the eleventh century to negotiate basic guarantees from a condition of weakness. Indeed, between 1122 and 1916, concordats had been primarily used to settle ongoing disputes.[51] Legally speaking, they were valid only before ecclesiastical law, which defined them as privileges granted by the Church in virtue of the superiority of her aims. As Pacelli argued in his wartime tract, the meaning of concordats should be altered. Concordats should no longer be defined as privileges granted by the Church. Instead, they should be recast as bilateral treaties to which two sovereign entities, the Vatican and the signatory state, were party. In legal terms, concordats should be considered valid not only before ecclesiastical law, but before civil and international law as well.[52] Building on a technical treatise he had written in 1912, Pacelli drew on Saint Thomas Aquinas, and argued that church laws and decrees could extend well beyond the strict territorial limits to which they had traditionally been circumscribed. Pacelli further suggested that previous concordats had granted too many concessions to partner states: "Better no concordat at all," he noted, "than a concordat that limits the Church and provides it with no advantages of its own."[53] Pacelli's message was clear: concordats must be made to assume a central place in the emerging legal-political landscape of the early twentieth century. They would help the papacy reattain sovereignty, despite its loss of the Papal States, and regain a position of prominence on the continent. Concordats had the capacity to break down the divisions between the fields of international law, ecclesiastical law, and civil law. In the process, these remarkable treaties could be used to encode a new relationship between the Vatican and the European continent as a whole.

By the end of 1918 Eugenio Pacelli had drafted a model for a "veritable concordatory common law," a concordat revolution.[54] The model he had put together created a complex and richly interwoven tapestry of Church–state cooperation, which aimed to upend liberal and socialist secular fantasies. In an attempt to offset the imagined anti-Christian foundations of the new international order, the treaty leaned heavily on the 1917 Code of Canon Law, including a large number of provisions from the newly redrafted Code, in an attempt to make ecclesiastical law an integral part of national legislation.

As we will see in the following chapters, Pacelli's model would soon be exported and become the letter of the law throughout the 1920s and early 1930s in countries like Latvia, Lithuania, Estonia, Poland, Germany, Austria, and Italy. In order to undermine the imagined-as-imminent liberal separation between church and state, the concordats concluded by the Holy See after the Great War carved out vast spaces for the operation of the Church in domains that had been key sites of controversy during the nineteenth century, like education and family law. They sought to expand the Church's presence in civil society, by providing state protection for a network of Catholic youth and adult organizations. In a bid to challenge the principle of equality before the law, they legislated privileges and exemptions for clergy and religious orders. The new treaties would also play the critical function of putting the shaky legal status of the Holy See on firmer ground. They recognized that the Church had a "true legal personality" and that as such it was "capable of exercising the rights that belong to it."[55] This meant that all treaties recognized the sovereign status of the Holy See, and provided diplomatic recognition to papal officials.[56] In this way, concordats would use international law as an instrument in the re-Christianization of Europe, as they overturned secularizing initiatives of the nineteenth century and increased the Vatican's cultural, social, legal, and economic power.

However, for all its innovativeness, Eugenio Pacelli's new theory of concordat diplomacy could well have remained just that: a theory. In the spring of 1918 the Holy See received the opportunity to try out the new tool. That opportunity was afforded by a major development in the war: the conclusion of the Treaty of Brest-Litovsk. In the spring of 1918, in the immediate aftermath of the treaty, Pope Benedict XV decided to turn Pacelli's legal tract into a plan of action. The testing ground would be the eastern part of the continent.[57] Using Eastern European countries as guinea pigs, the Holy See tried out its plans for reordering international affairs, and created a preemptive countersettlement to the imagined secular peace. As it did so, the Vatican elaborated on its own commitment to self-determination (present already in the papal peace plan), even as it pledged to assist Eastern European countries in their bid for international recognition and legitimacy. Buoyed by its success in Eastern Europe, the papacy would soon export concordats to Central and Western Europe. In this way Pacelli's tract helped inaugurate a new aggressive papal diplomacy, which was born during World War I and would remain the pope's privileged modus operandi for the better part of forty years.

2

A New Catholic Diplomacy

If the jurists and heads of state of the nineteenth century and the start
of the twentieth century—the anticlericals and simple liberals—could
return to earth . . . they would have trouble believing their eyes and
ears. They will crouch back down in their tombs rather than remain the
powerless witnesses of this toppling of their beloved work of legislative
secularization.

—R. P. YVES DE LA BRIÈRE, SJ, 1932

IN APRIL 1918, Pope Benedict XV summoned a charismatic, quick-
witted and sharp-tongued papal librarian to his chambers. Within a
month, the bespectacled cleric would be charged with the weighty task
of exporting concordat diplomacy to Poland, Latvia, Lithuania, and
Estonia. When Pope Benedict XV invited Achille Ratti to an audience,
the bibliophile had no way of knowing that he was about to be transformed from prefect of the Vatican Library to high-flying diplomat. It
was true that earlier in the war, Ratti—who held three doctorates and
enjoyed citing poetry in his native Milanese dialect—had earned the
friendship of the pope and provided him with advice and historical context for the war. But nothing in Ratti's biography really suggested that
he was ready for an adventure abroad in papal diplomacy.

In their April 1918 meeting, Benedict likely discussed Eugenio
Pacelli's vision for concordat diplomacy, Woodrow Wilson's recent
Fourteen Points address, and the signing of the Treaty of Brest-Litovsk
(on March 3, 1918). He may well have reminded the Milanese cleric that
the Holy See had just recognized Poland's independence in late March.

The pope then lodged his request. Would Achille Ratti consider serving as apostolic visitor to Poland to export concordat diplomacy and place the Catholic Church on firm grounding in Eastern Europe? While in Poland, Ratti could also reach out to Latvia, Lithuania, and Estonia, and get a closer view of the revolution and civil war under way in the vast Russian territories. The pope gave the librarian twenty-four hours to consider the request. On the next day he summoned Ratti for his second audience. As the story goes, the pope posed Ratti one simple question as he crossed the doorway: "When do you leave for Poland?"[1]

✻

Pope Benedict's decision to summon Achille Ratti and send him to export concordat diplomacy in Eastern Europe and the Baltic was a recent, risky one. As a result of the conclusion of the Treaty of Brest-Litovsk, the pope had decided that these territories were fertile ground for the concordat project. Negotiated by the Bolshevik regime and the Central Powers between December 1917 and March 1918, the treaty ended Russia's participation in the war and recognized the independence of six new states: Estonia, Latvia, Lithuania, Belarus, Ukraine, and Finland. It also put Poland's fate as an independent nation-state on firmer ground. In their bid to save the revolution, the Bolsheviks had agreed to shave one million square miles off the old Russian Empire, giving up Russia's control of 90 percent of the Empire's coal mines, 54 percent of its industry, 33 percent of its rail system, and 32 percent of its agricultural land, including almost all of its oil and cotton production.[2] On the face of things, Brest announced the broad shift that would soon shatter the old Europe of empires and usher in a continent of nation-states. The new premise was that peoples of the same race or ethnicity should be considered part of the same "nation," and have the right to a state of their own. But in fact, in the dictated peace the Bolsheviks had agreed to give up a great deal of land and help realize the German Empire's dream of expanding its power in the east. With Brest, the Bolsheviks had handed Latvia, Lithuania, Russian Poland, and most of Belarus, over to Germany, as client states. In a supplementary treaty on August 24, 1918, Russia renounced sovereignty over Estonia as well.

From Germany's point of view, Brest-Litovsk was a clear win, for it was in keeping with the German Empire's long-standing policy of revolutionizing the East and seizing control over vast swaths of land for agricultural development, settlement, and the creation of a military buffer zone held with "sword and plow."[3] German negotiators at Brest considered "self-determination" in Eastern Europe synonymous with a call for German hegemonic influence through the creation of a bloc of smaller Eastern European states under German protection. As the German chancellor, Bethmann-Hollweg, archly put it, "The times are no longer for annexation, but rather for the cuddling up of smaller state-entities to the great powers, to mutual benefit."[4] Influence without formal annexation not only would be cost-effective; it was also geopolitical commonsense. As several key German politicians argued, influence without formal annexation would be the best way to prevent the expansion of French, British, and especially American political and economic influence in Eastern Europe. Europe's future horizons could thus retain the contours of phantom empires and ward off new threats.[5]

To guarantee what ended up being the favorable result at Brest, just ten days before negotiations kicked off, German military authorities put strong pressure on future client states in Eastern Europe. After having threatened independence leaders with turning Lithuania into a marginal border zone of the German Empire, military authorities pressured the Lithuanian parliament to declare "a firm and permanent alliance with Germany," in the form of a military convention and a currency and customs union.[6] They also signed a separate treaty with the Ukrainian delegation, in which the new republic pledged to supply Germany with a million tons of bread annually. As a final blow, in late 1917 General Hoffman informed the shocked Russian delegation at Brest-Litovsk that Poland, Lithuania, and Latvia had already split from Russia and were planning for a future of close collaboration with Germany. In response to these moves, Leon Trotsky, heading Russia's delegation, stormed out, announcing his revolutionary formula of "No peace, no war." German armies resumed military action. By February 1918 they had conquered all of Latvia, Livonia, Estonia, Belarus, and Ukraine. As the kowtowing Bolsheviks were agreeing to reopen talks at Brest-Litovsk, Germany was rebuffing Estonia's claims to independent rule, refusing to allow Lithuanian delegates to participate in the resumed conference, and confiscating all newspapers that had reprinted a February 16, 1918, declaration, made by an embittered Lithuanian parliament, reversing the "alliance" with Germany, and announcing Lithuania's complete independence, without ties to any foreign powers.[7]

The papacy followed the conclusion of Brest-Litovsk closely, and was quite taken by Germany's understanding of the treaty, which was given its first extended airing by the Germany's chief negotiator, Matthias Erzberger, in July 1917. In a speech before the Reichstag, the Catholic politician called for peace without territorial gains, and celebrated self-determination as a pragmatic strategy. Eugenio Pacelli—who had arrived in Germany just a month and a half earlier—was enthralled. He noted that Erzberger's proposal was fascinating, not least because it had the singular virtue of being "devoid of that blinding nationalism which disoriented so much of the [German] hierarchy and Catholic nobility." The Roman cleric affirmed, "Erzberger's will be the position that is destined to win out and gain ground after the inevitable fall of the Empire, and it will be this position with which the Church will need to reckon [quella con cui la Chiesa dovrà fare i conti]."[8]

With the idea of ensuring that Erzberger's vision receive the best reception in papal headquarters, Pacelli brought the German Catholic politician into the process. Might Erzberger have collected favorable reactions to his Reichstag speech, Pacelli wondered, reactions that Pacelli could in turn send to the Vatican secretary of state?[9] The idea was to present papal officials back in Rome with the picture of a Germany united behind the Catholic politician. The reality was otherwise: on two occasions within a year, Erzberger would have to argue his case before German military courts staffed with officials eager to prosecute the Catholic Center politician for ditching classical imperialism and defending the independence of Eastern European territories such as Lithuania and Ukraine.[10] On the opposite end of the political spectrum, left-wing activists in Germany accused Erzberger of violating the spirit of self-determination—a term they understood as a call for imperialism's overthrow rather than its continuance under a new guise.[11] But despite the fact that Erzberger had become a persona non grata in several circles, Pacelli stood by him. "I can't abandon him," the Italian diplomat noted, "because he is intelligent, good, animated by the best of intentions, and of phenomenal and spontaneously provided assistance, past and present (perhaps alone of all the politicians of the Center Party), to the nunciature and the Holy See."[12]

Woodrow Wilson—who of course had hegemonic aims of his own—was following Brest-Litovsk closely, and he, like Pacelli, was taking his cues. In 1918 Wilson began speaking the language of self-determination. This was by no means a given. As late as December 1917 (the first month of negotiations at Brest), Wilson still bragged that he might conclude a separate peace with the Austro-Hungarian Empire, announcing in his State of the Union address, "We do not wish in any way to impair or to rearrange the Austro-Hungarian Empire." But by early 1918 Wilson had come around to a new position. He noted that peoples living in the Russian, Austro-Hungarian, and German Empires "should be accorded the freest opportunity of political development." Then, for the first time, the United States embraced the nationalist dissolution of the Habsburg Empire. Finally, Wilson proclaimed self-determination as a universal principle.[13] He was well aware that in doing so he was joining a chorus of new defenders of the phrase—from Bolsheviks to Austro-Marxists, from German imperialists to the pope himself.

"A Phrase Loaded with Dynamite"

Since the early twentieth century, key Russian revolutionaries, with Vladimir Lenin first in line, had been advocating national self-determination as a way to attract non-Russian nationalities and convince them that the Bolsheviks were their allies—and not Great Russian chauvinists bent on imperial rule. The tsarist system, they claimed, was a "prison house of nations" and the Bolsheviks were the prison house's liberators. In their theoretical works, the Bolsheviks tried to reconcile the defense of national self-determination with Marx's key insights on supranational working-class solidarity. They argued that despite appearances to the contrary, national self-determination could help realize the Marxist dream of worker unity, insofar as the overthrow of empires by national independence movements would be a stepping-stone toward transnational anticapitalist revolution. As Lenin put it, "Just as mankind can arrive at the abolition of classes only through a transitional period of dictatorship by the oppressed class, it can achieve the inevitable integration of nations only through a transitional period of the complete emancipation of all oppressed nations—i.e., their freedom to separate." This position caused some friction within the radical left in Russia, with figures like Nikolai Bukharin and Georgy Pyatakov instead insisting that internationalists should want, not "nations," but instead an immediate union of proletarians and the abolition of all frontiers.[14] But Lenin and many Bolsheviks on his side replied that self-determination would help galvanize revolution. It was "a phrase," as the U.S. secretary of state, Robert Lansing, aptly put it, "simply loaded with dynamite." On November 15, 1917, one month before the start of Brest-Litovsk negotiations, Lenin issued a Declaration of the Right to Self-Determination of all non-Russian peoples of Russia. The Declaration recognized the equality and sovereignty of the people of Russia, including their right to secede and form independent states.[15]

Woodrow Wilson followed Brest closely, and his February 1918 hymn to national self-determination was doubtless a way to pull the rug out from the feet of both the Bolsheviks and the Germans. But what precisely the American president meant by the phrase was not clear. He had hardly used it in his writings or public speeches to date (his earliest recorded usage was in 1914), and all that listeners could divine was that Wilson imagined a connection between "national self-determination" and three ideas to which he had devoted much more attention: that the peace in Europe depended on the extension of democracy; that the United States had a moral duty to liberate "mature" peoples from autocratic forms of government; and that, in keeping with the Anglo-American tradition of civic nationalism, communities had a right to self-government. Wilson's use of the phrase "national self-determination" was not systematic. Unlike the Bolsheviks, whose concept of self-determination had a decided anti-imperialist tinge, Wilson was no anti-imperialist, not only because he showed "little interest" in the "theoretical aspects of imperialism," but also because he had only recently responded enthusiastically to the rise of American imperialism in the late nineteenth century in territories like the Philippines.[16] Wilson's use of the word "national" also perplexed observers. Sometimes he seemed to be referencing a community sharing the same language or history, at other times a particular ethnicity. At war's end,

Wilson admitted that his understanding of the phrase was blurry, adding that implementing the idea of national self-determination was an extraordinary challenge—and one he had not properly thought through during the war itself. He sheepishly noted that he had issued his proclamation that all nations had a right to self-determination before he gained an awareness "that nationalities existed" and that these nationalities would "come to him day after day" to demand their rights.[17] Men quite close to Wilson privately expressed their annoyance with the president's lack of foresight. "Does national self-determination mean national sovereign determination—that is, that each nationality is entitled to possession of its own sovereign state—or does it mean autonomy within the given state structure? Does the same policy apply to all nationalities, great and small?" What was to be done in cases when nationalities made competing claims, or "when pursuit of peace without victory is in contradiction with a settlement that rests on the consent of the governed?" Throwing up his hands in frustration, Wilson's secretary of state, Robert Lansing, noted that the principle provided no helpful guidance for him and other policymakers: "The needle of one's compass swings around erratically and points in no single direction."[18]

Nonetheless, Wilson's February 1918 endorsement of national self-determination did have its importance, not least because of the short-term military advantage derived from the use of the phrase.[19] By mid- to late 1918, France, Italy, Japan, and Great Britain had all joined Woodrow Wilson in piously invoking the principle. Now it was not just the Bolsheviks and the German imperialists who were talking the national self-determination talk. Watching Wilson and his allies (watching Brest), Vatican diplomats reacted predictably. They quickly wrote off the rush to endorse the principle of self-determination as an instance of naked cunning. Citing their German interlocutors approvingly, they said that Wilson's new phrase of choice was simply a way for the United States "to attract peoples within its orbit and turn them against Germany," so as to better appease "the yearning [of the Allied powers] to expand their territories." "The fact that today Wilson ascribes a huge importance to the principle of nationalities as a condition for the settlement of the conflict should be understood as a special sort of demand," they noted: namely, as a ploy.[20]

At the same time, unwilling to let himself be left behind, the pope began to embrace the principle of national self-determination himself. That he did so was revolutionary. Popes had been among the concept's fiercest critics since French revolutionaries had affirmed the principle that "the source of all sovereignty resides essentially in the nation," thus undermining traditional Catholic understandings of sovereignty as divinely granted. Well into the Great War, the Vatican gave no indication of a change of heart. In 1916 the Vatican's cardinal secretary of state, Pietro Gasparri, operating within the *status quo ante* of a Europe of oversized empires, had rebuffed the claims of nationalist movements in the German and Austro-Hungarian Empires, and had even remarked offhandedly that an independent Poland was an unrealistic idea.[21] At that point Benedict may well have agreed with both Gasparri and with the journal *Civiltà Cattolica*, which in 1915 riffed against the rise of nationalist movements in Europe, noting that nationalism had its roots in the Greco-Roman "worship of the state" and, before that, in "paganism."[22] But by 1917 the pope had changed his tune. Benedict now argued that empires come and go but "nations don't die." According to the pope's new mantra, some European nationalities—particularly those in Germany's orbit, in Eastern Europe and the Baltic—had "rights and just aspirations" to self-rule. It was the papacy's task to support those aspirations and foster their realization.[23]

The papal defense of self-determination was never unpacked through a papal circular, encyclical, or other statement of doctrine. But from what we can piece together, it was closest to the German vision and distant indeed from Bolshevik or American understandings. Like the German, the papal celebration of self-determination was not universal: it was always qualified and used in reference to only a handful of peoples in East-Central Europe. Additionally, Benedict seemed to believe that more developed ethnicities or nationalities had the right to their own qualified independence—a supervised independence in which they could learn from and continue to enjoy the protection of more established and "advanced" states. Unlike Wilson, the pope gave no indication that he saw an essential and necessary linkage between self-determination, democratization, and self-government; indeed, democracy and self-government would not be conditionally embraced by the papacy until the 1940s. Finally, the pope's conception of self-determination was intimately religious. As he saw it, there was something providential about the explosion of nation-states after World War I—something that, in turn, indicated a necessary correlation between the rebirth of Catholicism during the Great War and the "resurrection" of select national states. The revival of "Christian civilization," Benedict hoped, would be actualized through the construction of really-existing Christian nation-states. As those nation-states took their "first steps" with the Church, they ensured that "their own boundaries" would be blessed in the future, and that these states and Catholicism together would enjoy "greatness and good fortune" in the years to come. Expanding the Church's authority, growing the Catholic faith, and fostering national self-determination were all of a piece.[24]

In April 1918, on the heels of Brest-Litovsk, the pope bit the bullet and counseled his diplomats to become spokespersons for national self-determination. Benedict asserted: "We see from this great upheaval many entirely new states appearing suddenly." Papal diplomats, he added, must show their support for "the new political reality that has emerged from the recent cruel war."[25] Soon enough, these clerics—who included Eugenio Pacelli himself, the Jesuit Antonino Zecchini, the titular archbishop Francesco Marmaggi, and Achille Ratti, future Pope Pius XI—were shipped abroad, in a bid to conclude concordats and change the shape of a portion of Europe before Woodrow Wilson and other politicians could do the same. For the pope and these clerics, the Treaty of Brest-Litovsk was a source of inspiration, because it was a brilliant example of how it was possible to turn defeat into victory and redraw Europe's boundaries before the Allied powers could do so. Brest, in fact, provided the papacy with an important model for how it might draft a new European order before the conclusion of the war.

To signal the imperative of Christian reconstruction in the region, Achille Ratti took the name Titular Archbishop of Lepanto, a reference to the defeat of the Ottoman Empire at Lepanto in 1571. His new title was supposed to conjure up the following association: Just as Christians had defeated the infidels in the sixteenth century, so would they defeat the new infidels of the twentieth century. Just as they had rebuilt Lepanto and turned it into a Christian city, so would Eastern

Europe be rebuilt in God's image. For Ratti, the mission was an exciting one. He effused in a letter to a friend, "Few things would be capable of inspiring in me a more lively and deep interest than the resurrection and progressive reconstruction of this great state."[26]

※

Just a few months after the conclusion of Brest-Litovsk, the German Empire imploded, and the new and newly reconstituted nation-states in the Brest zone entered a prolonged period of uncertainty. Even after the official end of the Great War with the November 1918 armistice, war continued. Violent border disputes exploded in succession, as Poland, Latvia, Lithuania, and Estonia struggled to agree among themselves on new state boundaries, and as Soviet troops and the German Freikorps continued armed incursions, oblivious to the armistice. Tensions within new nation-states were also high. For despite a tidal wave of nationalist sentiment, most of the territories in the Brest zone were divided internally, torn between warring political factions and divergent conceptions of what "Polishness" or "Lithuanianness" might mean. Socialist parties vied for power with right-wing agrarian movements; social-democrats, ethno-nationalists, and communists butted heads.

Within a few years it became apparent that the Vatican was benefiting from the situation, and that its new concordat diplomacy was proving a success. The appeal of concordats in the shadow of Brest-Litovsk depended on the intersection of Vatican and local interests. Vatican interests were not highly context-dependent: everywhere papal diplomats traveled, they sought to export similar Church-state treaties that would swing open the doors to Catholic influence over family law, education, and civil society, and buoy the papacy's claims to sovereignty. Though diplomats were sensitive to the differences between Catholic-majority countries (like Poland and Lithuania) and Catholic-minority territories (like Latvia and Estonia), the fundamental demands they made did not vary significantly from context to context. For this reason, the chief challenge papal diplomats faced was to show that concordats could be useful in advancing on-the-ground aims and adjudicating local disputes.

In fact, concordat diplomacy was successful because it genuinely appeared to be a path to satisfy the leading goals for state leaders in countries like Poland, Lithuania, Latvia, and Estonia. These goals included obtaining international sovereign recognition for their new nation-states, consolidating borders, and winning over the loyalty of borderland populations. Additionally, in the pitched battles of the early postwar years, new state leaders were interested in coming out on top and ensuring that their own political parties emerged triumphant in internal battles for influence and power. In country after country, the Vatican was able to win support for concordats when it showed local state leaders that these treaties could be helpful tools for achieving legitimacy in the international sphere and at home. Indeed, local actors quickly realized that the papacy's presence could be useful in domestic terms, for to have papal diplomats open talks with one or another political movement, and thereby confer their legitimacy upon that movement, would, they recognized, provide a crucial boost in a period of internal jockeying and infighting.

Furthermore, as new state leaders and papal diplomats understood well, formal declarations of independence were well and good, but in the era of mass politics, they were not sufficient to bind diverse populations to the new myth of a unified nation. Thus, papal diplomats presented concordats as important tools for facilitating the integration of Catholic-majority borderland regions from the bottom up, helping advance the myth that Catholicism and nationalism went hand-in-glove. At the same time, concordats, they emphasized, could help control borderlands from the top down, insofar as they mandated the appointment of state-approved bishops to contested regions. In practice, this measure guaranteed that, for instance, Polish clergy sympathetic to the ruling party would be placed at the head of local church hierarchies in the contested eastern territories of the new nation-state, or that Russian-language clergy in Lithuania would be replaced with clerics eager to challenge Russian influence on the ground. In this way, the papacy not only helped consolidate new nation-states; it helped fortify the imagined community of the nation through both bottom-up and top-down methods.

Enablers of the Polish Concordat

The very first country in which papal diplomats got to work was Poland. Poland was high on the Vatican's postwar priority list because it had the largest population of Catholics in Europe, after Italy, France, and Spain, and because, of all the new and emerging countries in the Brest zone, it had long been considered the linchpin of the East by the Great Powers.[27] Just over a month after Brest, Benedict recruited Achille Ratti as Poland's first wartime nuncio; by May 29, 1918, the Milanese cleric was already installed in Warsaw. Local members of the population gave him a jubilant welcome, as the apostolic nuncio got to work to figure out which interlocutors to cultivate as he sought to sell concordat diplomacy in a region that was, for him, entirely novel.

When Achille Ratti arrived in Poland, the Italocentric cleric knew little to nothing about the local political situation. Once on site, he gleaned only piecemeal information, and his opinions of local politicians were largely shaped by first impressions and intuitions. The politician with whom Ratti first established strong bonds was an unlikely friend. In addition to being a war hero and leader of Poland's independence movement, Józef Piłsudski was an erstwhile socialist, who in the course of his university studies had become a leader of the Polish Socialist Party and renounced the Catholic Church, formally adopting the Evangelical-Augsburg confession instead.[28] Immediately after the Great War, Marshal Piłsudski was appointed Chief of State of the independent Second Republic, a post he held until 1922. On the eve of taking power, Piłsudski reconverted to Catholicism and officially broke ties with the Socialist Party. Nonetheless, most of the country's Catholic upper and lower clergy held him in suspicion, and cast their lot instead with Piłsudski's leading domestic rival, Roman Dmowski, who headed up a nationalist and anti-Semitic right-wing political party, the National Democrats. In 1923, worn out by the contrasts with Dmowski, the Marshal temporarily retired from active politics. In 1926 he returned on his own terms, through a coup d'état. Piłsudski would rule Poland with an iron fist until his death in 1935.

Józef Piłsudski and Achille Ratti first met in 1918. The Polish general, by all accounts, made a superb impression on the Milanese cleric. On a personal level, the two resonated—both were rather gruff and direct in their style, and both were ambitious warriors, each for his own cause. It helped that one of Piłsudski's only friends in the Catholic Church was the archbishop of Warsaw, Aleksander Kakowski, a man Ratti held in high esteem. Together, Kakowski and Ratti decided that Piłsudski's faith (or lack thereof) had been misunderstood. Both bought the idea that Piłsudski had temporarily abandoned Catholicism for pragmatic reasons, and both believed his renunciation of socialism to be genuine. They gushed over the respect Piłsudski paid the Church in public ceremonies and Piłsudski's personal devotion to the Blessed Mother of Ostra Brama, the protectress of Vilna. (Piłsudski famously made no important decision without first praying to the Blessed Mother, whose icon hung above his bed. Even as head of state he would tear up when official ceremonies were held at Ostra Brama's shrine.)[29] Finally, the Polish politician in no way opposed Ratti's bid to strengthen Catholicism's place in Poland, increase Church–state ties, and get concordat negotiations under way. Piłsudski did not object when, in line with a great personal interest in supporting the expansion of Catholic civil society structures, Ratti encouraged the founding of Catholic lay organizations that militated actively to "bring the Kingdom of Christ on Earth."[30] Piłsudski let Ratti have free reign as he encouraged local Catholics to found publications tightly bound to the pope and set up a Vatican relief organization, which rivaled the future U.S. president Herbert Hoover's on-site branch of the American Relief Administration.[31]

Soon after his arrival to Poland, Ratti began conversations about the need for a concordat. The fact that the concordat ended up being negotiated and signed emerged from Ratti's capacity to understand the goals of secular politicians and present the concordat as a tool capable of satisfying those goals. The concordat, Ratti claimed, would help consolidate Poland's official borders, inform Poland's neighbors that those borders were set in stone, and grow the loyalty of residents in borderland regions. The concordat would facilitate the secular border-consolidation project because it would redraw diocesan lines in conformity with Poland's new map. This was very important because even though Poland's borders were eventually internationally recognized (in 1923), neither Germany nor Lithuania accepted the new status quo. Having diocesan lines redrawn to correspond to Poland's

Achille Ratti (right) with Poland's new chief of state, Marshal Józef Piłsudski (left). Credit: Rzeczpospolita Archive

new official borders would be a way to further send the message to Poland's neighbors that the new borders were nonnegotiable. For this reason, Poland's leaders quickly became convinced that they needed to move fast, and have a concordat signed before Berlin or Kaunas did the same. Along similar lines, they hoped that the concordat could help send the message that the still-contested Free City of Danzig was truly Polish, using the concordat to assert Polish ecclesiastical authority over this territory.

The secular project of nation-building, particularly in borderland regions, could also be buttressed by the concordat. Specifically, figures like the minister of education, Stanisław Grabski (a member of the National Democratic party), were thoroughly convinced that Catholicism and the Church should serve as instruments of Polish assimilation in regions where ethnic Poles were a minority. Indeed, throughout the 1920s and 1930s the government's Polonization campaign to win local populations over to a new identification with the Polish motherland was "heavily dependent on the Catholic Church, that is, on 'Poloni-zation through Catholicization.'" Furthermore, even as the central government adopted a range of means to achieve Polonization, local administration officials continued to show clear preferences toward using the Catholic Church as a leading instrument of the campaign.[32] Ratti favored this move, and in letters home to friends and papal offi-cials he often referred to Polish national identity as fundamentally Catholic. Poland's Cardinal Hlond, for his part, celebrated Ratti's at-tempts to lift up Catholicism and strengthen Church–state relations, affirming:

> The state cannot be atheistic, it cannot govern as if God did not exist. Rather, it ought to worship God and respect religion . . . A Church lowered to the status of an association, existing within civil laws, would be an oppressed Church.[33]

There was one last selling point for secular politicians interested in the concordat: it could be a helpful way to guard against Poland's perceived enemies. For Grabski and other National Democrats, those enemies were cast as individuals living in Poland who were "not really Polish," including Jews, communists, Russians, and liberals (oftentimes, these four categories had considerable rhetorical overlap). Grabski regarded the Kresy of eastern Poland as particularly vulnerable to foreign influ-ence due to its proximity to Russia and the elevated Jewish presence in those lands.[34] Here, he was especially interested in getting Polish say over the appointment of bishops, for he believed this would be a way to guarantee their loyalty to the Republic.[35]

Despite the many indications that Poland and the Vatican were nearing agreement on the importance and utility of a concordat, two key episodes did threaten to bring negotiations crashing down. The first concerned the contested Upper Silesian region, rich in mining and industry. Many Catholic Poles—including prominent members of the Polish clergy—accused the Vatican of favoring Germany in the lead-up to the 1921 plebiscite that was to settle the status of this region. The Poles' worries were not groundless: in keeping with the Vatican's at-tachment to the Brest-Litovsk model, the Vatican secretary of state, Pietro Gasparri, had affirmed that it was not realistic to imagine that Poland could guarantee its own autonomy and independence if it was not under German control. Furthermore, Gasparri personally supported retaining the German archbishop, Adolf Betram of Silesia, despite the fact that this polarizing cleric strongly supported Germany in the plebiscite. The Polish hierarchy crossed swords with the papacy again regarding Western Ukraine, opposing the papacy's support for the use of a new Byzantine-Slavonic rite in the region, in a move that was intended to signal the papacy's openness to the Russian Bolsheviks.[36] Ratti was caught in the middle of the fray and left for the northern Italian city of Milan, where he was given the prestigious title of Archbishop, as a reward for his good service in Eastern Europe. Luckily, the storm clouds passed quickly. By the mid-1920s, the papacy and the Polish government were back on good terms. Indeed, the Polish concordat would end up becoming a model for the Holy See moving forward, granting a set of additional guarantees than it had not received elsewhere.

The shift back to Rome was already palpable in the country's new constitution (ratified in 1921), which affirmed that "the Roman Catholic denomination [occupies] in the state a leading position among the denominations." The Catholic Church alone, the constitution further stated, had the right to "govern itself by its own laws." Other religions, by contrast, would need to conform to the dictates of civil law. The affirmation that Poland was a Catholic state was in keeping with the demands of the majoritarian Polish center-right parties, who saw eye-to-eye with the papacy. Lambasting liberalism, they argued that the separation of Church and state was contrary to national tradition and therefore unthinkable. Only a confessional state could guarantee the preservation of "national tradition" and the health of the Catholic Church.[37]

In addition to articulating a vision of the state aligned with the Holy See's, the 1921 Polish constitution promised a future concordat. Local center-right politicians were eager to conclude a concordat with the Holy See for state and nation-building purposes. As they saw it, a concordat would help consolidate the Polish state, particularly because Germany (to the west) and Lithuania (to the northeast) had not yet accepted Poland's new borders. A concordat could help by drawing diocesan lines to coincide with Poland's borders, thus further invalidating German and Lithuanian territorial claims. In particular, they urged the creation of a Polish metropolitanate with its seat in Vilna (a city Poland seized from Lithuania in 1920), as a way to consolidate this city as a Polish stronghold. Polish politicians were hopeful that a concordat would help Poland obtain control over the port city of Danzig, and thus weaken Germany's continued claims on the city. Such an act had an added bonus, too: it would help Poland thumb its nose at the postwar "international community," which had attempted to resolve the Polish-German dispute by declaring Danzig a Free City under the authority of a newborn supranational institution, the League of Nations.[38]

The concordat was concluded after several years of negotiations and twenty-three meetings in Rome. The year was 1925. In the intervening time, much had changed in the ruling structure of the central government of the Roman Catholic Church. On January 22, 1922, Benedict XV had died of pneumonia. An unprecedented wave of public mourning followed—saying more, perhaps, about the new stature acquired by the Holy See than about Benedict himself.[39] The time had come for the College of Cardinals to elect Benedict's successor, and the core question animating the clerics was whether the new pope should follow his predecessor and continue Benedict's diplomatic crusade. The cardinals answered in the affirmative, and the man they chose as the new pope was none other than Achille Ratti. Thanks to his unflagging work to export concordats in Eastern Europe, Ratti had received the support of many members of the papal diplomatic corps, including Benedict's secretary of state, Pietro Gasparri.[40] To underline Ratti's ground-laying work for concordats in Eastern Europe, one of the new pope's co-consecrators was the Polish Bishop Pelczar, a bishop who had long declared that Catholics in Poland "want the Catholic religion to be the ruling religion, and the Church to get the rights and freedoms that belong to it by divine appointment."[41]

Once crowned as pope, Achille Ratti (now Pius XI) intervened repeatedly in the final phase of concordat negotiations with Poland. The project, he emphasized, was still very much the result of his personal hard work, sacrifice, and diligence. When the concordat text was finally complete, the pope made it widely known that he had personally given his blessing to "every comma" of the treaty. On February 10, 1925, the treaty was officially signed. Both sides were pleased. Rome obtained "full freedom" for the Church and a slew of other guarantees regarding religious instruction, the organization of civil society, and family law—all of which seemed to suggest that the liberal ideal of separating church and state would get nowhere in the new Eastern European country. Poland, for its part, received further confirmation of its identity as a "Catholic State" and that religious minorities (such as the Jews) would have to work out their own status. The city of Danzig was assigned to Poland's papal nunciature, not Germany's, and Poland received the guarantee that "no part of the country would be under the jurisdiction of a foreign ordinary." The Vatican also granted that the Polish metropolitanate take its seat in Vilna, in a real affront to Lithuanian claims to the city. Poland had shown up Germany and Lithuania—a fact much celebrated by favorable voices in Poland's lower house of parliament in March 1925.[42] In these ways and more, the concordat achieved the state-building and nation-building goals envisioned by Polish negotiators.

Polish newspapers hailed the event as good for church and state alike. "The pope has the power to lead humanity to transcendent, eternal goals," commentators noted, while "the king or president [has the power] to lead his one nation to earthly goals." For this reason, "because these dual powers hold sway over us, it is important and right that the commands of one power do not contradict the commands of the other power; that what the spiritual power commands is not forbidden by the secular power, and vice versa." A concordat, Poland's local press averred, was essential to ensuring a healthy partnership between "the spiritual power" and "the secular power."[43] Other papers celebrated the fact that the concordat helped Poland with her nation- and state-building goals, repeating the idea that the concordat would help Poland achieve the consolidation of its state boundaries. One Polish paper affirmed shortly after the conclusion of the concordat, referencing the Upper Silesian controversy:

> Now, the dioceses will be organized so that the boundaries of the borderland dioceses will correspond to the boundary of the state. This way, neither will our bishop rule over parishes in another state nor will a bishop residing in a foreign country rule over parishes in Poland, which was what, unfortunately, happened in our borderland with Germany.[44]

Polish journalists, politicians, and local papal diplomats agreed that concordats could help Poland fully consolidate its new statehood, and override the mis-settlement of the Upper Silesian question. The country's papal diplomats had signed on to the Holy See's vision for a re-Christianized continent and aligned with the wishes long expressed by Bishop Pelczar and many others that Catholicism become Poland's "ruling religion."

Following the coup of 1926, Piłsudski returned to power and became one of the concordat's staunchest defenders, even though many members of his faction in government opposed the concordat, seeing it as an "unacceptable concession granted by a clericalist government." Nonetheless, the Marshal not only defended its existence: he worked to faithfully implement all of its articles throughout the 1920s and early 1930s. Indeed, for the Polish politician, upholding the concordat became a crucial way to flaunt his relationship with papal diplomats and undermine the claims of the National Democratic Party to being the representative of Polish Catholic interests at home. Thanks to Piłsudski's personal commitment to upholding the concordat, this period marked the high point of interwar Polish–Vatican harmony. The harmony was based on a simple quid pro quo: Piłsudski would guarantee the essential interests of the Church, and in return Rome would encourage Poland's Catholics to favor Piłsudski over the National Democratic Party.[45] Both the conclusion of the Polish concordat and its successful implementation were examples of how crucial it was to get papal, state, and local church interests aligned in order to guarantee a positive outcome.

Papal Reactions to the Paris Peace Conference

The papacy's activism in Poland and the conclusion of the Polish concordat took place against the backdrop of the Paris Peace Conference and the birth of a new institution charged with guaranteeing the postwar peace: the League of Nations. Both the Conference and the newborn League confirmed many of the papacy's worst fears about the coming Wilsonian order. The conference, which ran its course from January 1919 to January 1920, brought together the victorious Allied powers to set the peace terms for postwar Europe as a whole. Four political leaders, known as the Big Four, dominated the conference. Among them, the American president, Woodrow Wilson, was the star of the show. Hailed as "the messiah" and "the Moses from across the Atlantic," Wilson happily donned the mantle of the man who would single-handedly build a permanent peace in Europe. By contrast, the pope was officially shut out from the conference proceedings—despite a spate of last-minute lobbying efforts and a series of private meetings arranged between papal diplomats and European state leaders at the conference gates.

In keeping with Benedict's official recommendations, Ratti and his on-site assistant minced no words in condemning the Paris Peace Conference during their time in Poland. They spoke in unison with the Jesuit journal *Civiltà Cattolica,* which denounced Wilson and liberal internationalism, and echoed Cardinal Gasparri's views—expressed in the official Vatican daily, the *Osservatore Romano*—that Wilson in person bore the final and ultimate "responsibility" for the "odious offense" of excluding the pope from the meeting.[46] The Vatican daily synthetically noted that the world's populations now faced a stark choice between the "light of Rome" and the "moral nullity" [*nullismo morale*] of Paris, whose "menacing darkness" lurked ready to swallow Europe whole.[47] In Rome, the Paris Peace Treaties were promptly written off as the opposite of instruments of peace—as settlements that "represented a colossal failure of human judgment and expertise."[48] If only the "weak and unheeded voice of humanity," as channeled by the pope, had been invited to Versailles, all would have been otherwise.[49] Only select members of the Curia dared to propose that perhaps the League could be compatible with Catholic visions, as did a number of lay Catholics on the Italian peninsula.[50]

The Paris Peace Conference resulted in a series of major decisions which shaped Europe and the wider world for decades to come. Meeting participants drafted five peace treaties with defeated states, penalizing these states harshly. Germany was singled out for the worst treatment. According to section 231 of the Treaty of Versailles, Germany was saddled with guilt for starting the war. Its imperial territories were withdrawn and harsh financial reparations imposed. Many of its former territories in Europe were granted the right to self-determination, according to which each "nation" (defined in ethnic, linguistic, or cultural terms) was to occupy its own "state," or distinctive political unit. To enforce its new vision for Europe, the Paris Peace Conference created the League of Nations, a supranational organization whose aim was to put an end to war and provide a forum for dialogue between the world's member states. The League began its activities on January 16, 1920, and held its first working meeting on November 15, 1920, with the participation of forty-two member states. Modeling itself on a parliamentary democracy with a tripartite division of power, the League had the equivalent of a legislative branch (a League Council, populated by Great Power permanent members, and a one-member, one-vote assembly), an executive (the League's Office of the Secretary-General), and a Permanent Court of International Justice. In many senses, the League embodied the dreams of nineteenth-century liberal internationalists, for it was a secular, democratic space for resolving intrastate disputes.[51] However, the League was weaker than these liberal internationalists might have wished, for it had no real enforcement mechanisms. It lacked an army of its own (the French proposal for one had been rejected), its Court was not very powerful, and the best that it could do with defiant member states was subject them to boycott or sanctions. Even though the League was formally committed to national self-determination as a universal principle, most of the organization's key movers and shakers were imperialist powers who had no intention of giving up their empires. As a result, though the winners of the Great War reluctantly acknowledged the rising tide of anti-imperialist sentiment, they remained quite vague when it came to providing a route to independence for those African, Pacific, and Middle Eastern colonial territories they had seized from Germany and the Ottoman Empire.[52]

Achille Ratti and papal officials across Europe spoke out strongly against the League of Nations from its first day in operation. Papal officials and propagandists were impervious to the concerns of anticolonial activists and uncritical of the preservation of European empires; the chief reason they dismissed the League was that they saw it as an instrument for propping up the Great War's winners as the new arbiters of international affairs. The fact that Wilson voiced unconditional support for the organization soured many on the project, as did the strong support of Liberal parties in Europe. The liberals' "sacred egoism," *Civiltà Cattolica* thundered, had "broken the unity created by Christianity," forging "an international law" whose aim was "to oppose Christian international law" and bolster a "pagan conception" devoid of all religious meaning.[53] The choice of Geneva as the seat for the League's activities also troubled Catholics—after all, as members of the papal Secretariat of State grumbled, Geneva was a city for "international Freemasons" and was strongly identified with both the Protestant Reformation and the Enlightenment. To add insult to injury, it was in front of the city's statue of Jean-Jacques Rousseau that a large crowd had welcomed delegates to the first League of Nations assembly. If only Vienna had been chosen as the League's headquarters, officials said, that would have felt less as though Wilson and his allies were rubbing salt into an open wound.[54]

The Vatican daily also thundered against the League. As the *Osservatore Romano* put it in 1920, the "moniker League of Nations was a false claim," masking the "largest ever violation of the rights of populations to make decisions on their own."[55] Picking up on the idea that the name "League of Nations" was a bid to mislead the credulous, papal functionary Giovanni Battista Montini (who would become Pope Paul VI) polemicized: "The Church is the only true League of Nations—the only League of Nations that can escape a stillborn death, and the only one that can unite all men in 'one heart and one soul.'"[56] Writing in the Catholic conservative *Das Jahrbuch*, the final minister-president of the Habsburg Empire agreed, urging Catholics to form a faith-based League of Nations in response to the Wilsonian gambit—a so-called Catholic International League.[57] The idea was much praised by figures close to the Holy See, including no less than the director of the Vatican daily, who penned several letters to the papal secretary of state asserting that a Catholic International League had a greater chance of success than the League of Nations, and that it would go far in solving the Roman Question and circumventing liberal opposition to the pope.[58]

Though a rival Catholic International League never materialized, suspicions about the League of Nations remained strong. The League's minority rights regime was cause for particular concern. From the late nineteenth century, liberal internationalists had been advocating for a new set of legal instruments to protect religious and ethnic minorities, and with the creation of the League's minority rights regime, these internationalists had their day in the sun.[59] The League's regime was based on the notion that minorities deserved protection and support, not least because "minorities would be willing to integrate into the majority culture so long as the state granted them legal equality and protected their civil and political rights as citizens."[60] The League's minorities protection system was run by the League Council, and it sought to impel a dozen states in Eastern Europe and the Balkans to agree to protect national, ethnic, and religious minorities, as the price of sovereignty and membership. In a historic first, and in ways that caught the attention of new papal lawyers and new functionaries, the League's regime brought the question of minority rights into the purview of international law—thereby reframing understandings of state sovereignty. As the jurist Hans Aufricht noted, the minorities rights regime was a "striking example" of what was heretofore considered a more delimited domain for international law, for it declared "subject-matter that had previously been considered within the exclusive domestic jurisdiction of a State as a matter of international concern."[61]

The Minority Treaties were concluded by a string of Central, Southern, and Eastern European countries, including Poland, Czechoslovakia, Greece, Romania, Lithuania, Estonia, and Latvia. Poland signed the first Minority Treaty in June 1919; this was accompanied by an American-led fact-finding commission tasked with investigating instances of anti-Semitism in Poland in the summer of 1919.[62] For papal diplomats, that the fact-finding commission and the Polish Minority Treaty—which was tellingly known as the "Little Treaty of Versailles"—contained provisions protecting the Jewish minority in Poland was distressing. The Vatican believed that fostering the rights of non-Catholic minorities in Eastern Europe would breed conflict, and that it was best to curb the attempts of European powers "to strengthen the work of the [Minority] treaties."[63] The new Polish prime minister, Jan Paderewski, agreed, presenting the Minority Treaties as a clear instance of foreign meddling. Via a memorandum presented to the League of Nations, he argued that "Poland has already experienced the nefarious consequences which may result from the protection exercised by foreign powers over ethnical and religious minorities." In fact, if the League insisted on applying minority rights provisions, it would "fatally provoke excitement against the minorities and become the cause of incessant unrest."[64]

The papal position regarding the rights of Jewish and Catholic Poles was complemented by the announcement by Benedict XV that it was necessary to "protect the just rights of Christians" in Palestine, and ensure that "the rights of Jews should never and in no way override the just rights of Christians."[65] These were not just words: in these same years the pope was working with Polish diplomats to create a Catholic bloc (composed of Brazil, France, Italy, Spain, and Portugal) at the League to protest Britain's Balfour Declaration, which signaled Britain's support for "the establishment in Palestine of a national home for the Jewish people." Leaning on a similar logic as that used to protest the Minority Treaties, Benedict's secretary of state argued that the Balfour Declaration was a deeply faulty text, which "subordinate[d] the indigenous population for the advantage of other nationalities."[66] The pope, for his part, publicly warned that "it would be a terrible grief to Us and for all Christian faithful if infidels were placed in a more prominent position" in Palestine.[67]

Statements such as these endeared the papacy to many local Polish politicians, particularly in the anti-Semitic and ethno-nationalist National Democratic camp. They redoubled the conviction that it was necessary to fight the liberal model of the separation of church and state—a model that supposedly privileged national, ethnic, and religious minorities at the expense of national, ethnic, and religious majorities.[68] As a counter to those "builders" who were "unbelieving or did not follow Christ," local newspapers celebrated the pope's calls to "rebuild everything based in Christ" and "instill Catholicism into the reconstruction of the Polish state."[69]

Starting from the Paris Peace Conference, Woodrow Wilson and the United States lost ground in Eastern Europe—ground that would be occupied by the pope. In Paris, the United States had signaled that despite its calls for national self-determination, it was unwilling to take the steps necessary to robustly support national independence in Eastern Europe. The proposals of Polish delegates regarding the precise shape their new state should take were rejected out of hand, as American officials hid behind vague formulas (e.g., Poland "should get neither too much nor too little, but just what belonged to her"). What emerged was a compromise in which Polish leaders had little say—and one about which they were not pleased. The sense of shock at the United States' admittance that it would not be following through on past promises was palpable.[70]

If Poland was slighted, new nation-states like Estonia, Latvia, and Lithuania fared even worse: Woodrow Wilson questioned wholesale their right to self-determination, asserting that these states might not be "morally justified" in proclaiming independence, at least prior to the conclusion of the Russian civil war.[71] He noted that national self-determination, if applied throughout Eastern Europe, could be disastrous, for "pushed to its extreme, the principle would mean the disruption of existing governments, to an undefinable extent." At the same time, Wilson demurred, noting that "all such detailed questions" should be left to "the League of Nations to decide."[72]

In May 1919 one of the American president's closest advisors, William Bullitt, publicly resigned from the American peace commission in Paris after having articulated his disapproval of Wilson's waffling behavior.[73] Figures like the Polish politician Jan Paderewski and Karlis Ulmanis, Latvia's first prime minister, were similarly shocked by the gulf between Wilson's words and his actions. Both men had lived in the United States and acquired an inflated sense of America's importance in the making of postwar Europe. Ulmanis—who remained a central figure in Latvian politics from 1918 to his death in 1942—had famously declared himself a "son of America," and felt particularly humiliated by Wilson's snub. Similarly, Paderewski—a musician-composer hailed as a hero by many Americans—was sorely disappointed by the disinterest Washington showed toward his new nation-state. Local newspapers began railing against Wilson's hypocrisy, suggesting that the American idea of national self-determination had been a self-serving propaganda stunt all along.[74]

By 1919–1920 Wilson had already lost much of his messiah status in Eastern Europe. Papal diplomats benefited from the American president's demise. By presenting themselves as defenders of national self-determination but opponents of the Paris Peace settlement and the Minority Treaties, diplomats in Eastern Europe cast themselves as spokespersons for an alternative postwar Europe. In particular, they capitalized on the fact that the Holy See, unlike the United States, was ready and willing to grant recognition to new nation-states in the East. At a time when postwar boundaries were still fragile and labile, the Holy See's recognition of newly independent countries amounted to a stamp of approval of national sovereignty and a ticket to join the so-called international community.

Securing Latvia, Lithuania, and Estonia

Ratti, Benedict, and other papal officials quickly seized on the opportunities afforded by the moment and moved fast. The Vatican recognized Estonia's independence early and began to negotiate a concordat right away.[75] Already in 1920 they had won the prized agreement—the first concordat in the new Eastern European countries created by Brest-Litovsk. Interestingly, of all of the countries in the Brest zone, Estonia was the one with the smallest Catholic population (0.2 percent of Estonians were Catholic, according to a 1922 census). Here too, what enabled the concordat's success was the intersection of papal interests and those of secular state leaders, who saw the concordat as a way (in this case) to buttress Estonia's claims to independence and win over the country's small but economically significant Catholic population, based in the capital city of Tallinn.[76] Additionally, the fact that the papacy had aligned itself with the German Empire during World War I was not troubling to Estonian leaders, who were happy to grant rights and cultural autonomy to the German minority populations in Estonia (8.2 percent of the population) and consider postwar Germany a potential ally.[77]

As Ratti pushed on with concordat diplomacy in Lithuania and Latvia, he worked overtime to get the papacy to extend *de jure* recognition to these two countries before many of the Great Powers did the same. In the official documents recognizing the Latvian Republic, the Vatican made its intentions explicit. It strongly and unequivocally gave Latvia full diplomatic recognition, even as it noted the tit-for-tat aspect of its decision to do so:

The Holy See without hesitation completely and formally recognizes this republic [and] is convinced that the noble Latvian people and their government will see in this recognition new evidence of how very interested the Holy See is in the new republic's civic and moral well-being.[78]

The Vatican's declaration contrasted starkly with the United States' belated recognition of Latvia, Estonia, and Lithuania. In the official triple declaration of recognition, issued in 1922, the United States seemed unwilling to shed its earlier hesitations about recognizing the Baltic states in the hour of Russia's weakness. It even indicated that the recognition of these new territories did not preclude a future change of course. The document tentatively announced:

> The United States has consistently maintained that the disturbed conditions of Russian affairs may not be made the occasion for the alienation of Russian territory, and this principle is not deemed to be infringed by the recognition at this time of the Governments of Estonia, Latvia, and Lithuania, which have been set up and maintained by an indigenous population.[79]

Local state leaders reacted coolly to the United States' mealymouthed text. But the contrast between papal resolve and American shilly-shallying was not enough to win over local populations. Local politicians also needed to feel that concordats would help them deliver on some of their core aims. As in Poland, the chief concerns had to do with how the concordat would help with secular postwar priorities, which included consolidating borders, winning over local populations, and emerging victorious from internal power struggles.

Latvia, nestled between Estonia to the north, Lithuania to the south, the Baltic Sea to the west, and Russia to the east, had several live border questions. The small state had just waged war against both the Russians and the Germans, and it was eager to strengthen its diplomatic position and consolidate its borders. Papal diplomats quickly presented the concordat as a way to achieve these ends. The treaty not only made diocesan lines coincide with those of the new state. It also pledged that the Holy See would help Latvia in its project to diminish Russian influence on site, by constructing an Archdiocese of Riga, which would separate the Latvian ecclesiastical hierarchy from the Russian one (and the diocese of Mohilev). Additionally, the concordat would help local politicians integrate a potentially unwieldy periphery: the Catholic-dominated region of Latgale. As the government explained to its population, the treaty was "certainly necessary" for nation-building reasons, and particularly "in relation to Latgale, where most of the inhabitants are Catholic, differ the most from the rest of Latvia with regard to their cultural and ethnographic traits, and are subject [to] foreign influences that could significantly affect our Catholic residents—a situation which no patriotic Latvian politician would want."[80]

The concordat was signed in the Vatican on May 30, 1922. On November 3, 1922, it was approved by Latvia's parliament. The treaty was faithfully implemented by Latvian politicians in the 1920s and 1930s, both during a period of social-democratic leadership under Minister Skujenieks (1926–1928) and then under the period of nationalist and authoritarian rule, under Kārlis Ulmanis (1928–1940). As in Poland, loyalty to the concordat helped Latvia's leaders assert their own power and authority over rival factions and groups. Thus, the defense of the concordat by the country's social democrats became a way for them to demonstrate their loyalty to the Latgale region, and particularly to the Catholic organizations heavily represented there. Subsequently, the implementation of the concordat by Ulmanis helped this strongman make the case that he had the Latvian people's best interests and basic freedoms in mind—even as he suspended civil liberties, closed down newspapers, and imprisoned a large number of politicians on the right and the left.[81]

Despite the work of Ulmanis and others to convince Latvians that the concordat was advancing nation-building goals, portions of the population remained suspicious. Some commentators thundered against the "antinational" and "pro-Lithuanian" agreement, noting that "in a country where Lutherans are 76.6 percent of the population" the concordat was, quite simply, "unjust."[82] Others worried that the concordat would not only sanction the rise of Lithuania, but also "give Jesuits free license to convert the Lutheran Latvians and the unbelievers into faithful Catholics, because they believe that only in this way will the 'sinners' be forgiven."[83] Still others gave the agreement a satirical spin, through poems such as this: "Praise be to God and the concordat given by the Pope/With a bishop the Catholics are blessed/And a donkey's tail, too./But my mind has a holier thought:/Send the pope and Rome to the devil."[84] Local opposition nonetheless failed to block or overturn the Latvian concordat.[85] In Latvia, as across Europe, concordats were not concluded through popular plebiscites: they were signed over the heads of everyday residents by state leaders and papal authorities.

Like Latvia's, the story of Lithuania's concordat was also one of winning over local politicians and making them see the concordat as a way to deliver on local priorities. The Catholic-majority country was ruled from 1918 to 1926 by a clerical Christian Democratic party, which enjoyed the strong support of the local Church. Initially this party worked to win the papacy's favor, and to present Catholicism and Lithuanian nationalism as mutually reinforcing. In the first constitution of the newly independent Lithuanian state (1922), Catholics were granted various rights and privileges, including financial support for religious instruction. The Church was given the right to register births, marriages, and deaths, among other secular functions.[86] However, though the Christian Democrats showed themselves interested in a concordat, they would not see the treaty through. In 1925 a major controversy exploded between the papacy and the Lithuanian government when Achille Ratti concluded the Polish concordat. With the Polish treaty, Ratti had tacitly underwritten Polish claims to the city of Vilna—a city which Lithuanians considered their spiritual capital.[87] Partly as a result of the Christian Democrats' failure to sway the papacy on this matter, in May 1926 the party lost power. The big winners in the spring 1926 elections were the Social Democrats and the Peasant Populists, who promptly signed a treaty of neutrality and non-aggression with the Soviet Union, and granted amnesty to left-wing political prisoners. The moves troubled the Lithuanian right wing, and in December 1926 a group of Lithuanian army officers overthrew the left-wing government, with the support of two charismatic strongmen: Augustinas Voldemaras and Antanas Smetona.

Immediately after the coup, Voldemaras became the country's new prime minister, and Smetona the country's new president. The two men proudly defined themselves as "anti-liberal," a phrase they used to signal their opposition to parliamentary democracy. In 1928 Voldemaras and Smetona scrapped Lithuania's 1922 constitution without following constitutional procedures. Unapologetic about their moves, Voldemaras and Smetona argued that a reversion to parliamentary democracy would constitute "a relapse of a political illness." They also asserted that "parliamentarism" had failed across Europe, not just in Lithuania, and that it had given rise to "unstable and ineffective governments," "weakening the strength of the state both internally and externally." Thus, they concluded, "the deified democratism had failed," and "thoughtful postwar leaders of European states" were moving beyond parliamentarism in the search for stability.[88] The Christian Democrats, in protest, left the government.

As Smetona and Voldemaras consolidated power, they decided to turn back to the concordat question. Doing so, they reasoned, could help win over the Catholic masses still faithful to Lithuania's Christian Democratic party, all the while undermining the party's exclusive claims to being the Church's best protector. In 1927 Voldemaras traveled to Rome, where he met with papal diplomats and negotiated and signed the Lithuanian concordat. The move was controversial, and even the Vatican representative in Lithuania opposed it, on the grounds that the Vatican should not be buoying Lithuanian claims to sovereignty: as he saw things, the Lithuanians were incapable of governing themselves—the only answer was for Poland to absorb Lithuania. The Lithuanian clergy were also divided on the concordat. Many complained to Vatican diplomats that with the parliament dissolved, President Smetona and Prime Minister Voldemaras did not have the juridical right to ratify the concordat. In response, the papacy forced the Lithuanian government to confirm that the parliament was unnecessary for the ratification of the concordat and itself ratified the concordat on December 8, 1927. Following this move, Lithuania's new authoritarian regime did push back on some key components of the agreement, particularly pertaining to the freedom of organization of Lithuania's Catholic organizations.[89] However, by and large the Lithuanian concordat was faithfully implemented—much as was the case in Poland, Latvia, and Estonia.[90]

Concordat diplomacy succeeded in Latvia, Lithuania, Estonia, and Poland due to the intersection of papal interests and the goals of local politicians. In those territories where these conditions were absent, negotiations failed. In Czechoslovakia, for instance, the left-wing politicians who rose to power after World War I were strongly and openly anticlerical. The country's new leaders understood the Great War as a war against the "theocratic autocracy," embodied by the Central Powers,

which "ha[d] been defeated by democracy, resting on the principles of
human morality." After the war, with the state's tacit consent, several
religious statues, including Our Lady on Prague's Old Town Square,
were knocked down. Crucifixes were removed from Czechoslovakia's
schools. The papal diplomat in Czechoslovakia left in protest, but the
major conservative party in Czechoslovakia, the Agrarian Party, did
not raise its voice, and maintained a neutral attitude toward the Catholic Church and Catholicism. Neither did Czech Catholic newspapers
univocally rally to Rome's side. At the same time, Catholic dissident
movements were sprouting up left and right. For instance, the Czech
Jednota movement of priests decided to use the opportunities afforded
by the early postwar upending of norms to push for radical reforms,
including services in the vernacular and the abolition of clerical celi-
bacy. When Benedict XV condemned the movement and its requests,
Jednota responded by breaking ties with Rome and forming its own
schismatic Church, which of course was condemned again, this time
by the Vatican's Holy Office.[91] Small wonder that in a democratic
country where the elected powers were not sympathetic to Rome, and
where the Catholic Church and Catholic opinion were divided on many
issues dear to the papacy's heart, the Vatican was unsuccessful in its
concordat bid. The best it could do was conclude a *modus vivendi* with
Czechoslovakia, in which it was granted certain minimal privileges
in exchange for staying out of political life.

The Yugoslav case is similarly helpful in understanding the necessary conditions for the success of concordat diplomacy. Here too, as in
Czechoslovakia, the political and social climate was unfavorable to the
pope. Yugoslavia, like so many countries in the region, emerged from
World War I as a new state facing a serious challenge: that of politically integrating the country's many religious and ethnic groups. For
a period, Yugoslavia's King Alexander believed that concluding a
concordat with Rome could help in this project. In the hopes of simultaneously weakening separatist movements (particularly those
spearheaded by Croatian Catholics) and lessening the power of the
Serb Orthodox opposition, the royal dictator not only engaged in talks
with papal diplomats: over the heads of opposition members and impervious to their objections, he signed a concordat with the pope. However, King Alexander was not a popular figure at home, and in 1934 he

was assassinated by a Croatian separatist. Following the king's death, the concordat became a political liability. The country's new leaders were uninterested in rallying behind the text. Thus, despite years of negotiations, the concordat remained unratified by the Yugoslav upper house of parliament. As in Czechoslovakia, the problem was also with the local Catholic Church. Yugoslav Catholics, by and large, rejected the Vatican's political tutelage and were disturbed by the support of the Church of Rome for Italy's annexation of Istria, which they saw as non-Italian territory. Additionally, Catholic Croatian nationalists, including many members of the Catholic bishopric, worried that the concordat would weaken Croat claims for political autonomy. They argued that instead of getting involved in the messy business of signing treaties and forging alliances with state leaders, the Church should focus on economic and spiritual issues, and leave politics to the politicians.[92]

A Concordat Crusade

Despite the setbacks in Czechoslovakia and Yugoslavia, by the late 1920s the concordat crusade had scored a string of victories in Eastern Europe, in the countries most impacted by the conclusion of the Treaty of Brest-Litovsk in March 1918. The Vatican's new Catholic diplomacy had succeeded in Estonia (1920), Latvia (1922), Poland (1925), and Lithuania (1927). The revolution was pioneered by a new generation of functionaries within the papal diplomatic corps who had a keen interest in capturing the nascent field of international law and branding it Catholic. They had cut their teeth on the Code of Canon Law, which through concordat diplomacy they sought to insert into the legal frameworks of Europe's new and newly reconstituted nation-states. Their work caught the attention of European observers, who came out in large numbers both for and against the papacy's legal revolution.[93]

The speed of the papacy's legal revolution was unprecedented, and a new "concordat Europe" seemed in the making. In direct response to the school battles waged in European countries in the nineteenth century, what contemporaries termed the new "concordat common law" affirmed that henceforth European states would protect the teaching of the Catholic religion in public schools. The treaties specified that local high-ranking members of the clergy would be able to appoint teachers and determine curricula.[94] In some cases, clergy even received this power at the university level. Several concordats affirmed that private religious schools, founded and directed by clerics, could have the character of public schools.[95] All concordats gave bishops the right to run diocesan seminars or schools of philosophy or theology, thus effectively freeing the training of members of religious orders from state oversight.[96] All of these efforts were in keeping with an integral Catholic understanding of education, according to which schooling must be the "natural" outgrowth of education received within the bounds of family life, and a "subsidiary gift of the paternal household."[97] As such, Catholics deemed it necessary to limit as much as possible the influence of the state, favoring instead of "natural" units, like the patriarchal family and the Church.

Concordats signed after the Great War also challenged older regimes of state oversight by affirming the right of the Catholic Church to maintain, build, and develop religious institutions, which were granted legal personality.[98] Relatedly, they granted the Church freedom of communication and of the press. This was a huge win for the Church: in many countries, what was still on the books was a regime of strict censorship, which called for the government's authorization of any sort of text that the Church sought to distribute.[99] The Vatican's new treaty diplomacy promoted an expanded network of Vatican-supervised Catholic civil society organizations—organizations that actively militated against the idea that Catholicism was for the private sphere alone.

In another bid to erode the feared liberal public/private divide, the papacy's post-1918 treaties all contained provisions pertaining to family law—to marriage, divorce, and the rearing of children. Most concordats affirmed that the state would recognize religious marriages as civil marriages, and promised that the state would validate marriages between Catholics and non-Catholics, so long as they were contracted in the presence of a Catholic priest and conducted "according to the laws of the Church."[100] Many concordats specified that the rulings of ecclesiastical tribunals would be recognized by the state, especially in matters pertaining to marriage.[101] In practice, this meant that particularly sticky marriage questions, up to and including marriage annulment, must be handled by the reactionary Sacred Roman Rota, the Holy See's highest internal court of appeals. Some concordats laid out laws regarding mixed marriages, and some went a step further by insisting that the children of mixed marriages should be educated in the Catholic religion.[102]

Concordats responded to secularizing initiatives of the late eighteenth and nineteenth centuries by specifying that all Church properties should be exempt from taxation. Most treaties affirmed that in no circumstance would it be legal for the state to appropriate or confiscate religious sites or properties.[103] Many concordats also promised extensive financial support, in the form of clergy pensions and state donations, to be put toward churches, hospitals, and schools (new and old).[104] All concordats asserted that clergy and members of religious orders were exempt from appearing before secular tribunals. They also exempted clergy and monastics from military service and from certain civil functions.[105] Many of these provisions were directly lifted from the new 1917 Code of Canon Law, which outlined an entirely separate accountability structure for clergy and members of religious orders.[106] Indeed, the new concordats often simply referenced canons of the Code, which was treated as a go-to source for further elaboration of treaty articles.[107] In this way, as a contemporary observer noted, concordats amounted to a "consecrating of the Code of Canon Law . . . by secular law."[108]

In response to the wave of post-World War I concordats, many celebrated the pope's "extraordinarily active and varied legal work," and noted how far the pope had come since the days of the *Kulturkampf*.[109] The pope, bombastically, asserted that the rulers of practically every nation, motivated by a desire for union and peace, had turned to the Holy See in order to settle legal questions of interest to both Church and state.[110] This was a huge overstatement, of course, but for the Eurocentric pope, Europe was the world—and in continental terms, the papacy was doing quite well for itself indeed.

Soon enough, concordat diplomacy would travel from Eastern to Western Europe. As concordat diplomacy grew wings, local diplomats would continue to do their best to adapt to new circumstances, and present concordats as attractive to state leaders. Their success would hinge on their ability to build trust, respond to local state leaders' concerns, and develop a protean narrative on the utility of concordats and their capacity to solve local problems. As was the case during the Great War, Germany remained a centerpiece of the Holy See's efforts. The experiences of papal diplomats in this country would ultimately have a profound impact on Rome, and, in the long term, transform both the meaning of concordat diplomacy and the papacy's geopolitical designation of diplomatic friends and existential enemies.

3

Papal Officials Build Local Bridges

There are a few possible new European orders at this moment. Some—
informed by clear Christian principles—will guarantee freedom and
peace. Others—based on disbelieving secularism and atheism—will
be instruments for the creation of the worst forms of tyranny . . . [The
choice:] Either Wilson or Lenin [or] Christian civilization, led by the
Father of our great Christian family.

—*Osservatore Romano*, JANUARY 1919

As PAPAL DIPLOMATS moved from Eastern to Central and Western
Europe, they began attaching an additional set of symbolic valences to
the concordats they sought to export. This was not least because much
had changed in the time that elapsed between the original concordat
proposal formulated by Eugenio Pacelli in the midst of the Great War
and the conclusion of the first wave of successful concordats in Western
Europe in the mid- to late 1920s. During this arc of time, left-wing
radicalism had emerged as a new and powerful force, not just in
Russia but also in Germany, Austria, Hungary, Italy, and Spain. As
papal representatives built local bridges in these countries, they went
native—and, without direct input from their superiors, began to sell
concordat diplomacy not only as a way to resist the Paris peace settlement and advance nation-building goals, but also as a way to fight
against socialist and communist political forces that were gaining
momentum.

It was not as though socialism was a new enemy for these diplomats. Most of them saw socialism and liberalism as two sides of the

same coin, and were quite familiar with the fact that the socialists had gathered in international organizations since the mid-nineteenth century. In 1864 the International Workingmen's Association—or First International—was founded in London, and by the late nineteenth century, national socialist and labor parties had become important political players in Europe. Riding high on their electoral successes and buoyed by the existence of a thick web of socialist after-school and after-work associations, in 1889 they declared May 1—May Day—as International Workers' Day. Papal diplomats also identified socialists as leading anticlericals; after all, it was through their work, often in partnership with Liberal parties, that the pan-European *Kulturkampf* gathered steam. The countryside was fertile ground for socialist anticlericalism, due to the association between local clergy and the landowning class. The establishment of socialist assistance and mutual credit societies also undermined previous forms of charity and assistance provided by the Church, all the while reiterating the socialists' baseline commitment to the abolition of private property.

The rise of socialist internationalism in the late nineteenth century was deeply discomfiting to European clergy and the pontiff. In the first year of his pontificate, Leo XIII issued an encyclical, *Quod Apostolici Muneris*, that loudly condemned socialist parties and practices in Europe, arguing that socialism was fundamentally anti-Christian in that it opposed moral values and core Catholic principles, including respect for authority and private property. The socialist propensity to organize across borders also bothered the pope, who thundered against the socialists as "bound together in an unholy league" and bent on spreading a "deadly poison . . . into human society" as they sought "to uproot the foundation of society."[1] Socialists were extremists, the pope later noted, and in concert with liberals and "the sect of Freemasons," they aimed to undermine "reverence for divine laws."[2]

However, after nearly forty years of activism, just as the Great War got under way, socialist movements in Europe began to show signs of weakness. In 1916 the Second International dissolved. The proximate cause of the dissolution was the Great War, and more specifically the decision in August 1914 of most European socialist parties to rally to their countries' war efforts. Nationalism, many lamented, had beat out internationalism, and shown that the pre-1914 unity of socialists "was a sham." Then came the Bolshevik Revolution, which had a profound impact on left-wing movements in Central and Western Europe. It caused a sharp rupture between reformists and revolutionists and inaugurated a major crisis in the socialist movement. When after the war the Second International reconstituted, it was weak and ill-populated as compared to its prewar predecessor.[3] By contrast, newborn communist parties—forged by revolutionary socialists—were on the rise. As the founder of the Italian Communist Party, Antonio Gramsci, put it, the Bolshevik leader Vladimir Lenin had stirred the consciences of Western European socialists; he was the "awakener of sleeping souls."[4] The Polish-German activist Rosa Luxemburg emphasized that all signs indicated that the time was ripe for "socialist revolution."[5] In Germany, the Russian example would help inspire the Bavarian Soviet Republic, the Spartacist uprising in Berlin, and the expansion of revolutionary sentiments and actions across the entire German Empire, between November 1918 and August 1919. Austria and Hungary experienced revolutions as well. Across much of southern Europe, anarchist and socialist movements led by workers and farmers stopped short of full-blown revolution, but engaged in large-scale uprisings, seizing factories and farmland. Italy would experience the *Biennio Rosso*, the "two red years" of unrest in both urban and rural centers, which were followed by the Fascist seizure of power. In Hungary, Bulgaria, and Spain, and eventually Germany and Austria too, the postrevolutionary stabilization of the 1920s and 1930s would take reactionary and authoritarian forms. By contrast, in places like Czechoslovakia, Switzerland, Scandinavia, France, the Low Countries, and Britain, socialist and social democratic parties would go the ballot-box route. Their electoral successes would be impressive, and once in power these parties would work to strengthen parliamentary democracy and expand workers' rights under the law.[6]

Taking stock of the rise of socialist and communist movements in Europe, and concerned in particular by the growth in revolutionary sentiments, papal diplomats on the ground in Central and Western Europe began to modify the meaning accorded to the concordat project. In continuity with the wartime years, they still framed concordats as tools for Europe's re-Christianization—in other words, as opportunities for the creation (or "restoration," as they would have it) of a theocentric continent. But in conversation with local political forces, especially on the center and radical right, these functionaries grew increasingly convinced that left-wing radicalism was a serious and immediate threat to Europe's peace. Particularly in countries like Germany, which remained the crown jewel for the Holy See in the early postwar years, as well as in Italy, Spain, France, Austria, and Hungary, the rise of a new brand of racist and nativist anti-leftism left a mark on papal officials. Soon enough, these same papal officials began presenting concordats to their local interlocutors as socio-legal measures capable of stalling or undermining the plans of left-wing revolutionaries. Over the course of the late 1920s and early 1930s, this new justificatory framework for concordats was relayed back to Rome through missives, memos, and telegrams. The framing—which had been spontaneously adopted by papal diplomats in response to conditions on the ground— began to have its effect, slowly pushing the papal diplomatic establishment as a whole toward a frontal confrontation with the state most identified with left-wing radicalism in this period, the Soviet Union. Beginning in the early 1930s, under the influence of papal diplomats and local political forces, and under the weight of a new Great Depression era strand of apocalypticism, the central government of the Roman Catholic Church would launch a far-reaching crusade against international communism—a crusade that initially was peppered with anti-liberal and anti-American motifs but that would eventually take on a life of its own.

The 1930s papal anticommunist crusade was not inevitable. It marked an important shift for the central government of the Roman Catholic Church. To be sure, from the mid-nineteenth century, Pontiffs had condemned "socialism" or "communism" in some form. But socialism and communism initially were not presented as the only threats to the Church or, much less, the most dangerous ones.[7] From 1917 through the mid-1920s, the pope even instructed his men to keep open channels of communication with Russian revolutionaries and seek to forge a working relationship with them. It was only as a result of developments in the 1920s—and the new meanings that papal diplomats ascribed to concordats in Central and Western Europe—that the Vatican started changing its tune.

Engaging the Bolsheviks

In 1917 the hot fever of the concordat moment led the Holy See to look upon the Russian Revolution with a mix of fear and curiosity. Fear, because Catholics were still spooked, as they had been throughout the nineteenth century, by the ghost of 1789 and anticlerical revolutionism. Hope, because even as the Bolsheviks started unveiling a secularizing project that rhymed with that of the French revolutionaries, the clearly stated target was not the Catholic Church but the Russian Orthodox Church. When, starting in 1918, the Bolsheviks began nationalizing Orthodox religious property, removing religious instruction from public schools, and creating a secular bureaucracy to register births, marriages, deaths, and divorces, now constituted as civil acts, the moves were intended to clear away Orthodox influence from Russian society.[8] The early legislation of the Bolsheviks favored Catholics and the Catholic Church, granting them rights they had not enjoyed under the Romanov autocracy.[9] For this reason, the same Catholic commentators who fretted about the similarities between 1789 and 1917 simultaneously held open the possibility of concluding a concordat with the Bolsheviks. Perhaps, they noted, this was the moment to reconquer the vast Russian territories for Christ.[10] As the Superior General of the Jesuit Order put it, Russia was populated by "120,000,000 people with no shepherd" as a result of the eclipse of the Orthodox Church. This could only be good news for the Vatican.[11] According to the *Osservatore Romano*, even if the staying power of the Russian Bolsheviks was unclear, concluding an agreement with them seemed like a good idea, in that it would put the status of the Catholic Church in Russian territories on firmer ground.[12]

In keeping with the postwar concordat imperative, as early as 1918 Pope Benedict XV asked Achille Ratti, in his capacity as nuncio in Poland, to open avenues of communication with the Bolsheviks.[13] In his conversations with Ratti, the papal secretary of state, Pietro Gasparri, recommended that the cleric stay close to official Church policies at the time, which held that "the Church has—theoretically speaking— no prejudice against a communist form of government . . . The Church requires only that states, regardless of what kind, do not attempt to hinder or attack the free development of the religious and sacramental life that is the purpose and obligation of the Church."[14] Ever the loyal diplomat, Ratti did as he was told and opened regular contact with Vladimir Lenin and other Russian Bolshevik leaders by telegraph. He helped lay the foundations for Soviet-papal talks, which began in the early 1920s and continued through 1928. Given Ratti's pursuit of dialogue with the Russians, no potential occasion for tightening relations could be missed. Thus, when in July–August 1920 the Red Army invaded Poland, Gasparri instructed Ratti to stay at his post in Warsaw, just in case the Bolsheviks won the war. This way, the Milanese cleric would be in a good position to immediately establish diplomatic contact with the Bolsheviks.[15] Ironically, several years later this episode would be repackaged and presented as proof of papal bravery in the face of international communism; the new hero-narrative held that Ratti had decided to stay in Warsaw to invoke the protection of the Virgin Mary and "encourage the resistance of the good people of Poland" against the Red Army.[16] Polish Catholic papers repeated the myth, affirming that Ratti "remained, looking at the wild horde of Muscovites, which approached the Polish capital with torches in their hands and menaced to annihilate our nation, faith, and civilization."[17] But the new version of the story was far from the truth: the real motivation for Ratti's presence in Warsaw during the Red Army invasion was anything but anticommunist in spirit—Ratti stayed in the capital in order to strengthen ties with the Bolsheviks.

The papacy worked to show its goodwill toward the Bolsheviks through other measures as well. It founded the Russian Papal Relief Mission, which helped combat what from 1921 had become the worst famine in Russian memory. "[Do] not act in a way which might compromise the image of the Holy See in the eyes of the Russians," the Mission's leader, the Jesuit Edmund Walsh, was carefully instructed.[18] These actions to build, not burn, bridges helped lay the foundations for the presence of papal diplomats at the Genoa conference (April 10–May 19, 1922), the historic post–World War I meeting that was attended by representatives of thirty European countries, and that aimed to better the economic situation of Central and Eastern Europe while simultaneously improving relations between Soviet Russia and the West. At Genoa, the pope's men engaged in lengthy meetings with the Russian commissar of foreign affairs, Georgy Vasilyevich Chicerin,

Eugenio Pacelli (far left), en route to Breslau, 1926. Credit: Sueddeutsche
Zeitung Photo / Alamy Stock Photo

indicating that the Vatican was ready and willing to conclude a concordat or a less-binding *modus vivendi.* Soviet leaders, eager to gain
de jure recognition of their new country through the conclusion of an
international agreement with the Vatican, extended a willing hand and
promised to conclude a general deal and allow the Vatican to set up
schools, provide religious instruction, and implement other expressed
desiderata.[19]

As members of the papal diplomatic establishment instructed lower-
level officials, in face-to-face encounters with their Soviet counterparts, officials must stay calm, cool, cordial, and do what they could
to preserve "the goodwill of [the] Soviets." Out of deference to the rigid
ecclesiastical hierarchy in which they were trapped, most of the diplomats nodded in agreement. However, one of them—Edmund Walsh, the
leader of the Russian Papal Relief Mission—confided to the sympathetic Superior General of the Jesuits, Włodzimierz Ledóchowski, his

"surprise and disappointment" upon hearing this charge. The Vatican had embarked upon a "false track," he fretted. The "world [will] think the Vatican is compromising with [the] Soviets."[20] In fact, it was. From 1922 through 1928, papal and Soviet officials were knee-deep in diplomatic negotiations.

By the late 1920s these negotiations were showing serious signs of wear, however. This was not least due to the fact that local diplomats in Western Europe—deeply embedded in local discursive communities—started shifting the meaning accorded to concordats in response to a wave of anticommunist sentiment sweeping countries like Germany, Italy, Spain, France, Austria, and Hungary. As with the story of how the Vatican came to embrace the new concordat diplomacy during World War I, the story of how the Holy See began to shift against the Soviet Union begins in Germany. Initially, it was a classic anti-liberal tale.

Building Bridges in Bavaria

On April 13, 1917, exactly one week after the United States declared war on Germany, the main lifeline between Germany and the Holy See fell silent. When the Holy See's foreign ambassador in Munich died suddenly at the age of fifty-five, Matthias Erzberger zipped off a letter that came immediately to the point. The pope, he urged, must replace the not-quite-cold apostolic nuncio, for Europe was experiencing a "delicate moment," making papal support for Germany all the more essential.[21] By May 25, 1917, the new papal nuncio, Eugenio Pacelli, was in Munich, putting faces to names and buttering up prominent members of the Bavarian Catholic intelligentsia.

At this point, having a papal representative in Bavaria was the key to Germany as a whole—not to mention to Central Europe, insofar as papal-Austrian and papal-Hungarian relations would be reaffirmed only at a later date. Bavaria was Germany's second largest state, and the only one where Catholics were in the majority, at 70 percent of the population. It alone had enjoyed formal diplomatic relations with the Holy See since the late eighteenth century—relations that had remained uninterrupted even following Germany's unification. Prior to the mid-1920s there was no equivalent relationship with Berlin. It was for this reason that German anticlericals disparagingly referred to Munich as the "secret Rome," while proud natives celebrated their historic protection of "the Holy See's activities" and Bavaria's "better and deeper understanding of the Catholic Church and its relations with the State."[22]

As the new nuncio settled in, the person who emerged as his first and closest interlocutor was the man who had urgently wanted him there: Matthias Erzberger. The nuncio was initially quite taken by the German Catholic politician and his vision for self-determination—that is, the Brest model of hegemony without territorial annexation. But following a honeymoon period, relations between the two men soured. Troubles started by late 1918, when Erzberger decided to embrace Woodrow Wilson and support the League of Nations, pushing all majoritarian political parties in Germany to do the same. Pacelli was troubled, not least because Erzberger began emphasizing what he saw as the manifold similarities between Wilson's vision for postwar Europe and Benedict XV's.[23] Many papal officials remained convinced that a deep gulf separated Benedict XV from the calculating "liberal hypocrisy" of Woodrow Wilson. Furthermore, how could the League of Nations be trusted, when it was nothing but a Trojan horse for anti-Catholic, Wilsonian interests? Erzberger got the message quickly and stopped reaching out. In 1918 he had sent 117 letters to Pacelli (one every three to four days); in 1919 he sent only 14 missives. Between January 1920 and mid-August 1921, not a single note of his reached the nuncio's desk.[24] When on August 26, 1921, right-wing extremists shot Erzberger dead, Pacelli was certainly shocked by the murder, but he also must have felt some relief knowing he had burned his bridges with the politician in time.

Well before Erzberger's murder, Pacelli had begun building an alternate community of friends and informants. The figures within the nuncio's emergent discursive network had key features in common. All were resolutely anti-liberal and fawningly pro-papist; all espoused love for Bavaria and their love for Rome. All supported monarchies and were particularly enamored with the Bavarian monarchy, the House of Wittelsbach. Few had much confidence in democracy as an ideal and as a form of government, but none had strong objections to the creation of political Catholic parties—so long as they stayed true to their Catholic origins. Pacelli's new interlocutors were also staunch regionalists, who romanticized Bavaria's pre-urban rural traditions and believed it was imperative for Bavaria to stay independent from Germany's "fallen" capital.[25]

A key figure in Pacelli's new network was Michael von Faulhaber, who in July 1917 became archbishop of Munich. Hailing from a sleepy town in rural Bavaria, the German cleric had gained a name for himself on the battlefield, as military chaplain on the Western Front. Faulhaber had seen it as his noble duty to participate in the Great War, which he understood as a "crusade" and "holy war" against atheism, liberalism, and modernism. Even after Germany's 1918 defeat, Faulhaber affirmed: "It is my conviction that when it comes to the ethics of war, this war will constitute for us a classic example of just war." Faulhaber saw no contradiction between his nationalistic loyalty to "the Fatherland" and his love of Rome and the Holy Father. Indeed, he dreamed of the day when Church and state would come together as a single power and reinforce one another's actions. In this he was joined by many conservative Bavarian Catholics.[26]

In his early speeches in Munich, Pacelli sowed the seeds for a future concordat, emphasizing that the Holy See was eager to lend a hand "in this grave hour," to help "reconstruct human society on the solid ground of Christian justice." "A lasting peace," Pacelli informed a crowd soon after his arrival, could be "grounded solely on the solid bases of Christian law."[27] But as the nuncio settled into his new home, the comforting Old Europe he had known fell apart all around him. In late October and early November 1918, the German Empire imploded, the German Kaiser abdicated, and Germany became a republic. For the papal nuncio, the developments initially demonstrated that the Wilsonian settlement was bearing fruit.

On November 7, 1918, Munich was shaken by the revolutionary wave as well, with the eruption of the first Bavarian revolution. Within a day, what had started as a mass demonstration to demand the war's immediate end turned into a full-blown changing of the guard. Revolutionaries occupied Munich's government buildings, transportation, and communication centers. Workers' and soldiers' councils formed. With dizzying speed, the last king of Bavaria, Ludwig II, abandoned the throne. At 10 p.m. that same evening, the revolution's leader—a Jewish freelance journalist and independent social democrat by the name of Kurt

Eisner—climbed to the presidential podium in Bavaria's state parliament. He proclaimed Bavaria a free state and a republic, affirming: "The Bavarian revolution is victorious. It has put an end to the old plunder of the Wittelsbach kings. Now we must proceed to build a new regime."[28] Soon the rest of Germany followed suit, and by month's end all of the royal rulers of Germany's states had abdicated. Then the Austrians threw out the Habsburg monarchy, and the king of Hungary, Charles IV, relinquished his hold on power. Austria and Hungary— Germany's old allies—had also become republics overnight.

The German Catholic hierarchy responded to the new developments with hard-line, uncompromising tones. Faulhaber declared the new republics illegitimate, even as Prussian bishops encouraged their flocks to rise in resistance: "You need to defend yourselves by standing united. Be inflexible and invincible."[29] Bavaria's Catholic conservative press—the official diocesan weekly, the *Münchener Katholische Kirchenzeitung*, and the conservative *Bayerischer Kurier*, Pacelli's chosen paper for publishing the papal view on pressing questions of the day— expressed similar sentiments.[30] Echoing a long tradition of papal anti-republicanism, Pacelli joined the chorus. He argued that the republics that had come to light were illegitimate creations: the children of "perjury and high treason," born of "the revolution's overturning of all thrones." The "crime" of German republicanism, he said, was of a piece with the sin committed by French revolutionaries.[31]

Despite the hostility in Catholic circles to the new Republic, Bavaria's new social-democratic leader, Kurt Eisner, repeatedly sought out formal relations with the Vatican. To send the clearest possible signal that he was uninterested, Pacelli gave Eisner the cold shoulder by heading to the charming town of Rorschach, in Switzerland, on the south side of Lake Constance. He did not consult anyone in papal headquarters prior to leaving, and only belatedly informed the Vatican secretary of state of the trip.[32] The Bavarian Catholic conservative milieu was united behind Pacelli's decision: they were convinced that talking to Eisner meant accepting the end of the monarchy and the rise of republics in Germany. (To demonstrate its total and complete disapproval of the new Republican Bavaria, in late November the Bavarian representation to the Holy See swore allegiance to the Bavarian people, not the Bavarian government.[33]). The papal secretary of state, Cardinal

Gasparri, was angered by Pacelli's bold and independent actions. In letters to the nuncio, Gasparri suggested that Pacelli needed to act only following consultation with his superiors, and that he was overplaying the threat and missing a historic opportunity to win protections for the Catholic Church.[34]

Pacelli deflected Gasparri by putting forward his interpretation of recent history. He argued that the November revolutions would have never happened if German politicians had done more to support Benedict's peace plan and fight against Wilsonianism. "If Germany had listened to the suggestions of the Holy See, it would not have come to such a sad end," he lamented.[35] Monsignor Lorenzo Schioppa, Pacelli's assistant at the nunciature in Munich, harped on similar themes, emphasizing that the United States had gotten what it wanted: Germany's crushing defeat and the country's total destabilization.[36]

The letters to Rome were not simply reiterations of the classic papal anti-Wilsonianism. They contained evidence that the nuncio and his assistant were internalizing a new variety of racialized and anti-Semitic anti-republicanism present in Bavarian Catholic circles. Many of the Bavarian Catholic newspapers the nuncio regularly perused announced that the 1918 revolutions were best understood as "invasions" carried out by "foreign" Jews, and that the republics that followed in the revolution's wake were illegitimate creatures.[37] Reviving the nineteenth-century notion that Jewish emancipation had been a mistake, conservative journalists argued that Jews did not have the right to assume leadership positions in Germany, given their unreliable traits and their questionable "Bavarian-ness."[38] Finally, the Bavarian Catholic right increasingly characterized Kurt Eisner as a "sleazy Jew" who along with his "pack of unbelieving Jews" had destroyed the God-given order and ushered in what might well be the beginning of the end of Europe as a whole.[39]

Pacelli and his assistant expressed similar sentiments. As they announced in letters back to Rome, dialoguing with Kurt Eisner was unthinkable: after all, he was a criminal, "an atheist, a radical socialist," and crucially, "to top it all off, a Galician Jew"—that is, a foreigner, from the Polish region of Galicia.[40] They affirmed that the people with whom Eisner surrounded himself were "bestial" and cunning, just like he was.[41] Both in general terms and when it came to the particular figure of Kurt Eisner, Pacelli and his assistant interbraided tropes borrowed from centuries of anti-Semitism (which cast Jews as untrustworthy, unclean outsiders), with the notion that there was some essential link between Eisner's "radical socialism" and his Jewishness. This interbraiding was increasingly common in Bavaria, and in France, Hungary, Poland, Russia, Austria, and Italy as well. Starting in the late nineteenth century, propagandists had cast Jews as republicans, democrats, liberals, Freemasons, socialists, and capitalists who through newfangled political and economic ideas were seeking to disrupt and overturn the old order. Catholics were not immune to this discourse, and many emerged as foremost turn-of-the-century exponents of it.[42]

If the success of concordat diplomacy in Poland was connected to the idea that Catholics were the "deserving" and "proper" members of the Polish national community, in Bavaria, similarly, concordat diplomacy received local buy-in thanks in no small measure to its ability to gel with anti-Semitic and nationalistic motifs. According to a view that was gaining followers in this period, concordats could be a way to reaffirm Catholic authority over Bavaria and prevent Jews—cast as "invaders" and "outsiders"—from laying claim to the mantle of Bavarian belonging. Just a few days after the declaration of the Bavarian Republic, a Catholic political party that received the immediate endorsement of local clergy and papal officials began pushing exactly this line—and it would be thanks to this party that in the early 1920s, Eugenio Pacelli would conclude his first successful concordat in postwar Germany.

Counterrevolutionary Consolidation

On November 12, 1918, the Bavarian People's Party (the Bayerische Volkspartei, or BVP) was founded. A rightist alternative to the Catholic Center Party, the BVP affirmed its desire to become the official representative of interests of the Catholic Church in Bavaria, and to translate Catholic social teachings into counterrevolutionary, antirepublican policy. It asserted its continued support for the dethroned Wittelsbach monarchy, and loudly criticized the "accommodationist" politics of Center Party politicians like Matthias Erzberger vis-à-vis Woodrow Wilson. In keeping with the bigotry increasingly salient on the Catholic right, it wove together anti-liberalism, anti-leftism, and anti-Semitism, celebrating Bavaria's independence from Berlin, which it referred to as the city of "Jews and asphalt." Immediately after its founding, the Bavarian People's Party won the enthusiastic support of the Bavarian episcopacy, Eugenio Pacelli, and key Catholic newspapers.[43]

Within just a few months, the worst fears of the BVP were realized, with the launching of a second revolution in Bavaria and the founding of the short-lived Bavarian Soviet Republic. The new Republic was a manifestation of a form of left-wing radicalism that demanded public ownership and workers' control over production and contested the Socialist Party's gradualist project of trying to capture parliamentary and state institutions through the ballot box. As exponents of the nascent "council communist" movement—in which worker councils or "soviets" defined themselves as different from unions because they sought to undermine capitalism directly—radicals in Bavaria drew inspiration (but not directives) from the Russian Bolsheviks. Once in power, the revolutionaries of the Bavarian Soviet Republic placed factories under worker ownership, expropriated some property from Munich's wealthiest landlords, and even formed a small "Red Army."

The experiment would not last long, however. On May 3, 1919, a force 39,000 strong—composed of members of the German army and two right-wing paramilitary organizations, the Freikorps and the Bavarian Civil Guard—entered Munich to bring down the revolutionary government. The BVP gave its strongest support to the action, which was seen as a local act with global resonance: 1919 was the year in which many countries across Europe (including Hungary, Spain, and Italy) were swept by left-wing radicalism and revolutionism. Some 1,000 enthusiasts of the Bavarian Soviet Republic were killed on the spot, and 700 were summarily executed in the following days, including hundreds whose sole crime was being Jewish, or being perceived as such.[44]

Among Catholic conservative circles, the bloody end of the Republic elicited sentimental, joyous reactions. The official diocesan paper, the *Münchener Katholische Kirchenzeitung*, called upon Munich's Catholics to celebrate the troops that had freed them from "foreign elements" and restored order. In an article entitled "Citizens of Munich, Be Thankful!" the paper justified the extreme violence by asserting that "[the few] mistakes that may have been made pale in comparison

Revolution in the era of mass politics. The Bavarian Soviet Republic. Crowd gathering on the Karlsplatz, Munich, 1919. Credit: Ullstein Bild/Getty Images

to the terrorism under which we still suffered only a few days ago."[45] The leader of the Bavarian People's Party, Georg Heim, concurred.[46] Pacelli, for his part, declared the end of the Bavarian Soviet Republic "magnificent." None, he wrote, could contain their "emotion and applause" as "the red flag was lowered on all public buildings." Without any reservations, Pacelli clearly suggested that the extreme violence of the German army and paramilitary forces had been necessary.[47] Time would only harden these views. In the months and years to come, the papal nuncio would repeatedly revisit his defense of Bavaria's paramilitary forces, presenting them as the leading reason for Bavaria's "liberation" from Bolshevism, and arguing that it was a wise defensive move for Bavaria to violate the terms of the Treaty of Versailles and refrain from disbanding the units.[48]

As the Bavarian Soviet Republic rose and fell, a new counterrevolutionary conspiracy theory was born. This theory held that the Bavarian uprising had been caused by "Eastern" Jews, who were stirring up global revolution on the Soviet model in order to seize global domination.[49] On the eve of the Bavarian Soviet Republic's defeat—on April 30, 1919—Eugenio Pacelli and his assistant demonstrated how they had begun to integrate this framework of analysis when they declared the Bavarian Soviet Republic a "harsh Russian-Judaic-Revolutionary tyranny."[50] As proof, they (like many in their circles) pointed to the fact that the revolution's leaders included Eugen Leviné, a Russian-born Jew; Max Levien, whom they believed was Jewish (though he was not); and "squadrons of young Jews, who sit in the [government] offices, with provocative looks and dishonest smiles." In letters to Gasparri, Pacelli and his assistant obsessively emphasized the "revolting spectacle" of the new government. Max Levien, as they saw him, was "a young man, Russian and Jewish like the others": "pale, dirty, with dull eyes, and with a hoarse and vulgar voice, and yet with an intelligent and clever physiognomy." Similarly, the revolutionary government, which was seated in "what used to be the Wittelsbach royal palace," was characterized by "the most chaotic confusion, the most nauseating squalor, the continuous coming and going of soldiers and armed men, shouts, ugly words, [and] cursing." In sum, the revolutionaries had "transformed what used to be the favored residence of the King of Bavaria into a truly infernal pit."[51]

The newspapers Pacelli regularly consulted repeated similar heavily racialized descriptions, affirming that the Bavarian Soviet Republic's "swarms of Jews and foreigners" were participating in a plot to take over the world, in collaboration with their "racial comrades" elsewhere. Papers like the *Bayerischer Kurier* and the *Allgemeine Rundschau* went a step further, calling for appeals to defend the "Christian *Volk*" against Jews and the revolutionary politics they promoted.[52] In the former Austro-Hungarian Empire, conservative writers noted, "It was as though the city had for years devoured countless [Jewish] Galician immigrants and now vomited them forth in sickness. How sick it was!"[53] With surprising synchronicity, the Vatican nuncio in Hungary—with whom Pacelli entertained a regular correspondence— similarly condemned the short-lived Hungarian Soviet Republic of 1919 as a "Judeo-Communist" plot carried out by a "small minority of delinquents."[54]

The Bayerische Volkspartei also made free use of the association between Jews, Russia, and Eastern Europe in its electoral propaganda. In one of its 1919 posters, for instance, the BVP features a man with caricatured features and yellowish skin, who is dressed in red and adorned with a hat similar to the French revolutionary Phrygian cap. The unseemly character sits straddled over a map of Europe, his center of gravity comfortably situated in the eastern part of the continent, his arms looming over Germany. A smoking firebomb in his right hand has already ignited the city of Berlin; his left hand, which holds a fire torch, is poised menacingly over the city of Munich and the whole of Bavaria (recognizable through its color scheme, which is that of the Bavarian flag). The caption below the image reads: "Bavaria, the Bolshevik is out and about! Out with him on election day!"

The Munich revolution helped consolidate a new counterrevolutionary myth: the myth of "Judeo-Bolshevism."[55] The term was intentionally ambiguous and used in at least two ways. In the mouth of certain counterrevolutionary propagandists, "Judeo-Bolshevism" was tossed into sentences to make the case that the two component parts of the phrase—"Judaism" and "Bolshevism"—were interchangeable and synonymous. This enabled writers to imply that all Jews were Bolsheviks, and all Bolsheviks Jews, without providing any evidence to substantiate these categorical statements. Other Catholic counterrevolutionary propagandists in Central Europe used the term "Judeo-Bolshevism" to draw back the curtain for their readers. As they saw it, the phrase "Judeo-Bolshevism" was supposed to jumpstart the readers' understanding of what Bolshevism really was and had been all along: a Jewish trick or ruse. According to this view, Jews were simply promoting Bolshevik-style revolution as a way to advance their true aims: the destruction of Christianity and the conquest of the world. On this view, Jews did not really care about communist principles at all—communism was just a cover, in the same way that capitalism had supposedly been a cover for the advancement of naked Jewish interests. If capitalist control allowed Jews to make money, communist revolution allowed them to topple the existing order and seize power more quickly. This is what led promoters of this view to improbably claim that, say, the Rothschild family was not only amassing tremendous wealth for itself, but also funneling money into communist movements worldwide.

BERLIN

MÜNCHEN

BAYERN, DER BOLSCHEWIK GEHT UM!
HINAUS MIT IHM AM WAHLTAG!
BAYERISCHE VOLKSPARTEI

1919 Bayerische Volkspartei (BVP) propaganda poster. The caption reads:
"Bavaria, the Bolshevik is out and about! Out with him on election day!"
Credit: Ullstein Bild/Getty Images

The notion that communism was terrifying because it was international and transnational was central to the Judeo-Bolshevik myth, as was the existence of the Comintern, or Communist International, founded in 1919. As a descendant of the First International, born in London in 1864, and the Second International, founded in Paris in 1889, the Third International, or Comintern, was proud of its historic claims to first usage of the term. It announced that "the first congress of our new revolutionary International" had taken place in the first week of March, in Moscow. The congress was small, drawing only 52 delegates, but they hailed from 35 organizations in 22 countries. A quarter of the delegates came from Asia, drawn, not least, by Lenin's strong defense of national self-determination and his promise to revolutionize and decolonize the non-Western world.[56] After a discussion of the world capitalist order and the need to forge a "new and higher workers' democracy" in place of moribund socialist and liberal democracies, the congress issued a series of detailed statements. One of them, the "Manifesto of the Communist International to the Proletariat of the Entire World," emphasized the global and international ambitions of the communist movement:

> We summon the working men and women of all countries to unite under the communist banner under which the first great victories have already been won. Proletarians of all countries! . . . Under the banner of workers' Soviets, under the banner of revolutionary struggle for power and the dictatorship of the proletariat, under the banner of the Third International—proletarians of all countries, unite![57]

In addition to laying claim to the mantle of communist internationalism, the Comintern, unlike its predecessors, aimed to be a superparty. A centralized international organization, it demanded strict discipline and the use of the label "communist" in all organizing efforts. Additionally, the Comintern called upon national parties to remake themselves in the Bolshevik image and support the Soviet Republic. From its first 1919 congress, the Third International sent the message that the interests of the Soviet regime and those of worldwide communist parties were identical.[58]

Though the prospects for the organization's short-term ability to deliver on its ambitious goals were limited, the radicals who attended the congress were hopeful.[59] They felt that they stood on the cusp of a new era. Communist self-confidence was also buoyed by the fear of revolution palpable among their opponents. In Germany, conservative Catholics were particularly terrified by the Third International's recommendations (in place from 1919 through at least 1926) that called on European communists to abandon the sectarian anticlericalism of yore and work instead to peel off "left-wing Catholics" and bring them into the Communist Party. More worrisome still, around this same time a few Catholics *were* beginning argue that socialism and communism had much to teach Catholics. "We used to argue with the Reds every day in the factory over religious, moral, and political questions," asserted a prominent Catholic trade unionist, for instance. "Now all that has ended and we recognize together only one enemy: Capitalism!"[60] A minority of Catholic intellectuals was also drawn to a groundbreaking new collection of writings by Karl Marx, edited by Siegfried Landshut and Jakob Peter Mayer. This "young Marx" suggested an alternative vision for social change—one less premised on bloody class war, revolution, and anticlericalism, and more focused on the radical transformation that would come about in the psychic and social lives of individual workers. In these writings, Marx discussed how capitalism had created workers "alienated" from their abstract "species-being," which constitutes the essence of human being in general; only through the abolition of capitalism, he said, could this "self-estrangement" be superseded and human flourishing be realized. This Marx seemed to rhyme with the Catholic emphasis on the need to fight liberalism through crafting a personal alternative to the crippling and "dehumanizing" cult of hyperindividualism that capitalism encouraged.[61]

Even still, Catholic interest in communism in these early postwar years remained a minoritarian affair. In Bavaria, most were drawn to counterrevolutionary tendencies, exemplified by the region's new political forces. In 1920, riding the first wave of this counterrevolutionary sentiment, the Bavarian People's Party swept the polls, and the ultraconservative Gustav Ritter von Kahr took the reins as Bavaria's new prime minister. He assured both Pacelli and Faulhaber that under his watch, Church and state would work together in perfect harmony.[62] It was in this favorable climate that the BVP's minister of education and the arts, Franz Matt (whom Scioppa described as "an exemplary Catholic"), began negotiating with Pacelli.[63] At first Gasparri was not pleased by the news, for he worried that concluding an agreement with Bavaria first would incite Bavarian separatism and undermine the Holy See's attempts to reach an accord with Germany as a whole. Concordat diplomacy was intended to show that the Holy See embraced the new Europe of nation-states—not a Europe of micro-states or regional entities.

In response to Gasparri's worries, Pacelli emphasized that a temporary privileging of Bavaria would be a good way to contain the tangible threat of "Bolshevism" in Germany as a whole. In letter after letter, Pacelli emphasized that recent events showed that a "Bolshevik bloc" connected Russia to Hungary, Austria, and Germany. According to Pacelli's trusted contacts in the German diplomatic corps, the Russian Bolsheviks were considering capturing Germany to bring about a worldwide revolution, with Vienna, Linz, and Innsbruck as the bases for this expansionistic "Bolshevik movement," which would first "spread toward Bavaria" and then "take over all industrialized cities."[64] "The triumph of this revolution would consecrate the union between Bolshevik Russia and Bolshevik Germany," Pacelli's contacts in the BVP noted. Small wonder that Bavaria's new prime minister considered "Bolshevism the gravest world question at the moment," or that the electoral propaganda of the BVP focused narrowly on the Bolshevik threat to Bavaria.[65] In this climate of heightened anxiety, reflections on what might happen and predictions of what would surely arise got intermingled. The leader of the Bavarian People's Party warned the German nuncio that a "Bolshevik Germany" was a distinct possibility. Within this "Bolshevik Germany,"

> Locals who do not agree to the revolution will be immediately destroyed. A few machine guns in every city and in the railway hubs, along with a manifesto that threatens to kill those who don't deposit their arms will be enough to scare the masses. All the rest will unfold programmatically as was the case in Bavaria with the difference that the Bolsheviks will attempt to avoid the errors committed in Bavaria and Hungary.[66]

Marshaling these frightening stories for Gasparri's consumption helped Pacelli make the point that it would make good sense to conclude a concordat with Bavaria immediately. Pacelli reasoned that a concordat could better insulate the southern German Catholic stronghold from the damaging winds of revolution. Bavarian separatism—buoyed by a concordat, which would reaffirm Bavaria's distinctiveness—could be a useful short-term strategy to resist the imminent Bolshevik incursion from the north. He noted that in the not-unlikely case that there was another "Bolshevik revolution" in Germany, it would be advisable for Bavaria to break away from Germany.[67] Echoing recent conversations with the leaders of the Bavarian People's Party, Pacelli affirmed: "Bavaria, along with the other states in southern Germany, can constitute an effective base against the Bolshevik tidal wave (*la marea bolscevica*)."[68] In his letters to Pacelli, the head of the Bavarian People's Party was underscoring the same point, arguing that it was necessary for "the Catholic south to be reinforced against the Protestant north." "Bavaria can easily combat Bolshevism," he noted, "so long as it continues to do battle against centralizing Berlin."[69]

The year was 1920, and Pacelli did not have the papal diplomatic establishment in Rome with him when it came to anti-Bolshevism. In August of that year, the Vatican secretary of state had urged Achille Ratti to stay in Warsaw during the Polish-Soviet War so as to be in a better position to engage in dialogue with the Bolsheviks. In his responses to the German nuncio, Gasparri emphasized that the pope was committed to presenting the Holy See as open to an agreement with the Russians. He also suggested that the German nuncio was overplaying the gravity of the threat.

Gasparri proved more responsive to a different line of reasoning: the idea that a deal with Bavaria first made good sense because it would give the Holy See more leverage in its negotiations with Berlin and other social democratic, Protestant strongholds. Pacelli knew well that Prussian diplomats wanted the Holy See to help it maintain, at all costs, a large, unified, Germany. They were worried about the potential of a union between Bavaria and Austria.[70] Thus, using fear as leverage, Pacelli proposed to use his good relations with Bavaria as a trump card.[71] At last Gasparri conceded, and concordat negotiations between Bavaria and the Holy See began in earnest. By March 1922 the draft concordat was complete, and in 1924 the Bavarian concordat was signed.

The Bavarian concordat was a thoroughly maximalist concordat—and for this reason it was, according to papal diplomats, a "masterpiece," and a model for future concordats.[72] The agreement was composed of sixteen articles. It promised that Bavaria would protect the free and public exercise of Catholicism, and that religious congregations and orders would operate freely, without the control of the state. Matters of education were resolved squarely in favor of the Holy See's demands. Religious instruction at the primary, middle, and high school levels was made mandatory in public schools. Clerical influence was also expanded at the university level, in disciplines like history, philosophy, pedagogy, sociology, and politics. The Church received the power of appointing teachers and controlling curricula. The "exemplary" concordat specified that the state would provide considerable funding for churches, clergy pensions, and "spiritual services" to be offered in prisons and hospitals. The Church was guaranteed a steady annual stream of funding, as it was granted the right to levy taxes.

As was the case with the Polish concordat, the Bavarian treaty specified that bishops should be Bavarian—not "foreigners." Furthermore, the agreement stipulated that civil powers would be consulted prior to the Church's nomination of bishops, to ensure that there were no political objections. In keeping with Bavarian demands, the treaty asserted that Church diocesan lines would conform to the political lines of *status quo ante* Bavaria. Like other concordats of the early postwar years, the Bavarian agreement helped reinforce state boundaries, through the expansion or reinstantiation of diocesan borders. At a more abstract level, the BVP's conclusion of the concordat with Pacelli helped fortify the idea that Bavaria was first and foremost a Catholic territory. In these ways and more, the concordat was not only a tool for Bavaria's consolidation in the here-and-now. It also promised to be an instrument for the promotion of confessional exclusivism in the foreseeable future.

※

The larger meaning of concordats—and of the Vatican's countersettlement after World War I—began to shift in the aftermath of the Bavarian agreement. The agreement suggested that concordat diplomacy might end up being more than what it was imagined to be by its advocates early on—namely, a strategy to protect and restore Church rights; a way to offset the potential liberal separation of Church and state; and a way to get the new Code of Canon Law integrated within national legal frameworks. For though the legal treatise between the Holy See and Bavaria did not mention "Bolshevism" or "Judeo-Bolshevism," the fact that the German nuncio and his leading interlocutors in Bavaria were in agreement on the treaty's anticommunist purpose was significant. It signaled that the highest on-site representative of the Holy See had adopted a locally crafted conspiracy theory, and that he was ready, through concordat diplomacy, to help local communities in what he deemed their "inevitable" future battles with "Judeo-Bolshevism."

Papal attitudes toward both liberalism and communism continued to evolve over the course of the 1920s, even as concordats increasingly became the law of the land. With the rise to power of Achille Ratti as Pope Pius XI in 1922, the concordat crusade was confirmed. Pius XI was an even stronger supporter of the concordat project than Benedict XV had been, and he advocated for the conclusion a string of new concordats in Europe—including the two most controversial concordats in history. Chapter 4 will trace the lead-up to the Lateran Agreements with Fascist Italy and the Reichskonkordat with Nazi Germany. It will also shed light on how the rise of left-wing radicalism in Italy further transformed papal perceptions of the concordat project. By the time the Italian and German agreements were concluded (in 1929 and in 1933), the papal diplomatic establishment as a whole had begun reorienting itself against a new enemy: the Soviet Union and international communism.

4

The Fascist Temptation

Let's give [Benito Mussolini] a few months' credit, before passing judgment on the revolutionary coup d'état, which he carried out in a masterly way.

—PIETRO GASPARRI, 1922

LIKE GERMANY, ITALY WAS undergoing tumultuous political and social changes after World War I. In 1919–1920, a wave of demonstrations, strikes, and factory occupations seized the Italian peninsula, traversing both the city and the countryside. By the end of 1919 the country had witnessed 1,800 strikes, carried out by at least one million and a half strikers.[1] The *Osservatore Romano* and *Civiltà Cattolica* both sternly condemned the events. The Jesuit journal noted that the demonstrations were "a threat to all national life and a warning of more serious disorders directed at the state," adding that the workers were wrong to protest and demand salary hikes: they would be better off economically if it was not for the "scant productivity of workers, who are always in a constant state of agitation." The Vatican daily similarly condemned the strikers, claiming that workers were striking because they were actually *too* well paid and comfortable: "The worker eats well, dresses well, and has fun in ways that were unimaginable before the war. This ease and frivolity also permit the worker to engage in extended strikes, demonstrating that he possesses considerable resources."[2]

In 1920 the civil unrest brought back to government one of the Vatican's great Liberal nemeses: Giovanni Giolitti. Seeing the developments through a conspiratorial lens, the Vatican secretary of state, Cardinal Gasparri, affirmed that the left-wing unrest of 1919–1920 must have been intentionally exacerbated by the "Masonic" forces in Italy's Liberal government, which were keen on elbowing their way back to power. Accordingly, Gasparri told Italy's upper clergy that they should encourage their flock to support only those political movements that respected "justice, order, and religion" and avoid those parties that were "contrary to the Church and to good social order." The *Osservatore Romano*, for its part, cast aspersions on the Liberal government's "unwillingness" to repress left-wing agitation—another sign, it intimated, that the two were in cahoots.[3] Unsurprisingly, when negotiations to address the Roman Question kicked off between papal officials and Italian state leaders, they quickly broke down in a climate of mutual suspicion.[4]

Unlike in Bavaria, where the Bavarian People's Party was a natural choice as a counter to both liberalism and left-wing radicalism, in Italy papal officials were unsure where to turn. The Socialists, who were scaling the polls and had endorsed the strikes of 1919–1920, were clearly not an option. Newer political parties on the scene did not seem like natural allies either. In papal headquarters, some abhorred—and only a small number supported—a newly founded political party, the Italian Popular Party (PPI), which, though inspired by Catholic social teachings and led by a Sicilian priest, consistently called itself secular and nonconfessional, and came out in support of the League of Nations and other elements of the postwar Wilsonian order.[5] In response to queries coming in from clergy to the Holy See about what to make of the PPI, top-ranking Vatican officials responded coldly, noting that "the Holy See is and wants to abstain from any political competition, and from [supporting] any political party."[6] At the same time, through one-on-one correspondence and pastoral letters, clerics close to the Holy See asserted that the party's "amorphous aconfessionalism" amounted to "a mockery of the Church and of God." Revisiting the tropes of wartime anti-Wilsonianism, the archbishop of Genoa, Cardinal Tommaso Pio Boggiani, rhetorically asked *popolari* in a pastoral letter: "How could you, who call yourselves Catholics . . . combat, as is your strictest duty, the dominant error, the error which is responsible for all of the ruins that we lament, that is: the separation of Church and state; the secular state? How can you combat all the other errors of liberalism? What is it that the liberals have always wanted and said, if not this: freedom of religion in public and political life?"[7]

The Holy See was also tepid when it came to another new political movement that had burst on the scene in 1919: the nationalist, anti-leftist Fasci italiani di combattimento. On April 15, 1919, the thuggish new movement gained national notoriety when its members used fire-arms to disperse left-wing demonstrators in Milan, and then attacked the headquarters of the Socialist Party's newspaper, *Avanti!,* killing three and destroying printing machines and other materials. This orgy of violence soon became the rule, not the exception: throughout the fol-lowing years, Fascist militants—dressed in black shirts, and known as *squadristi*—would torture, shoot at, destroy the property of, and hu-miliate anyone they deemed an "enemy of the state." "The Fascists devote themselves to manhunts," the police inspector of Rovigo Prov-ince, in the Veneto region, affirmed in 1921. "There is no end to their breaking into homes, destroying furniture, documents, and objects, lighting fires, shooting into houses at night, [and] patrolling in armed groups; and all this in order to keep in a perpetual state of intimidation people who truly, in some places, are so traumatized and frightened, one could even say terrorized, that they completely avoid public places and never leave their homes."[8]

The vigilante justice of the anti-leftist Fascist squadrons alienated many, but it also attracted supporters. Alarmed by the strikes and land seizures of 1919–1920, local landowners and factory owners began pro-viding financial support to the Fascists, and this money helped the movement turn itself into a political party in 1920–1921. During this time, Fascist propagandists began to present their leading task as that of solving the "demo-Bolshevik" crisis of a postwar Europe forced to decide between two bad options: liberalism and communism.[9] The pa-pacy and the Italian church hierarchy reacted with ambivalence. On the one hand, they applauded the Fascists' indictment of left-wing rad-icalism and liberalism. On the other hand, they worried that Fascism might be yet another manifestation of the "exaggerated nationalism" of World War I, and that too many Fascists nursed anticlerical tenden-cies. After all, up through May 1920, the movement had pronounced itself in favor of "the expropriation of all properties of the religious congregations and the abolition of all bishops' revenues," and was wont to affirm that Fascism was neither black nor red, but instead "immune" to the "encyclicals" that were being "sent out from two Vaticans: Rome and Moscow."[10]

Beginning in the spring of 1920, however, the Fascist Party began to take a new approach to Catholicism and the Church. In a real *volte-face*, it began celebrating the Vatican and promising to solve the Roman Question. At the second congress of the Fascists, in May 1920, Benito Mussolini announced that because "the Vatican represents some 400 million people scattered all over the world . . . no one in Italy, unless he wants to unleash a religious war, can attack this spiritual sovereign." By June 1921 the Fascist Party's transformation was complete. In his parliamentary debut following the appointment of thirty-five Fascist MPs to the Chamber of Deputies, Mussolini dismissed the movement's erstwhile anticlericalism, asserting that "in the history of Fascism there are no invasions of churches." "Fascism does not preach and does not practice anticlericalism," he added. On church-state relations, he said that Italy "must furnish the Vatican with material aid, material concessions for schools, churches, hospitals, and so on." By way of conclusion, Mussolini suggested that papal universalism was a praiseworthy continuation of imperial Rome's traditions—"I affirm here and now that today the Latin and imperial tradition of Rome is represented by Catholicism"—noting that "the only universal idea that exists in Rome today is that irradiated by the Vatican."[11]

The change of tone and the clear endorsement of the papacy's new internationalism was pleasing to those papal officials who were paying attention—not least because they were short on allies in Italian politics. Partisans of the Italian Popular Party were not as impressed: they denounced the Fascist strategy as pure instrumentalism, and highlighted the "pagan foundations" of Fascism, which was, if anything, interested in creating a religion of its own—a secular, "Fascist religion" of the state.[12] But despite these objections, starting in 1921 Achille Ratti, the former nuncio of Poland who was serving a brief stint as archbishop of Milan, opened dialogue with the Fascists in Milan to begin entertaining the possibility of working with the Fascist Party toward the solution of the Roman Question. He authorized Fascist Blackshirts to attend religious celebrations in uniform, and even to enter Milan's Cathedral carrying pennants and draped in Fascist symbols. On November 4, 1921, Ratti and Mussolini would meet in person for the first time, and according to reports from both sides, the conversation would be cordial, and forward-gazing.

In February 1922, Achille Ratti was elected pope. He took the name Pope Pius XI, and, in a historic move, signaled his desire to make peace with the Italian state by giving his blessing from the central balcony of St. Peter's—facing outward, to the crowd. Since his return from Eastern Europe, Ratti had repeatedly hammered on the need to solve the Roman Question as a way to restore Italy's grandeur in the wider world. "Amid the current turning of all states to the pope," Ratti announced, "one would have to close one's eyes to the evidence to deny what prestige and advantages our country [Italy] could obtain from his presence, once his status as an international and supranational sovereign were recognized." "The pope is the greatest medal of honor for Italy," Ratti added. The new pope was keen on emphasizing that Rome, for him, was "truly the capital of the world."[13] Much to Mussolini's liking, Ratti presented himself as an internationalist dressed in Italian clothing. He was proud of being born and bred on the Italian peninsula— so much so, that observers promptly called him *l'italianissimo*, the "most Italian," pope.[14]

In October 1922, a few months after his ascent to the Throne of St. Peter, Ratti enjoyed a front-row seat to the Fascist seizure of power, watching as King Victor Emanuel III made Benito Mussolini prime minister and refrained from ordering Italian troops to fire on the Blackshirts converging on Rome. The Vatican's *Osservatore Romano* issued no comment, but the papal secretary of state—still Pietro Gasparri— applauded the king's decision in a mid-November interview with a French journal. Gasparri emphasized that prior to the Fascist march on Rome, Italy was on the brink of anarchy, and that the Fascists might well help restore order and discipline to the country. In a conversation with the Belgian ambassador to the Holy See shortly thereafter, Gasparri added that Mussolini seemed well disposed to the Church. "Let's give him a few months' credit, before passing judgment on the revolutionary coup d'état, which he carried out in a masterly way."[15]

Just a few weeks earlier Gasparri had sent Italian bishops a letter stating that the Italian Popular Party had received no official backing

from the Holy See and that it could not be considered the true "expo-
nent of Catholics in the Parliament and in the country." Through this
message, the papal secretary of state invited the clergy to help delegiti-
mize the Christian Democratic movement and crush the Popular Party's
electoral chances.[16] Like many Catholics and lower clergy in these years,
Gasparri and Pius XI had little desire to align themselves with the
liberal-leaning Popular Party and held out more hope for the Fascist
movement, which had consistently presented itself as besieged by and
opposed to a "clique" of Freemasons, capitalist plutocrats, and "Jewish
Bolsheviks."[17]

In December 1922 Pius XI issued his first encyclical, which clearly
articulated his priorities. In unison with the late Benedict XV, the text
began by denouncing the failure of the Paris Peace Conference to bring
about "true peace." Since the Wilsonian settlement had been inaugurated, the text asserted, obscene and lawless behavior was on the
rise, as were "famine and epidemics." The Wilsonian model of liberal
democracy was partly to blame, in that only "kings" and "kingdoms"
(mentioned on twenty-four occasions) were capable of bringing about
peace; parliamentary deputies and democracies were not. "Contests
between political parties beget threats of popular action, and, at times,
eventuate in open rebellion," the encyclical affirmed. Thus, "our
modern democratic states" are "most exposed to the danger of being
overthrown by one faction or another." Indeed, the text continued, it
was liberal-democratic complicity that had fostered a "restless spirit
of revolution" after the Great War—a spirit that, dangerously, kept
alive the "threat of war." The time for true peacemaking—the time to
abandon the false peace of Paris—was now. Otherwise, the text
warned, Europe would "lapse back slowly but surely into a state of
barbarism."[18]

The encyclical then outlined a familiar solution to this chaotic state
of affairs: concordat diplomacy, and the recognition of the Holy See as
a privileged partner of European states. The idea that the liberal League
of Nations was up to the task of building a permanent peace in Europe
was wrong, as only the universal government of the Roman Catholic
Church was "divinely commissioned to lead mankind." Through concordat diplomacy, the Church would "safeguard the sanctity of the
law of nations" and rebuild the European continent. Indeed, the idea

of international law without papal input was deeply problematic, for "no merely human institution of today can be successful in devising a set of international laws that will be in harmony with world conditions." The League of Nations was bound to die a stillborn death. Only human beings of "the Middle Ages were in possession of that true League of Nations," and its name was "Christianity."[19]

Though Pius XI's first encyclical refrained from explicitly mentioning Fascism, its anti-League and antidemocratic message constituted a clear disavowal of the Italian Popular Party, whose raison d'être was to reconcile Catholic social teachings with democracy, and whose members had come out strongly in favor of the League of Nations from the day of its founding. At the same time, the pope was informing the Fascists that without papal assistance, their attempts to build peace in Italy would surely fail. The Vatican, Pius XI asserted through his first encyclical, was the only institution that "is a part of every nation [and] at the same time, [that] is above all nations."[20] As the text drove home, in the era of the nation-state, it was possible—and indeed necessary—to be both a fervid nationalist and a Catholic internationalist at the same time.

Working with the Fascists

Mussolini got the pope's message immediately, and from his first days in office he showed a great willingness to work with him to turn Italy into what the quasi-respectable thug-turned-statesman called "a Catholic State and a Catholic Nation." Much to the delight of the anti-liberal Catholic intelligentsia, Mussolini affirmed that the Fascist state had "repudiated both the principle of the state's religious agnosticism, and the principles of separation of church and state," thus disposing of "liberalism and its prejudices" for good.[21] He simultaneously took his distance from notable Fascists and outspoken anticlericals, claiming that Catholic education, culture, and morality should play a shaping influence in Italian affairs.[22] To underscore his claims, Mussolini accredited the Catholic University of the Sacred Heart in Milan, which would soon become the most vibrant center of papal-sanctioned Catholic intellectual life outside of Rome. In a private letter to the future leader of Christian Democracy, Alcide de Gasperi, Father Gemelli, the rector of the Catholic University, noted that he would do anything to preserve and promote his university—even if he "earned the undesirable reputation" of being a Fascist sympathizer.[23]

During his first five years in office, Mussolini did several things to ingratiate the Holy See. He consistently took a strong stance against liberalism, Freemasonry, and Protestant missionary activity, along with divorce, contraceptive devices, pornography, and blasphemy. He worked to return the crucifix to schools and other public buildings and create tax exemptions and state subsidies for clergy. The Italian leader also unveiled a series of intellectual undertakings that were meant to provide a stage for the fusion of Catholic and Fascist ideologies, such as the Istituto fascista di cultura. In all these undertakings, the Fascist regime carefully, intentionally, and loudly invited prominent Catholics to play a leading role in shaping Italian intellectual life. The Jesuit journal *Civiltà Cattolica* was delighted, noting that the regime was giving "writers full freedom to express Christian and Catholic views, and judge facts according to criteria established by the tried-and-true ecclesiastical method," a method far superior to the "secular scientific method" so haloed in liberal circles.[24]

On repeated occasions, Mussolini took his cues from what was unfolding further east, in concordat lands. He recognized religious feasts as civil holidays, and reintroduced religion as a compulsory subject in schools. The official text of the Gentile education reform asserted that "the teaching of Christian doctrine in accordance with the Catholic faith shall form the foundation and capstone of elementary education in all grades."[25] Religion, for Fascist education reformers, would assist the new movement in its state and nation-building goals because Roman Catholicism was "a peculiarly Italian institution" and a "storehouse of national tradition." It would also teach the value of obedience and deference to figures of authority.[26] *Civiltà Cattolica* applauded, noting that Mussolini had decisively shown that he stood against atheism and liberalism and for the Catholic Church. On the Italian political scene, bringing back religious education was a leap backward to 1859, after which point liberal governments in Italy had deliberately ended the teaching of religious subjects in state schools, privileging instead other ways of "turning peasants into Italians" and fostering national cohesion. But for papal officials, members of the Italian high clergy, and Catholic civic leaders, the Fascist educational reforms were a gigantic leap forward—a point they made in countless congresses, articles, and speeches, even as they emphasized that Fascism must continue to distance itself from its early anticlericalism.[27]

Soon enough, Pius XI showed he was willing to "give Mussolini some credit" for his work in favor of the Catholic Church. In July 1923 the pope encouraged the Popular Party's leader to step down, in what was widely interpreted as a Vatican attempt to dissolve the Italian Christian Democratic Party, one of the Fascist Party's leading competitors. The following year Pius XI helped doom one of the only possibilities to resist the Fascist Party's imminent capture of the state by issuing a strong condemnation of any possible alliance between Catholics and socialists in Italy as "contrary to the teachings of the Church." The socialists, in Pius XI's eyes, were the main force behind the "two red years" (1919–1920), and the idea that a Catholic political party could ally with them was anathema.[28]

Mussolini, for his part, showed that even now that he ruled Italy, destroying the Socialist Party remained a top priority. Informing his public that "Fascist violence must be reasoned, rational, surgical," he sanctioned a whole-scale intimidation and terror campaign against parties of the left. He called Fascist violence "child's play" compared to the "real" political terror of the anarchists, socialists, and "Bolsheviks," the latter of whom had executed "two million people," and thrown "two million more" in prison.[29] By 1923 the Fascist Party had broken the spine of the Italian Socialist Party. The Fascist Interior Ministry, pleased with the results of its terror campaign, turned its attention to the just-founded Italian Communist Party. By year's end the police had arrested thousands of Communist political leaders and militants, including the secretaries of provincial youth organizations, trade union leaders, and many others. Activists were held for months and even years, awaiting trial for the presumed crime of trying to "overthrow the state" or "incite class hatred."[30] In June 1924 Giacomo Matteotti, a Socialist deputy who in a speech to the Chamber of Deputies had taken a public stand against the Fascist use of violence, was brutally assassinated by Fascist thugs. A public outcry against the Fascist Party followed, and the remaining leftist parties received a temporary boost. Antonio Gramsci, the leader of the newly minted Italian

Communist Party, wrote to his wife on June 22, 1924: "Our movement has made a huge step forward: our newspaper has tripled its circulation, in many centers our comrades have started leading the people . . . in these days I think that our Party has really become a mass party."[31]

On January 3, 1925, however, in a chilling speech, Mussolini took responsibility for the murder and asserted, "If Fascism has been a criminal association, then I am the boss," and "If all acts of violence have been the outcome of a certain historical–political, moral climate, then the responsibility is mine, for I created this climate."[32] Immediately afterward, the Italian leader gave orders to shut down opposition party offices and newspapers. Non-Fascist ministers were excluded from the government, and Italy became a one-party, dictatorial state. Floods of new activists and presumed leftist sympathizers were once again jailed or forced into a new form of internal exile, known as the *confino*. The *Osservatore Romano* hardly batted an eyelash, and the pope's emissary to Mussolini, Father Tacchi Venturi, commemorated the developments by gifting Mussolini the book *Zionism and Catholicism*, which made the familiar point that "Judeo-Bolsheviks" must be rooted out because they sought "to destroy current society and dominate the world by themselves, as the Talmud prescribes."[33] *Civiltà Cattolica*, at the height of the Matteotti crisis, explained to its readers that it was the duty of Catholics to support the Fascist battle against socialism, insofar as socialists were atheists while Fascists were not.[34]

After the Matteotti affair, Mussolini promptly received another justification for further consolidating the Fascist dictatorship. On October 31, 1926, the Duce was inaugurating a new sports stadium in the northern Italian city of Bologna when a young man of fifteen fired a gun straight at his head. The shot just missed—it perforated Mussolini's lapel and zipped through the top-hat worn by Bologna's mayor, Umberto Puppini. Fascist squadrons in attendance immediately pounced on the teenager, torturing and lynching him on the spot.[35] Pope Pius XI showed his solidarity with the Duce, condemning the "criminal assassination attempt" but not the brutal killing of the young perpetrator. "Just thinking of [the attempted murder], saddens us," the pope added, "and it makes us thankful to God for its failure." Italian churches exalted with Te Deums of thanksgiving, and the *Osservatore Romano* thanked "the Divine Goodness that had intervened to render [the attack] vain."[36]

Mussolini promptly used the assassination attempt as an excuse to hack apart what remained of Italian democracy. A set of new "Laws for the Defense of the State" called for the dissolution of all political parties (save the Fascist), the removal from office of 120 opposition deputies, and the creation of new forms of domestic repression, including the Voluntary Military for National Security (Milizia Volontaria per la Sicurezza Nazionale, or MVSN). Strikes were banned outright, as were all non-Fascist trade unions. Press censorship was tightened another notch. On November 9, 1926, the Fascist police arrested Antonio Gramsci, despite his parliamentary immunity. Within the year the Italian Communist Party had been destroyed. In his very first letter from prison, Gramsci said he would survive the murderous Fascist prison sentence, but faced with the reality of the Italy unfolding around him, he soon fell into a depression: unable to sleep, and racked by physical pain, Gramsci's own body wore the signs of his party's deep malaise and undoing.[37] Limited sectors of Catholic opinion in Italy began quietly expressing their concerns about the new turn Fascism had taken.[38]

With the destruction of any credible threat from the socialist or communist left, Fascist propagandists elevated the violent anti-leftism of Fascism's early years into a self-legitimizing feature of the regime. It helped that from 1926 on, Fascist attempts to reach mutually beneficial economic and geopolitical agreements with the Soviet Union were floundering, which meant that the Soviets would no longer object to the resurgence of anticommunism in Fascist propaganda.[39] Under the influence of thinkers like Giovanni Gentile, a more sophisticated theoretical apparatus also began justifying Fascist anticommunism. Fascism was cast as a worldview that stood at communism's antipodes. In place of the Soviet "Workers' State," the Fascists affirmed that they were building an "Ethical State" that was the only lasting response to capitalism's "dramatic contradictions." The Fascist "Ethical State" would be a source of morality, peace, and harmony between employers and employees, in stark contrast to the violence and strife advocated by the communists.[40]

Severing Ties with the Soviet Union

In the late 1920s, Fascist-induced hysteria about the need for national security against the left was at an all-time high, and Vatican-Soviet relations were at an all-time low. Since 1917, papal officials had doggedly pursued a diplomatic relationship with Bolshevik officials. In 1922 Soviet-papal negotiations had officially kicked off, as papal officials hoped to conclude a concordat or *modus vivendi* with the new regime. Eager to make progress more quickly, in the mid-1920s Pius XI shifted papal-Soviet negotiations to Berlin, where they were put in the hands of Eugenio Pacelli, who had already gained a reputation as a skillful diplomat. Fascist Italy had no objections when this took place—it, too, at the time, was eager to reach an economic accord with the Soviet Union. But the German nuncio struggled under the weight of the diplomatic task he had been assigned. For a man who had come to see concordat diplomacy as a way to fight left-wing radicalism in general and what he called "Judeo-Bolshevism" in particular, friendly chit-chat with Russian emissaries did not come naturally. The situation worsened when Soviet authorities discovered a plot to smuggle Catholic priests into Russia. Two months later (in November 1926), two of the trafficked Jesuits were apprehended and deported. As one of the two men—the Franco-Canadian Joseph-Henri Ledit, to whom we shall return in Chapter 5—packed his bags, he sadly commented in his diary that "all hope of remaining in Russia has, for now, vanished. It is with regret that I leave this immense country where there would be so much work to do to expand God's glory."[41]

Seizing the moment, Eugenio Pacelli sent a stream of hard-hitting letters to Pietro Gasparri. He informed the Vatican's secretary of state that although he was loyally trying to follow the Vatican's suggestions to "not break ties with the Soviet Union," the task was becoming more difficult by the day. In exchange for granting some freedoms to the Catholic Church, the Soviets were making demands that Pacelli could not accept. Without mincing words, Pacelli confessed that he found meeting his Soviet interlocutors "unpleasant" and "almost repugnant"—using descriptors that rhymed with those he had applied to what he had called the "dirty" and "revolting" "Judeo-Bolshevik" leaders of the Bavarian Soviet Republic. "It would be a vain illusion to hope to reach an agreement with the present government of Moscow," the nuncio editorialized.[42] Upon being asked to comment on Pacelli's report, experts in Rome on Russian affairs "concurred with the judgment of the Berlin nuncio," and informed the pope that "any relation and appearance of negotiations with [the Soviets] was very dangerous, and left little hope of bearing fruit."[43] The pope's emissary to Mussolini, Father Tacchi Venturi, was pleased; he had long argued that the Bolsheviks—in league with the Protestants, the Jews, the Masons, and other exponents of "Anglo-Saxon hegemony"—were a direct threat to the Catholic Church and the Italian government.[44]

The tide was turning for the Soviets, too. In the mid- to late 1920s, Soviet leaders had inaugurated a new project that struck deeper than earlier attempts to separate Church and state and foster a new Bolshevik culture of atheism and scientism. Russian officials and dedicated organizations, such as the 1925 League of the Godless (after 1929, the League of Militant Godless), pioneered the effort via a series of antireligious campaigns aimed at "unmasking" members of the clergy as penny-pinching counterrevolutionaries. The antireligious furor involved everything from pro-atheism poster campaigns to the inauguration of antireligious museums; from the creation of anti-Christian study groups to the hosting of theater performances foregrounding the triumph of science over superstition. In the eyes of Soviet state leaders, antireligious work would aid a far-reaching economic development program: the first Soviet Five-Year Plan (1928–1932). Stalin's Plan focused on developing heavy industry, collectivizing agriculture, and removing any obstacles in the way—including clerics who would be unwilling to relinquish religious properties. By 1928–1929 a marked uptick was noticeable in the closure of churches, as local cells of the League of Militant Godless were being told to "take measures for the mass exit of laborers from religious communities."[45] The state-run Soviet secret police agency, the NKVD, was brought into the battle as well. An April 1929 decree on religious organizations made all public displays of religion illegal, shut down monasteries and religious charity organizations, and suppressed religious works. A secret Party circular of the same year announced that the actions were necessary because "religious organizations are the only legally existing counterrevolutionary organizations, with which it is essential to wage a merciless war."[46]

The measures were of limited success—Russian religious life continued—but the die had been cast.[47] From 1929 on, many Bolshevik leaders were now openly identifying themselves as leaders of a movement to eradicate religion from the public sphere and from private life.[48]

The papacy received the news in bits and pieces, but it was enough to tip the balance. Concordat negotiations were not going well anyway, and for months Eugenio Pacelli had been calling for an end to the whole business. In 1929, under pressure from his own diplomatic corps and from his base in Fascist, anticommunist Rome, the pope officially broke off negotiations with the Soviet Union. In early 1930, in a public letter published in the *Osservatore Romano*, he announced that any hope of concluding a Vatican agreement with the Soviet Union had become impossible, given the antireligious campaign in the U.S.S.R.—a campaign whose fundamental aim was "to destroy and defile religious buildings and symbols."[49]

Pius XI's words were harsh, but they focused on practices internal to Russia. A series of key events separated this protest from the pope's later decision to launch a cultural and diplomatic crusade presenting the Soviet Union as a global threat. Many scholars have run together these two moments, casting the papal crusade against the Soviet Union as a simple action-reaction story—that is, as a response to the uptick in anticlericalism among Soviet officials in the late 1920s. This explanation is incomplete. To understand how the papacy got from closing down diplomatic negotiations with the Soviet Union in 1929–1930 to defining itself as the leader of an anticommunist Catholic International, starting in 1933–1934, we need to broaden our vistas. A new battle for global control was raging in the late 1920s and early 1930s, and the Holy See was responding to the changing tides.

Forging a New World Order (Again)

The Paris Peace Conference, the Russian Revolution, and the papacy's concordat bid in the years just after World War I unleashed a flurry of ideas for how to forge a new world order and build bonds across national borders. Internationalism—already a feature of European intellectual, social, and political life—came of age. The currents unleashed were not only visible in parliaments, foreign chancelleries, and the League of Nations; the 1920s also witnessed the birth of myriad international organizations, including some of the earliest nongovernmental organizations (NGOs), the beginning of an international ecumenical movement, the rise of international voluntary organizations, and the formalization of international networks of academics, athletes, feminists, pacifists, anti-imperialists, and more. For this reason, some scholars have argued that modern international society first emerged in the 1920s. Contemporaries felt the winds of change, noting that the new enthusiasm around international cooperation and problem solving was part and parcel with a new awareness of globalism—that is, a sense of being a citizen of the world, not just of one or another nation or empire. "The main world event of the twentieth century," asserted the Spanish diplomat and pacifist Salvador de Madariaga, "is the birth of the world. The world did not exist before."[50]

A key question posed by internationalists in the 1920s involved who deserved the title of governing the world, and how they would go about doing it—over the heads of everyday citizens, or through their intimate participation. In Geneva, a group of secular politicians answered the question by suggesting that diplomats, acting without citizen input but in their best interest, were well-equipped to define the shape of the new international society and build a permanent global peace. Through their conclusion of the Locarno Treaties and the Kellogg-Briand Pact, these politicians sought to solve the unresolved questions from the Paris Peace Treaties (and particularly the status of Germany in Europe), while making future war impossible. The Locarno Treaties aimed to establish a new status quo that would allow Europe to build unity, and set right the problems of the Treaty of Versailles. Signed by Germany, France, Belgium, Great Britain, and Italy, the agreements fixed the German-Belgian and Franco-German frontiers as inviolable, and pledged that Germany, Belgium, and France would never attack each other except in "legitimate defense" or as a result of a League of Nations obligation. In the words of "one of the most fervent supporters of the 'new internationalism,'" the French Socialist prime minister of France, Aristide Briand, Locarno marked "the beginning of a magnificent work, the renewal of Europe . . . by means of a general union in which all nations will be invited to participate."[51] Welcoming Germany back into the community of nations came with a price, however. Locarno forced Germany to renounce the use of force to change its western frontiers, but its eastern frontiers were still underdetermined. According to the terms of the treaty, Great Britain promised to defend Belgium and France, but not territories like Poland and Czechoslovakia, whose relations with Germany were to be settled only by means of arbitration. The shadow of Brest-Litovsk still hung over the international order.

Whereas the Locarno Treaties had been textbook examples of diplomatic realism, the Kellogg-Briand Pact, by contrast, was an exercise in idealism. The agreement, also known as the Pact of Paris, again placed the French Socialist politician Aristide Briand in a leading role. Signed by nearly all of the nations in the world, Kellogg-Briand vowed that states would renounce war and settle all disputes by peaceful, juridical means. However, the pact contained many qualifications and exempting clauses and failed to establish a means of enforcement. It was, in the long run, ineffective in preventing the recurrence of Europe-wide war. But in the late 1920s it was a model for global peace that neither Mussolini nor the pope could afford to ignore.[52]

As Mussolini worked to present Fascism as an international force, he attempted to show that he was a reasonable diplomat, willing to work with rival modes of internationalism enshrined by the Locarno and Kellogg-Briand agreements. Thus, Fascist Italy signed on to both pacts. But Mussolini was not enthusiastic—his "last-minute dash by special train, racing car, and speedboat to Locarno fooled no one." Once on site, Mussolini was confronted by anti-Fascist demonstrators and received a frosty reception from fellow European state leaders. Because of what had happened with Locarno, Mussolini did not even attend the signing ceremony of the Kellogg-Briand Pact.[53]

The Holy See was similarly divided on these major 1920s agreements. Some papal officials participated in the Locarno honeymoon and were pleased to see Germany treated as a Great Power once again.[54] Others were skeptical about the new internationalism and "spirit of peace" invoked by liberal and socialist leaders, among others. They were uncomfortable with the fact that the Soviet Union had signed onto Kellogg-Briand, and disliked the leading role played by French socialists. Briand and his men were part of a French coalition known as the "Cartel des Gauches," which united socialists, radicals, and republicans and since 1924 had wasted little time in reviving a dominant strand in French political culture—namely, anticlericalism.[55] The cartel had immediately earned the rebuke of the French hierarchy and the French Catholic right, and helped get a new militant Catholic civil society movement off the ground: the Fédération Nationale Catholique (FNC). Nationalistic, antidemocratic, anti-liberal, antisocialist, and with the strong support of the French Catholic hierarchy, the FNC quickly won over conservative Catholics for its large-scale mobilizations against French radicals, republicans, and socialists allied with Briand. The papacy showed its support for the new organization early on as well.[56]

In tandem, the papacy expressed its dislike for one of Briand's close collaborators: the German politician Gustav Stresemann. When Stresemann accepted the Nobel Peace Prize in 1927 as a tribute to his work to reconcile "national solidarity and the idea of international cooperation," figures close to the Vatican grimaced.[57] Taking a jab at both Stresemann and Briand, *Civiltà Cattolica* derided the "ingenious utopianism" of the "improvised peace-makers." It came out strongly against the Kellogg-Briand Pact, mocking the agreement as an "illusory paper edifice." Foregrounding Catholic anti-Americanism as the prism through which to understand the new geopolitical reshuffling of alliances, the Jesuit journal termed Kellogg-Briand a "disposable American trinket" that, despite its high talk of "peace, disarmament, and international union," was a "hypocritical" way of hiding the "morbid germs of an implacable bellicose spirit." Europe, it cautioned, should wake up and start opposing the "hegemonic tendencies that press on her from the other side of the Atlantic."[58]

Many within the Holy See doubled down on their old skepticism toward the League of Nations. The bishop of Lausanne penned the Vatican secretary of state, promising to keep an ear to the ground "so that the Holy See, even as it continues to remain completely external to the events [at the League of Nations], will be in-the-know about what is being done." Over and against the urgings of those lay Catholics eager to build a stronger Catholic presence within the League and open up lines of dialogue with Protestant pacifists, papal officials answered that the "form of internationalism" endorsed by the Church was the only one that had a clearly "diocesan" and Catholic character—and that Catholic internationalism should not get mixed up with the liberal-socialist internationalism of the League. The "Holy See will remain faithful to the reservations it has always had about the League of Nations," they affirmed.[59] But despite the papacy's hard-line attitudes, and indeed because of them, a growing chink was opening up between some Catholic laypersons and lower clergy, who were sympathetic to the League, Locarno, and Kellogg-Briand, and the intransigence of many members of the Holy See.[60] The rift would grow larger in the 1930s, during the Spanish Civil War, and become a gaping chasm by the years of World War II.

In the late 1920s it was not just the liberal and socialist diplomats of Europe and the United States who were proposing a new model for governing the world; the Communist International was doing so as well. Rather than simply relying on signed agreements between well-positioned diplomats, however, the Communist International was pioneering a different model: one that relied on the proliferation of communist political parties and on the fostering of communist civil society organizations for individuals of all social classes and ages. But for all its encouragement of international activism, the Soviet Union was keen on casting itself as communism's nerve-center. In the late 1920s, Soviet leaders began putting great energy into presenting Moscow as the heart of a new global culture that could, it was hoped, directly reach the working masses. Moscow, the "fourth Rome," was "to be the capital of a different, post-Christian, belief system." Intellectuals and party officials joined forces in a bid to Bolshevize the global left—for instance, by turning Moscow's International Lenin School into a hub for radical activists from across the world. Russian was advertised as the emergent *lingua franca* of the international left, as Soviet officials engaged in a sustained attempt to woo artists and intellectuals at home and abroad. New energies and monies were pumped into the creation of films, posters, traveling exhibitions, and other cultural products, which sent the message that the Soviet Union was a Workers' State that stood at the head of an international communist movement for radical change. Soviet propaganda intended for foreign audiences focused in particular on communist opposition to imperialism and racism, and across the Euro-American imperial world, communists began cooperating with nonaligned actors and actresses with "flexible solidarities" to achieve the end-goal of overturning imperial rule. Stalin in these years was focused on consolidating his power at home, however. His ambitions to control the global communist movement had limited effect, and historians tend to agree that although the Comintern eventually evolved into a highly centralized, hierarchical, and authoritarian organization, it did not already have this character in the 1920s and early 1930s.[61] Nonetheless, observers at the *Civiltà Cattolica* bought the hype of the "fourth Rome," and took stock of developments with concern. Doing Stalin a favor, they asserted that "behind the thin veil of the Third International *(Comintern),* the Bolshevik Government aims to ignite everywhere the fire of revolution."[62]

Unfolding events seemed to corroborate this interpretation. Between 1928 and 1933, trade-union mobilizations and demonstrations ricocheted from Bombay to Paris, and though many of these protests were not communist-led, the Comintern was happy to have global anticommunists claim responsibility.[63] European institutions like the Committee for the Defense of the Black Race (founded in Paris in 1926) or the League Against Imperialism (founded in Berlin in 1927), which did have robust communist participation, gave the sense that a transborder movement was on the rise.[64] Commenting on these developments in 1930, the pope noted that Bolshevik ideas were making worrisome progress among both African-Americans in the United States and anticolonial activists overseas—something that made the task of Catholic missionaries all the more indispensable.[65] Apart from making passing mention of the importance of missionary activity and the need to train indigenous clergy, the Vatican's principal response to anticolonial and antiracist movements of the 1920s was to highlight their "revolutionary" and hence dangerous potential. As we will see in subsequent chapters, the Vatican's response to the explosion of anticolonial nationalism and internationalism would cause problems in the coming decades.

The papal answer to the explosion of communist civil society activism was to strengthen, consolidate, and centralize a civil society culture of its own. Pius XI was the great pioneer in this, so much so that many judged his unique contribution as pope to be his capacity "to enlist large cadres of the Catholic laity into an army of religious defense commanded by the hierarchy."[66] Pius XI branded his program to mobilize and organize the Catholic masses "Catholic Action."

Though Catholic Action took different shapes in different contexts, the basic idea was to encourage lay Catholics to bring home the mission of re-Christianizing society through a range of after-school and after-work activities—activities that would be social and fun but also serve the purpose of training future warriors of Catholicism to defend their turf. Women and men, boys and girls, university students and factory workers were all invited to participate, and all were given unique roles and responsibilities. A key component of Pius XI's Catholic Action revolution was structure—specifically, a structure that tightly bound the laity to the hierarchy. Thus, for a Catholic civil society organization to be branded "Catholic Action," it would have to conform to a set of rules that ensured its oversight by not just the parish priest, but bishops and archbishops too, on up to an ecclesiastical assistant based in Rome and appointed directly by the pope.

In the mid-1920s Pius XI approved new statutes governing Italian Catholic Action. The statutes, which Pius XI later sought to universalize, put the Vatican at the head of Catholic civil society. As Pius saw it, the papal-sanctioned "Catholic Action" would help the Catholic Church protect concordat wins and fight against its enemies by inscribing a new code of action into the lives of everyday Catholics. As a figure close to Pius XI put it, "the Church must make extensive use of the liberties now conceded to it," and, working in tandem with friendly states and local members of the Church hierarchy, "it must encourage the proliferation of lay Catholic organizations, so as to bring about the supreme goal of the Christian penetration of the entire population."[67] The new Catholic Action was to provide Catholics with a worldview, a culture, and a repertoire of collective actions that they could participate in "from the cradle to the grave," and help advance the papacy's earthly agenda.

The papacy's new push to activate civil society clashed with the increasingly totalitarian ambitions of the Fascist regime. In 1926 Mussolini cut the ribbons on a new Fascist youth organization, the Opera Nazionale Balilla, and sharply limited the activities of a key branch of Catholic Action in Italy: the Gioventù Italiana di Azione Cattolica. Pius XI was incensed and expressed his concern that a wing of the Fascist movement (not the Fascist movement as a whole) seemed committed to the "primacy of politics" over the "primacy of the spiritual,"

The Italian female youth branch of Catholic Action, *Gioventù femminile*, in Piazza San Pietro, celebrating its twenty-year anniversary in 1938. The woman dressed in black on the left-hand side of the photo, Armida Barelli, would be the organization's president until 1946. Credit: Isacem-Institute for the History of Catholic Action and the Catholic Movement in Italy Paul VI, Luigi Gedda Fund, Series Civic Committees

and to a conception of the state that "turns the state into an end, and makes the citizen a means, monopolizing and absorbing him in the process."[68] Some theologians close to the pope went a step further, calling upon Fascists to denounce a conception of the state that "claimed that nothing is above the state, and no limitation can be placed on its activities. There is no real law other than the one that is created by the state and recognized by it." They quipped that if Fascism did not clean up its house, its "totalitarian" wing, which sought to deify the state, would lead to the entire regime's demise.[69]

Catholic critiques of conceptions of the "total state" were not new. Back in 1922, as it lambasted the League of Nations, *Civiltà Cattolica* had described liberals as beholden to a conception of the state that contradicted "natural law, which comes before, and is superior to, the State."[70] In 1923 Luigi Sturzo, the founder of the Italian Popular Party, had been the first to apply the anti-liberal slur to the Fascist phenomenon. In 1924 he noted that Mussolini's "totalitarianism" sought "to subsume everything moral, cultural, political and religious [into] something new: 'Fascism.'"[71] In 1927, when Pius XI condemned a defiant French civil society organization, French Action, for its insubordination and its privileging of politics above religion, *Civiltà Cattolica* suggested that the pope's veto had meaning beyond France. The pope, the journal noted, had raged against a secular "conception of the state" that synthesized "the old pagan idolatry and the modern liberal conception"—a vision that good Catholics could not underwrite. The following year, in a speech to Catholic activists in September 1928, the director of the *Osservatore Romano*, Giuseppe Dalla Torre, extended the warning. Some Fascists, he suggested, seemed committed to a vision of "a state . . . which nothing can escape from: neither souls, nor things, nor ideas, nor works." But to erect the state as the source of all "moral law" and as the "only reality of social life" was not only anti-Christian; it risked turning the state itself into a religion. If the Fascists did not change their ways, "the state," he cautioned, "will become the Church for those who have repudiated the Church, or better still, it will be the God of those who have broken with or failed to recognize the Kingdom of God!"[72]

Toward the Lateran Pacts

The papacy and its allies were concerned about the rise of state totalitarianism within Fascist circles, and turned to concordat diplomacy as a solution. The conclusion of a concordat with the Italian state, Pius XI reasoned, would oblige the Italian dictator to embrace a "conception of the state that conforms to Catholic doctrine."[73] Mussolini promptly responded to the idea by saying that the Fascist Party was ready and willing to embrace the Catholic model, not least because it had long ago "repudiated both the principle of the state's religious agnosticism, and the principles of separation of church and state."[74] Many papal observers took Mussolini at his word. They began to believe that Mussolini and Fascism could be "reformed" and brought into line with Vatican

Premier Benito Mussolini reading the Lateran Agreements, just before
signing them with the papal secretary of state, Cardinal Pietro Gasparri
(facing the camera). Vatican City, February 11, 1929. Credit: AP Photo

fantasies, on the condition that the regime sign on to the Catholic and
concordat vision of the state, and protect Catholic prerogatives in civil
society and elsewhere.[75] After several years of preparing the ground
through behind-the-scenes conversations, Pius XI charged one of his
legal counselors, Francesco Pacelli, a prominent Vatican lawyer and
Eugenio Pacelli's younger brother, with formally opening negotiations
in August 1926. The negotiations were halting and difficult. But finally, on February 11, 1929, Vatican Secretary of State Gasparri and
Mussolini signed the Lateran Agreements.[76]

The Agreements were composed of three interlinked texts, including a concordat. In ideational, legal, and financial terms, the pacts
fulfilled many of the papacy's core demands, and strongly suggested
that Italy would become a confessional state, characterized by a deep
cooperation and collaboration with the Holy See. Like the concordats

that preceded it, the pacts had the status of treaty under international law; they were not simply an Italian bill. The pope in person had pushed hard on precisely this point, insofar as he wanted his lead negotiators to use the Agreements to restore the papacy as an official international, independent player on the diplomatic stage.

The Agreements began with a conciliation treaty, whose first article prominently announced, "The Holy Catholic Apostolic and Roman Religion is the only state religion." Additionally, the treaty restored territorial sovereignty to the pope. Per the pope's express and repeated requests, the land received would henceforth be called a "state."[77] According to the pacts, the 108 acres of the newborn Vatican City State were a "neutral territory" that was independent from Italy, even though Italy would supply the city-state with water and basic infrastructure (railroad, telephone and postal services). The second key component—the concordat—laid out in forty-five articles the sacralization of the Italian state, specifying the fusion of religious and civil holidays, the preeminence of the Church in matters of marriage and divorce, and the role of the Church as "the basis and crown of public education" at the primary, secondary, and tertiary levels. Catholic Action was also protected in the concordat, which asserted that the organization would "go about its activities regarding the dissemination and actualization of Catholic principles outside of the bounds of a political party, and under the immediate dependence of the Church hierarchy."[78] As the pope repeatedly emphasized, the concordat was the core of the settlement, and the conciliation treaty and financial settlement assumed meaning only when read alongside the concordat.

The third component of the pacts—the financial agreement—promised that Italy would provide the Vatican with a cash payment of 750 million lire and investments in Italian government stock worth one billion lire. After many years of financial uncertainty and dependence on the fluctuating donations of the faithful, the Vatican had become financially secure, and with the hefty income of up to 87 million lire per year and the freedom to invest in companies both at home and abroad, it "would never be poor again."[79] Irrespective of its critique of economic liberalism, it had also become a key player in the emergent global capitalist marketplace.

Much hullabaloo surrounded the conclusion of the Lateran Agreements in 1929. Flags were flown, church bells rung, and hymns sung to Mussolini, the "man from Providence" who had enabled this historic overturning of the "nightmare" of a Church and state divided. Fascist politicians announced that Italy was seizing the mantle of the defunct Habsburg Empire, as Europe's new leading Catholic power.[80] The Catholic Action press deemed 1929 "a truly epochal year."[81] On the evening of the conclusion of the Agreements, the *Osservatore Romano* issued a special edition. Since 1870 the newspaper had printed the Latin phrase "Non Praevalebunt" (They will not prevail) as its heading, but that evening, February 12, 1929, the heading was gone. In its place was an announcement: "Today at noon, in the popes' Hall of the Apostolic Lateran Palazzo, a Treaty was signed between the Holy See and Italy."[82] The president of Italian Catholic Action noted that the *Conciliazione* had definitively laid to rest the concern that Fascism was idolatrous and that it considered "religion purely as an *instrumentum regni*."[83]

Within six days of concluding the Agreements, Pius XI encouraged Vatican representatives to pressure the Fascist regime so as to ensure that "worthy representatives of a confessional state" come to power in the upcoming parliamentary elections. As papal diplomats specified, this meant that Parliament should be purged of "undesirables," which included individuals with "any tie with Freemasonry" and "the anticlerical parties." Jews and Protestants should also be kept at arm's length.[84] As was the case with Poland, Pius XI's basic position was that religious minorities should not be allowed to wield "undue" social and political influence in predominantly Catholic countries. Mussolini complied with many of the requests, while grumbling that the Church's worries were exaggerated and possibly bent on "suppressing freedom of worship" entirely.[85]

Commentators took stock of the new state of affairs and concluded that Church and Fascist state were now in perfect concord. But in fact the Lateran Agreements are best understood as an unstable truce, or a working agreement, established between two competing hegemonic regimes.[86] Curiously, both sides saw the pacts as a clear win for their side. That they did so is proof of the oddity of Catholicism and Fascism in the late 1920s. Both were riding high, whether it was because of recent concordat victories and the expansion of Catholic Action, or because of the consolidation of the Fascist dictatorship and the sense that Mussolini had successfully constructed a "bloc of consensus" that would give him freedom to maneuver in Italy and abroad.

For the papacy, the Lateran Agreements were seen as a crucial chapter in the resurgence of a muscular papacy—flush with money; endowed with power over civil society, law, and education; and with its own independent state. The pacts, Pius XI believed, would guarantee the papacy's independent powers as an international actor and enable the papacy to keep Fascism's totalitarian wing in check. Immediately following their conclusion, the pope encouraged the development of extensive plans to build up Vatican City into a model micro-state, to expand the internationalization of Catholic Action, and to strengthen the papacy's stature as an international power. The Lateran Agreements, for the Holy See, signaled that Italy could become a model confessional state. The ecclesiastical assistant of the leading male branch of Catholic Action put the sentiment thusly: "Italy has been remade Catholic. Now, we will remake Catholic the souls of Italians." Along similar lines, the editorial board of a leading Catholic Action journal noted that the pacts represented the end of anticlericalism in Italy, and the birth of a new "religious and political conscience of the Italian people." Thanks to the Lateran Agreements, they said, Catholic Action could now hold out "the promise of spiritual resurrection for all Italians." Catholics close to the pope understood the pacts as opening up a possibility for Catholicism's eventual overtaking of the "bad" elements of Fascism—insofar as they would force statist Fascists to abandon their totalitarianism, and bow to a model of the state imbued by Catholic teachings. Many Catholics optimistically noted that the pacts had provided the basis of the "Christian restoration of society" and demonstrated that the risks of Fascist statolatry had been "transcended and rendered defunct." As they saw it, the Lateran Agreements represented an opening and an opportunity for Catholic internationalism.[87]

The pacts indicated that the Vatican was not alone, and that it had a partner in its battle against the forces seeking to undermine Catholicism in Europe. Pius XI's motto to summarize the relationship was "collaboration, but not confusion." He counseled that Catholic internationalists must work *with* the Fascists, but never at the cost of sacrificing their own distinct identity, and their own plans for Europe.

For a minute but crucial group of Catholic observers in Europe, however, the Lateran Agreements were not a win at all—they were a major loss. For in place of taking a hard line against Fascist totalitarianism, the Agreements suggested that the papacy was willing to compromise with Fascism and sanction its violent and repressive tactics. The French theologian Yves Simon, bursting with anger, noted: "Imbeciles have been in key positions [in] the Vatican, the bishoprics, the universities, the Catholic press [and] given free rein to criminals." He added that with the conclusion of the Lateran Agreements, "totalitarian regimes . . . are accomplishing with a growing efficacy a more redoubtable infamy than any persecution: *the corruption of the Catholic world from within*." "We are in full Catholic crisis," he concluded.[88]

Luigi Sturzo and other *popolari* were similarly crushed by news of the Lateran Agreements, which convinced them that the papacy would never turn against the Fascist regime.[89] The founder of the Italian Popular Party decried "the new agreement," which, he said, "represents the complete triumph of the Fascist State over the Church." Along similar lines, Guido Miglioli, a former Popular Party leader in exile in France, affirmed in an interview with *Le Monde*, "These two years have witnessed the gradual but inexorable submission of the pope to the demands of the regime."[90]

Some observers took the Lateran Agreements as an opportunity to take a step further and express their skepticism about the concordat revolution as a whole. Alcide de Gasperi, who would emerge as the leader of Italy's Christian Democratic Party in the early postwar years, voiced the fear that observers would henceforth confuse Fascism with Catholicism. "The Church will be compromised," he informed a friend, noting further that this was bigger than a Fascist-papal problem: the "real danger," he noted, "lies in the policy of concordats" itself.[91] The socialist historian and writer Gaetano Salvemini, who was also a friend of Luigi Sturzo, took the critique further still: "We refute the very idea of the concordat as an idea that creates a privileged religious organization in a society that, according to us, ought to grant no privilege of any sort to any single religious organization."[92]

But despite this opposition, the Vatican's commitment to the Lateran Agreements did not waiver. To appease critics, Pius XI did use his new platform on several occasions to remind Mussolini that with the conclusion of the pacts, the Fascist totalitarian wing had received a fatal blow, and he repeatedly lambasted Fascist attempts to limit the Church's presence in civil society. In a strongly worded assertion of the priority of Catholic internationalism over Fascism, Pius publicly affirmed: "If there is a regime that is totalitarian, totalitarian in reality and according to the law, that is the regime of the Church . . . Man belongs wholly to the Church, and must belong wholly to it, insofar as he is a creature of God. [Thus], the Church really has the right and duty to claim the totality of its power over individuals: every man in his entirety belongs to the Church, because in his entirety he belongs to God."[93]

In response, members of the Fascist secret police emphasized that Italy must neither "fall into the hands of the Jewish and communist international, [nor] into those of the Catholic international, which works more silently, it is true, but not less intensely than the former."[94] But despite the tug of war over who had full rights to claim power over the hearts, minds, and bodies of Italians, the Lateran Agreements would remain on the books. In fact, as the years went by, they would become ever-more important to the papacy, not least because the Great Depression would consolidate the conviction that a partnership with the Fascists was necessary in order to resist the growth of radical left-wing movements and the dangerous internationalism of the Soviet Union.

5

Launching the Anticommunist Crusade

If Moscow's Comintern is at the head of the Communist International, Rome is the center of the Catholic International!

—*Lettres de Rome*, MAY 1935

IN 1930–1935 the unprecedented economic crisis known as the Great Depression hit Europe hard. All the major countries in Europe suffered serious economic damage. Stock market values collapsed and foreign trade declined. Unemployment in many countries soared above 25 percent, resulting in a precipitous decline in standards of living.[1] Face-to-face with six million jobless men and women in Germany, the writer Rudolf Ditzen (writing under the pseudonym Hans Fallada) depicted the forlorn victims as "dressed in gray, pale in the face," and "waiting, but even they don't know what they wait for. Who is it that expects a job anyway?"[2]

The Great Depression would usher in a new international order, and mark the perceived rise of the Soviet Union as the papacy's leading competitor on the global stage. It would also result in the temporary retreat of the United States from the continent. Until the Depression, the United States had remained, as one British diplomat put it, the "ghost at all our feasts." But in the early 1930s the United States moved to a position of detachment, succumbing to a "great isolationist temptation," and retreating from Europe for a decade. At the same time, the League of Nations stopped serving as an effective forum for international politics. Liberal internationalism, it seemed, was no longer a viable model or a credible threat in Europe, insofar as it had been unable to withstand the disintegrative effect of the Great Depression.[3]

If the old order, based on the "absent presence of U.S. power," was breaking apart, would the Holy See—which from 1917 had positioned itself as the mascot of an alternative, anti-liberal, and anti-American international order—be able to take advantage of the new situation? Though somewhat insulated from the crisis, it too had suffered in the course of the Great Depression. As a result of the Lateran Agreements, the Vatican was now a major investor in European stocks, and in 1930–1931 it experienced a significant decrease in its earnings due to stock depreciation. The Vatican also registered a visible decline in annual contributions to the Church. The decline was particularly sharp when it came to contributions from Catholics in the two countries that had recently become its biggest donors: Germany and the United States.

As several of the pope's regular interlocutors attested, global economic matters soon became the pope's preferred topic of conversation. When speaking of the unfolding crisis, Pius XI, with no hint of irony, declared the Great Depression "the greatest human calamity since the Flood."[4] A close advisor recorded: "The pope is often quite interested in discussing with me the topic that worries him most: the world economic crisis. He speaks with almost greater enthusiasm about the fall of the dollar than about the decline of morality; he laments with more palpable bitterness the loss of money than the ruin of souls."[5]

Distressed by the Vatican's decline in income, the pope mandated a general reduction in wages for all Vatican employees. He allowed his leading financial advisor to redirect investments and engage in ethically questionable arbitrage schemes, which had as their purpose, as the advisor explained, "the profit from the greater depression of the New York market in comparison with the London one."[6] In a blow to the grand plan to take back Rome after the Lateran Agreements, he regretfully halted the rebuilding of Vatican City.

The notion that the Great Depression marked the end of an era and the beginning of a period of great uncertainty was a key theme in clerical circles. The leader of the Dominican order in Italy informed Pius XI, "The economic crisis is tied with a thousand strings—some more visible, some less—to a global moral crisis."[7] Many fretted about the impact of the Great Depression on individual psyches; Hans Fallada noted that a desperate, hopeless, unemployed, and broken "little man" (kleiner Mann) was becoming the mascot of the European moment. In the words of the artist and intellectual Ernst Jünger, Europe was traversing a "dangerous moment." Did a promising, "transformed world" lie just around the corner? Or would the old order—blown apart by the Great Depression—be supplanted by something even more frightening?[8]

From 1930 onward, concerned letters began pouring into Vatican City from the pope's most trusted interlocutors. Responding to the uptick in strikes, demonstrations, and left-wing radicalism, the letters had a common thread: all expressed the worry that the retreat of the United States would coincide with the rise, not of the Vatican, but of the Soviet Union. The respected German Jesuit Father Friedrich Muckermann wrote to warn that the current economic situation would quickly devolve into a "world revolution" that would directly benefit the Soviet Union. As Muckermann saw it, the Soviet Union's "policy is to drive Germany to the side of Bolshevism" and thus create "a victorious united Soviet Germany and Soviet Russia." "Germany and Europe must be unified through an anti-Bolshevik movement," centered in Rome, which "can be the savior of Europe once again, as it was at the time of the Turks." "It is still possible to achieve something like this, but it will not be possible much longer."[9]

German bishops informed their superiors that they were considering various options, including excommunication, to prevent Catholic workers from joining left-wing unions or being involved in communist movements.[10] In tandem, German Catholic civil society movements began positioning themselves against communism. The most active groups in this effort became Quickborn (led by Romano Guardini), Neu Deutschland (founded with help from German Jesuit activists), Windthorstbund (the youth organization of the Center party), and Volksverein für das Katholische Deutschland (the People's Association for Catholic Germany, which received the strong support of the German higher clergy).[11] In Austria the Catholic civil society organization known as Internacio Katolika, or IKA, also put itself at the forefront of the opposition to "Bolshevism's battle against religion and Christian culture both inside and outside Russia," and worked to unite Catholics in Germany and Austria in common cause.[12]

Though initially these movements were small and isolated, they shared some common themes. All presented themselves as primarily interested in defending the Church and the family from "anti-Christian" attacks. They explicitly stated that they were most concerned about the ideological and political straying of young people, who were vulnerable because they were not yet "fully formed" and thus were more subject to "propaganda."[13] The Volksverein pioneered a series of conferences and summer courses "against atheism," which advocated, among other things, the creation of a "Catholic International of the Working Class."[14] IKA sponsored international conferences in Austria, Luxembourg, Germany, Switzerland, Hungary, and Great Britain, which focused on themes such as "Bolshevism's world propaganda," "Religious persecution in Russia," and "The destructive influence of Bolshevism on human civilization, and especially on the family and education."[15] The Windthorstbund helped establish a Committee for the Struggle against Bolshevism (composed of lawyers, journalists, union leaders, Catholic politicians, and members of the clergy), and got to work through the creation of "a comprehensive strategy of training, public demonstrations and lectures" that aimed to warn everyday Germans of the threat posed by "the Soviet star." Soon enough, the organization was averaging 2,000 themed events per year and making use of both print and radio to spread its anticommunist message.[16] The Volksverein even set up an anticommunist intelligence-gathering bureau, which began drawing on the resources of a vast network of Catholic youth associations as it collected information about the form and effectiveness of communist penetration in Germany.[17]

If German Catholics were alarmed by the growth of communism and left-wing radicalism in the aftermath of the Great Depression, so were influential Catholics in Poland, who noted that the Great Depression had caused an "extremely dangerous" rise in communist power. They affirmed that not just Germany and Poland, but Spain, France, and other countries too were all tottering on the brink of communist revolution. Like stacked dominoes, if Germany fell, so would the rest of Europe, and "that," they said, "will be the moment that Bolshevism invades Europe as a whole."[18] Papal officials agreed, noting that Moscow's aim was most certainly global conquest and destabilization. In order to carry out that aim, it "satanically attacks the weakest point in any given nation: while in one nation it might raise the social question and distance the working masses from religion, in another, for instance, England, it ranges its diabolical weapons against marriage; in Spain, it topples the Government; in the colonies it foments the spirit of revenge and nationalism."[19]

The panicked letters streaming toward the pope were not cries in the dark: they were symptomatic of a general reorientation in the wider European Catholic world. Many intellectuals in France, Germany, Spain, Italy, Poland, and elsewhere had by the early 1930s begun embracing an emerging trope that cast the continent as locked in a struggle between a communist and morally deprived Eastern Europe and a noncommunist and religiously grounded Western Europe. A flurry of new books revisited the old Orientalist East/West binary in this new anti-Soviet key. Devoured by Catholic intellectuals and exhaustively reviewed on the pages of Catholic journals, these books began to construct a myth of Catholicism and communism at the antipodes—a myth that became central to the papal anticommunist crusade of the 1930s. Soon enough, many of the continent's most prominent Catholic writers and intellectuals were echoing this myth, all the while fretting about how the Great Depression had ushered in what they called a "crisis of civilization" that might hand Europe to the Bolsheviks and destroy the continent as a whole.[20] Catholic anticommunism became prominent in American Catholic circles as well, whether it came to articles in the American Jesuit mouthpiece, *America,* conference themes addressed by professors of canon law at the University of St. Louis, or speeches delivered in a range of venues—including the American Historical Association—by figures like Father Edmund Walsh, the first key figure entrusted by the papacy to travel to Russian lands after the 1917 revolution.[21]

The pressure was mounting—not least because the papacy's own most trusted diplomats, like Eugenio Pacelli, had for years warned of the threat of communist expansionism. In 1930–1931, Pius XI decided to take action. He informed high-level papal diplomats that upon careful reflection, he had reached the conclusion that "it is most especially the expansion of the Bolshevik ideology that constitutes a danger."[22] Accordingly, the Catholic laity in general and Catholic youth groups in particular must reposition themselves at the forefront of a battle against "godless" communism.[23] Pius XI then appointed the staunchly anticommunist Eugenio Pacelli as secretary of state, rejected the possibility of a *modus vivendi* with the Soviet Union, and tapped a series of known Catholic anticommunists to write a public diagnosis of the present moment. Mussolini promptly made it known that he and conservatives across Europe read the moves "as an invitation to launch a political campaign" against the Soviet Union. At the same time, the Duce added that because he had already destroyed communism in Italy, he had nothing to gain by being leader of the pack. Passing off the responsibility of a global anticommunist campaign to the pope, while simultaneously showing that he shared the desire to continue combatting communism, Mussolini affirmed: "If other powers throw in the ball, I will be one of the strongest footballers."[24]

In 1931 Pius XI suggested that he was ready to play ball. First, he began loudly protesting commercial treaties signed by European countries with the Soviet Union, on the grounds that the "corrupting thirst for gold" was leading European powers to "give money to the Soviets" and thus help fund their global gamble for hegemony.[25] In tandem, he encouraged Pacelli to start a diplomatic initiative, targeting American, German, and Italian diplomats, to prevent the Soviet Union from joining the League of Nations.[26] In a further indication of his change of course, Pius XI sent an enterprising Jesuit, Joseph Ledit, who as a younger man had been deported from the Soviet Union, to the United States, on a mission to learn more about how American Catholics were mobilizing against communism.[27]

In lockstep, the *Osservatore Romano* began increasing its coverage of international communism, reporting, for instance, on purported Soviet plans to export the League of the Militant Godless to Europe, via the creation of "centers of instruction and propaganda in every city or village," known as "cells of atheism," and via the translation of weekly publications into German, English, and French.[28] A former Vatican official working as a Fascist spy, Umberto Benigni, noted with pleasure the change in tone: "The papacy and his press were silent for a long time on the antireligious horrors of Russian Bolshevism," he noted in a confidential secret police briefing. "Suddenly, that undignified silence has ended, and the *Osservatore Romano* and *Civiltà Cattolica* have, in unison, started protesting on behalf of the Christian world."[29]

On the fortieth anniversary of Leo's landmark social encyclical *Rerum Novarum*, Pius XI established closer ties to a handful of well-known clerics connected to the German anticommunist Catholic movement, the Volksverein. Since the late 1920s Eugenio Pacelli had been keeping the pope abreast of the activities of this movement, not least because the German upper clergy were fully informed about, and in complete support of, its anticommunist activities.[30] Through the launching of so-called Weeks for God *(Gotteswochen)*, conferences, and demonstrations, the clergy were cooperating with the Volksverein, so that they together could "bring alive in the great masses of faithful the full joy that accompanies Catholic truth, and in this way warn them against the insidious propaganda of the 'Godless.'"[31] Following this stamp of approval by the German hierarchy, the work of the Volksverein was repeatedly cited in the marbled halls of the Vatican by officials who noted that, "The methods followed in Germany by the Volksverein [in] the organization of propaganda against the dangers of Bolshevism [are] very effective." Indeed, the work of the Volksverein was being presented as something worthy of emulation by the papacy itself.[32] In 1931 Pius XI tapped a group of German Catholics from the Volksverein to help draft a landmark encyclical on social issues.[33]

The text would be no less than Pius XI's follow-up response to Leo's 1891 *Rerum Novarum*. Włodzimierz Ledóchowski, the Superior General of the Jesuits, also played an important role in the drafting of the encyclical, and did what he could to "inject a powerful dose of anti-communism in the notable 1931 social encyclical."[34] Given the robust participation of German and also French anticommunist clerics in the project, that "extra boost" was hardly necessary, however.

The new encyclical would tackle three key questions: What had caused the Great Depression? How had the Depression led to the spread of communism? What could everyday Catholics do about it? In the spring of 1931 the Vatican's daily newspaper, the *Osservatore Romano*, began foreshadowing the encyclical's core arguments. The Great Depression, it said, had been caused by liberal democracies and the "poison" of economic liberalism, which in turn had led to the rise of communism and communist-inspired "antireligious organizations" across Western Europe and beyond.[35]

Liberalism and its cognates were condemned in sharp tones on thirteen occasions in *Quadragesimo Anno,* a move that placed Pius XI in strong continuity with the views articulated by Benedict XV during and immediately after World War I. The encyclical started off by emphasizing that in most countries in the West, "human society was clearly becoming divided more and more into two classes": the haves and the have-nots. "One class, very small in number, was enjoying almost all the advantages which modern inventions so abundantly provided; the other, embracing the huge multitude of working people, oppressed by wretched poverty, was vainly seeking escape from the straits wherein it stood." Following this stark characterization, the encyclical strongly implied that the United States and its capitalist credo had caused the "shipwreck" of the Great Depression. Liberal "individualism," the text asserted, had turned greed into a virtue, allowing for the spread of unethical financial speculation and the destruction of any genuine commitment to public life and community goods. The "right ordering of economic life cannot be left to a free competition of forces," the text thundered. "From this source, as from a poisoned spring, have originated and spread all the errors of individualist economic teaching." Indeed, liberalism "had proved that it was utterly unable to solve the social problem."[36]

After the extended harangue against liberalism, Pius XI then expounded upon the intimate relation between liberalism, socialism, and communism. Socialism, the pope argued, had emerged historically and in dialectical fashion. Liberalism had "come first," providing one bad answer to the social question (one "thesis"), and socialism had "come next," as an attempt to negate the principles of liberalism (it was the "antithesis"). However, both liberalism and socialism were "twin errors" and "twin rocks of shipwreck"—and both of them "must be carefully avoided" by good Catholics. The socialist cure to the evils of liberalism was no cure at all—instead, it was a "dangerous" and "alluring poison." Pius XI instructed his readers that socialism was wholly unacceptable because of its commitment to class warfare and materialism, as well as its call to abolish private property. For these reasons, "religious socialism, Christian socialism, are contradictory terms." "No one can be at the same time a good Catholic and a true socialist."[37]

As had Leo XIII, Pius XI affirmed that class warfare was the wrong way to understand human relations: the Bible taught that all classes and peoples must live harmoniously, and that all were equal in the eyes of God. With reference to socialism's materialism, Pius XI noted that Christianity held that human beings are placed on the earth so that they "may fully cultivate and develop all their faculties unto the praise and glory of their Creation." By contrast, socialism "wholly ignore[s] and [is] indifferent to this sublime end of both man and society," focusing exclusively on the here-and-now. Thus, Catholics must understand that socialism "is based on a theory of human society peculiar to itself and irreconcilable with Christianity." Regarding private property, Pius XI referred readers to Leo XIII's (and Thomas Aquinas's) discussion of private property as a "natural right" that emerged from the pater familias's need to care for his offspring, not just in the present (through the provision of food on the table), but also through the transmission of private property from one generation to the next. Pius XI noted that owning private property helped men support not just their children but their wives, too. This enabled women to avoid the situation "to be abolished at all costs," of mothers taking jobs "outside the home to the neglect of their proper cares and duties, especially the training of children."[38] Pius XI's paternalistic calls to exclude women from the workforce, camouflaged behind the idea of the "protection of motherhood," were amply echoed in mainline Fascist policies and positions at the time.[39]

Following the resolute condemnation of socialism, Pius XI moved on to link liberalism, socialism, and communism. "Let all remember that Liberalism is the father of this Socialism that is pervading morality and culture; and that Bolshevism will be its heir," Pius XI announced. Communism and socialism had much in common: both were materialistic, opposed to private property, and committed to class warfare. Furthermore, both were "openly hostile to the Holy Church and to God Himself." As compared to socialism, however, communism was more focused on "winning the hearts and minds" of youth, and more successful, thanks in no small part to its tactics. "Unrelenting" and "absolute," Pius XI noted, communists were targeting youth in the attempt to train their "mind and character." Indeed, "under the guise of affection," communism was working "to attract children of tender age and win them to itself." Communists pursued their aims "by employing every and all means, even the most violent." They were "incredible and portent-like in [their] cruelty and inhumanity." Through "horrible slaughter and destruction," Bolshevism had already "laid waste to vast regions of eastern Europe and Asia [sic]." For all these reasons and more, communism was evidently a "grave and imminent evil."[40]

Because the "Bolshevik poison" was a real and imminent danger, Pius XI concluded, readers must take action. Catholics were asked to spread the word: "We cannot without deep sorrow contemplate the heedlessness of those who apparently make light of these impending dangers." Catholics must push local and state government representatives to be more proactive, for too many of these figures "with sluggish inertia allow the widespread propaganda of doctrine which seeks by violence and slaughter to destroy society altogether." They must help Catholic lay organizations grow their numbers, because communist associations were "flourishing everywhere," and even often "surpassing in numbers" their Catholic equivalents. The encyclical outlined a way to carry out a Catholic "reconstruction of the social order" through the backing of a corporatist economic system, which was neither capitalist nor communist. This state-controlled system of syndicates and corporations, for Pius XI, had "obvious advantages," in that "the various classes work together peacefully" and "socialist organizations and their activities are repressed."[41] However, the encyclical was silent on the key question of whether Fascist corporatism and Catholic corporatism were aligned.[42] Additionally, the text did not encourage Catholics to engage in a "strong fight against the crimes of capitalism," as at least one key papal adviser had hoped it would.[43] For these reasons and more, some Catholic commentators grumbled that the text was confusing, and that it lacked "a precise orientation or answer to the questions raised by modern-day economic life."[44]

The critics made a good point. However, the purpose of *Quadragesimo Anno* was not to outright condemn capitalism, much less the Fascist regime. Instead, its aim was to argue that tight historical and ideological bonds linked liberalism, socialism, and communism, and that therefore the fight against one must be the fight against all. This core message stood in stark contrast to Leo XIII's *Rerum Novarum*, which had placed more emphasis on socialism than liberalism, and had steered clear of arguing for any intimate relation between the two. Additionally, Leo XIII had not named communism in his encyclical or clearly distinguished it from socialism. By contrast, the premise and point of *Quadragesimo Anno* was to claim that the "war against liberalism" must continue in a new guise, and morph into a battle against international communism.

Quadragesimo Anno was the opening salvo of what would soon become the Vatican's anticommunist crusade of the 1930s. As such, it was no accident that the text was intended for a global audience. In May 1931 the Tipografia Vaticana was reassuring the pope that it was poised to issue translations of the text in twelve different languages, even as the head of the Jesuit order scurried behind the scenes to find the very best translators for some of the languages into which papal encyclicals were not typically translated, such as Chinese. Once printed, the text was disseminated with extraordinary speed and efficiency by members of papal diplomatic corps and leading religious orders.[45]

Unsurprisingly, Catholics noticed. As the American archbishop, Cardinal Hayes, happily informed Pacelli, the encyclical aided him tremendously in his work to convince many a Catholic of communism's dangers. It had even helped him convert a difficult type: a "history professor teaching at one of the most prominent secular universities" in the United States. Not long ago, Hayes noted, this professor "had become a communist, because he had thought that communism was a solution to certain social problems." But then, "having read and carefully studied *Quadragesimo Anno* and *Rerum Novarum*, the professor came to recognize that communism was a destructive force, while the Church, by contrast, defends social justice and proposes safe and well-informed solutions."[46] Catholic journalists similarly celebrated the encyclical, which they characterized as "a magnificent, energetic, and wise encyclical against Bolshevism."[47] A few enthusiasts of the anticommunist turn, wedded to the Judeo-Bolshevik myth, expressed their disappoint at the fact that the pope had "not expressed even a word against Jews," despite the fact that (so they believed) "Jews are the organizers and sustainers of Bolshevism" and their real project is not to build communism but instead to "destroy the Church of Jesus Christ."[48]

Announcing the Campaign

In the aftermath of *Quadragesimo Anno*, the Vatican launched a far-reaching crusade against international communism. It did so independently of its concordat partners, but in close communication with them. Its aim was to disseminate a cohesive Catholic anticommunist ideology and simultaneously put pressure on state leaders to marginalize the Soviet Union from the international state system. The campaign catapulted the papacy into an era of new media experiments. By decade's end, the Vatican had helped sponsor anticommunist novel competitions, anticommunist traveling exhibitions, and anticommunist radio programming. It had also placed anticommunism at the center of its work in civil society. By the mid-1930s the campaign was active across much of Europe, North America, and Latin America, and in parts of Asia and Africa. It mobilized millions of people and strengthened new partnerships, including with states like Fascist Italy. Furthermore, the campaign successfully disseminated a new framework for understanding communism as a fundamentally atheistic force, and suggested that because communism was violent and extreme in its tactics and aims, war against it was probable and morally justifiable.

The papacy's anticommunist campaign was a clear example of the power of transnational activism in the era of mass politics. However, the Vatican campaign has received little scholarly attention. Experts have tended to treat Catholic anticommunism as a given, rather than as something that needed to be built, both from the ground up and from the top down.[49] Those few scholars who have made passing mention of the papacy's interwar campaign have downplayed its highly centralized nature, its transnational reach, and its ambitious scope.[50] They have also missed the fact that the Vatican's decision to launch a full-scale campaign against the Soviet Union and international communism took shape in response to contingent developments in the interwar years, including the rise of communist internationalism in the late 1920s, the crisis of the Great Depression, and the disproportionate influence of Catholics in places like Bavaria and Italy in shaping papal policies.

The Vatican's global campaign against the Soviet Union transformed Catholic internationalism in profound ways. Starting from the 1930s, a focus on capturing airwaves, flooding the literary marketplace, and developing a lasting presence in civil society began to overshadow the papacy's earlier interest in laying claim to legal structures and Catholicizing Europe's nation-states through legal means. Now the pope was supporting the global expansion and centralization of Catholic Action organizations, the production of glossy anti-Soviet comic books, and wide-ranging attempts to censor and block the import of Soviet films. In 1929 the *Osservatore Romano* transitioned from being principally interested in "matters Italian" and tightly censured by the Italian state, to being a self-consciously international—and internationalist—newspaper.[51] In 1931 Pius XI cut the ribbons for Vatican Radio. In the same year, the papacy inaugurated a first-of-its-kind internal news agency, which took a distinctly anti-Soviet tack from the moment of its founding. In the era of internationalism, the anticommunist media offensive enabled the pope to present himself as the most plausible leader of a campaign against an enemy of the European right— an enemy whose "internationalism" was cast as its leading point of strength.

When it came to the transformation of Catholic internationalism in the 1930s, the media *was* the message. Radio, film, literature, children's books, and news agencies all suggested several things to consumers. They helped popularize the idea of the pope as a familiar, intimate presence, and as a figure who was both critically aware and of-the-moment. Additionally, new entertainment media meant that Catholicism could be integrated with leisure time through the reading of novels or fun magazines. Most crucially, the existence of an ever-expanding, extensive, transborder Catholic media empire signified "internationalism" and "universality" to listeners, viewers, and observers. It reinforced the Vatican's claim that the "Catholic International" led by

Guglielmo Marconi (left) and Pope Pius XI (right) listening to an early
broadcast of Vatican Radio. February 20, 1933. Credit: De Agostini Picture
Library / Getty Images

the pope constituted the most credible response to the Communist
International, headquartered in Moscow.

Beginning in 1931, anticommunist references became an ever-more-
visible component of papal encyclicals, and in April 1932, leaders in
the Catholic Church based in forty-three different countries received
a ringing appeal. The circular letter, written by the pope's new secretary of state, Eugenio Pacelli, sought to raise consciousness among
leaders in the Catholic Church about the gravity of the communist
threat. It informed readers that the Vatican would soon launch a public
and large-scale campaign against international communism. This
campaign would permanently and definitively shut down the possibility for diplomatic negotiations with the Soviet Union, and loudly
announce that the Church was the leader in a nascent battle against
the communist enemy.

The letter presented the case for communism's threat to Catholics and the Catholic Church. It stressed that communists aimed first and foremost at destroying Christianity and disseminating atheistic teachings. For these reasons, communism was "a grave danger for the social order in general, and for the Catholic religion in particular."[52] Reiterating points familiar to careful readers of the pope's most recent encyclicals, the circular noted that communists had been able to expand successfully due to the Great Depression. Presenting themselves as the world's leading critics of economic liberalism, they targeted a range of social classes and nationalities. Communist propaganda had spread like wildfire—through film, radio, and other means—during the economic crisis. Soviet agents had moved quickly, setting up a range of youth and adult organizations—many of which directly competed with Catholic counterparts. Comintern agents had targeted individuals who moved fluidly and frequently across national borders, such as sailors, merchants, university students, soldiers, postal system employees, train conductors, and pilots, in order to internationalize their message. With speed and clever use of media and agents, communism had become a global reality. It had won converts not only across Western, Central, and Eastern Europe, but in North and South America, Australia, China, and India as well.

Responding to this dire reality, the Vatican proposed to launch an anticommunist campaign with two key components: surveillance and propaganda. The circular advised that the Vatican would pioneer a vast information-gathering operation about communist methods in order to effectively combat the communist menace. In particular, information was needed on the precise tactics employed by communist forces, as they infiltrated and penetrated local and regional organizations. Recipients of the letter from Secretary of State Pacelli were encouraged to distribute a lengthy questionnaire to lower clergy in order to gather crucial intelligence from them as well as and raise consciousness among members of the Church hierarchy as to the elevation of communism as enemy number one.

Clergy were asked to report back to Rome regarding the political manifestations of the communist party in their geographic locales and the extent to which "signs of secret communist activity" were visible, "particularly in schools and ports." They were told to take note of communist films, newspapers, flyers, and journals circulating locally. The questionnaire encouraged clergy to consider whether politicians and opinion makers were critical, indifferent, sympathetic, or curious toward communism. Were there any state-run counterpropaganda efforts under way? Did anticommunist governments understand the vehemence with which communists targeted religion, and did state propaganda sufficiently "highlight the need to protect religion and religious orders"? More importantly, clergy were asked to evaluate the mobilization of Catholics at the local level against communism. Did local Catholic Action branches understand that their task was to mobilize against communism?[53]

The first major component of this new papal undertaking was active vigilance. Regular clergy must become regular informants, reporting back to Rome the suspicious activities, government actions, and civil society initiatives they had observed. The second component was the launching of a Catholic cross-border anticommunist media and civil society campaign. To be sure, the campaign should make use of traditional means long employed by the Catholic Church, such as "acts of reparation, pilgrimages, expiatory communions, [and] prayers for the persecuted." But, taking a page out of the communist playbook, the papacy should also employ new technologies and new media. The Catholic presence in civil society must be exploited in novel ways to combat the expansion of communist organizations. In this way—through a combination of grassroots activism, vigilance, and propaganda—the Vatican hoped to be able to fend off the communist menace.

In the 1932 circular, Pacelli referenced anticommunist initiatives under way in Spain and Germany as sources of inspiration. Since the early 1930s, Pacelli and his superiors had in fact been following the work of smaller anticommunist initiatives across Europe—particularly in Spain and Germany. A key example of how to put Catholic civil society structures to good use, for instance, was represented by the Spanish Centro Español Anti-Bolchevista. The Centro had been established in Madrid in 1925 by members of the Associación Católica Nacional de Propagandistas (ACNP), an elite lay organization that trained Catholics for public life. The Spanish group's main activities centered around the publication of anticommunist materials, including an anti-Bolshevik review, an anti-Bolshevik handbook, and an information bulletin, all of which were packed to the brim with condemnations of communist activity worldwide and with stark depictions of life in the Soviet Union.[54] The Superior General of the Jesuits, Włodzimierz Ledóchowski, was delighted with the work of the Centro, urging Spanish Jesuits to expand its work and "foster Catholic Action more and more" so as to defend "the Christian concept of the family and the state" and combat "the present dangers of communism."[55] German Catholic initiatives to combat communism, such as the Volksverein, also left a lasting mark on Pacelli, and were celebrated in the 1932 circular.

These nationally circumscribed initiatives appealed not only because they had pioneered usable models, but also because they represented a confessionally pure form of anticommunism.[56] As Pacelli and many others saw it, the papacy must lead a transnational anticommunist crusade, not least because the initiative must be first and foremost a *Catholic* project.[57] Pius XI advised Pacelli, with respect to the largest anticommunist interconfessional initiative in Europe, the International Entente Against the Third International, "the Holy Father does not want to appear as connected to these organizations. Do not respond to their letters. Do not even say you have received them."[58] This did not stop the Curia from sending money to the organization in order to receive its twice-weekly Bulletin, a practice that continued from 1930 through 1935.[59] Neither did the desire to identify anticommunism primarily with the Catholic Church and Catholicism prevent the Vatican from entering into pragmatic partnerships with cross-confessional political parties that defined themselves in starkly anti-Bolshevik terms. In particular, Pacelli's April 1932 circular was issued on the heels of a crucial shift taking place in Vatican City and among the higher clergy in Germany, which enabled a short-lived but highly consequential opening to National Socialism.

Reinterpreting National Socialism

The Nazi Party had its origins in the same environment of violent counterrevolution that had given birth to the Fascist movement, and contributed to the radicalization of Eugenio Pacelli's views on communism. From its early days, the party (originally known as the German

Workers' Party) had defined itself as anti-liberal, anti-Bolshevik, and opposed to the Versailles Treaty and the Paris peace settlement. It was thuggish, violent, antidemocratic, and virulently anti-Semitic. Between 1919 and 1928, it had not enjoyed a great deal of success, failing to poll above 3 percent of the vote. But in just two years—in the aftermath of the Great Depression—the party's appeal soared. In the 1930 Reichstag elections, the Nazis won 18 percent of the vote, and became the second party in the Parliament, after the Socialists.

The German Catholic response to the Nazi Party fluctuated over time. A network of Catholic activists was central to the founding and early expansion of the National Socialists in Bavaria in 1919–1923.[60] But when in 1923–1924 the party took a strong anticlerical line in newspapers such as the *Völkischer Beobachter* or *Heimatland*, German Catholic bishops took note, and in March 1931 they issued a condemnation of National Socialism as "irreconcilable with Catholic doctrine."[61] The party was a socialist party, which meant that it was incompatible with Catholicism "in the same way that all socialist parties are incompatible with Catholicism."[62] Additionally, the party's calls for "positive Christianity" worried many Catholics, in that the vague ideal of "positive Christianity" (referenced as early as the 1920 Nazi Party Platform) was premised on the rejection of the Old Testament, on German exclusionary nationalism, and on the idea that it was necessary to overcome confessional differences. Beginning in 1929 the Nazis had emphasized that they believed in "positive Christianity" as a way to forge a united, interconfessional front against communism. However, as Bavarian bishops put it, what the Nazis called Christianity was not the Christianity of their Church and of Christ.[63] Neither did the Nazi calls to interfaith dialogue match with the Church's longtime aversion to ecumenism. Nazism's hypernationalism and its cult of the state betrayed an ideal of rule that was different from that espoused by the Catholic Church.

But even as the German upper hierarchy came out against the Nazi Party, the papacy was careful to refrain from issuing final judgments. In 1931 Eugenio Pacelli let a Center Party representative know that he was making it a rule to "always respond in an evasive manner" when he was asked by interlocutors about the Holy See's views on Nazism.[64] Doing so was in keeping with the advice of the new papal nuncio to

Germany, Cesare Orsenigo (nuncio from 1930 to 1945), who recommended "a patient and careful wait-and-see attitude on the part of Catholics." After all, according to Orsenigo, the Nazi Party—much like the Italian Fascist Party—contained two wings: one Catholic and one anti-Catholic. The anti-Catholic wing had "totalitarian" tendencies, as did some Italian Fascists who sought to subsume the Church under the state. But there was also a wing that sympathized with the Catholic Church. For this reason—and particularly because National Socialism was not a "transient phenomenon"—the German nuncio counseled that the Vatican would do best to wait and hope that the Catholic-sympathizing wing of the National Socialist movement would emerge victorious.[65] Indeed, there were signs that it might. As Orsenigo indicated, local chapters of the National Socialist party were coming out strongly against the corrupting influence of secular education, and in favor of putting education in the hands of the Catholic Church.[66]

In 1931–1933 the rising pan-European anticommunist tides began to further shape perceptions of National Socialism both in Germany and beyond. The declaration of the Second Spanish Republic on April 14, 1931, was met with alarm by the Spanish hierarchy, which harped on the newborn Republic being a covert Bolshevik plot for global conquest and "a methodical Masonic-Bolshevik plan of action intended to de-Christianize Spain."[67] The editor-in-chief of *Civiltà Cattolica* wrote that the world was witnessing a massive social apostasy and moral corruption that struck at the very heart of Spain's "true" and "natural" identity as a bastion of Catholicism.[68] German clergy looking at Spain were similarly alarmed, affirming that "Lenin's prediction that Spain was the country most susceptible to (communist) revolution has been peculiarly fulfilled." "Bolshevization is spreading across Europe," they concluded.[69]

German bishops began seeing the fight against Bolshevism as *the* battle of the twentieth century. They insistently urged the faithful to found Catholic organizations to fight "communist atheism," insofar as the Comintern was planning "to drive Germany to the side of Bolshevism."[70] In 1930–1931 the Katholikentage (Catholic festivals) formed a Committee for the Struggle Against Bolshevism, which soon built up a surveillance wing, known as the Bureau of Research and Information

on Bolshevism and Freethought. The purpose of this Bureau was to
maintain active monitoring of the spread of Russian and German anticlerical and communist-inspired organizations, and develop strategies
for combating them.[71] A pleased German bishop explained, as he provided an example of the work performed by the Bureau, "Clerics who
had been entrusted with seaman's service in the German port cities"
were now tasked with such tasks as keeping "a watchful eye on the
Bolshevik propaganda on ships," and "reliable Catholic sailors," who
were capable of "observing the agents of Bolshevism" and "distributing
anti-Bolshevik flyers on the ships," had been brought into the effort. In
sum, the Bureau had launched a multipronged surveillance effort,
which united lay Catholics and clergy in a far-reaching project to mon-
itor and block the work of "the agents of Bolshevism."[72]

Despite the work of the Bureau (or perhaps because of it), in 1931–
1933 longtime anticommunist Catholics in close contact with the Holy
See began sending in ever-more-panicked notes, affirming that communism was at Germany's gates. Conservative political figures in
regular contact with papal diplomats were making the same points.
Crown Prince Rupprecht and his son, Albrecht of Bavaria, for instance,
noted that "Communism is more widespread here than we had
thought."[73] The Bavarian chargé d'affaires to the Holy See, Groenesteyn,
went a step further, asserting that the "invasion of communism" was
imminent.[74]

In tandem, the conservative old guard, terrified of losing their grip
on power, was coming around to the idea of working with the Nazi
Party. On January 28, unable to find a majority in the Reichstag, Germany's ruling chancellor, Kurt von Schleicher, resigned. Two days
later, on January 30, 1933, Germany's president, Paul von Hindenburg,
appointed Adolf Hitler Chancellor of the Reich. He and the other
members of the old guard were convinced that they would retain
power: "We've engaged him for ourselves," affirmed the new vice-
chancellor under Hitler, Franz von Papen.[75] After all, the Cabinet only
contained three Nazis, and Hitler was unqualified and inexperi-
enced. Despite such hopes, the National Socialist Party showed itself
a force to be reckoned with. Within five months, it had established a
dictatorship and swept away German democracy.

As these dramatic and fast-paced developments unfolded, members of the Catholic upper hierarchy appeared tone-deaf. They continued sending letters to the pope expressing worries about how the German churches would be impacted by communism—not by National Socialism. Even the papal nuncio to Germany, Cesare Orsenigo, focused on drafting a lengthy, detailed, and troubling report on the spread of communism in Germany immediately following Hitler's rise to the chancellorship.[76] Shortly thereafter, Pacelli followed up with a letter asking German and Bavarian bishops "whether and in what way they think it might be opportune for the Holy Office to issue a condemnation" of communism and of those organizations in Germany disseminating it.[77] The response was that a formal condemnation would be "superfluous" because Hitler was already doing so much to fight communism. In the aftermath of the arson attack on the Reichstag just one month after Adolf Hitler was sworn in as chancellor, "the [German] state had used all of its means to suppress the communist danger."[78] Perhaps "an authoritative word encouraging the battle already busily undertaken" would be more appropriate.[79] Indeed, it was important to "recognize the merits of the present government in the fight against communism."[80] Following the Reichstag fire, the new chancellor had severely limited freedom of the press, political meetings, and marches, and the right to electoral campaigning. On March 23 the Reichstag passed the Enabling Act, which abolished democracy and the constitutional state. Only the Social Democrats cast dissenting votes against this law, which was officially known as the Law to Relieve the Distress of Volk and Reich.[81] German bishops who witnessed the events stayed focused on the Reichstag fire, expressing the concern that the act of arson really was a communist plot to overthrow the state, as Hitler said it was. For this reason they called on the Holy See to applaud Hitler's bold actions, instead of lamenting the beginning of the end of German democracy.

In early March 1933 Pacelli affirmed in an audience with Pius XI that "Hitler is the first (and only) statesman who has to date spoken publicly against communism. Until now only the pope had done so."[82] Soon enough, this way of reading German political developments rubbed off on the pope. Three days after his audience with Pacelli, in a meeting with the French ambassador, François Charles-Roux, Pius XI affirmed that he had modified his opinion of the leader of the National Socialists especially because he believed Hitler to be "an ally against Bolshevism."[83] The pope made similar statements to the cardinals in a consistory on March 13, and in private settings as well.[84] German bishops in mid-March affirmed that they were amenable to retracting the condemnation of National Socialism "if the new government demonstrates in fact that the fears of the bishops were unfounded," and "if in addition the new government continues to remain strong in the battle against advancing Bolshevism and public immorality." There was so much to be praised in Hitler's commitment "to 'crush' Marxism in whatever form, particularly communism as an economic and state principle."[85]

On March 23, the day when he gave German democracy its final blow with the Enabling Act, Hitler also engaged in moves modeled on Mussolini's courting of the Holy See. Hitler delivered a speech in which he asserted that Christianity was "the most important factor in the maintenance of [Germany's] national identity." In an apparent tiptoe away from his commitment to a fusion of Protestantism and Catholicism in a "positive Christianity," the German chancellor promised to honor the Holy See's concordats with individual German states, maintain government support of Catholic schools, and uphold religious education in public, while simultaneously doing battle with "atheistic organizations" undermining the Christian churches. The rights of the churches, he said, would "not be infringed upon." Hitler promised to "maintain and further friendly relations with the Holy See."[86] In response, five days later, the Fulda Bishops' conference formally lifted the existing ban on Catholic membership in the National Socialist party.[87] "The occasion for this revision," the German nuncio informed Pius XI, "was offered by the calm speech delivered last Thursday at the Reichstag by the head of government [Hitler], but the true determining cause, I believe, is to try to do something about the attitude of increasing sympathy by the Catholic masses, young and old, for the new regime."[88] (The bishop of Linz, Johannes Maria Gföllner, was not as impressed, and immediately reissued the existing bans against Austrian Catholics joining the Nazi party.)

Nonetheless, as he privately informed Pacelli, Pius XI was satisfied with what he called Hitler's "good declaration" of March 23. So was the *Osservatore Romano*, which praised the speech, highlighting in particular Hitler's double commitment to concordats and anticommunism.[89] The next day the Center Party agreed to sign the Enabling Act, which granted Hitler dictatorial powers. And less than a week later, German bishops retracted the condemnation of National Socialism, declaring that the general "bans and admonitions" were no longer necessary.[90] On April 1, Pius XI informed the Berlin nuncio that he was aware of "anti-Semitic excesses under way in Germany," and that it would be a good idea to find a way for him to "say or do something," particularly because "there will come a day in which we can say that something was done."[91] Exactly one week later, the Holy See was entertaining "potential negotiations about a concordat with the Reich." The central government of the Holy See was still suspicious of Nazism, to be sure. But they had come around to the view that Nazism, like Italian Fascism, could likely be "righted" and "domesticated," so as to ensure the victory of its supposedly "good wing," which was populated by individuals sympathetic to the Catholic Church. They had come to endorse the view that there was "no way other than to join the Hitler movement in order to save Germany from Communism." On April 8, less than two months after the Reichstag fire, the concordat drums were already beating; by April 15, the negotiations were under way.[92] All of this despite the fact that on April 1, 1933, the Nazi regime announced the first nationwide boycott targeting Jewish businesses and professionals. The boycott was followed a week later by a law restricting employment in the civil service to "Aryans." In compliance with this law, Jewish professors at the university level, teachers in the public school system, and government employees were fired. Among the German Catholic hierarchy and members of German Catholic religious orders, almost no one lodged a protest against the regime's treatment of the Jews. To the contrary, the focus remained on Catholic rights—and on getting those rights protected by a concordat.

Launching the Campaign

It was in this context of fear of communist revolution, and the rise of antidemocratic reaction, that plans for the launching of a papal anticommunist campaign got off the ground. The initial blueprints were drawn up in the aftermath of Pacelli's 1932 circular. It took about a year and a half for papal officials to translate those plans into practice. During this arc of time, Hitler became Germany's chancellor and the Holy See signaled its support of his suppression of the communist movement. Additionally, within Vatican City a change was under way. In 1932–1933, key officials who had proposed a more conciliatory approach to the Soviet Union were sacked. As they were let go, some were "blamed for the current situation in Russia and even in part in Spain."[93] The Superior General of the Jesuits, Father Ledóchowski, played an important role in the process of maligning the old guard, lining up replacement experts with astounding speed, and personally drafting the official *Osservatore Romano* announcement regarding the termination of once-powerful employees.[94]

Simultaneously, functionaries in the Secretariat of State close to Eugenio Pacelli worked to convince high-ranking members of the Catholic hierarchy to come on board with the new turn against the Soviet Union. Papal officials noted, "Moscow, in a hundred and million different ways, destroys religion and all of the institutions founded on Christian civilization, not only in Russia, but in other nations, too."[95] The responses to Pacelli's 1932 circular—which soon came pouring in from the four corners of the world—helped functionaries build their case. So did the content of Pope Pius XI's speeches during the Holy Year, which was held from Easter 1933 through Easter 1934. Pius XI informed huge crowds of pilgrims, "The destructive efforts of Militant Atheists are on the rise." Action was necessary, in that "these depraved men are endeavoring to destroy not only all religion but every vestige of civic culture and true refinement."[96] The fact that many in attendance were Catholic journalists and filmmakers who had been specifically asked to take part in an "international pilgrimage of journalists to Rome" was important. Not only were the media key to the pope's nascent anticommunist crusade, but having thousands of journalists as witnesses to the pope's speech meant that his words would receive greater amplification than in any previous time. Per the express wishes of Pius XI, the Holy Year was even documented in a film—Paolo Salviucci's *Jubileum*—which was produced by the newborn Catholic Cinema Center (Centro Cattolico Cinematografico).[97] Pius XI's repeated references to the Soviet Union and international communism and his use of the binary "communist atheism vs. Catholicism" had their effect. In 1933–1934 the rigid frameworks employed in the pope's addresses during the Holy Year began to get more coverage in European papers. On December 7, 1933, the phrase "godless communism" made its first appearance in the *New York Times.*

In the meantime, behind the scenes, key figures within the papal diplomatic corps sorted out the details of how to institutionalize the nascent campaign. The Superior General of the Jesuit order, Włodzimierz Ledóchowski, volunteered to have the Jesuits captain the initiative. Papal diplomats agreed that this would be a good idea, given the Jesuits' multilingual skills, their pioneering work in Germany and the United States to fight communism, and their long-standing interest in increasing the Catholic media presence. It helped that Ledóchowski was one of Pacelli's close friends and a proven ally of Pius XI. Loyal, meticulous, and solidly anticommunist, Ledóchowski had been personally responsible for inaugurating an era of close partnership between the Jesuit order and the Secretariat of State, starting from the 1920s, and for tucking anticommunist references into Pius XI's encyclicals in 1931 and 1932.[98]

In early 1933,Ledóchowski selected the dynamic Franco-Canadian priest, Father Joseph-Henri Ledit, to lead the nascent papal anticommunist institution.[99] Ledit had traveled to the Soviet Union in the early 1920s and had come back disgusted with what he had seen. Ledit's impressive language skills and his already-demonstrated capacity as a project manager made him a natural choice. That Ledit moved fluidly across the Atlantic—and seemed equally at home in Catholic Europe and North America—was an added bonus. So was the fact that the Franco-Canadian Jesuit had no strong anti-Fascist or anti-Nazi feelings. The point was particularly relevant following Hitler's appointment as chancellor in January 1933, the March passage of the Enabling Act, and Hitler's subsequent elimination of Marxist parties and left-wing secular movements in the spring of 1933. Father Ledit watched these developments with interest and may well have shared the conviction of Father Ledóchowski (and many other high-ranking clergy) that Hitler's moves against the radical left were worthy of applause. There is certainly no archival evidence that he found them problematic.

In 1934 the Superior General of the Jesuits in Rome sent a note to provincial fathers, announcing that Rome was about to unveil "a plan of concerted action against communism."[100] Within the year, the ribbons were cut on the new institution. Its name would be the Secretariat on Atheism. Given the growing popularity of the "communist atheism versus Catholicism" binary, the decision to cast the institution as focused on expunging atheism seemed like a good idea. The choice of the term "Secretariat" was no accident either, as it served as a clear institutional-rhetorical response to the Soviet Union's Secretariat of the Central Committee of the Communist Party. Naming the new papal institution a Secretariat elevated its internal importance and placed it on the same footing as older and long-established secretariats within the Holy See, such as the Secretariat of State.

The American Jesuit, historian, and founder of Georgetown University's School of Foreign Service, Father Edmund Walsh, SJ, was an early fan of the newborn institution. As Walsh saw it, the Secretariat would be valuable because the battle against communism was a battle for hearts and minds—it was "an ancient conflict in which the protagonists are not men but principles."[101] The border-crossing Secretariat would be a great boon because the battle against communism must be waged internationally. As Walsh explained, the Soviet Union's ambitions were "not limited by national frontiers," and thus the Bolsheviks' "militant political philosophy" was duty-bound to "leap traditional limits of sovereignty, since [its] claim is to rule mankind in the mass."[102] For these reasons, the Church's response must be international too. All of the Secretariat's members agreed: the Soviet Union was dangerous precisely because it was a transnational power. "The word 'Russian' today, after the Bolshevik revolution, no longer has the specific geographic meaning it used to have," they asserted.[103] In response, Catholics must redouble their expertise as boundary-jumpers and border-crossers.

The strategy of the newborn Secretariat on Atheism was internationalist not only because it had international aims, but because the institution broadcast the Vatican as the international power best capable of fending off the leading transnational, cross-border threat of the day. As many of the campaign's early materials asserted, communist activism demonstrated that the capacity to move across and between nation-states was the way of the future. Thus, an international power—not constrained by national borders—was best equipped to combat the communist menace. In the words of the Secretariat on Atheism's flagship journal, *Lettres de Rome*, "The Communist International is the only dynamic and truly global organization, other than the Catholic Church, which is above all nations and nationalities."[104] "If Moscow's Comintern is at the head of the Communist International, Rome is the center of the Catholic International!"[105]

In the spring of 1935 the Secretariat on Atheism entered into operation. The institution functioned as a branch of the Vatican's foreign policy apparatus, and was put in charge of an astounding range of anticommunist initiatives. The Secretariat would work closely with Catholic civil society organizations, in a bid to make the mobilization against communism the center of Catholic lay life.[106] It announced that it would raise awareness of the extent of the Soviet threat through traditional print media, including its monthly journal, which was published in French, Spanish, German, and English. It also launched the papacy into the production of radio, literature, and multimedia traveling exhibitions. Through its many cultural products, the Secretariat disseminated a vision of communism that was in continuity with *Quadragesimo Anno*. Communism was presented as the grandchild and logical outgrowth of liberalism. The Secretariat's journal articles and exhibitions sent the message that the fight against communism was something that only Catholics, led by the Holy See, could do well. This was because the Vatican was an internationalist power, and as such, it was interested in and capable of combating the communists on their same cultural turf through exhibitions, comic books, film, and radio.

Enlisting the Masses

The Vatican's anticommunist campaign helped Pope Pius XI convince the Catholic hierarchy to begin making use of a range of new, nonprint media—including radio. The trouble was that radio had for quite some time made most members of the Catholic hierarchy uncomfortable. As late as 1927 the Giunta Lombarda of the Catholic Church of Italy had forbidden the installation of radio receivers in religious schools and even in the homes of priests.[107] As the Giunta saw it, radio was a cor-rupting influence, not least because it used emotions to sway its lis-teners and change their minds. In the 1920s, papal officials had echoed these fears, noting that radio and new media should be shunned because they tended to "rip from the heart any Christian sentiment."[108]

But behind the scenes, Pius XI, Pacelli, and a small number of papal officials were busy in an effort to overhaul the Church's attitude toward new media. This was unsurprising to those who knew Achille Ratti well. As early as 1904, in a sung mass, the young Ratti had hailed the father of radio, Guglielmo Marconi, as "our glory," celebrating radio and the "human progress" that had enabled it as proof of "the ascending movement of humanity towards truth and goodness, which is to say, toward God."[109] This precocious interest in radio meant that by the early interwar years, the pope was absolutely tuned into the fact that thanks to new technologies and mass production methods, radio was being transformed, as Victoria De Grazia has noted, "from a specialty item with a limited audience into a major commodity of industrial production and one of the most important sources of popular enter-tainment."[110] In the late 1920s, as part of the secret and closed-door negotiations in the Lateran Accords, Pius XI had personally instructed papal diplomats to fight hard for special provisions regarding the pro-tection and funding of a yet-to-be-built Vatican radio station.[111] Pacelli had been particularly keen on this too, and had personally started dis-cussing the possibility of a Vatican radio station with none other than Guglielmo Marconi himself. Immediately thereafter, Pius XI moved with lightning speed to ensure that the new radio station would get built, even before the exchange of the sanctions of the Accords, in June 1929. Marconi—Ratti's longtime hero—accepted the job with pleasure.[112]

A few months later, in December 1929, the general Catholic public was informed that the shift was under way when Pius XI told the faithful that being a good Catholic was compatible with listening to the radio. Through his encyclical *Divini Illius Magistri*, the pope was toeing a fine line. Because encyclicals needed, *per force*, to signal continuity rather than innovation, Pius XI began by trying to appease those clerics still uncomfortable with nonprint media, noting that, of course, "an extended and careful vigilance is necessary" regarding when, how, and why the faithful could be encouraged to take part in these new means of entertainment. However, the pope asserted, given the formidable enemies faced by the Church, it would be a shame to leave media aside, in that it "can be of great utility for instruction and education when directed by sound principles."[113] For these reasons, clerics should encourage their flock to tune in, not tune out.

Within just over a year, the papacy's very own radio station—Vatican Radio—was officially inaugurated. The Catholic press, buoyed by the tides of Catholic internationalism triumphant, celebrated the initiative immediately. At last, observers noted, the central government of the Roman Catholic Church had its own "mass mediated, unified voice."[114] The point was made repeatedly, including by Marconi himself, who in his inauguration speech noted, "For almost twenty centuries the Roman Pontiff has spread the word of his Divine teaching in the world; but this is the first time that His lively voice will be heard simultaneously on the entire surface of the earth."[115] The hymn to Catholic globalization was repeated by the *Osservatore Romano,* which emphasized the technological prowess involved in getting the pope's voice to travel the world over: "The Radio Station of the Vatican is among the first stations in Europe from which it is possible to speak telephonically in 'duplex' with other European, American, Canadian, and Australian stations. It can be considered the most advanced shortwave station in existence . . . Radio Vaticana not only enables Vatican City to directly connect with the most distant regions of the world; it also allows the voice of His Holiness to be radio diffused and listened to all over the world."[116]

As the *Osservatore Romano* and other Catholic newspapers emphasized, the pope could now speak directly to the globe. Catholics the world around, it seemed, were genuinely enraptured and eager to receive his message. Letters soon poured in from faithful who had heard the pope's voice for the first time and were profoundly moved by the miracle. Many—including a ten-year-old English boy who wrote directly to the pope—received personalized responses to their ebullient notes lauding the modernity of Catholicism and its transcendent, border-crossing powers.[117]

The Fascist press jumped on the bandwagon, too. Vatican Radio represented a golden occasion to sing the praises of Rome as the global center of progress—for it was a way to celebrate the Fascist cult of *romanità.* As the Fascist Forges Davanzati put it, the new radio station demonstrated that "God [had] placed Rome at the center of humanity," and that "Vatican Rome [was] reconciled forever with Fascist and Italian Rome." The *Gazzetta Del Popolo* gleefully chimed in, asserting that Rome had now unquestionably earned its title as a "metropolis of radio." The Fascist press seized on the opportunity to celebrate Vatican Radio as proof positive of the new mutually reinforcing bond between Church and (Fascist) state. The picture-perfect collaboration was driven home through sentimental snapshots offered by Fascist newspapers: "In Courmayeur [an Alpine resort town], Alpine guides gathered [around the radio] in a circle, with pictures of Pope Pius XI, Mussolini, and the King in hand. They genuflected, listening to the word of the Pontificate, himself a great rock climber."[118] As members of the Fascist press emphasized, kneeling before the miracle of radio, the Supreme Pontiff, Benito Mussolini, and Italy's King was one and the same act.

Vatican Radio was put in the service of the nascent papal anticommunist campaign immediately after its founding. Because of radio's capacity to make listeners feel as though they had invited the pope in for a midmorning espresso, members of the Secretariat on Atheism were convinced that it would be a key tool in their battle for hearts and minds. They took advantage of the new climate of cooperation with the Fascist regime, and in 1935 Vatican Radio was the only radio station Italians were legally allowed to listen to other than the state's.[119] By 1936 the anticommunist crusade and Vatican Radio had merged to such an extent that the director of the Secretariat on Atheism, Joseph-Henri Ledit, was appointed the head of Vatican Radio as well. By 1938 the Secretariat had helped Vatican Radio spawn a Catholic Information Service, for which the sole task was to combat atheistic propaganda. By this time, Vatican Radio was transmitting in ten languages in both short-wave and medium-wave. It was little surprise that by the mid- to late 1930s, "almost every program [on Vatican Radio] contained a segment devoted to Russia with specific details and directives for the ideological battle against communism."[120] In tandem with the work of the Secretariat, Vatican Radio took part in an ambitious plan to jam the signal of Radio Moscow.[121] In these ways and more, the new Secretariat on Atheism—the institutional expression of the pope's anticommunist turn—helped radio become a leading medium for the Pontiff's anticommunist message. And that message was reaching more people by the day. In Italy alone, the number of radio subscribers jumped from about 27,000 in 1926 to over one million by the end of 1939.[122]

Just as the Secretariat was taking radio on board, it was also turning to literature. Specifically, the pope's anticommunist campaign planners decided to produce a series of Catholic anticommunist novels. As a figure closely associated with this effort put it, literature was unique precisely because it could appeal "to both reason and emotion."[123] Another noted that literature was "seducing"—and that the idea of using literature "as a weapon in the fight against Bolshevism" was brilliant because of "the role that literature and novels play in contemporary life, [and] the profound influence novels can have on ideas and mores."[124]

In line with a new generation of Catholic literary theorists, proponents of the papacy's attempts to generate a Catholic anticommunist literature firmly rejected the idea of art for art's sake. Instead, Catholic literati called for a deep realism that could represent a way of engaging more deeply with "real life." In the words of a prominent Catholic Action layman and influential literary theorist, there could be "no opposition between literature and life" as both were essentially "instruments of self-search and thus of truth." The vision of Catholic literary realism endorsed here was not simply about reflecting reality. It was about transforming it. As another Catholic Action member put it, by unveiling the "profoundest roots" of life, a Catholic literary renaissance would help "reinvent our heroes."[125]

Pope Pius XI was a strong advocate of using literature in the anticommunist campaign. Since his youth, the erstwhile librarian-pope had been an avid consumer of both poetry and novels, and even as an adult he ranked massive sentimental tomes like Alessandro Manzoni's *I promessi sposi* among his favorite works. For this reason, Pius XI was particularly hard hit by the fact that even as literacy rates and the consumption of literature were on the rise, a specifically and distinctly Catholic literature was not keeping pace. As the pope fretted, basic Christian teachings were being polluted "by amorous and frivolous novels."[126] Instead of helping to promote Catholicism, literature was helping to undermine it.

In response to this situation, Pius XI and his advisers made a move similar to their adoption of radio: Rather than simply censoring literature, why not get ahead of the curve, and sponsor a Catholic literary renaissance, with a heavy dose of anticommunism? The pope soon put forward a concrete proposal, suggesting that the papacy launch a worldwide competition for the best religiously themed anticommunist novel.

As was the case with radio, Pius XI's idea won internal support and was implemented quite quickly as a component of the cultural attack on communism. Rather than unearthing hidden gems, the aim of the competition would be to create a new literary genre: the Catholic anticommunist novel. One of the competition's early supporters noted that the "international competition . . . would surely result in a flowering of compositions, which—even if they are not all given a prize— would appear in nearly all countries." For this reason, it was imperative to encourage the submission of novels "in any language." Even though papal personnel knew they would be unable to find competent judges with a very broad range of language skills, they nonetheless decided to push for compositions in many languages, and from all parts of the world.[127]

To incentivize writers, the prize needed to acquire legitimacy. For that reason, it was decided that the project should be officially administered by two respected and trusted Catholic writers, both of whom were members of the notable Académie française in Paris: Georges Goyau, a publicist known for his sympathies with French Action and the radical right, and Henri Bordeaux, a novelist outspoken in his support for leaders such as Benito Mussolini.[128] The former was a close friend of Cardinal Baudrillart—one of the leading anticommunist clerics in France, who would soon be one of the most vocal supporters of Marshal Pétain.[129] These two figures would be "introduced to the public as the promoters and organizers of the competition."[130] It would be up to them to pull together a jury composed of leading literary lights from across Europe.

Though carefully shielded from view, the Vatican would maintain direct control over the competition from start to finish, including having final say regarding the awarded novels. As a secret internal agreement specified, two "ecclesiastical officials" would be part of the jury in a way "that would be shielded from the public." They were the ones who held official veto powers, in case the proposed winning novels countered the spirit and message of the papacy's anticommunist campaign. Their power was reinforced by the fact that the pope controlled the funding of the competition. In the initial agreement, the Vatican promised to provide 80,000 lire to cover the entirety of the prize money, and more monies, of an unspecified amount, to cover the costs associated with evaluating, printing, distributing, and translating winning novels.[131]

Papal officials maintained control over the description of the competition. When prize administrators recommended amendments, those amendments were promptly shot down. The original description, handwritten by papal officials, specified that "contestants must, in whatever language they wish, present a novel that is capable of illustrating *from the point of view of Christian doctrines and morals*, the psychology of Sovietism, and the real consequences of Soviet conceptions on domains like the family, civic life, social and economic affairs, and international life."[132] The two main prize administrators—Goyau and Bordeaux—wanted stronger wording. Bordeaux, for instance, suggested that the description encourage expressly nationalistic works, in that he saw nationalism as a strong counter to communist internationalism. He also thought that it would be a good idea for the prize description to mention what he considered a patent fact—namely, that "democracy and democratic governments . . . both lead people slowly but surely to socialism and communism, in their search for equality!"[133]

Pius XI read the recommendations, and though he expressed "immense pleasure" at their contents, he informed prize administrators that their suggestions would not be integrated in the prize announcement. As the pope took pains to specify, he agreed that democratic "individualists" (that is, liberal democrats) were in the wrong, and that what was needed was "authority, order, and hierarchy, [based] on the principles of the Catholic Church." He also asserted that it would be a real shame "if the monarchist cause definitively disappears." However, Pius XI noted, it would be ill-advised to include a reference to nationalism and a condemnation of democracy in the prize description. Celebrating nationalism meant playing with fire, in that certain "Hitlerians" had taken nationalism a step too far, pitting German nationalism as something inherently "opposed to the supranationalism of the Church." Furthermore, condemning democracy outright would confuse the faithful, whom the pope had instructed (most recently through his 1927 condemnation of French Action) to become active citizens, even in democratic regimes.[134] Pius XI was keen on sending the message that Catholic internationalism could be compatible with all forms of government.

The prize administrators endorsed the original prize description and began distributing it to Catholic newspapers and Catholic Action offices. However, creating a Catholic anticommunist literary genre out of thin air proved a difficult feat, even in the age of "authoritarian fictions."[135] The issue was not quantity, but quality. Of the 400 novels from 31 different countries that flooded prize administrators' desks, nearly all were deemed to be of only modest literary and social value. As prize administrators noted with palpable concern in a letter to the Vatican, the French, Italian, Portuguese, English, and Spanish novels were particularly "mediocre" and insufficiently incensed against communism. This was worrisome because it indicated that Catholics "do not feel threatened enough by Bolshevism" and "have not yet realized its dangers." Even the literary works pouring in from "most Catholic Spain" were only tepidly anticommunist, which prize administrators found shocking, in that Spain had "just [been] a victim of Revolution"— that is, the 1931 declaration of the Second Spanish Republic.[136]

In consultation with papal officials, prize administrators decided to re-release the announcement of the competition but make sure that it landed on the right desks. To do so, they solicited authors well-known for their Catholicism and their rabid anticommunism. The new method insulated against chance submissions, and proved more effective. By late 1934, 109 novels had been received, 51 of which were in French, 25 in Russian, 19 in German, 9 in Spanish, and the remaining in Italian, English, Portuguese, Polish, Chinese, and Hungarian.[137] On balance, this time around prize administrators were pleased with the work that came in—though again, they grumbled a bit at the poor quality and insufficiently anticommunist tenor of some of the works.[138]

The gold and silver awards were doled out to Russian and Austrian writers. The competition's first-place novel was written by a Russian exile living in Vienna, Alja Rachmanova. Rachmanova was no unknown quantity at the time she was asked to submit something for the prize. The Catholic writer had gone to university in Russia prior to moving to Austria, and had struggled as the owner of a small shop before turning to full-time writing. As a young woman she had made a name for herself through a memoir—which became popular in several Western European countries—in which she described her experiences as a student in Russia during the Revolution. The unpublished manuscript she submitted for the Vatican competition was her second major *opus,* and it was entitled *The Factory of New Men.*[139]

The sentimental novel centers attention on two women living in the Soviet Union. Warriors for Christian purity, the two demonstrate that Christianity is capable of surviving the sullied stench of "Sovietism." Together, the two women engage in a series of noble acts: they save children who risk being torn from their families and raised collectively, they rescue young girls from falling into prostitution, and they fend off grotesque party *apparatchiks.* Throughout, the duo defends the right of Soviet citizens to profess the Catholic faith. "I want to keep my soul and body pure," one of the women affirms at the novel's climax, "especially because they ridicule these things; I want some religion, especially because they reject all religions."[140] Jury members loved the book and decided that it was deserving of the first prize—not least because it "maintains the hope of redemption for the Russian people alive."[141] The pope in person vetted the novel as well, and commended the author for assembling "a persuasive and impressive . . . collection of snapshots of a fierce tragedy."[142]

The silver medal in the competition went to a figure who had been tapped to submit something by prize administrators. The already quite noted Austrian anti-liberal theorist Erik Maria Ritter von Kühnelt-Leddihn was evidently honored by the solicitation. His fast-paced adventure novel, *Jesuits, Philistines, and Bolsheviks,* was a thinly veiled allegory celebrating an imagined anticommunist alliance forged between Germany, Italy, and the papacy.[143] The work follows the adventures of a trio of muscular, handsome, and clever men: a German Catholic journalist, an Italian Jesuit, and a German priest. The mission of the three men is simple: they want to show the world that there is only one viable alternative to the Soviet political model—an antiliberal, anticommunist political system that is informed by Catholic

social-economic and corporatist teachings. On their rambles through
Europe and North Africa, the men frequently show up (and beat up)
communists. Happily, they tend to emerge victorious from innumerable brawls and skirmishes, not least because the German journalist
has impressive jiujitsu skills, and the Italian Jesuit "packs a terribly
strong punch."[144] Written in 1933 on the eve of Hitler's seizure of
power, the novel bore a clear message: to combat communism, Italy,
Germany, and the papacy must band together, and not shy away from
using violent means. Given the extensive involvement of papal officials
in the awards process, we can surmise that the novel was deemed
worthy of applause.

Through new media like radio and new literary genres, the 1930s
papal anticommunist campaign broke new ground and showed itself
to be a pioneer in the art of transborder cultural diplomacy. But the fact
that *Jesuits, Philistines, and Bolsheviks* won the second prize in the
papacy's anticommunist book competition brought some key ambiguities to the surface as well. In the "battle for hearts and minds," how
should the Church position itself vis-à-vis movements like Fascism and
Nazism? In private correspondence with prize administrators, the pope
had made it clear that the novel competition should not explicitly frame
itself as sympathetic to extreme nationalistic movements on the
European right. However, the pope had approved two prominent individuals sympathetic to Fascism for the prize's administration. The
Vatican's ecclesiastical advisors had been on board with granting the
silver medal to a book that could easily be read as an allegory advocating a united German-Fascist-Vatican front.

Upon receiving word of the newborn Secretariat on Atheism, many
lay Catholics, members of the Vatican hierarchy, and key players in the
Jesuit order had cheered from the sidelines. Spaniards and Germans already mobilized in their nationally circumscribed Catholic anticommunist efforts were delighted that there would soon be a Vatican-led
initiative to fight communism across Europe, and beyond. Many American Catholics also hailed the birth of a "Christian front to combat
communism" and the arrival of a "Catholic answer" to the "Moscow
terror."[145] But not all were happy. When the German Jesuit Gustav
Gundlach was told about the initiative, his response was cool. As Gundlach saw it, the official Vatican campaign against the Soviet Union was

ill-timed. Onlookers might interpret the Secretariat on Atheism as proof of a deep bond between the Vatican and the Nazi movement, and the Secretariat on Atheism could end up giving unwelcome "moral sustenance" to Hitler and the Nazis. Indeed, "an undertaking of this sort" could have all sorts of negative repercussions—not least by "confusing Catholics in Germany and elsewhere weakening the moral influence of the Church."[146] Gundlach cautioned that the price to pay was too high, and suggested that the initiative take a different shape. Cardinal Faulhaber and a very small number of other high-ranking clerics voiced similar concerns.[147] But the archival evidence suggests that no one—not the Superior General of the Jesuits, not the secretary of state, and not the pope—took these concerns very seriously.

In fact, the publications and activities of the Secretariat on Atheism only exacerbated the worries of critics. In all its publications, the Secretariat went out of its way to insist that it would *not* oppose Nazism and Fascism. In its very first year of publication, the Secretariat's journal, *Letters from Rome,* took pains to clarify that even though the Secretariat was officially interested in the battle against atheism, its concern would be communism, while all other atheistic, anticlerical, or anti-Catholic movements would be "left aside."[148] In another issue, the journal informed its readers that to call oneself an anti-Fascist in the current political climate was analogous to declaring oneself a communist.[149] And in a range of early cultural diplomacy initiatives—from anticommunist novel competitions to attempts to jam the signal of Radio Moscow—the Secretariat leaned extensively on the support of Fascist and Nazi sympathizers and officials. It is little wonder that most followers of the Secretariat's work reached the conclusion that Mussolini had erected an effective barrier against "the pestilential heresy of communism" and created "a spiritual environment favorable to the Christian religious tradition."[150]

The notion that the papal anticommunist campaign signaled the pope's approval for Fascism and Nazism was reaffirmed in the context of a large-scale anticommunist exhibition organized by the Secretariat on Atheism on the eve of Franco's coup in Spain, to coincide with the World Exposition of Catholic Press at the Vatican. Like the anticommunist book prize, the exhibition received various forms of support from Fascist and Nazi sympathizers. But much like the anticommunist book

prize, the exhibition was officially presented as an entirely independent undertaking. It presented anticommunism as a distinctly Catholic global movement, led by the pope, and perpetuated the simple
binaries "communist atheism versus Catholicism," and "Godless
Moscow versus Catholic Rome."

As one of its first public large-scale initiatives, the Secretariat on
Atheism had decided to launch a traveling exhibition that would
teach visitors about communism through images, graphs, and text.
The key purpose of the exhibition, as announced by Father Ledóchowski
to fellow members of the Jesuit order, was threefold. It should use
the latest propaganda strategies to convince attendees that communism was synonymous with a global atheistic project. It should demonstrate that the Soviet Union was "daily making new conquests
throughout the world." Finally, Ledóchowski emphasized, the exhibition should highlight that the Vatican was the unquestioned leader
of a global campaign to fend off the Soviet danger. In sum, attendees
should be presented with a simple question: *Which side are you on:
Catholic Rome or Godless Communism?* They should walk away
from the exhibit convinced that "nothing is more to the point,
nothing is more necessary, than our [Catholic] war against atheistic
communism."[151]

The central theme—*Which side are you on?*—was neatly summa-
rized by a single image. The image was present in nearly all of the exhibition rooms and reprinted on the back of the visitor booklet. Three
objects hovered against a solemn black background: an enormous white
crucifix, a red blood-stained hammer-and-sickle, and a rather small
planet Earth. The crucifix and the hammer-and-sickle were vying for
control over planet Earth. The cross was depicted as gigantic, bright
white, and three-dimensional; it cast a long and comforting shadow
that seemed to embrace the earth's round globe (particularly, Italy and
Western Europe). By contrast, the hammer-and-sickle was depicted as
two-dimensional, with sketched contours outlined in white. Whereas
the crucifix had weight and substance, viewers could, quite literally,
see right through the hammer-and-sickle.

Below the image, viewers were presented with a simple question:
"Which sign will win?" Typographic cues suggested the answer. While
the words "Which sign" were written in black and white, echoing the

The image that became the symbol of the Vatican's anticommunist campaign. The caption reads, "Which sign will win?" On the crucifix is written, "In this sign you will win" (In hoc signo vinces). Credit: JESCOM 1038, DcA, fasc. SAR, © Archivum Romanum Societis Iesu

drawing style of the hammer-and-sickle, the word(s) "will win" seemed carved from the same block as the white, sturdy crucifix. Victory and the crucifix, the typographic cues led readers to conclude, were one and the same. Written in smaller type on the horizontal arm of the cross itself, was another message: "In hoc signo vinces" (In this sign, you will win). The reference, of course, was to Emperor Constantine, who had supposedly seen this phrase scrawled in the sky during a mythic march toward battle. The vision had led to Constantine's conversion to Christianity—and it had also supposedly ensured his victory. Thus, the crucifix presented answer to the question "Which sign will win?"—"This sign."

The exhibition covered about a dozen rooms, organized on two floors. Hallways and staircases were exploited for their pedagogical opportunities, and it was hard to find a blank wall—every available space was wallpapered from floor to ceiling with captions, maps, charts, newspaper clippings, and posters. Rooms corresponded to particular geographic locales. In keeping with the papacy's Eurocentric biases, European countries were typically honored with stand-alone rooms of their own.

Although the exhibition's logo suggested that the crucifix would emerge victorious in its battle against communism for planet Earth, the exhibition rooms themselves were not quite as upbeat. As the exhibitioners sought to show (and tell), communists were everywhere, and they were dangerous creatures indeed. By inundating the viewer with dark, overbearing montages of sensationalist communist propaganda posters, viewers were pushed to feel that communists were lurking in every corner. Furthermore, exhibition attendees were encouraged to believe that they were catching a secret glimpse of what communism "really was"—and that communism was even worse than what they had originally imagined. Just as radio and literature were created to reach "hearts and minds," the Secretariat's exhibition was an experiment in popular manipulation, as organizers deployed elaborate staging techniques to elicit particular emotional reactions from attendees—particularly, the feeling of fear. To reinforce the message of communism as Godless and violent, exhibition organizers intentionally chose—and, if necessary, selectively cropped—the most terrifying posters they could find. With some of

One small corner of the 1938 anticommunist exhibition organized by the Secretariat on Atheism. The images, drawn from communist pamphlets, were intended to reinforce the idea that the Soviet Union was a violent and expansionistic force. The handwritten caption in the right-hand part of the image reads, "Our army is the army of the world revolution—Stalin." Credit: JESCOM 1038, DcA, fasc. SAR, © Archivum Romanum Societis Iesu

these images they paired choice quotes from figures such as Lenin and Stalin, written out in large block letters.

The exhibition also emphasized that communism was becoming more threatening by the day. This was the message carried, for instance, by the staircase that linked the exhibition's two floors. As viewers ascended the staircase, they experienced in step-by-step detail the escalating horror of international communism. This effect was achieved by presenting attendees by repeated visual cues. The riser of each stair bore three evenly spaced pieces of information: the hammer-and-sickle logo, a specific year, and a reference to one historical episode that had taken place during that date within the Soviet Union. The lowest step represented 1917, and after a twenty-step ascent, visitors

The central stairway of the 1938 anticommunist exhibition organized by the Secretariat on Atheism. The ascending steps chart moments in the history of the Soviet Union, including "1923: Looting of the Churches"; "1927: Mass Arrests of Catholic Clergy"; and "1929: Antireligious Legislation." Credit: JESCOM 1038, DcA, fasc. SAR, © Archivum Romanum Societis Iesu

had been brought up through the present day. Each step announced a crime that the Soviets had committed in that year: the 1923 step, for instance, contained the stark text, "The Looting of Churches"; the 1927 step was that of the "Mass Arrest of Catholic Clergy"; 1929 was the year of "Antireligious Legislation." Even if visitors did not read every step, they would get the cumulative message quickly that communists were horrific, and that the closer things got to the present, the worse they got. The point that communists were escalating their tactics by the minute was repeated by graphs lining the staircase. In lockstep with the upward movement, graphs with simple upward slopes demonstrated the continuing increase in "circulation numbers of communist newspapers," or "numbers of communist world leaders."[152]

The 1938 exhibition room dedicated to France, juxtaposing Catholic internationalism (here represented by the marble statue of the Virgin Mary) with communist internationalism. A sign on a map bears the hammer and sickle and the caption, "The communist octopus extends its tentacles." The "tentacles" all lead to Moscow. Credit: JESCOM 1038, DcA, fasc. SAR, © Archivum Romanum Societis Iesu

As the visual cues of the exhibition suggested, communism would keep growing—unless Catholics united to stop it. But if there was communist terror, there was light, too. Through high contrast and spotlight effects, viewers were encouraged to see Catholicism as communism's truest and most successful opponent. Rooms exploding with communist propaganda, for instance, would often include a carefully positioned religious statue of the Virgin Mary, or Christ on the cross. Other rooms sent similar messages by splitting the space in half: to get through the first half of the room, visitors would need to pass by messy and chaotic piles of communist propaganda prior to reaching the second half of the room, which was bright and tidy and contained things like visually appealing displays of the latest publications of the Secretariat on Atheism. In keeping with Ledóchowski's initial description of the exhibition, rooms such as these made it very easy for spectators to answer the question "Which side are you on?"

On the surface, it seemed as though the entire exhibition was organized around a set of rather simple and predictable binaries: Moscow or Rome, godlessness or religion, dark or light, chaos or order, violence or peace. But the message of the Secretariat's exhibition went further. As many spectators realized, the Secretariat's exhibition suggested that Vatican anticommunism was compatible with movements on the radical right.

As insiders knew well and exhibition attendees readily guessed, the Secretariat's exhibition had been made possible by a preexisting climate of cooperation between the Secretariat and forces on the European right. By the time of the exhibition, Fascist secret police and the Gestapo were familiar with the Secretariat, and had already put their stamp of approval on the circulation of the Secretariat's anticommunist journal *Letters from Rome* within their borders. It was only thanks to special agreements with Fascist and Nazi ministries that the Secretariat had been able to import the communist posters, journals, and newspapers that cluttered the exhibition's walls.[153] Once the show had been put together but before it was opened to the public, the Secretariat's organizers had run the exhibition's contents by Fascist censors, who had liked it, noting that "everything is correct, according to civil authorities." In a tip of the hat to the climate of cooperation, the exhibition booklet had showered applause on countries at the forefront of anticommunist efforts, including Fascist Italy. When the first exhibition was inaugurated in Rome in 1936, numerous high-profile Fascist officials and at least three well-placed members of the Gestapo were among the visitors. All had expressed their approval of the exhibition's contents, and encouraged the show to travel to major European capitals.[154]

To further nurture this climate of mutual support and cooperation, shortly after the conclusion of the first 1936 Rome exhibition, Father Ledóchowski asked Father Ledit to pack his bags for a short trip to Munich to take part in the opening ceremonies of a Nazi anticommunist exhibition entitled "Bolshevism Unmasked" *(Bolschewismus ohne Maske)*. The exhibition was officially put together by the Coalition of German Anticommunist Associations, a creature of Joseph Goebbels's

Ministry of Propaganda and Popular Enlightenment. Father Ledit happily complied with Father Ledóchowki's request, and according to the accounts, he thoroughly enjoyed his time in Munich and liked the exhibition. So did Italian Catholic journalists, who traveled to the scene to report on the show. The reporter for *Avvenire d'Italia*, however, did note that the Nazis were clearly indebted to the "scholarly and universal touch" of the Vatican's exhibition, and that the exhibition they had put together was "much more cumbersome" than the Secretariat's. Father Ledóchowski, for his part, "did not hide his satisfaction" at the mutually reinforcing relationship that was forming at the grassroots level between Catholic and Nazi anticommunist initiatives.[155]

Through its traveling exhibitions, anticommunist novel competitions, radio programs, and print media publications, the Secretariat on Atheism sent the message that the Soviet Union was fundamentally atheistic, and that communist internationalism was violent and ruthless in its global war on religion. The Secretariat's many products suggested that the Catholic Church had gone international too, and that instead of standing idly by, it was doing everything in its power to combat communism, which represented an international menace. In 1936, when Pius XI issued a new encyclical urging Catholics to "claim their right" to "produce films that fully correspond to our principles," the circle of new media to which Catholics were encouraged to lay claim was complete.[156]

At the same time, however, the Secretariat's work left key questions unanswered. What was the precise nature of the relationship between the Catholic anticommunist campaign and the anticommunist efforts of forces on the European radical right? Were these entirely separate efforts motivated by different lines of reasoning and aiming at different postcommunist realities? Or were these anticommunist efforts mutually reinforcing, and indicative of the possibility of greater cooperation? Relatedly, what should be the relationship between military power and nonmilitary means of persuasion, like propaganda? For if the Vatican's anticommunist campaign was a struggle for influence over the airwaves, over the literary marketplace, and over "hearts and minds," the content of the Secretariat's output seemed to suggest that nonmilitary means were insufficient. Revisiting Thomas Aquinas, a figure very much in vogue in the interwar years, the Secretariat's flagship journal distinguished between a *pax vera*—a true peace—and the *pax apparens* ushered into global politics by the Soviet Union. This unreal or only apparent peace, this peace "not worthy even of the name of peace," was a farce and a façade—it was a way for the communists to advance their plot of global domination more quickly. Where did this leave the Catholic Church and its use of nonmilitary instruments? Were they adequate to meet the communist challenge?

The Spanish Civil War broke out a year and a half after the founding of the Secretariat on Atheism. The conflict served to reify the communism / anticommunism binary as the prism through which the Vatican encouraged its faithful to see the world. It bracketed papal antiliberalism, presenting communism as the world's leading evil. The violence in Spain also convinced millions of Catholics that nonmilitary power alone—while crucial—was insufficient in the struggle against international communism. Indeed, the anticommunist campaign crafted by the Secretariat on Atheism made millions of Catholics more willing to use violence against real and presumed communists on the battlefields of Spain. However, the Spanish Civil War also deepened a preexisting fissure within the European Catholic world between Catholics tolerant or supportive of Fascism and those who saw the papacy's willingness to cooperate with Fascist forces—and to prioritize Catholic anticommunism over Catholic anti-Fascism—as a terrible mistake.

6

Catholic Anti-Fascism, Silenced

Totalitarian regimes . . . are accomplishing with a growing efficacy a
more redoubtable infamy than any persecution: the corruption of the
Catholic world from within.

—YVES SIMON, 1940

THE PAPACY's decision to privilege the struggle against communism
above other threats to its survival was by no means a given. Indeed,
for a brief period in the early 1930s, papal anticommunism and papal
anti-totalitarianism overlapped. As we have seen, beginning in the late
1920s the Church had begun objecting to the fact that both Nazism
and Fascism (or sectors therein) nursed totalitarian ambitions. Furthermore, as the Nazi and Fascist states consolidated, their leaders became
ever-more impatient with granting the Church the rights it was owed
as a result of concordats—particularly when it came to freedom of the
press, freedom of association, and the right to educate the country's
youth. In the push-and-pull between the Church and Nazi and Fascist state leaders, papal officials contemplated taking a strong stance.
They even briefly underwrote a robust Catholic anti-totalitarianism
through the drafting of a new Syllabus of Errors, which would have
condemned Nazi-Fascist statolatry as heretical. The effort—which
clearly distinguished Catholicism's vision of the state from Nazism's
and Fascism's—would have provided some ideological ammunition to
small-scale Catholic anti-Nazi and anti-Fascist movements in Italy,
in Germany, and in exile (in France, Austria, Great Britain, and the
United States). However, the Syllabus of Errors project would never be

167

completed. By the mid- to late 1930s, the papacy's anticommunist crusade had foreclosed any possibility of a genuine Catholic anti-Fascism or anti-Nazism from becoming a significant force. This foreclosure was quite literal, and involved the extraordinary appropriation of nascent Catholic anti-Nazi and anti-Fascist discourses by the leaders of the papacy's anticommunist crusade.

Taking a Stand against Nazism and Fascism?

In February 1929, Pope Pius XI was feeling hopeful about Vatican-Fascist relations in the aftermath of the Lateran Agreements; but by the early 1930s, tensions with the Fascists had returned. In 1930–1931, on the heels of the *Conciliazione,* Fascist state authorities attacked various branches of Catholic Action. Pius XI responded with anger (and the requisite caution), as did the papacy's daily newspaper, the *Osservatore Romano,* which read Fascist actions as part of a broader trend to increase the state's power at the expense of the Church. In a text on the "Christian education of youth," Pius XI affirmed that the family and the Church had rights over the education of youth that were prior to those held by any state.[1] In a public letter to the cardinal and archbishop of Milan, he added that a state that demands the allegiance of the "entirety of the citizen body" and presumes to control all "private, domestic, spiritual, and supernatural matters," is "totalitarian [and] a manifest monstrosity." Additionally, the pope affirmed: "Fascism declares itself to be Catholic. Well, there is one way and one way alone to be Catholic: obey the Church and its head."[2] Next, through an encyclical entitled *Non Abbiamo Bisogno,* Pius XI urged Fascism to better comply with the promises it had made in the Lateran Agreements. "Catholics cannot accept a conception of the state that seizes hold of youth entirely and without exception," the pope asserted, adding that "this conception is not reconcilable with Catholic doctrine." Furthermore, the pope noted, "an ideology that clearly resolves itself into a true, a real pagan worship of the state . . . is in contradiction with the supernatural rights of the Church."[3] In an article for *Civiltà Cattolica* that was a response to Fascist attempts to suppress Catholic civil society organizations, the pope warned that Fascism's totalitarian wing risked destroying Italy's "true religiosity," as well as its "morality" and "civility."[4] In instructions to papal diplomats, he harped on the "totalitarianism" of some Fascist party members, arguing that it needed to be toned down; otherwise "the pope would out of necessity have to intervene" by more loudly naming and shaming Mussolini on the international stage.[5] He informed his secretary of state that he was considering condemning Mussolini's party "as the German bishops had already done with Hitler's party" in 1930.[6]

A similar back-and-forth dance took place in Germany. In March 1933, Pope Pius XI had expressed his tepid support for Hitler as German bishops lifted the ban on Catholic participation in the Nazi Party. Just one month later, many upper clergy expressed their concerns about whether the Church had acted wisely. Many stressed how unfriendly the regime seemed toward Catholicism, and how, despite the existence of the Reichskonkordat, the Nazi Party displayed a great deal of hostility toward Catholic schools and Catholic youth associations. Clergy also worried about a marked uptick in the number of priests arrested and imprisoned.[7] The pope supported German clerics who thundered against figures like Carl Schmitt and his defenders, who in these same years were defending the need for a "total state"—that is, a modern state in which the distinctions between "nonpolitical" civil society and the political sphere fall away.[8] Rather than accepting the Catholic vision of the nation-state as an entity grounded in natural law and subordinate to other entities (such as the Church and the family), clergy charged, the advocates of "totalitarianism" called for states that were makers of their own norms and morality. Rather than understanding the state as a means to end, totalitarians saw states as ends in themselves.[9]

In the spring of 1933, in response to concerns that Nazi Germany and Fascist Italy were not respecting the obligations laid out in the concordats, the pope decided to make a bold move. He encouraged the Holy Office (formerly the Supreme Sacred Congregation of the Roman and Universal Inquisition) to place a small number of key Italian and German theorists of the "total state" on the Index of Forbidden Books.[10] Soon thereafter, on the heels of Nazi and Fascist attacks on Catholic youth groups in the early 1930s, the pope asked Holy Office clerics to update Pius IX's sweeping Syllabus of Errors, which had gone untouched since 1864, by adding a section on Nazi and Fascist statolatry. Catholics could not accept "the deification of the state," and "the absorption of the individual by the state," the draft Syllabus affirmed. "The spirit that animates these errors is not just *pagan* but *antireligious* and most especially *anti-Catholic*."[11]

In 1934 Pope Pius XI tasked the Congregation of the Holy Office with condemning the "totalitarian conception of the state."[12] Drafting a new anti-Fascist Syllabus of Errors was a tall order, but in good speed Pius XI convened a dedicated team of Austrian and German theologians to get to work. They immersed themselves in the writings and speeches of the German chancellor, Adolf Hitler, and in those of Benito Mussolini. By early 1935 they had completed a draft of the new Syllabus. Their text focused entirely on Nazism and Fascism, and explained why Nazi and Fascist theories of the state were totalitarian and inimical to the Catholic Church and Catholicism. In this initial draft, communism was entirely absent: the pope's new Syllabus of Errors would be a loud denunciation of Nazism and Fascism alone.

The Syllabus began by condemning totalitarianism, which was defined as a worldview that elevated the state above the individual, the Catholic Church, natural law, and God himself. Through explicit references to the works of Hitler and Mussolini, the draft Syllabus hammered home the point that "all theories that teach the 'total' state are full of error."[13] In so-called total states, the text explained, "nothing is completely exempt from the state's oversight." "Proclaiming the principle of the 'total state,'" Nazi and Fascist movements sought to justify the state's "total dominion" over everything, allowing "public powers the inherent right to control all things."[14] In totalitarian states, "individual human beings are not thought to possess any rights prior to those granted to them by the state, either in virtue of divine law, or in virtue of natural law." Indeed, totalitarian states do what they can to stamp out the human person's "right to true religion and to attain a supranatural end."[15]

In their 1934 Syllabus the Holy Office clerics were interbraiding several new and old Catholic perspectives, as they argued that totalitarian states represented the inversion, in all respects, of Catholic states and Catholic theories of the state, most recently and famously defended by concordats. According to Catholic teachings, the state could be justified only through its respect for and grounding in divine and natural law. Indeed, the concordat moment that flourished after World War I was entirely based on the fundamental premise that European states could be provided this grounding and justification anew, through the conclusion of treaties with the Holy See. "According to those Christian principles which the Church has always taught, and which popes have recently repeatedly noted, the state has a different origin, and a different purpose," the Syllabus affirmed. Both Thomas Aquinas and the Church taught that "citizens do not have the state as their end; instead, it is the state that is made for citizens." Furthermore, the state never can "completely remove individual rights, insofar as it is not the source of those rights."[16] As popes since Pius IV had declared, according to Thomist teachings, human beings did have rights—though those rights were derived, not from the state, and much less from the revolutionary principle of liberty, but instead from the Thomist rule to live life in accordance with reason and in devotion to God.[17]

In their draft Syllabus, Holy Office clerics argued that totalitarian states were running roughshod over a series of basic human rights Catholics had defended for centuries. Just as Pius IV condemned French revolutionaries for misunderstanding the sources of human rights—and Leo XIII had done the same, in the context of the rise of Liberal Europe—now too, in the mid-twentieth century, the papacy's theologians were interested in clarifying what Catholic teachings indicated as the true source of human rights and the true nature of the state. Following in the tracks of French revolutionaries and nineteenth-century liberal states, totalitarians sought to interfere in "the right to educate children" by limiting Catholic education in public schools and curtailing the rights of Catholic schools. As was the case during the pan-European *Kulturkampf,* twentieth-century totalitarian states were also disturbing "the right to association"—that is, the right of the Catholic Church to "exercise full independence in civil society," specifically through its work with Catholic Action.[18] These states deprived human beings of the "right to life and the integrity of the body," through practices like eugenics, and when they violated "the right to procreate" through population control and forced sterilization measures.[19] Total states suggested that state laws trumped divine and natural law and basic human rights. (As we will see in Chapter 7, during and after World War II, Pius XI's successor would expound upon this incipient language of Catholic human rights, as would newborn Christian Democratic parties keen on condemning both Nazi-Fascist and communist "totalitarianism.")

Had the draft Syllabus of Errors been published immediately, it would have helped boost Catholic anti-Nazi and anti-Fascist movements across Europe and in the Americas. However, this prospect greatly worried an important group of clerics closely connected to the Holy See. Through the concerted actions of these powerful figures—who included Secretary of State Eugenio Pacelli and the head of the Jesuit order, Włodzimierz Ledóchowski—the draft Syllabus of Errors was first placed on the back burner, then buried, then fundamentally altered, and finally published in a new and barely recognizable form. The bits and pieces of the Syllabus draft that eventually saw the light of day emphasized that communism—not Nazism, and certainly not Fascism—was totalitarian, and that *it* was the greatest existential threat to the Catholic Church.

⚙

In July 1935, per standard practice, the Superior General of the Jesuit Order received the final draft of the Holy Office Syllabus of Errors project. His task was to give the Syllabus a quick final glance and pass it along to the secretary of state and the pope for publication. This Ledóchowski did not do. Instead, he sat on the project for almost a full calendar year. Only in April 1936 did he pick up the file once again. His aim was not to get the Syllabus published, but to use recent history to encourage the pope to radically alter its content and purpose.

It was true that much had transpired between July 1935, when Ledóchowski received the draft Syllabus, and April 1936, when he finally picked up the file again. In July–August 1935, the Seventh Congress of the Communist International had taken place in Moscow. The Congress, attended by more than 500 delegates, had settled upon an official new *modus operandi* for communist parties around the world: the "Popular Front" strategy. Henceforth, communist forces would be encouraged to stop maligning social and social democratic parties, and instead band together to combat the threat of Fascism in Europe. Matured on European soil in countries like Spain and France, the Comintern's new policy of creating a broad anti-Fascist front had now received official institutional backing.

Important figures in Rome were paying attention. Eugenio Pacelli, the leader of the papal Secretariat of State, raised the specter of a potential communist take-over of Europe in his conversations with high-ranking figures in the Curia, whom he encouraged to pore over a specially commissioned and annotated Italian translation of the Seventh Congress's results.[20] The Popular Front strategy received attention in the first few issues of *Lettres de Rome*, the publication of the newly founded Secretariat on Atheism, which gave ample coverage to the Comintern Congress as well. Its interpretation of what had happened in Moscow was unequivocal: the Comintern had developed a new deceptive strategy. As the journal noted, the "conniving communists" had designated all governments not directed by the Third International as Fascist. The real goal of the Popular Front strategy, *Lettres de Rome* informed its readers, was not to abolish Italian or German Fascism, but instead to use the label "Fascist" to destroy all noncommunist governments worldwide.[21] The *Osservatore Romano* made similar points, claiming that under the banner of anti-Fascism, the Comintern was making a concerted push for "world revolution."[22] The inauguration of the Popular Front strategy was without a doubt the event that most caught the papacy's attention in these months— months that were also marked by Fascist Italy's violent invasion of Ethiopia.

In early 1936 the Popular Front won the elections in Spain. As careful observers readily noted, the electoral front was not a Comintern creation but instead the revival of an older Republican-Socialist coalition, similar to the one that had come to power in Spain in 1931. Communists were a minority of the newly elected representatives, having won just over a dozen of the 473 seats of the Cortes Generales.[23] But for the Spanish Catholic right, the electoral results demonstrated the influence of the Comintern's efforts. This understanding was promptly endorsed by the papal nuncio on site, who announced that the results of the Spanish elections were due, quite simply, to the direct intervention of the Soviet Union.[24] Following the 1936 elections, according to many conservative Catholic Spaniards with whom the

Holy See was now in regular conversation, the Second Spanish Republic had lost its legitimacy and could be understood only as a cover for communist conquest.[25] Leaders of the Secretariat on Atheism thundered against the election in Spain as a charted point in a "global campaign of the Godless."[26] In panicked notes, clerics asserted that now that communist forces advocating "radical atheism" were in power, the "future of the Church" was unknown.[27]

Those few Spanish Catholics who took part in the Popular Front payed a heavy price. When the Christian Democratic Basque Nationalist Party, the oldest and largest Basque political party, joined the Popular Front coalition,[28] proto-Fascists in Spain were incensed, announcing that the Basque part of Spain was a "cancer in the body of the nation. Fascism, the cure for Spain, has come to exterminate [it]!"[29] The higher clergy issued a stream of sermons in only slightly less inflammatory tones, condemning Basque Catholics for their "errors." The sermons were promptly collected and published in both Spanish and French, in an early attempt to shift international opinion against the new Spanish Republic.[30] When in late February 1936, shortly after the Popular Front victory at the polls, a group of Basque pilgrims arrived in Rome, they were given the cold shoulder. The pilgrims were informed that because they were Basque, they would not be received by the pope or the secretary of state. Even their Peter's pence contribution of 25,000 Italian lire would be returned to them. Cardinal Pizzardo—the sole figure who agreed to briefly receive the pilgrims—explained: "It is well known that the program of the *Frente Popular* leads to the ruin of the Church, [and] it is the duty of Catholics to unite for the defense of religion and the established order, and not help the enemies of the Church." Deploying a form of black-and-white reasoning that was emerging as a pervasive feature of the papal anticommunist campaign, Pizzardo added: "[Your] refusal to unite with the Right necessarily means that [you] are providing an indirect, but effective, assistance to the Left."[31] The victory of the Popular Front in Spain was still fresh in the minds of papal officials, and the Basque "sin" would not be easily forgiven.

In February, March, and April, in direct response to developments in Spain, Rome issued a slew of warnings about communist internationalism. After all, elections were coming up in France in the spring of 1936, and there, too, the Popular Front seemed poised to make major gains. In March 1936, fifty-eight countries received a warning from the pope (drafted by Pacelli): When Catholics headed to the polls, they should not be duped by communist promises for economic and social equality. Instead, they must remember that communists worldwide were narrowly in pursuit of a single "truly diabolic" aim—namely, the "systematic and totalitarian destruction of every religion."[32] In a follow-up text immediately sent for publication to all major French Catholic periodicals, Pius XI repeated the warning, adding that communism has "systematically declared war on God and on Christ" and that "Bolshevik machinations aim at nothing less than sapping the foundations of Christian civilization. Pastors and sheep, be on the alert: the roaring lion is on the prowl, searching for its next victim."[33] Throughout March and April, French clerics, now in a frenzy, denounced the Popular Front from the pulpits. They warned of an imminent communist take-over in France, and called for the monitoring of French Catholics who were sympathetic to communism.[34] French Catholic intellectuals also hurriedly penned books that warned their fellow brethren: "We can't collaborate with communists, because we don't see eye-to-eye with them on anything: anti-capitalism, anti-Fascism, the war against war, revolution, or culture. Communists understand these issues in an entirely different way than we do."[35]

It was against this backdrop that Ledóchowski scheduled a series of meetings with the pope to discuss the anti-Nazi and anti-Fascist draft of the Syllabus of Errors. The Superior General emphasized that the universal Catholic Church now stood at the crossroads. With "atheistic communism" on the rise and the Soviet Union spreading "ever-more intense propaganda" across Europe, the pope was duty-bound to respond, and respond clearly and powerfully. An encyclical outlining why communism was antithetical to Catholicism might be a good place to begin, the Superior General suggested. Such an encyclical would send a clear signal to "Catholics and others to unite in a more energetic and better-organized resistance." Convinced that the myth of Judeo-Bolshevism provided a way to understand the Popular Front moment, Ledóchowski added that such an encyclical should make "at least a passing and veiled reference to the Jewish influence" over the international communist movement, insofar as, globally, "Jews are the first makers and promoters of communist propaganda."[36]

The pope, unsure what move to make in response, demurred. Then, on May 3, 1936, the Popular Front seized 61 percent of seats in the French Chamber of Deputies. Though the Communist Party was not at the top of the charts (it won 72 of 610 seats), hard-liners nonetheless concluded that the Popular Front victory in France was really a victory of the Comintern and foreign communists. The entreaties of the French Communist Party leader Maurice Thorez to French Catholics both before and after the elections—"We offer you our hand, Catholic worker . . . because you are our brother"—only added fuel to the fire, insofar as Catholics close to the pope were unwilling to seize the communist "extended hand" (main tendue) or engage in any sort of shared collaboration.[37] By contrast, French Catholics more distant from the pope were interested, with the Catholic socialist paper Terre Nouvelle going so far as to proclaim "Pour le régne de Christ, votons Rouge!" (For the reign of Christ, vote Red!).[38]

In a speech shortly after the elections, the pope affirmed that communism was "a common danger, threatening everything and everyone, including the sacred space of the family and the state and society."[39] The next day, on May 12, 1936, speaking to Catholic journalists on the occasion of the Exhibition of the Catholic Press, the pope made the Holy See's new priorities clear: "Communism in all of its forms is certainly the first danger, the biggest danger, and the more general danger, because it takes over everything, it infiltrates everywhere, openly and covertly, and it menaces everything: individual dignity, the sanctity of the family, social order, and especially religion, going so far as to openly negate God, and especially the Catholic religion."[40] Speaking to representatives of Catholic Action of various countries, the Pontiff emphasized that one of the key tasks of Catholic Action was to fight communist internationalism, a menace that struck at the heart of civil society.[41] The Secretariat on Atheism moved into high alert, and promptly convened Italian, German, French, Spanish, English, American, Czech, Yugoslav, and Polish Jesuits in Rome to discuss and compare notes on how they could do a better job in the bitter war against "Atheismo et comunismo."[42]

The Popular Front victory had not just terrified Catholic anticommunists: it was hardening their ranks. This, Ledóchowski's realized, was his moment. Seizing it, he tapped two clerics (Father Gillet and Father Tardini), and asked them to write up an authoritative judgment on the draft Syllabus of Errors before the project moved any further. The two external consultants quickly produced a slim analysis, which concluded that communism was inexplicably absent from the Syllabus. If communism was no heresy, then what was, they asked?[43] When Ledóchowski brought the recommendations to Pius XI, he found the pope amenable. Pius XI promptly agreed to commission an anticommunist "amendment" to the Syllabus. Per Ledóchowski's advice, the figure he tapped to do so was Joseph Ledit, the head of the Vatican Secretariat on Atheism. Ledóchowski was delighted, and privately informed Ledit that he must use this new platform in the Holy Office to encourage the Vatican to step up its activities against communism once and for all. The circle was complete. From the early 1930s, Pacelli and Ledóchowski had sought a papal institution expressly dedicated to combating communism. Now, in the spring of 1936, the leader of that institution was being entrusted with the task of explaining why communism was a heretical doctrine, on a par with Nazism and Fascism.

Joseph Ledit was the man asked to draft the papal condemnation of communism for the Syllabus of Errors project, but there was only one problem: Ledit was not a theologian. Throughout his career, he had distinguished himself as a doer, not a thinker. He was the one who had traveled to the Soviet Union in the 1920s; he was the one who had successfully worked with the Nazi and Fascist regimes to get permission for the Secretariat on Atheism to open its doors and disseminate its publications. In 1936 Ledit was stretched very thin with administrative duties. He really did not have time to spare to draft an official theological condemnation of communism.

For these reasons, Ledit played it safe. Rather than develop an analysis *ex novo*, he carried out a cut-and-paste operation. Catholic anticommunist *matériel* was not lacking, and in 1934–1935 a small but formidable group of Catholics had begun drafting a new variety of antitotalitarianism. These figures—hailing primarily from France and Austria—had sought to diminish the appeal of Nazism, Fascism, and communism by branding all three as inimical to Catholicism. Thus, in

1934 the French Catholic intellectual Pierre Lucius, for instance, had argued that Nazi Germany, Fascist Italy, and Bolshevik Russia were all regimes where "the state is everything for everyone: it is 'totalitarian.'" His compatriot Jacques de Brozes affirmed that the Catholic state was the only proper reply to Germany, Italy, and Russia—that is, to "the totalitarian states," which by definition display "the greatest contempt for the rights of the person."[44] Drawing freely on these texts, Ledit argued that communism was guilty of all the same sins as Nazism and Fascism. It, too, was "totalitarian," in the sense that it espoused a conception of the state that was antithetical to Catholic teachings. It, too, violated rights—the very same rights that the Syllabus had accused Nazi-Fascism of violating. Like these other political movements, communism similarly trampled the right to education, the right to a religious marriage, the right to the priesthood, and the right to worship the Catholic religion.[45]

In this way, thanks to Ledit's plagiarism and the behind-the-scenes maneuverings of the Superior General of the Jesuit order, communism made it into the draft Syllabus of Errors as one of now *three* totalitarian heresies of the modern age. In the fall of 1936, clerics in the Holy Office submitted the Syllabus of Errors to a final round of editing. The project was, at last, complete. All told, it had mobilized over a dozen clerics and taken several years of hard work. Catholic internationalism, it seemed, was poised to make a powerful statement against "totalitarianism," defined as a theory of the state that was antithetical to Catholic visions of the state, and that had become a reality in Germany, Italy, and the Soviet Union. However, instead of hitting the printing press, the Syllabus was shoved deep into a desk drawer. While it lay there, three encyclicals would be published. They would entirely subvert the Syllabus of Errors project. Once again, as had been the case with the papacy's *volte-face* on Nazism, it was developments in Spain that proved decisive—this time, in sealing the fate for Catholic anticommunism and putting the nail in the coffin of the revised Syllabus of Errors.

The Spanish Civil War

Since 1931 considerable swaths of Spanish society had looked upon the Second Spanish Republic with suspicion. In 1936, with the election of a Popular Front government, many had moved from suspicion to out-right rejection. Rightist paramilitary organizations were gaining fol-lowers by the day, and many began openly plotting for the government's overthrow.[46] One of them, led by Generals Francisco Franco and Emilio Mola, swiftly rose to the fore; on July 17, 1936, they issued the long-awaited *pronunciamento*, a written and oral manifesto launching the coup.

Members of the Spanish Catholic hierarchy and papal officials were not unequivocally with Franco in July 1936, but by the end of autumn they had come to support him. This was not least because of the actions of a disorganized group of anticlerical Spaniards embittered by the coup and drawn into the vortex of civil war. The Republican govern-ment had promised to build a secular Spain—but because of the strong opposition it had received in Catholic quarters, it had stopped short of its goals. In the summer and fall of 1936, anticlerical activists acting of their own accord, without government support, took it upon themselves to complete what they saw as the "unfinished business" of the Second Spanish Republic. They blasted and shot up religious statues made of stone and marble, and burned wooden sculptures of saints to keep warm. They appropriated churches and turned them into schools, cinemas, hospitals, and popular kitchens. Their vindictive vio-lence was not just exercised against religious objects. Throughout Republican-controlled Spain, thousands of clerics and members of re-ligious orders were forced to take part in parodic weddings and fake rituals. Many were tortured and killed. Soon enough, Spain's "Cath-olic heartlands" decided to side with Franco, welcoming the coup with cries of "Long live Christ the King."[47]

Catholic Action newspapers under the pope's watch promptly re-acted, and in the process helped turn the Spanish Civil War from a local conflict into a global one. The papers affirmed that what was under way was not just a civil war but a war of religion. Furthermore, Spanish loy-alists as a bloc were to blame, because with the Popular Front victory they had handed the Republic over to rabid communists, who were church arsonists and cold-blooded assassins.[48] "The reality is worse than our fears," Catholic youth groups fretted, praising Pius XI's foresight in warning against "Godless" communism.[49] The Italian cardinal who was serving as Apostolic nuncio to Spain, Cardinal Tedeschini,

commented, "Christianity and communism have become two opposite and contradictory realities . . . two powers that work and do battle
against one another in the modern world."[50]

The pope initially stayed neutral—but how he exercised and displayed his neutrality favored Franco more than it did the Spanish government. Through a flurry of notes and telegrams, the pope informed
the Republican government that he considered Spain's ruling politicians responsible for the wave of anticlerical violence. The anti-
Church behaviors afflicting Spain were unfolding "under the eyes of
the central government, which is still in power and in control of the
situation," but which nonetheless "[does] not intervene to repress these
crimes."[51] Soon enough the Osservatore Romano took these accusa-
tions a step further. The official Vatican daily proclaimed that the Holy
See had lodged a protest with Madrid regarding the "barbaric" persecution of priests and members of religious orders by "elements armed
by the government itself." In what constituted a not-so-veiled endorsement of the Nationalist coup, the article concluded that "a dawn of
justice and peace will come," and that "the blood of the new martyrs"
would not have been shed in vain.[52]

The coup's architects caught the way the wind was blowing, and
General Emilio Mola promptly "moved to take advantage of Catholic
backing."[53] Mola, who had already gained a name for himself by proposing that the purpose of the Civil War was the elimination, "without
scruple or hesitation, of those who do not think as we do," now began
identifying as a born-again Catholic.[54] Framing his actions in religious
terms, the general suggested that he and his fellow Nationalist insurgents were rising up to defend "the true Catholic Spain" against its
attackers. He asserted that if "the Popular Front has brought blood,
fire, and tears down upon us," then the insurgents would "retrieve the
Cross from the rubble of Spain" and restore "our religion and our
Faith" from the "barbarism" of the Popular Front. Drawing freely on a
mix of anti-Jewish, anti-Bolshevik, and Catholic internationalist language, Mola and fellow rebels began to loudly proclaim their aim as
saving Spain from communism and turning it into a model "Catholic
State."[55]

Mola's words were not just empty rhetoric. By August the first cities
captured by the insurgent forces began the process of repealing the an-

ticlerical laws of the Republic, rehanging crucifixes in schools, and purging antireligious teachers.[56] Vatican Radio trumpeted the "great religious reawakening happening in Spain, in the battle against communism and anarchism, which have sworn to destroy the Catholic Church."[57] The Spanish upper clergy applauded as well. Cardinal Isidro Gomá, archbishop of Toledo, was among the most fervent in his defense of the insurgents' uprising against the Republican government. "This most cruel war is at bottom a war of principles, of doctrines, of one concept of life and social reality against another, of one civilization against another. It is a war waged by the Christian and Spanish spirit against another spirit."[58] Gomá and others resuscitated moribund Catholic theories of just war, to argue that the Nationalists were right to pick up arms because they were rebelling against a tyrannical and unjust government. For these reasons, "the Spanish National war is a holy war." Indeed, it was "the most holy war registered by history." Whereas in previous wars Christians had clashed with other believers in God, in this war Christians clashed with the "Godless"—with militant atheists.[59] Spanish bishops made it clear that this was no normal battle, but a twentieth-century re-evocation of the medieval Crusades, in which the Nationalists were best understood as modern-day Crusaders, carrying the torch of Western, Christian civilization.[60]

By July 1937 Spanish bishops as a whole were endorsing the ahistorical analogy via a collective pastoral letter. The move promptly found its echo in the letters of the papal nuncio to Spain, Monsignor Ildebrando Antoniutti, which similarly harped on modern-day parallels to the medieval Crusades.[61] Other prominent Catholic clergy chimed in as well, using the reference to the Middle Ages to incite prompt action. "Spain was the barrier against which Islamism broke," they noted, "and now we hope that it will be the barrier that blocks Communist Bolshevism from claiming ownership over the European West."[62] In the past, "Spain delivered Western civilization from the Oriental peril," and now Spain was called upon to defeat "a subtler Orient" (namely, the Soviet Union).[63] Given the gravity of the situation, observers concluded, "it would be disastrous to counsel pacifism." Pacifism in this context would be antireligious, and an affront to Catholicism and the long history of the Catholic Church.[64] The French Catholic Church rallied to this position, as did the conservative

Fédération Nationale Catholique, which hailed Franco's rebels as "defenders of the social order, Christian civilization, and spiritual supremacy by the reign of Christ's gospel."[65] The *Osservatore Romano* concurred, noting that the Spanish Civil War was "a holy war, something that, for spiritual reasons, is inevitable."[66]

A flurry of well-publicized Catholic books and pamphlets issued in 1936–1937 helped internationalize this position. In Latvia, Poland, France, Italy, and other European countries, Catholic defenses of the insurgent violence were a dime a dozen. Brochures like *The Religious Philosophy of the Communist Party*, *The Pope on the Spanish Terror*, and *The Martyrdom of Spain* were assiduously promoted by Catholic periodicals and magazines.[67] The speeches and pronouncements of the warmongering Cardinal Gomá were repeatedly translated and disseminated as well: in 1936–1938 alone, over fifty books and translations under his authorship appeared on both sides of the Atlantic. While it is well known that the Spanish Civil War became one of the first and most important arenas for transnational collaboration between European Fascists, it also—quite significantly—became a concrete site for transnational cooperation and dialogue between Catholic internationalists, who through their exchanges hardened their interpretation of the Civil War as a struggle between Catholicism and communism, and as a local manifestation of a global, Manichean conflict.[68]

American Catholics joined the conversation too. In a collective letter, in a display of interest in European affairs they had rarely shown before, American bishops expressed their sympathy and admiration for Franco and his fight against communism. American Catholics formed lobbies to sway congressional opinion on Spain and influence political asylum policies regarding Spanish refugees.[69] American politicians took note, and as a result of this activism, they began, for the first time, to consider American Catholics as a distinctive voting bloc that it was necessary to win over. As the American president, Franklin Delano Roosevelt, put it in 1938, Catholic involvement in the Spanish Civil War had taught him that "in his whole policy, domestic and foreign, it was necessary to carry along the Catholic Church."[70] This new perspective would lead the United States to seek out a diplomatic relationship with the Holy See in the late 1930s, as Europe as a whole tumbled toward war. The activism of American Catholics would also bring the

Vatican to further let down its anti-liberal guard, open more dialogue with American interlocutors, and, in 1937, undertake its own "Atlantic crossing" via an anticommunist encyclical intended for American audiences.

In the fall of 1936, just as anticlerical violence in Spain was reaching fever pitch, Pope Pius XI fell sick, and his tasks were passed to his secretary of state, Cardinal Eugenio Pacelli. On November 18, 1936, Fascist Italy and Nazi Germany officially recognized Franco and his Junta Técnica del Estado as Spain's rightful leaders.[71] The next day, on November 19, 1936, the Cardinal Assessor of the Holy Office received the cryptic news that the pope was still concerned about the heresies condemned by the draft Syllabus, but that he was going to "do something on his own" about them.[72] Three more months passed—and still, all was silent. In the meanwhile, thanks in large part to Nazi-Fascist involvement, the Spanish Civil War was growing bloodier by the day. Mussolini had sent more than 78,000 men to Spain, and Hitler was now deploying the Luftwaffe as a dress rehearsal for what he imagined would be the imminent European-wide war. Jubilant Spanish Fascists informed their brethren in Germany and Italy, "Dawn is breaking in Spain. Fascist enthusiasm is great . . . Our totalitarian time is drawing near."[73]

In early March 1937 the Holy Office finally received word from the pope regarding the Syllabus of Errors: the Syllabus would be indefinitely postponed. The note informed the clerics that the pope was getting ready to release a series of encyclicals in place of the Syllabus.[74] Almost all of the members of the Holy Office project were shocked, save one. Joseph Ledit had been advised of these developments in advance, not least because he had played a leading role in drafting one of the three encyclicals. Ledit had had no binding intellectual commitment to the anti-totalitarianism frame and had always seen communism as being more dangerous than both Nazism and Fascism. For these reasons, he likely shed crocodile tears when he received final word that the draft Syllabus of Errors was not to be published.

In Praise of Concordats

The triple encyclicals of 1937 not only supplanted the Holy Office project; they entirely subverted it. The first encyclical, on Nazi Germany, was written only in German and was intended for a small audience. It eschewed any sort of robust Catholic anti-totalitarianism, abandoning the joint attack on Fascism and Nazism of the Syllabus project, and saving Fascism from reproof. Neither did the encyclical engage with the writings of key Nazi theorists, nor, much less, with those of Adolf Hitler himself. Instead, the text was principally concerned with advancing a stale justification for Catholic legal internationalism and the concordat revolution. The second encyclical, on the Soviet Union, was intended for global consumption. It made the case that communism was a heretical doctrine and that communist internationalism was the world's biggest threat to Catholicism and the Catholic Church. The third encyclical defended the necessity of just war, asserting that if and when left-wing radical and anticlerical groups and governments posed a threat to the Catholic Church and to individuals, it was acceptable to use violence against them. The text, which focused on current events in Mexico, was clearly intended to offer guidance on the Spanish Civil War as well.

On March 14, 1937, the first of the three encyclicals was published. Instead of being drafted with assistance from the clerics of the Holy Office, it had been written by two figures: Eugenio Pacelli and Pacelli's old friend from his time in Germany, Cardinal Faulhaber. Of all Germany's bishops, Faulhaber was the most attached to the Reichskonkordat, and throughout the harsh years of Nazi persecution, he retained the conviction (which many other clerics had lost) that the concordat was still the best defense for the Catholic Church. Pacelli was in complete alignment with Faulhaber on this point, and in the summer of 1936 he suggested that the pope issue a low-profile document cataloguing Germany's violations of the concordat, with the aim of bringing the Nazis back into line. Though Pacelli much preferred that the document be a pastoral letter, by early 1937 Germany's most powerful bishops had successfully lobbied the pope to issue an encyclical instead.[75]

The resulting text, *Mit brennender Sorge* ("With deep anxiety"), bore almost no resemblance to the Holy Office draft. Its main purpose was to defend the concordat revolution in general, and the Reichskonkordat in particular. Written in German and addressed to German bishops alone, the encyclical presented itself as an internal document, directed at Germany. It omitted mention of Germany's support for Dollfuss's murder and its treatment of Germany's Jewish population. Nazi "hyper-statism" and "hypernationalism" were mentioned only in passing, and the words "totalitarian" and "totalitarianism" appeared nowhere in the text. Only in one passage was there a glimmer of the Holy Office's Syllabus of Errors, when the pontiff asserted that "man, as a person, possesses rights that he holds from God and which must remain, with regard to the collectivity, beyond the reach of anything that would tend to deny them, to abolish them, or to neglect them." Furthermore, the encyclical spoke out against the Nazi privileging of categories like "nation," "race," and "the people" over and above all else. Other than this, the text did not present what was going on in Germany as a general trend or, much less, a global threat. Neither did the encyclical employ terms typically used in papal condemnations of doctrine, like "heretical," "immoral," or "offensive to pious ears."[76] In this way, the real force of the Syllabus of Errors was lost. For while the Syllabus had argued that Nazism was heretical and fundamentally incompatible with Catholicism, *Mit brennender Sorge* suggested that the Nazi regime and the Church *could* reach a working agreement.[77]

Even though Hitler was infuriated by the text, several scholars and commentators since have noted that *Mit brennender Sorge* reads as weak, disappointing, and a missed opportunity.[78] Emphasizing the text's failure to strongly condemn racism and anti-Semitism, they have concluded that the Holy See, in 1937, was "silent" on all fronts. However, although it is true that the text was not strong on racism, anti-Semitism, or totalitarianism, the text did speak up about one key topic. The authoritative circular letter was dominated by an attempt to explain and celebrate Catholic legal internationalism, and to use that explanation as a way to bring Nazi Germany back into the fold.

The 1937 encyclical began by emphasizing that concordats were good and necessary instruments for the universal Catholic Church, and for nation-states as well. Concordats assisted the church in her "universal evangelical mission" because they secured "the freedom of the Church's beneficent mission and the salvation of the souls in her care." Christian legal internationalism enshrined "Christianity as a model and guide to the world, which is sick to death and clamors for directives." Additionally, concordats directly benefited European nation-states, anchoring them "in the holy will of the eternal God and His commandments." By providing clear guidance over "the organization of social and political life," they actively militated against the possibility of "spiritual spoliation and degradation." They helped states avoid the pitfalls of positive legal systems built exclusively upon "man's subjective opinion, which changes with the times." Instead, concordat diplomacy enabled states to protect "the immutable laws of God" and avoid the error of drafting "human laws in flagrant contradiction with the natural law." Concordats did so, for instance, by protecting the "primary right" of (Catholic) parents—that is, the right "to the education of their children in the spirit of their true Faith, and according to its prescriptions"—in addition to protecting the rights of Catholic youth and adults to take part in "religious associations" without "seeing the loyalty to [their] country misunderstood" or "being hurt in [their] social or professional life." These legal treatises, the encyclical reminded its readers, represented a defensive wall against secularism—and thus, they were praiseworthy and even indispensable tools. For these reasons, the German government was making a mistake when it violated the concordat. "True and lawful authority is invariably a bond of unity, a source of strength, a guarantee against division and ruin, a pledge for the future," the encyclical lectured. By acting "unlawfully," through its violation of the concordat, Nazi Germany was putting its own future at stake.[79]

Mit brennender Sorge recycled a series of well-known justifications for Catholic legal internationalism, even as it sunk the possibility of a robust Catholic anti-Nazism. Just three days later, Pius XI issued a second encyclical, *Divini Redemptoris.* An exercise in alchemy, the text carried out the transformation of Catholic anti-Fascist and anti-Nazi anti-totalitarianism into Catholic anticommunism. In the process, it provided the final stamp of approval on the papacy's anticommunist campaign, turning anticommunism into a credo, and making the papal campaign against the Soviet Union near-irreversible.

A Bold Stand against Communism

Unlike *Mit brennender Sorge, Divini Redemptoris* was absolutely unambiguous about the gravity of the threat posed by communism to the

Church. The text's first section affirmed that communism was in no uncertain terms a heresy—a "satanic scourge." Erasing the difference between communism and the Soviet Union, the text explained that the Soviet government was evil because it made no room for God and "refuse[d] to human life any sacred or spiritual character." There could be no confusion that Christianity and communism stood at the antipodes, and that the Soviet Union, through its internationalization of communism, put the fate of the Church in jeopardy. In fact, "the most persistent enemies of the Church [are] from Moscow directing the struggle against Christian civilization." The battle, therefore, was global, and the Soviet Union was pulling the strings.[80]

From here, the encyclical went on to reveal what communism "really was." This section of the text bore so many similarities to the draft Syllabus of Errors that members of the Holy Office painstakingly took note of them, through a line-by-line comparison.[81] In keeping with the draft Syllabus, the encyclical affirmed that the leading crime of communism was "to defraud man of his God-granted rights," thus overturning the precepts of both natural and divine law. The encyclical proved this point by providing a laundry list of the rights violated by communist Russia, which included the right to marriage, the right to education, the right of association, and, of course, the right to private property. Referencing the notion that the Soviet Union was a totalitarian state, the encyclical affirmed that "there is no recognition of any right of the individual in his relations to the collectivity," adding that in the Soviet Union, each citizen was "a mere cog-wheel in the Communist system."[82]

The encyclical then juxtaposed the absolute darkness of Soviet communism to the light of the ideal Catholic state. The ideal Catholic state, as defended and interpreted by the Church, was a "vigilant and provident defender" of divine and natural law, and of the individual rights derived therefrom. Led by "the social doctrine of the Church," this state could achieve harmony between social classes, and guarantee the protection of a range of rights for their citizens, including "the right to life, to bodily integrity, to the necessary means of existence," and to things like freedom of association and private property. By contrast, the Soviet state was dark, violent, and squalid: a place where no self-respecting man, woman, or child would want to live.[83]

But if the Soviet Union was a formidable international foe, it met its match in the Vatican. Indeed, the Vatican could provide crucial guidance in this dark moment because it, too, had a handle on internationalism in a way that no power (save the Soviet Union) did. The Vatican, like the Soviet Union, was principally concerned, not with the national, but with the "international" (a word that appeared three times in the encyclical), the "universal" (five times), and the "world" (mentioned thirty-nine times). If the Soviets had "great financial resources, gigantic organizations, and international congresses," so did the pope. Similarly, only the pope was capable of responding to the Soviet propaganda machine—a machine that "the world has never witnessed before," which was "directed from one common center" and "shrewdly adapted to the varying conditions of diverse peoples." The Vatican's Catholic International was well versed, like the Comintern, in the art of "propaganda on a large scale," which put media new and old in the service of "an intensive program of social education to procure the widest possible diffusion of the teachings of the Church."[84] Communist internationalism, in sum, had met its match in Catholic internationalism.

The concluding section of *Divini Redemptoris* was a wrap-up of the core themes addressed throughout the text: Communism was the modern incarnation of ancient evil; if left unopposed, it would destroy religion and the world itself; luckily, one power was capable of countering its influence—namely, the Roman Catholic Church. Given the papacy's manifold services in the fight against international communism, the encyclical noted, states would do well to help the Church, and allow her "full liberty" to pursue good and fight (communist) evil. Because the Church was the world's best resource against communism, it should be allowed to survive and thrive.[85]

It is hard to overemphasize the importance of *Divini Redemptoris*. By presenting international communism as evil incarnate, the encyclical explained, celebrated, and tacitly imposed the Vatican's turn against the Soviet Union on the Catholic and non-Catholic world. It helped enshrine the antithesis "Catholicism versus communism" as a mainstay on the European political scene. The text tidily swept away its own origin story—its roots in a draft Syllabus of Errors that would have condemned Nazism, Fascism, and communism alike as heretical, totalitarian, doctrines. In the process, it purged the associations that had originally bound Catholic anti-totalitarianism to Catholic anti-Nazism and anti-Fascism. Through its ringing attack on *communist* totalitarianism alone, the encyclical suggested that there was only one real threat to Catholicism. Finally, the text buoyed the myth of a Catholic International, and endowed that International with one leading purpose: fighting communism.

Divini Redemptoris was significant for a last reason, too: it prepared the ground for a further radicalization of the anticommunist crusade. Through a flurry of bellicose words and images—including repeated mentions of words such as "battle," "war," "fight," and "blood"—it called upon Catholics worldwide to respond to the Soviet "war on all that is God," and go forth and "fight the battles of the Lord."[86] Nine days later, through the encyclical *Firmissimam Constantiam*, Pius XI made a clear statement in favor of the use of violence to defend Church interests and fight left-wing elements.

The pope's third encyclical of 1937 officially focused on Mexico, a country of particular interest not only to Central American Catholics, but to North American ones as well. The Vatican's decision to speak out loudly about Mexico—which shared a long border and deep history with the United States—was part of its attempt to begin speaking to American Catholics during the late 1930s and 1940s. As part of this reorientation, Eugenio Pacelli had taken a trip to the United States in 1936, where he zipped from one political-diplomatic appointment to the next, meeting with American politicians, Catholic archbishops, and Catholic lay organizations. During his travels, he learned of U.S. anxieties over the rise of the radical left in Mexico.

While it was true that Mexico was in the midst of an anticlerical moment, communist revolution was not a real possibility.[87] From the conspiratorial point of view of Mexican clergymen, however, an ambitious nationalization and public education project, which Mexico's new president, Lázaro Cárdenas, had launched in 1934, was proof of extensive communist influence.[88] Mexican clergymen were convinced that the Cardenas government was a front, and that their country was being taken over by many "authentic Russians," whose "ultimate aim" was "to create a new communist generation."[89] They were concerned that should the situation continue to escalate, the United States would not intervene, given Franklin D. Roosevelt's repeated adherence to the Good Neighbor Policy and his insistence on renouncing the United States' "right" to military intervention in Latin America.[90] The Mexican Church felt it was being left to fend for itself.

Hence, starting from the mid 1930s, several high-ranking members of the Mexican hierarchy began writing to the pope to ask him to approve the same "liberty of action against communism" accorded "to Spanish Catholics": that is, "armed defense."[91] In the words of the bishop of Chiapas, "Faced with the danger of communism and the fear that its deeds succeed, everyone understands that it is necessary to be ready to defeat force with force, and that this defense is legitimate."[92] With the intent of riling up local opinion, the Spanish hierarchy began to discuss the anticlerical campaign in Spain from the pulpits, and to disseminate the collective pastoral of Spanish bishops, which called the Civil War a crusade. Mexican Catholic publications similarly gave the Spanish Civil War extensive coverage, emphasizing that Mexico must be prepared to fight communism, not just with ideas, but with arms too.[93]

Firmissimam Constantiam was the pope's affirmative response to the Mexican clergy's request. Drafted by Giuseppe Pizzardo, with input from the omnipresent Ledóchowski and from the energetically anticommunist Father Alba of the Colegio Pio Latino Americano in Rome, the encyclical began by outlining the manifold threats to Catholicism posed by left-wing activists in Mexico.[94] It sang the praises of Catholic Action as "the educator of consciences and the molder of moral qualities," suggesting that the capture of civil society was the best way to guarantee the Church's interests in Mexico. Then, the encyclical took a sharp right turn, providing a clear justification for armed violence. "It is quite natural that when the most elementary religious and civil liberties are attacked, Catholic citizens do not resign themselves passively to renouncing those liberties," the text asserted. "It is not to be seen how citizens are to be condemned who unite to defend themselves and the nation, by licit and appropriate means, against those who make use of public power to bring it to ruin." The implication was clear. Picking up arms in "just defense" against one's own government was an appropriate action for Catholics—and one that the pope endorsed. To be sure, the encyclical specified, the armed revolt of Catholics must be "licit" and waged through acts that were "not intrinsically evil."[95] But to the question of whether armed revolt was appropriate and advisable, the papacy answered a clear yes.

A few clerics who read the text were concerned that the pope was taking an unwarranted position, noting that it would have been better for him to encourage Catholics to only engage in *"passive* resistance, through participation in Catholic Action,"* instead of encouraging "armed violence, which easily gets out of hand."[96] Most commentators, however, praised the text and aligned with the hale endorsement of *Civiltà Cattolica.* The Jesuit journal highlighted that the encyclical on Mexico, together with *Divini Redemptoris,* had done Catholics a great service in alerting them to the communist "de-Christianization of peoples," and in reminding them that the Vatican had the best response to the communist menace, through its "whole positive and practical 'program' of Christian restoration."[97]

In Mexico, *Firmissimam Constantiam* was released on Easter Day, coinciding with the most important festival of the liturgical year. In published form, it was paired in a two-cent pamphlet with *Divini Redemptoris,* making clear the link between Catholic anticommunist internationalism and the situation in Mexico.[98] The message was picked up both in Mexico and in the United States, just as the Vatican hoped it would be. The encyclical was meant to suggest to Central and North American Catholics that the Vatican was not just a European power concerned with European affairs; instead, it was prepared to bring its mission—and its anticommunist crusade—across the Atlantic as well. With evident enthusiasm, the Vatican nuncio in Washington, D.C., informed his superiors that American journalists had celebrated *Firmissimam Constantiam,* focusing in particular on its censure of "atheism and communism." The nuncio also noted that North American journalists had failed to grasp the import of the encyclical's core message, insofar as their articles "made no particular reference to the extremely delicate point, that of armed resistance."[99] As far as the nuncio was concerned, this was for the best—after all, in the 1930s Catholics were still imperfectly integrated members of American society, and if they came out loudly in favor of an armed insurrection against Cárdenas, this might incite Protestant and liberal opinion against them.

The Vatican was crossing the Atlantic with its anticommunist crusade, and the Americans received the message. In 1937 Jesuits in the United States launched a series of courses on international communism and "Christian sociology," even as local American media began giving ample coverage to Catholic anticommunism, including analyses of *Divini Redemptoris* and its implications for the United States.[100] In 1938 the Secretariat on Atheism began publishing an English-language edition of *Lettres de Rome*, entitled *The World Problem*, which included "a few small variations so as to better adapt its contents to America."[101] Soon enough, American Catholic intellectual heavyweights like Edmund A. Walsh, the founder of the School of Foreign Service at Georgetown University, and Father Fulton Sheen, who had obtained a PhD in philosophy from the Catholic University of Leuven in Belgium, lent their services to the project of building a transatlantic Catholic anticommunist movement. Both Sheen's wildly popular weekly Catholic radio show, *The Catholic Hour*, and Walsh's lecture series (which included stops at the American Historical Society and at the American Academy of Political and Social Sciences), sought to "situate theology in the context of current affairs," even as they encouraged Catholics to hit the streets in a series of religious anticommunist demonstrations that swept New York, Cleveland, and other cities in the late 1930s.[102] "We have a new mandate," Edmund Walsh announced, jubilant.[103]

In these various radio programs and lecture tours, Catholic antiliberalism—which had been so important in shaping papal policy from World War I onward—did not feature prominently. Rather than emphasize the genealogical links between liberalism and communism (as had *Quadragesimo Anno*), American clerics went the path suggested by *Divini Redemptoris:* Communism's historical genealogy mattered little—what mattered more was that it represented a timeless evil incarnate, the work of Satan himself. This monumental shift—which took place as American Catholics and Catholics in Europe were establishing firmer ties—had important consequences. It would lead the Holy See, first, to seek closer contact with American politicians in the late 1930s; then to open informal diplomatic relations with the United States during World War II; and finally, in 1944–1945, to enlist the United States in the battle for "Christian Europe" and against Soviet expansionism.

❖

Much had changed between 1935 and 1937 for the universal Roman Catholic Church. As a result of the victories of the Popular Front, the launching of the Spanish Civil War, and, most crucially, the interpretations accorded to these events by influential clerics in Spain, France, Italy, Poland, Hungary, Mexico, the United States, and elsewhere, the papacy had decided to make anticommunism its focus. It ceased presenting American-style liberalism as a credible threat, and silenced the possibility of a robust Catholic anti-Fascist or anti-Nazi movement framework from receiving Rome's official endorsement. A telltale sign that this reorientation was under way was the sinking of the draft Syllabus of Errors and the issuing of the triple encyclicals of March 1937.

The triple encyclicals crystallized for the faithful what it meant to be Catholic in the mid- to late 1930s. Celebrating the triumphal concordat moment of the early post–World War I years, the first of the three texts, *Mit Brennender Sorge*, stood by the old-fashioned idea that Catholic legal internationalism was the way forward. Indeed, the pope's primary response to wayward partners like Nazi Germany was to praise the concordat—and request that concordats be respected and honored, according to the letter of the law. In other words, the best defense against Europe's de-Christianization was again and still the concordat.

The 1937 encyclicals announced that communism and communism alone was "totalitarian," and that it was the greatest existential threat to Catholicism and the world.[104] By casting communism as the modern incarnation of absolute evil, and juxtaposing its terrifying internationalism with the noble internationalism of the Holy See, the triple encyclicals confirmed the antithesis between Catholicism and communism as a fixture of modern Catholic political discourse. The texts suggested that good Catholics, when faced with the communist menace, should feel warranted in their use of violence to quash this nemesis. Through their explicit references to Spain, Mexico, and the United States, the texts announced that papal anticommunist internationalism was not just a European affair, but one that must expand to the Americas as well.

Thus it was that in 1936–1937, in the context of a war on European soil, Catholic anti-totalitarianism took a backseat to a concern about the erasure of Catholicism *tout court* in a supposedly imminent European-wide Bolshevik revolution. Though it was true that the Holy See had no standing army in Spain (or elsewhere), its "words, too, could destroy."[105] Hundreds of Catholic volunteers flocked to Spain's shores to fight what they understood as the battle for Christian civilization against Bolshevik barbarism, holding *Divini Redemptoris* high in their hands. The Vatican, though it refrained from explicitly condoning Franco, showed its sympathy for him early in the conflict. No wonder that when, in November 1938, a rather under-informed Roosevelt administration approached the Vatican to propose that the two powers work together to end the Spanish Civil War and appoint a three-man provisional ruling government for Spain, with figures handpicked by the United States and the Holy See, Pius XI politely turned down the offer.[106] This war was one in which the pope was not neutral, and he was not interested in brokering peace until an enemy of anticlericalism came out on top.

One year later, the Second World War broke out. The conflict was not a fundamental turning point for the Holy See in the way that World War I had been. The Great War had, after all, revolutionized papal diplomacy and led the Vatican to present itself as a champion of an anti-liberal and antisocialist postwar order, in both Eastern and Western Europe. Over and against the legal internationalism of the League of Nations and the innovative civil society work of the Communist International, the Vatican had propped itself up as a Catholic International, with a legal and cultural strategy of its own. During the Great War, close friendships with partners like the German Empire had given the pope not only a confidence boost but also a model for how to think through issues like national self-determination, post-imperial hegemony, and left-wing revolutionism. During the course of the 1920s and 1930s, events such as the Great Depression and the Spanish Civil War only hardened the papacy's commitment to concordat diplomacy and anticommunist mobilizing. Rather than listening to countervailing tendencies within the Holy See and within the broader Catholic world—

tendencies that called for a vocal protest of Nazism and Fascism, or the jettisoning of concordat diplomacy—the papacy had done what it could to shut those conversations down.

By contrast, World War II had a surprisingly neutral impact on papal diplomacy and on the core planks of its interwar internationalism. Unlike during World War I, the Vatican did not try to claim center stage, nor did it present a novel vision of how to organize the postwar order. Furthermore, unlike during World War I, the Vatican lacked natural allies. In this conflict—which dramatically began with the conclusion of a nonaggression pact between Nazi Germany and the Soviet Union and continued with the double invasion of "most Catholic" Poland—the Holy See found itself unmoored. It still wanted the Soviet Union gone, but it was not willing to countenance the sacrifice of Poland and much of Eastern Europe in the process. Furthermore, because the policies of Nazi Germany vis-à-vis the Catholic Church grew increasingly harsh over the course of the war, the papacy did not feel protected by the Axis powers. As a result, the Vatican continued with its late-1930s praxis of bracketing anti-liberalism, and showed itself cautiously open to talks with the United States. However, it did not embrace a fundamentally new diplomatic agenda. It did not indicate that it was willing to rethink concordat diplomacy, and it did not suggest that its anticommunist crusade had been a mistake. Thus, unlike during World War I—when the Vatican seized center stage, turned its weakness into strength, and emerged as a harsh critic of the European order emerging from the war—during World War II the pope played it safe. He stuck to his core internationalist planks of anticommunism and concordat diplomacy, but he also tried as best as he could to lie low and not draw attention to his tentative openness toward the Allies. In the process, he chose, time and time again, to proffer silence more than guidance during events like the invasion of Poland, the occupation of France, and the genocide of European Jewry. Silence, the pope informed skeptics in his immediate circles, would be more effective than words, in that it would diminish the likelihood of retaliatory actions and help the papacy emerge from the conflict unscathed.

This decision ultimately cost the pope a heavy price. Starting from the Spanish Civil War years, the pope butted up against a phenomenon that his actions had helped generate: the creation of an alternative Catholic internationalist movement that was highly critical of the two planks of papal activism—namely, concordatory intrigue and anticommunist derring-do. This alternative form of Catholic internationalism was eager to speak out clearly against both Nazism and Fascism. It was unconvinced that communism was the only existential threat to the Catholic Church. And it was interested in the possibility of building a new post–World War II order that was fundamentally committed to democracy as a form of government, and to the creation of a new and more effective League of Nations.

Members of this alternative Catholic international were few and far between in the late 1930s and early 1940s. Connected by ties of friendship and informal solidarities, these dispersed figures resided in countries like France, Austria, Italy, Great Britain, the United States, and Canada. Many were political refugees and recent converts to Catholicism. The experience of Fascism, Nazism, and authoritarianism had led them to definitively reject dictatorial political systems and embrace democratic forms of government—forms of government that emphasized the individual liberty of citizens over and above the authority of the state. Like the papacy's men, they too were fervid Catholics, convinced that "politics must be moral or fail in its purpose." "There can be no sound politics," they argued, "without the application of the Church's social teachings."[107] However, unlike the Holy See, they saw the Church's social teachings as indicating a fundamentally anti-totalitarian and pro-democratic road—one that shied away from concordat diplomacy and the compromises it inevitably entailed and that tended to present communism as one of several evils plaguing the contemporary world.

7

The War for the Soul of Catholicism

[The Church] maintain[s] itself only by remaining immobile, for the smallest crack might bring down the whole edifice.

—JEAN GRENIER, 1938

WHEN IN 1936–1937 the universal government of the Roman Catholic Church decided to quash the Syllabus of Errors project and present communism as being more dangerous than both Nazism and Fascism, this decision had disastrous consequences for those European Catholics who remained strongly opposed to both right-wing authoritarian movements and who, increasingly, felt abandoned by the Holy See. This feeling led to the quiet expansion of a fringe dissident Catholic movement, and initiated a profound, and fraught, struggle for the soul of Catholicism—a struggle that would continue against the backdrop of World War II and throughout the postwar reconstruction years.

Beginning in 1936, a small but powerful contingent of anti-Fascist and anti-Nazi European Catholics rejected several of the component parts of the emergent Catholic rightist narrative regarding the Spanish Civil War. They began arguing that Catholics must not perforce back Franco and that the Spanish Civil War was not a religious war, pitting Catholicism against atheistic communism. In a bold move, these dissenting Catholics—who lived in Spain, England, France, Austria, and the United States—rallied under the banner of "neither Nazism, nor Fascism, nor communism."[1] In doing so, they announced their neutrality in the Spanish Civil War and their interest in cultivating an alternative conception of Catholicism that stood a few steps removed from that of the Holy See.[2] It is important to stress that in these years these Catholic dissidents were few in number. Nonetheless, they launched a movement that would, in the long run, have a profound impact on the European continent as a whole.

Catholic Dissidents Speak Out

All the key figures in the emergent movement were hardened anti-Fascists and anti-Nazis. An important reference point for them was Luigi Sturzo, the Sicilian priest who after the Great War had founded the Italian Christian Democratic Party. A staunch critic of the Fascist regime from 1923–1924, Sturzo was one of the first people in Italy (and Europe) to use the label "totalitarian" in reference to the new Fascist phenomenon.[3] Having run into trouble with the Holy See for his commitment to secularism and democracy, in 1924 Sturzo left Italy for London, a choice perhaps dictated by his desire to escape Vatican control.[4] In 1929 the Sicilian cleric fumed against the conclusion of the Lateran Agreements, which he fretted put the Catholic *imprimatur* on Italy's new murderous regime. At every major crime and foreign gamble perpetrated by the Fascists in the 1920s and 1930s, Sturzo spoke up. In response to Fascist military operations in Ethiopia and the outpouring of Italian Catholic support for Mussolini's actions in the fall of 1936, the Italian cleric announced that the mass rallying of Italian Catholics to the Fascist imperialist war was "extremely sad," not least because the war was "an unjust war," and one "won through aerial bombardments and poisonous, choking gasses." He wondered, "How can military chaplains and bishops exalt the war and encourage it through their speeches and their benedictions of the troops?"[5] "The tragedy of Abyssinia," Sturzo wrote, "fills me with sorrow, as a Catholic and as an Italian. And the *Te Deum* that will be sung in Italy (along with inopportune speeches) increases my indignation . . . I cannot conceive of a violation of law and morality graver than that which brought Italy to victory."[6]

Writing in exile first in Britain and then in the United States, Sturzo kept a close watch over developments in Spain, a country he visited in 1934, forging important ties with fellow left-Catholics and many future members of the emergent Catholic dissident movement.[7] In line with his radical Catholic pacifism and his profound distrust of any power that sought the help of Fascist Italy and Nazi Germany, Sturzo made up his mind early on regarding the Spanish Civil War. "Every day, at Mass, I pray for Spain," the Italian cleric informed a friend in early 1937. "I do not believe that the victory of one side or the other can bring peace and an end to the present crisis." Indeed, Sturzo affirmed, "the Church of Spain, which should have worked for peace, has in its majority aligned itself with one of the parties, even to the extent of declaring a holy war and a crusade." He lamented that "the whole of the Catholic Church, including the pope himself," seemed to be going along with the game. Sturzo concluded that only a genuine Catholic neutrality would bring the conflict to its end.[8]

Sturzo's position lay well outside the Catholic mainstream, but a small group of Spanish, Italian, and French Catholics agreed with him. In the winter of 1936 the Spanish cleric Gallegos Rocafull expressed similar sentiments in an article published in Barcelona, entitled "Why I Am with the People." The article explained to readers that the Spanish Civil War had been misrepresented to Catholics, and by them. "Holy War? Crusade? Evidently, this is not either," Rocafull affirmed. The Spanish intellectual asserted that if Catholics joined Franco's side, then they would help usher in a Fascist Europe, which would work to undermine the Catholic Church rather than protect it.[9] Father Rocafull's unwavering opposition to Franco's coup and his support of the Republic would cost him his livelihood: Spanish Catholic superiors would suspend his ministry, and the defrocked Spanish father would be condemned as the "unhappy scum of the Spanish clergy."[10]

Despite the high stakes involved, a small group of French Catholics rallied to positions close to those espoused by Rocafull and Sturzo. The French Thomist philosopher Jacques Maritain played an important role in this effort. An erstwhile fan of the ultranationalist, anti-Semitic, Fascist-sympathizing French Action, the French layman had reformed his views and had gone so far as to cultivate an interest in reading Marx, all the while remaining firmly committed to a fiercely anticommunist worldview. By the mid- to late 1930s Maritain was ready to take a stand that would, he knew, run counter to that of mainstream Catholic clergy and the Church of Rome. In an article published in the summer of 1937, Maritain argued against the idea that the Spanish Civil War should be understood as a "holy war." Wars could never be holy, Maritain explained, because war and violence secularize values instead of sacralizing them. The fact that the Nationalists carried out acts of terror under the sign of cross made them at least as bad as their opponents. "It is a horrible sacrilege to massacre priests out of hatred for religion, for even if they are 'Fascists,' they are still ministers of Christ. It is another sacrilege, horrible also, to massacre poor people in the name of religion—be they 'Marxists,' they are still the people of Christ."[11]

Echoing Sturzo's outrage at leaders of the Catholic Church, Maritain emphasized that while it was "understandable" that many Spanish Catholics found themselves in a state of confusion, the warmongering behavior of the "leaders of the Church" was beyond the pale. "The Catholic world is falling into an abyss, the blind leading the blind," he informed a friend.[12] Some French Catholics came forth even more strongly. Emmanuel Mounier, the French Catholic personalist, asserted: "A Franquist Spain, with its horrible cortège of spying, of terror, and of lies: and it's with this that one wants to solidify the destiny of our Church?"[13] In 1938 the Catholic writer Georges Bernanos picked up pen and paper to denounce the Church's hypocrisy through a novel on the atrocities of the Spanish Civil War, *The Great Cemeteries under the Moon*. In the same year, more intellectuals spoke out against a Catholic Church that was "stiff," "intransigent," and attempting to "maintain itself only by remaining immobile, for the smallest crack might bring down the whole edifice."[14] The movement to delineate a Catholic but nonpapal response to the Spanish Civil War was growing.

Rocafull, Maritain, and others warned their readers that the real risk of the Spanish Civil War was that it would lead to Fascism's takeover of Europe.[15] Mounier's journal *Esprit* expressed sympathy with the Spanish Republic and condemned Franco and his troops.[16] Georges Bidault, who would soon emerge as one of the leading lights of France's new Christian Democratic Party, used his platform at the newspaper *L'Aube* to express his sympathies with Basque Catholics and to advocate resistance to Nazi intervention in the conflict.[17] A more radical group of progressive Catholics, organized by Marc Sangnier in a group called the Jeune République, openly supported the Spanish Republican government, sending both food and clothing to the Spanish Loyalists, as did the journal *Terre Nouvelle,* which even called for military aid to the Republic.[18]

Individuals connected to these efforts were not just brave writers— they were also astute publicists and movement builders. Through their actions, a small but intellectually powerful transnational network was forming.[19] Its members retained their opposition to totalitarianism in its Fascist and Nazi forms, while simultaneously breaking with orthodoxy regarding the Spanish Civil War. This group of Catholic dissidents—which remained a loose gathering of individuals rather than a formal or named group—focused on changing opinions by influencing the international Catholic media. They worked to get key texts of the group translated and dispersed to a wide audience, which starting in 1936–1937 connected people not just in Spain and France, but also in Great Britain, Belgium, Italy, Poland, Mexico and the United States. Members of this growing network of Catholic pacifists worked so fast that oftentimes the hand-typed Spanish-language translation of a French Catholic antiwar article would start circulating in Barcelona and other major urban centers even before the official French edition hit newsstands.[20] Their membership within a broader Catholic anti-Fascist community could cost them some friends closer to home, however: When in April 1937 the American Catholic journal *Commonweal,* whose managing editor had close ties with Sturzo and other Catholic dissidents, published an article critical of Franco, journal subscriptions immediately fell by 25 percent, and the journal's director was sharply attacked for allowing the article to make it into print.[21]

In the spirit of constructing an alternative to the Vatican's Catholic International, these figures made great use of lecture tours and a series of international appeals meant to generate discussion.[22] In these appeals, the "international," was an explicit object of attention and concern. The *Appel espagnol* signed in Paris by the Spanish contingent of this group in April 1937 appealed to the "international community" to launch a double entreaty to both the League of Nations and transnational Catholics. "If the international community really exists," the statement implored, "it must help our country to find peace again, instead of aiding and abetting a contest that threatens to bring down the whole of Europe."[23] Along similar lines, a manifesto against the bombing of Guernica (entitled "For the Basque People: An Appeal to

All Men of Heart"] had the explicit aim of rallying opinion, not just of
the French and Spanish, but of Catholics across the continent. As Catholic dissidents emphasized, the Spanish Civil War was an opportunity
for the resurgence of a different sort of Catholic social creed: one that
counseled pacifism, and that stood up against Fascism and Nazism.[24]

The Spanish Civil War not only strengthened an alternative form
of Catholic internationalism: it also helped popularize a new Catholic
theory of Church-state relations. Jacques Maritain broke ground in this
respect. In the 1920s the French philosopher had hewed close to the
pope and been convinced that the Church could and must wield indirect
power over temporal affairs via the instrument of the concordat. However, in the early 1930s Maritain began to develop a new perspective
on Church-state relations. He argued that the Church must focus
simply on directing consciences, not directing states by signing concordatory agreements that bound the Church closely to particular
countries and their rulers. Maritain believed that the Church should
gain influence over states through the actions of "the most evolved
politically and the most devoted part of the Christian laity." For him,
Catholicism was the only "true" religion, and all states must be "oriented toward the perfection of natural law and Christian law." But
relying on the state and its coercive and legal apparatus was no longer
an acceptable path. Concordat diplomacy could not be the way of the
future.[25]

Maritain's landmark 1936 work, *Integral Humanism*, defended
what he called an "integrally" or "vitally" Christian" body politic and
decried coercively Christian states—that is, states made Christian
through "legal constraints." He suggested that the legalistic-concordatory
vision of a Christian sacral society imposed from on high was "incapable of existence" in the modern world. Any state that literally or
juridically cast "unbelievers outside the walls of the Christian politic" was "unacceptable" and a thing of the past. "A Christian body
politic in the conditions of modern times can only be a Christian body
politic within whose walls *unbelievers and believers live together and
share in the same temporal common good*," the philosopher asserted.
In place of "Catholicizing" Europe, Maritain was calling for Catholics
to accept pluralism: a Europe forged in cooperation with non-Catholics,

Jews, and even atheists. In another jab at the concordat vision, Maritain argued that Catholics could no longer focus on states as entities governed primarily by hierarchy and law. Instead of trying to capture power and legal authority, Catholics should put their energies into civil society—into cultivating a presence within religiously plural states in the realm of associational activity. Acceptance of pluralism and activism in civil society was, for Maritain, the best way for Europe to retain its "integrally Christian" character.[26]

Taking a step further, the Jesuit father Henri de Lubac noted that the twentieth century was the era in which the Holy See must assert its "directive power over *consciences*," not states. The idea of indirect power, wrote de Lubac, was "a bastard and untenable compromise between the theory of direct power and the so-called theory of directive power"—that is, the idea that the Church had the right to exercise direct power over state affairs, and the idea that it merely wielded the power of moral suasion over individuals. Only the idea of directive power over individual consciences, according to the Jesuit scholar, prevented the Church from at once abasing itself by prostrating itself before the state—or, just as dangerously, perverting the state by trying to lead it to confessionally pure waters.[27]

In addition to challenging Catholic legal internationalism, de Lubac, Maritain, and their allies increasingly also used their writings to question the Holy See's anticommunist crusade. Maritain, for one, agreed that Catholics should not succumb to the communist temptation, but he urged them to read Marx closely, to see how communism was best understood as a wrong turn emerging from "misdirected Christian values." For this reason, the proper reply to communists was not to excoriate or massacre them, but instead to read communist texts, establish dialogue with communist activists on social justice issues, and ultimately, bring communists into the Catholic fold.[28] This was radical thought from a devout Catholic in the 1930s.

Predictably, many clerics in France, Spain, and elsewhere in Europe did not take well to these recommendations. In addition to fretting over the birth of a new transnational movement that called into question many of the core tenets of the Vatican's recent diplomacy, they were distressed by the calls for either neutrality or support of the Republicans in the Spanish Civil War. Members of the Catholic upper hierarchy in Spain responded to the writings of these dissenting Catholics with vehement tones, accusing them of, among other things, a lack of religious fervor and a disrespect for the "martyrs" of "Western Christendom."[29] In France, neologisms like "Maritainist" quickly emerged as terms of abuse on the Catholic right.[30] The well-known Russian Catholic émigré and anticommunist pioneer Nicolai Berdyaev thundered against Maritain and his ilk, asserting that the universal Roman Catholic Church "has nothing in common . . . with Marxist orthodoxy."[31] Prominent theologians closely bound to Pius XI, such as Réginald Garrigou-Lagrange, questioned whether these dissident Catholics had a handle on theology, casting doubt, for instance, on whether they had ever read or understood Thomas Aquinas.[32] The Superior General of the Jesuit Order spoke in heightened tones against these "traitorous Catholics" as early as November 1936. Between 1936 and 1939, he encouraged Jesuits across Europe to compile a massive archive on the "troubling" activities of pacifist and anti-Franco Catholics.[33] The papal nuncio in Paris was asked to go on high alert; he soon began sending reports to Rome, lamenting the proliferation of periodicals that, "despite the fact that [they] are published by practicing Catholics, are nonetheless oriented toward the left, and even on the Spanish question they have shown themselves to be more favorable to the Reds than to the Nationalists."[34] Ledóchowski, for his part, reminded his fellow Jesuits that all those who stood against Franco stood for communism, even as he urged all Jesuits in Italy to celebrate the fact that "thanks to God's grace, the Italian government opposes all communist propaganda," diminishing the possibility that the "terrifying ruin witnessed in Spain" might touch Italy as well.[35] Right-wing organizations such as French Action took public positions, referencing Pius XI's anticommunist speeches to lambast what they called the "Catholic left" for its inability to heed the pope's warning and recognize that "since communism is the enemy, it is everyone's duty to treat it like the plague" rather than "indulge" it.[36]

The Vatican's Congregation of the Holy Office was asked to address the "confusions" of dissident Catholics. Readily, it took a strong stand against the supposed infiltration of Catholic ranks by communist forces, condemning a string of Catholic journals and books deemed too sympathetic to the Soviet Union, and putting several others under investigation—including ones in which Maritain, Mounier, and Sturzo regularly published.[37] Even before the issuance of the triple encyclicals of 1937, the new climate created by the Spanish Civil War pushed leading members of the Catholic hierarchy in Rome to deny the possibility of a Catholic anti-Nazi and anti-Fascist movement from ever receiving the Holy See's official institutional backing.

At the same time, Pius XI did personally attempt to address some of the complaints of Catholic dissidents. In March 1938, on the heels of the Anschluss of Austria to Nazi Germany—*Finis Austriae*—the pope revisited the buried Syllabus of Errors and decided to incorporate bits and pieces of it into an Instruction to Catholic Colleges. The text was released with little fanfare, but it nevertheless constituted an important relic of the Catholic anti-totalitarianism that might have been.[38] In the meantime, in a last-ditch attempt to preserve the peace at all costs, in late September 1938 France, Italy, and the United Kingdom concluded the Munich Agreement with Nazi Germany, permitting Germany's annexation of the Sudetenland—the parts of Czechoslovakia that had a high density of German-speaking residents. As with Austria, Germany's justification was that the local German minority was really a part of the German nation, and that it was being oppressed—not only by local Slavs, but also and more importantly, as Hermann Göring put it, by "Moscow and the eternal Jewish-Bolshevik rabble."[39]

Starting in 1937–1938, German authorities began taking the legislative persecution of German Jews to a new level. As of 1938 all German Jews were obliged to carry identity cards and take new names to explicitly flag themselves as Jewish. Following the Kristallnacht pogrom, a new wave of Nazi legislation barred Jews from public schools, universities, theaters, and sports facilities. At the same time, Fascist Italy began issuing racial purity laws targeted at Italian Jews. These laws banned foreign Jews from attending Italian schools; annulled "interracial" marriages between Jews and Aryans; required Jews to carry an identity card; forbade Jews from serving in the military; and prohibited Jews from owning real estate.

As these events were unfolding, Pius XI secretly commissioned an antiracist encyclical, *Humani Generis Unitas*, which was written by the American Jesuit John LaFarge and two fellow Jesuits, Gustav Gundlach and Gustave Desbuquois.[40] Rumors that Pius XI was getting ready to take a stand against both Fascism and Nazism started swirling around Europe. A well-connected Austrian anti-Fascist gushed that he had heard that "the Holy Father, troubled by the pressure Hitler is exerting upon Europe, has spelled out his policies in a new encyclical . . . in which he underscores the church's opposition to the new Nazi paganism, which will be officially condemned and placed on par with Bolshevik atheism."[41] Catholic dissidents—and particularly those who denounced Catholic anti-Judaism and anti-Semitism and asserted that the measures taken against the Jews in Nazi Germany were "contrary to civilization and to Christianity"[42]—were hopeful that they might have a potential ally in Rome.

As it turned out, *Humani Generis Unitas*, had it been published, would have condemned Nazism and race thinking. However, as John Connelly has noted, perhaps it was for the best that the text never saw the light of day. It clung to the idea that states were allowed to take legal action to ensure that Jews not be allowed to enact their "age-old hatred towards Christianity," and recited a host of anti-Judaic assumptions, including the supposed association between Jews and capitalism, and the notion that Jews in some way deserved their suffering because of their "refusal" of Christ. The text also troublingly suggested that only mass conversion to Catholicism could definitively solve the "Jewish problem."[43] Bigoted as it still was, *Humani Generis Unitas* would have nonetheless constituted a revolution in Catholic teachings on the Jews. In what would be the final year of his life, Pius XI was growing bolder in other respects as well, and even planned to speak out strongly against Mussolini at the upcoming tenth anniversary of the Lateran Agreements, in 1939. When Germany and Italy got wind of the news, they were not pleased. A prominent Fascist spy affirmed, "One hopes that the present pontiff is really on his last legs."[44]

In fact, he was. On February 10, 1939, Pope Pius XI died of cardiac arrest, at the age of eighty-one. Soon enough, the central government of the Roman Catholic Church would have a new official leader, and that man was none other than Eugenio Pacelli, Pius XI's former secretary of state. Pacelli was elected pope one month after Pius XI's death, in the swiftest conclave in 300 years. He took the name Pius XII. Most certainly because of Pacelli's intervention, Ratti's planned antiracist encyclical—which was sitting on the pope's desk at the moment of his death—was not published.[45] As one of the drafters of the text commented, his project had been "sabotaged" for "tactical and diplomatic reasons," despite the fact that the encyclical had been "a mission directly entrusted" by the pope. Pius XI's planned speech to Mussolini was, similarly, neither delivered nor published until long after Ratti's death.[46]

A New Bishop of Rome

During the entirety of his pontificate, Pius XII would stay true to what had been his two core commitments as secretary of state: the Vatican's anti-Soviet campaign and concordat diplomacy. The men with whom the new pope surrounded himself were aligned with these diplomatic priorities. They included figures like Giuseppe Pizzardo and Cesare Orsenigo, whose moderate views toward Nazi Germany were well known, and Borgongini Duca, an early fan of the Fascist regime.[47] Recasting Catholic internationalism as an antiracist or anti-Fascist movement was a far cry from how Pius XII and these men conceived the Holy See's mission. Neither were Pius XII and his men interested renegotiating power relations with the Catholic community, as dissident movements might have hoped. Instead, Pius XII worked to reassert a hierarchical definition of Catholic power, even as dissidents and newborn Christian Democratic political movements began claiming leadership over what John Boyer has termed the Catholic "social civilization"—the interlocking network of civil society groups over which the papacy, since Pius XI, had asserted its control.[48]

All of Pius XII's early actions spoke volumes about his redoubled commitment to centralizing authority in the person of the pope and protecting Catholic legal internationalism and cultural anticommunism. In one of his first acts as pope, Pacelli penned a letter to Hitler remarking on the goodness both of the Reichskonkordat and of relations between the Holy See and Germany. He made peace with French Action—the anti-Semitic, Fascist-sympathizing movement condemned in the 1920s by both Pius XI and Jacques Maritain. Then Pius XII celebrated the 1939 opening of the latest anticommunist exhibition of the

Pope Pius XII has his ring kissed by a general during an audience with Franco's troops at the Vatican on June 11, 1939. Credit: AP Photo

Secretariat on Atheism, whose success was due in part to the support it received from both Nazi German and Italian Fascist officials.[49] Following Franco's seizure of Madrid, Pius gave a warm welcome to Franco's troops, whom he treated to a formal audience. He sent a high-profile letter to the General, in which he asserted, "We sincerely give thanks, along with Your Excellency, for this long-desired Catholic victory in Spain."[50] Less than two weeks after Eugenio Pacelli rose to the Throne of St. Peter, when Germany invaded Czechoslovakia in violation of the Munich agreement, the new pope issued no response. These back-to-back words, actions, and inactions sent a clear message: papal anti-Nazism and anti-Fascism were definitively off the table. Distraught Catholic dissidents bitterly commented that Pius XII's early moves as pope were "enough to make one cry and laugh at the same time!"[51]

Then, on August 23, 1939, Nazi Germany and the Soviet Union signed a nonaggression agreement. The Molotov-Ribbentrop Pact partitioned Poland between Germany and the Soviet Union, and effectively sealed the fate of this Catholic stronghold in Eastern Europe. The pope was beside himself. How could a regime that had been built on anticommunism and had just helped "defeat communism" in Spain, reach a formal, written accord with the Soviet Union?

For many of the Catholic dissidents who adhered to an alternative view of the Church's international mission, Hitler's action came as no surprise. They saw Nazism and communism as totalitarian evils and did not find it shocking that these movements would find common cause. "The beast is revealing itself more and more," Jacques Maritain confided to a friend, adding that "from a spiritual point of view" the Molotov-Ribbentrop Pact might even be a net good, in that "it will illuminate the consciences and gain the Church fighters for liberation."[52] Emmanuel Mounier issued a similar response, as his journal *Esprit* asserted that "Russia's desire for power can no longer hide itself behind the working class, just as Nazi imperialism can no longer hide itself behind the German nation."[53] Luigi Sturzo was galvanized by the shock of the Molotov-Ribbentrop Pact to deepen his theorizing of a future international order that was Christian, democratic, and neither Nazi nor Communist.[54]

Pius XII's response to the Pact was more diplomatic in nature. Through an anxious string of meetings, letters, and telegrams sent to Berlin and Munich, he frantically tried to get the Pact repealed. He asked Italian officials to use their connections with Germany to apply whatever pressures they could to get Germany to overturn Molotov-Ribbentrop.[55] (The Italians, embarrassed, conceded that they had lost much of their influence over the Germans.) Then Pius XII implored German diplomats to rethink their actions. The German foreign minister, Joachim von Ribbentrop, informed the pontiff that his reactions were exaggerated. After all, he said, was Hitler not the world's leading anticommunist? Did it bear repeating that if Hitler had not risen to power to save Germany, "not even one church would have remained standing, as happened in Russia"? "National Socialism has prevented the triumph of communism in Germany," Ribbentrop asserted. "In the years 1930–1932 . . . communism was about to triumph. Hitler beat it."[56] Pius XII and papal diplomats informed Ribbentrop that even though the Nazi movement had crushed communism in the early

1930s, signing a pact with the Soviet Union could never be condoned. In a conversation with the Spanish ambassador to the Holy See, a close aide to Pius XII, Monsignor Domenico Tardini, expressed his concerns: "The Spanish know through painful experience what communism means. They thought they had delivered a serious blow to communism, defeating it in Spain. Instead now they see [that] . . . even he who had helped Spain against communism is entering into agreements with Stalin."[57] Like Tardini, many papal officials saw the Molotov-Ribbentrop Pact as a brazen betrayal of a core component of the Nazi-Vatican alliance and of the Holy See's anticommunist crusade. It meant that Nazi Germany could not be trusted, in that it was willing to put diplomacy over doctrine even on the most crucial issue of fighting international communism.

Papal perceptions of Nazi Germany only worsened when on September 1, 1939, Nazi Germany began its brutal invasion of "most Catholic" Poland. Hitler's aim with the invasion was to create new "living space," or *Lebensraum*, for the "German race." At 4:20 a.m., German airplanes began dropping seventy tons of bombs on the Polish city of Wielun—a city that was completely bereft of strategic significance. By the time a German administrator arrived on foot to survey the damage, most of the city's buildings had been destroyed, including the church, the synagogue, and the hospital. "There were more corpses than live people."[58] As German officials saw things, these massacres of Poles—Christian and Jewish—were essential in order to create the imagined Greater Germany. "For us," Heinrich Himmler asserted, "the end of this war will mean an open road to the east." But to usher in the new meant clearing out the old. "All Poles will disappear from the world," Himmler dryly asserted.[59] Though Himmler did not end up being quite right, Poland would be one of the four countries (along with Yugoslavia, the USSR, and Greece) that suffered the highest numbers of civilian and military deaths, in proportion to their populations. By war's end, Poland had lost about 20 percent of its prewar population, including a far higher percentage of the Polish intelligentsia.[60]

On September 17, 1939, the Red Army crossed the border into Poland. The Polish Republic had to fend for itself. For though Poland had secured guarantees of military assistance from Britain and France, these two countries were not ready to commit troops to battle. Out-numbered and fighting with the most rudimentary weapons, the Polish Army was quickly destroyed. Warsaw fell on September 27. The papal nuncio to Poland, Filippo Cortesi, abandoned the city, as did August Hlond, the Primate of Poland. National Democracy, the Catholic right-wing political movement that had established a close working relationship with the Polish Catholic Church and the Holy See, im-ploded. On September 28, 1939, a new German-Soviet treaty parti-tioned the country. Independent Poland, a shining interwar example of concordat diplomacy, was no more.

The Führer had ordered the elimination of all perceived enemies of Germany—and given the association between Catholicism and Polish nationalism, many German soldiers saw Catholics as enemies of *Lebensraum*. By the end of 1939 the Germans had killed more than 200 Catholic priests, and imprisoned about 1,000 more. They had also closed down Catholic churches, monasteries, and convents. By the end of the conflict, about 2,600, or 20 percent, of Polish clergy had been killed by the Nazis. From the autumn of 1939 through 1941, the Polish people experienced a reign of terror—and though Jews ranked lower than Poles in Nazi racial classifications, non-Jewish Catholic Poles were targeted aggressively as well, because of their prominent role in Polish society. (Of the 6 million Polish citizens who were even-tually killed during the war years, approximately half were Polish Gentiles.)[61]

Pius XII was regularly informed of developments by reports from high-ranking Polish prelates, who focused on Germany's anti-Catholic actions. The prelates argued that "Hitlerism aims at the systematic and total destruction of the Catholic Church in the rich and fertile ter-ritories of Poland." As these prelates saw things, Germany's actions in Poland were part of a broader plan to eliminate the potential threat of Catholic civil society to the Nazi dictatorship. Just a few months be-fore the start of the war, the last Catholic youth groups in Germany had been dissolved, and membership in Nazi youth groups had be-come compulsory for all boys and girls between the ages of ten and eighteen. With some reason, the Polish prelates saw Nazi behavior in Poland as part of a broader pattern.[62]

As a result of the Molotov-Ribbentrop Pact and the invasion of Poland, Pius XII, behind closed doors, belatedly reached the conclusion that Adolf Hitler was a calculating politician who cared neither about the destruction of international communism, nor about the protection of Catholicism.[63] Motivated by a desire to annul the effect of the Molotov-Ribbentrop Pact and reconstitute the anti-Soviet front, Pius XII briefly acted as a go-between for the British government and a group of German generals plotting Hitler's overthrow.[64] He quietly welcomed diplomatic talks with a personal representative of the American president, Franklin Delano Roosevelt, who since 1938 had been cultivating the papacy's attentions, in what Eleanor Roosevelt later characterized as "one of the wise preliminary steps in the preparation for war."[65] In response to inquisitive questions, the pope specified that the talks opening up with the United States were motivated by a desire to halt Soviet antireligious behavior, create a bulwark against international communism, and bring the emerging global conflict to a speedy end. The talks, he informed skeptics in his own ranks, did not indicate a change of course when it came to papal anti-liberalism.[66]

Ever the careful diplomat, in public Pius XII did not lambast liberalism, but neither did he highlight Nazism's crimes: instead, his focus remained, as before, on defending concordats and fighting communism. In the very first encyclical of his pontificate, *Summi Pontificatus*, he sang the praises of the concordat project. Released one month after the invasion of Poland and the start of World War II, the encyclical was oddly timeless in character. In keeping with the key precepts of the concordat moment, it affirmed that it is an "error . . . to divorce civil authority from every kind of dependence upon the Supreme Being . . . and from every restraint of a Higher Law derived from God." As St. Thomas Aquinas taught, the task of the state was to help individuals "reach their supernatural end." For this reason, "to tear the law of nations from its anchor in Divine law, to base it on the autonomous will of states, is to dethrone that very law and deprive it of its noblest and strongest qualities." Concordats, Pacelli suggested, were the key to ensuring that the "law of nations" would be anchored in "divine law." They protected human and Catholic rights, rights that were granted by the Creator insofar as human beings and their rights "are by nature anterior to the state."[67] As Pius XII underscored in the first Christmas broadcast of his pontificate, the "norms of divine law" and "natural law" must play a central role in the "new order in Europe" that would result from the war—something that concordats were adept at guaranteeing.[68] Meanwhile, through back-channel diplomacy, papal officials attempted to pressure Nazi Germany to honor the Polish concordat.[69]

When Polish Catholics read *Summi Pontificatus*, they were shocked and angered by the fact that the encyclical's only mention of the invasion of their country was in a passing allusion to "Our dear Poland," whose soil, the pontiff noted, had been stained by "the blood of countless human beings, even noncombatants." For Polish Catholics, the overly vague reference to the current war was wholly inadequate. After all, for months they had been pressuring the pope to speak. Added to this, Polish Catholics were disappointed that the Primate August Cardinal Hlond had immediately gone into exile, with many Poles wishing that he had instead followed the lead of clerics like the archbishop of Krakow, Adam Sapieha, who had remained at his post. The Polish president-in-exile, Wladislas Raczkiewicz, expressed his frustrations with the Vatican on more than one occasion. He and others wondered why the pope had forsaken them—and what side he was really on. There was even some conversation in Polish Catholic circles about breaking ties to Rome.[70]

As they read Pius XII's first encyclical, *Summi Pontificatus*, non-Polish Catholic dissidents were further disappointed—not least because of the presence of a passage pertaining to Italy. In a striking reversal of Pius XI's plan to speak out against Mussolini on the tenth anniversary of the Lateran Agreements, in 1939 Pius XII used this early public state-ment to send a different message. "Our heart is joyous especially at the thought that We can . . . rank among such friendly powers Our dear Italy, fruitful garden of Faith." In place of denouncing Italy for its failure to comply with the Lateran Agreements through its renewed persecution of Catholic Action and for its recent discriminatory Race Laws, Pius XII announced that "as a result of the Lateran Pacts, [Italy's] represen-tative occupies a place of honor among those officially accredited to the Apostolic See. 'The Peace of Christ Restored to Italy,' like a new dawn of brotherly union in religious and civil intercourse, had its beginning in these Pacts."[71] With this October 1939 message, Pacelli suggested that

Italy embodied the sort of perfect Catholic state to which the rest of his encyclical alluded. *Civiltà Cattolica* emphasized that "the encyclical includes a page that bestows high honors on Italy, Italy as she is today," adding that because "our totalitarian state is a Catholic state," there was no need to worry about potential contrasts between the Church and the Fascist regime.[72] Two months later, on December 28, 1939, Pius XII praised Italy again, announcing in a speech at the Palazzo Quirinale that "the Vatican and the Quirinal" were "reunited by the bond of peace." Witnessing this renewed peace, "Italy watches and exults, [and] the Catholic world watches and exults."[73] To be sure, statements like these were part of Pius XII's attempt to get Mussolini to restrain Hitler. But they also constituted a genuine hymn of praise for Italy's choice to go the concordat route.

The papal agenda to defend concordat victories and celebrate Catholic states was, it appeared, intact. So was papal anticommunism. In the autumn of 1939, Pius XII came out strongly against the Soviet occupation of Lithuania, which he called "the last Catholic stronghold in northern Europe."[74] He publicly denounced the Soviet invasion of Finland. Speaking out against what he called a "calculated act of aggression against a small, industrious, and peaceful nation," Pius XII showed himself more willing to praise the military defeat of left-wing rule than to oppose Nazism's ruthless aggression in the east.[75] Regarding Poland's invasion, Pius XII had been ambiguous on the question of guilt; by contrast, when it came to the Soviet invasion of Finland, he was crystal clear. Even the spring 1940 Nazi rampage through Western Europe and the fall of France elicited muted reactions from the pope. Partly this had to do with local circumstances. The fact that many Catholics in Belgium, the Netherlands, Slovakia, and Croatia accepted Germany's presence, and even sought to introduce the Nazi New Order, mattered, as did the rallying of the French Catholic Church and much of the French laity to the conservative and Catholic Vichy regime. (Indeed, even some prominent members of the dissident Catholic movement, like Emmanuel Mounier, showed interest in the Vichy experiment.)[76] But the pope's silence was also due to a lack of new thinking in trying times. In 1940 Pius XII gave a disturbing allocution in which he affirmed that the Paris peace settlement had not created a necessary basis for peace, alluding to Germany's "vital necessities."

Was Pius XII an apologist for the Nazi New Order or a critic of it? Many observers were not sure.[77]

At the height of World War I, Benedict XV had loudly presented himself as a figure eager to craft a new international order. During World War II, by contrast, Pius XII seemed content to play a backseat role. If the Nazi New Order did not elicit a clear reaction from the pope, neither did American plans for a new postwar international system. In January 1941 the American president, Franklin Delano Roosevelt, articulated his vision for a new "kind of world," defined as "the very antithesis of the so-called 'new order' of tyranny." FDR's vision was based on a call to social and liberal democracy and a disarmed peace—freedom of speech and religion, and freedom from want and fear. The pope had nothing much to say. His silence spoke volumes. He was unprepared or unwilling to counter either the resurgence of American internationalism or the Nazi New Order.

A rival brand of Catholic internationalism, which had grown stronger in the aftermath of the Spanish Civil War, stepped into the void. A group founded by Sturzo in London in the late 1930s, known as People and Freedom, was spawning the creation of similar groups in the United States and Italy, all similarly committed to upholding and expanding the Catholic democratic tradition, *contra* both Nazism and communism. Other venues for fostering transnational contacts were also proliferating. Anti-Fascist and anti-Nazi Catholics flocked, for instance, to a series of lectures and meetings organized by Jacques Maritain and other Catholics in New York City, at Hunter College and at the École Libre des Hautes Études, a "university-in-exile" for French intellectuals in New York.[78] Several Czech, Polish, Belgian, and French politicians also entered governments-in-exile, and began planning for postwar reconstruction.[79] The anti-Nazi and anti-Fascist Catholics who had forged alliances and protested the Church's support of Franco were now activating themselves.

As these new Catholic internationalists explained, the postwar order they imagined had several component parts. Democracy, regional cooperation, and the creation of a new and more effective League of Nations, they argued, all went hand-in-hand, and all were essential for the creation of a new and peaceful Europe. The trouble with the interwar order was that it had not given supranational institutions enough power to govern global affairs. Sturzo's People and Freedom group called for "A New League of Nations Now," and Maritain emphasized that "the nations must choose between the prospect of aggravated, irremediable chaos and a strenuous effort at cooperation, working with patience and perseverance towards a progressive organization of the world in a supranational community."[80]

In the United States, a petition that Maritain helped write—"In the Face of the World's Crisis: A Manifesto by European Catholics Sojourning in America"—called upon Catholics to fight totalitarianism (Fascist, Nazi, and Bolshevik) and create a new world order that defended democracy and human rights.[81] Maritain built on the manifesto, which was signed by forty-three Catholic intellectuals, in various wartime articles, emphasizing that Nazism and communism were secular ideologies that erroneously sought to "claim human rights and dignity—without God." He elaborated on these ideas again in a wartime pamphlet, *Christianity and Democracy*, which was one of the first documents to yoke the new language of rights with the claim that a natural bond existed between Christianity and democracy.[82] As an analyst for the U.S. State Department wrote in a confidential report, the pamphlet could be "of primary importance in such countries as France, Belgium, Spain, Portugal, and Italy, where the official propaganda line represents democracy as bourgeois, decadent, and anti-Christian, and tries to use the Catholic Church as a totalitarian tool."[83] Indeed, as a result of their commitments, Sturzo, Maritain, and many other left-Catholic refugees were enthusiastic about the 1941 Atlantic Charter, and its promise to build an international order that would defend human rights and the national self-determination of all peoples, including those in colonial empires. Additionally, thanks to their experiences in liberal-democratic countries, they favored the idea of Great Britain and the United States playing a leading role in the new organization.[84]

The pope, for most of the war, refused to take a stand on these new visions for international order. The contrast with the World War I years was dramatic. The papacy of 1915–1918 had presented itself as the dogged advocate of a postwar settlement that stood in sharp contrast to that delineated by figures like Woodrow Wilson. During World War II, Pius XII gave up on the project of outlining a clear vision for postwar Europe—despite the fact that a newly vocal set of Catholic internationalists was doing so. When the new Catholic internationalists begged the pope for a word of support, he politely demurred. When American interlocutors pressured the pope to express support for the Atlantic Charter, he fell mute.

On June 22, 1941, Hitler violated the Molotov-Ribbentrop Pact and invaded Russia, as well as Lithuania, Latvia, and Estonia—three countries that, according to the 1939 pact between Germany and the Soviet Union, were all within the Soviet "sphere." Mussolini promptly sent in Italian troops, as did Hungary, Slovakia, Romania, and Spain. The war that followed would be no regular conflict; instead it aimed at eliminating, in Hitler's words, "Jewish Bolsheviks" from vast swaths of territory in Russia and Eastern Europe. "We are joined by common ideals," Baldur von Schirach affirmed at the Hitler Youth championships before an international audience in Breslau, in the summer of 1941, as he spoke of the pan-European anti-Soviet coalition. "We are brothers and sisters in the fight for freedom of the European spirit and against the Bolshevik terror . . . We march and we fight for these ideals."[85]

Throughout the Nazi invasion of Russia (June 22–December 5, 1941), Axis propaganda drew heavily on themes from the 1930s Catholic anticommunist campaign. It emphasized that communism was Godless and opposed to basic family values.[86] It freely used the term "crusade," asserting that a "European crusade against Bolshevism" was advisable and necessary.[87] In Catholic-majority Axis powers, the war was even sold as a strategy for bringing about the mass conversion of Russians to Catholicism.[88] Finally, the Axis repeatedly and insistently referenced the Spanish Civil War, presenting Operation Barbarossa (the Axis invasion of the Soviet Union) as the Spanish Civil War's natural next step. Juxtaposing photographs of the burning and looting of churches in Spain with shots of recent Soviet occupation practices, wartime propaganda sought to encourage residents in Axis countries to connect the Spanish Civil War to the invasion of Russia. The soldier-protagonist of a Fascist radio play that was quite popular at the time asserted: "I saw Bolshevism in Spain . . . I saw churches blown up by a

"Victory: The Crusade Against Bolshevism." Vichy French propaganda poster presenting the war against the Soviet Union as a holy crusade. Credit: Alamy Images

mine placed at the altar by the reds. The church was full of women and children gathered there to pray after the city was taken. The Bolsheviks lit candles at the altar because they knew people would come looking for God's comfort. It was a cowardly massacre. For that we are here [in Russia]!"[89]

Many Catholics in Axis countries fell in line. German bishops repeatedly rehearsed the "Catholicism versus Godless communism" binary, as did members of the Italian clergy.[90] Some prominent Fascist-sympathizing Catholic intellectuals gave the invasion an apocalyptic luster, arguing that only through the Italian and German destruction of the Soviet Union would a new *societas christiana* come into being.[91] In France, one of Pius XII's close friends, Monsignor Mayol de Luppé, agreed to become chaplain of the anticommunist and philo-Nazi *Ligue des Volontaires français contre le Bolchevisme*.[92] In Spain, newspapers referred to the invasion of the Soviet Union as being analogous to the Spanish crusade against the Comintern.[93] In the United States, Catholic prelates freely quoted *Divini Redemptoris*, indicating their support for the invasion and their concern over the provision of American military aid to the Soviets. In Italy, the clerically supervised Catholic Cinema Center, run by Catholic Action activists, used the invasion as an opportunity to warmly recommend the viewing of several films on the Spanish Civil War, including Augusto Genina's *Siege of Alcazar*, which presented the Manichean story of how the royal palace of Séville, having been assailed by "Red hoards," was "saved" by the "troops of *Generalissimo* Franco."[94]

Given the preponderance of Catholic support for Operation Barbarossa, many observers assumed that the pope would jump on the bandwagon. Italy's Fascist officials were convinced that the Church would "return to the side of the [Fascist] regime" and issue a statement in support of the invasion.[95] The Germans were similarly hopeful that Barbarossa would win back the pope, who was, they thought, duty-bound to supporting this "crusade" against Bolshevism.[96] They were heartened when in August 1941 Pius XII failed to issue any statement in favor of the Allied cause and the recently concluded Atlantic Charter, despite repeated American urgings to do so.[97] Perhaps the pope was preparing the ground for his belated and expected endorsement of Barbarossa.

But contrary to Nazi and Fascist expectations, Pius XII did not endorse the invasion. By way of explanation, he told the flummoxed Italian ambassador to the Holy See that Nazism was persecuting the church, and that until the invasion of the Soviet Union in June 1941, the Third Reich had been Russia's ally.[98] This proved that the Third Reich was a fickle anticommunist power: the only genuine anticommunist power in Europe was the Vatican.[99] Papal officials went a step further, informing their Fascist counterparts that there was certainly a need for a crusade against the Soviet Union, but that the Nazis were "not the crusaders" the Church had in mind.[100] Revisiting a form of Catholic anti-totalitarianism that suggested more equivalence between Nazism and communism than the Church had thus far felt comfortable articulating, these officials added that "communism is really atheistic and condemnable—but very condemnable as well is Nazism." Privately, papal diplomats close to Pius XII expressed the wish that Operation Barbarossa would inaugurate "the end of communism and Nazism alike."[101] An incensed Hitler prohibited the Holy See from sending any Catholic missions into Russia, encouraged the Wehrmacht to issue a flurry of orders that forbade field chaplains "any official church activity or religious propaganda toward the civilian population," and barred civilians from participating in field services. The orders further recommended that "none of the Catholic priests remain in the country" following the conclusion of the invasion. The reasoning, as articulated in a memorandum of the Reich Security Office, pointed back to World War I, and specifically to the Treaty of Brest-Litovsk: Nazi Germany wanted to take preventive measures to ensure that the Vatican would not "become the actual war profiteer in Russian territory that is being fought for with German blood."[102]

American officials saw their chance. If the pope was not willing to underwrite the German invasion of the Soviet Union, perhaps he would help the United States? Specifically, it would be a great boon if the pope could help quell American Catholic opposition to the United States' decision to extend Lend-Lease aid to the Soviet Union. In a bid to curry the pope's favor, at the height of Operation Barbarossa—when American officials surely had more urgent matters to attend to—FDR issued a strongly worded request that urged Russia to protect religion and religious freedom and suspend its antireligious policies. In September

1941 the Soviets, already bled white by the war, complied. In a surprising move that demonstrated how badly Russia needed Lend-Lease aid (and how concerned the Bolsheviks were about losing the consent of Russia's still-religious population in the context of a brutal war), the Russian Communist Party pivoted 180 degrees. The main organ of the Communist Party, *Pravda*, announced that the Soviet Union was prepared to take a stand against the invading "barbarous Fascist hoards, drunk with blood," who were persecuting Christians, both "Catholics and Protestants," and "devastating churches and violating the sacred vessels."[103] The Russian newspaper carefully refrained from presenting the Soviet Union as the defender of *all* religious populations in Eastern Europe—that is, as a protector of the Jewish population as well, which was at that time being brutally interned, shot dead, and gassed. Nonetheless, FDR was pleased. His core aim had been attained.

Hopeful about the prospects of finally shifting Catholic opinion at home, FDR informed the pope that a change was under way in the Soviet Union. The antireligious campaigns had been suspended, he noted, adding, rather implausibly, "the churches in Russia are open." (In 1941 only two of the 1,195 Catholic churches that had been open in 1917 were operational.[104]) "I believe that there is a real possibility that Russia may as a result of the present conflict recognize freedom of religion," he concluded.[105] Papal diplomats were initially suspicious. Showing the persistence of anti-liberalism in the highest echelons of the papal hierarchy, Pius XII's close aide Domenico Tardini commented on FDR's enthusiasm as follows: "For anyone concerned only with the moral and religious interests of the Russian people, there is only one way to save it: the destruction of Communism. But that is not Roosevelt's idea . . . For him, as a good American, religion is quite apart from politics. That is the liberal and democratic theory. It is wrong, for even the state as such has duties to God."[106]

The pessimism of Pius XII's inner circle was soon put in check when one of only two Catholic priests still in the Soviet Union, an American Catholic by the name of Father Braun, began defending Roosevelt's claims. In a letter addressed directly to the pope, Father Braun announced that the American president had succeeded in getting Soviet leaders to bow under pressure and suspend their decades-long campaign

against Christians and Christianity. He counseled the Vatican to trust
FDR and also press the restart button with the Soviet Union. Perhaps
now was the time to pursue a concordat or *modus vivendi* with Bolshevik leaders. "This is, if ever, the time to act," he wrote. "We must
beat the iron while it is hot and obtain from these people what they
would be only too willing to grant."[107]

In light of these and similar reports, Pius XII belatedly agreed to
the American request, and said he would try to change American Catholic opinion on Lend-Lease aid. On the same day that FDR officially
signed into law the approval of $1 billion in Lend-Lease aid to the
Soviet Union, the pope compelled the archbishop of Cincinnati,
John T. McNicholas, to release a pastoral letter. The statement hinged
on a rereading of *Divini Redemptoris,* and the introduction of a new
distinction between helping communism, which no Catholic could
ever do, and helping the Russian people in their moment of need
(coded as an act of Christian charity). In late October 1941 the largest
Jesuit publication in the United States, *America,* issued its conditional
support for Lend-Lease. The journal argued that once Nazism was
crushed, communism would surely fall as well. At that point Russia
would turn into "one of the greatest missionary fields in the world."[108]
Soon enough, leading American Catholic clerics such as Monsignor
John A. Ryan, Monsignor Fulton Sheen, and Archbishop Francis Spellman
made similar points in their speeches and publications. Their words,
of course, proved of enormous utility for the United States' own
movement toward war.[109]

The autumn of 1941 marked an important moment for both the
Holy See and the United States. In a historic first, a pope and an American head of state had shown that they were willing to work together
to bring American Catholics into line with U.S. foreign policy priorities. The Vatican had accepted that the United States—through its
work to protect the "religious freedom" of Christians in the Soviet
Union—was a potential ally in the struggle against communist atheism
in Russia. The pope's fall 1941 actions confirmed what the Vatican had
made clear throughout the interwar years: that its primary concern was
not with humanity at large, but with the treatment of European Catholics. The fact that the most blatant case of religious rights violations
in 1941 did not pertain to Catholics but to Jews was of little matter.

The Jews were a group about which the pope said little for the entirety of the war.

The Papacy and the Holocaust

What came to be known as the Holocaust began with the invasion of the Soviet Union. In June 1941, four mobile killing units or death squads, the *Einsatzgruppen,* followed the German army as its invasion of the Soviet Union advanced. Drawing on local civilian and police support, they began by carrying out mass shootings, as a result of which as many as 2.2 million Jewish and Roma people were killed and thrown into hastily dug pits. At first only men were targeted, but by July, women and children were being massacred too. Beginning in the late autumn of 1941, gas vans appeared on the Eastern Front, and industrialized killing began. By war's end, some one million Jews residing in the prewar Soviet Union had been murdered, along with about 3 million Polish Jews. The next-largest groups massacred were Romanian, Hungarian, and Czechoslovak Jews.

The mass killing of what the Nazis contemptuously referred to as *Ostjuden,* "Jews of the east" (a phrase that was used to intentionally conjure up the Judeo-Bolshevik myth), was supposed to be phase one of the exterminatory project. Had the Nazis been able to reshape the European continent in the way they hoped, by the end of the winter of 1941–1942 the so-called Hunger Plan, which envisioned a programmed death-by-starvation, would have killed an additional 30 million people in Soviet territories. Horrifically, the Hunger Plan was, in turn, supposed to be a prelude to *Generalplan Ost,* which envisaged the elimination of an additional 50 million Slavic individuals as Nazi Germany completed its "colonization" of western Russia. In sum, Germany imagined that in its invasion of the Soviet Union, it would massacre and eliminate from view over half of the country's prewar population of 170 million people.[110] Ramón Serrano Suñer, the president of the Falange's political board and the Interior and Foreign Affairs Minister, was not misrepresenting Axis ambitions when he celebrated Operation Barbarossa and its accompanying violence as the "extermination of Russia," which, as the Axis saw it, was a "requirement of History and for the future of Europe."[111]

Starting from 1942, the Nazis began implementing the decision to murder all European Jews. According to the Nazi plan, the continent's Jews would be transported to death camps and work camps, where they would either be used for slave labor or killed immediately. By 1943 about 3 million Jews had already been murdered in death camps. Germany's acts of inhumanity and brutality did not lead most European Catholics residing in Axis territories to rise up in opposition. Indeed, many inhabitants in concordat strongholds were willing participants in the slaughter. In Poland, the episodes of barbaric anti-Semitic violence are almost too many too name, as are the numbers of local Catholics who willingly took part.[112] In Latvia, thanks to local assistance, 69,750 of the country's 80,000 Jews were killed by the end of 1941.[113] In Estonia, where Jews were few in number, locals killed all of the Jews they could find (963), and then proceeded to massacre about 5,000 non-Jewish Estonians as well, for the crime of ostensibly collaborating with the Soviet Union.[114] In Lithuania, where only 3.3 percent of the occupation administration was German, it was local residents who were responsible for identifying, rounding up, and killing both Jews and Soviet soldiers. Lithuanian Christians assisted, for instance, in the killing of more than 18,000 Jews in the city of Kovno, including more than 5,000 children. Before the violence occurred, the Jews of Kovno had appealed to the Catholic archbishop for assistance, but he had ignored their pleas.[115] Catholic-majority Western European countries also facilitated the slaughter. By the autumn of 1940, France had already excluded Jews from the civil service, as well as from the army, from education, and from the press. The laws were expanded through a supplementary decree of June 2, 1941, and applied to metropolitan France and Algeria, as well as to France's colonies, protectorates, and mandates.[116] In March 1942 the first transport of Jews left France. Beginning in September 1943, Italy was arresting and deporting Jews to concentration and extermination camps as well.

By early 1942 the Vatican became officially aware that Jews were being slaughtered in large numbers when the archbishop of Krakow, Sapieha, and the Metropolitan Szeptyckyj of Lvov sent detailed reports demonstrating the extent of the violence under way. In a report of February 1942, Metropolitan Szeptyckyj asserted that "the Jews are the first victims" of the Nazis' "horrible crimes, murders, robberies and rapes," and that "200,000 and more" Jews had been "killed in the first weeks" of the German occupation.[117] Reports from Slovakia, Germany, Latvia, Italy, Great Britain, and the United States soon poured in as well.[118] A few Lithuanian Catholic clergy raised their voices, charging that "anti-Bolshevik propaganda," interwoven with anti-Semitic motifs, remained a staple feature of Vatican Radio broadcasts to Lithuania, even though "such broadcasts only provoke the state authorities here" and provide "'information' that is after all very far removed from the true, exact reality."[119] By September 1942, Under-Secretary of State Montini (later Pope Paul VI) affirmed: "The massacres of the Jews have assumed atrocious and frightening forms and proportions."[120]

Initially Pius XII was skeptical about the veracity of the reports, as were leading figures in the Allied governments. But by the end of 1942, few "could seriously doubt that the Germans had, indeed, embarked on a final solution of the Jewish 'problem,' as they called it."[121] But instead of speaking out against anti-Semitism and the murder of Jews in Eastern Europe, the pope refrained from public comment. He came the closest in an annual address to the College of Cardinals, when he spoke of victims who were "destined sometimes, even without guilt on their part, to exterminatory measures,"[122] and in his Christmas message of 1942, when he declared, "Humanity owes this vow to those hundreds of thousands who, without any fault of their own, sometimes only by reason of their nationality or race, are marked down for death or gradual extinction." At the same time, the potential strength of the pope's message was diluted through his use of the burdened term "crusade," as he called for a "holy crusade" against those who declare war on the "darkness of alienation from God," highlighting the fact that the Church had "always condemned the various systems of Marxist socialism."[123] As several historians have concluded on the basis of documentary evidence from the time, "no one, certainly not the Germans, took [the 1942 Christmas address] as a protest against their slaughter of the Jews."[124]

Faced with the Holocaust's brutality, other members of the Catholic upper hierarchy limited themselves to condemning "human suffering" in the most general terms. The furthest that German bishops felt comfortable going was to inform the faithful that "killing is in itself a wrong," and that Catholics should have special regard for "the innocent people who are not of our *Volk* and blood," whom the bishops defined as "the resettled," "prisoners," and "foreign workers."[125] This same text, which studiously avoided any mention of the Jews, did say that racially mixed marriages were indissoluble—something that was in direct contradiction to the Nuremberg laws, and something that, again, demonstrated the Church's special concern for Catholics and Catholic converts.[126] As murderous violence raged under their windows, the papal nuncios to Slovakia, France, and Hungary all informed the Holy See of their disapproval of violent persecutions of Jews, even as they noted that a moderate "containment" of Jews was advisable, given their disproportionate influence in European society.[127] *Civiltà Cattolica*, along similar lines, approved of the Hungarian government's decision to limit the rights of Jews in economic and intellectual life by asserting that Hungary was within its full rights to take measures to ensure the "defense of national traditions, and the defense of the true liberty and independence of the Hungarian people." Hungary's anti-Semitic laws, according to the Jesuit journal, were praiseworthy in that they assisted with the fortification of this Central European "Catholic nation."[128]

It is important not to oversimplify the reaction of Pius XII and the Holy See to the Holocaust. In some cases and under certain conditions, the pope did intervene, with studied caution, to assist Jewish and Catholic refugees. In one famous case, the pope attempted to facilitate the emigration of Jewish converts to Catholicism from Germany to Brazil. He also provided a small sum of money—about $2,000—to assist Jewish converts to Catholicism in Vienna. When it came to the deportation of Jews from Slovakia and Hungary, the pope intervened repeatedly.[129] However, the fact remains that the Vatican could have done more to assist Jewish refugees across the continent. Not only did Pius XII and other papal officials fail to speak out clearly to condemn German atrocities; they also did not share in a timely manner the information they were receiving about the Holocaust, or provide financial assistance to a range of organizations (including Catholic resistance organizations) that were working to protect Jews on the ground.

The Response of Catholic Dissidents

The weakness of the official Vatican response to Nazi atrocities was noted immediately. Harold H. Tittman, the assistant to President Roosevelt's personal representative to the Vatican, reported in 1942 that Catholics in Eastern Europe had "no patience with arguments to the effect that intervention by the Holy See would only worsen their plight." The English minister to the Holy See, Francis d'Arcy Osborne, observed that the "continued silence of the pope on the moral issues of the day, especially in the face of one notorious Nazi atrocity after another, has alarmed many loyal Catholics." In the autumn of 1942, the governments of the United States, Great Britain, Brazil, Uruguay, and Belgium, as well as the Polish government-in-exile, informed Pius XII that his "policy of silence" would "necessarily involve a renunciation of moral leadership and a consequent atrophy of the influence and authority of the Vatican."[130]

Catholic dissidents were particularly sensitive to the Vatican's failure to speak out against Nazi terror. Figures like Yves Simon, Jacques Maritain, Henri de Lubac, Luigi Sturzo, and Paul Vignaux penned fiery tracks and letters, lamenting that the pope's behavior had left "Catholicity . . . very much compromised," and that it was becoming "more and more difficult, really impossible, to defend the neutrality of the present-day Vatican."[131] A group of American Catholics led by John A. Ryan founded the Committee of Catholics for Human Rights; its purpose was to argue strongly against racism and anti-Semitism, suggesting that "natural law demands that all human rights be afforded to all human beings."[132]

Some Catholic dissidents sought to use their positions of prominence to push the upper clergy to denounce the Nazi persecution of European Jews. In France, in response to the second round of anti-Semitic legislation passed in 1941, Henri de Lubac and some of his colleagues at the Faculty of Theology of Lyons informed all French cardinals: "It is not permitted to be silent, [for] even only our silence" signals approval of "the anti-Semitic propaganda disseminated throughout our country and the legislative measures against the Jews."[133] Striking a similar tone, the clandestine journal with which de Lubac was closely associated, *Cahiers du témoignage chrétien* ("Christian witness notebooks"), asserted: *"People of France, Christians, we are now solemnly breaking this silence.* Should it last any longer, this silence would overburden our consciences and force the world to conclude that we are complicit—all of France, and especially Christian France."[134]

Jacques Maritain joined the outcry, coming out strongly against anti-Semitism and "the tragic situation in which the Jews at present find themselves." If "a state resort[s] to the extermination of certain levels of its population," Maritain cautioned, it is not "offering proper political solutions" to the real "problem of national minorities" and their integration into national communities; instead, it is providing "only an apparent cure from a surgical operation not even aseptic but, in fact, infected with hate and injustice." Jews in Europe, he said, were being denied "purely and simply the right to exist," through appeal to specious stereotypes popularized by "the Hitler propaganda machine," which, among other things, "charge[d] the Jews with the sins of Bolshevism, [by] identifying Judaism and communism."[135] Instead, Maritain highlighted, what Catholics should do is recognize the historic "achievement of cooperation among men of different creeds," and support pluralist states, not exclusivist ones that "excised" non-Christians and massacred them in large numbers.[136]

These Catholic pleas had little effect on either the Holy See or most of the French episcopate. In August 1942 only five brave bishops in the French Catholic Church would speak out against Vichy's complicity in the deportation of Jews, arguing that "the Jews are our brothers," but in tandem the French Assembly of Cardinals issued a generic and weak call for respect for the human person and charity unto all.[137] The Vatican nuncio to France, Valerio Valeri, toed a similar line, limiting his protest of France's new anti-Semitic laws to a complaint to the Vichy government about the "grave inconveniences" from the religious point of view of the new legislation.[138] Meanwhile, behind the scenes the Holy See made it known that it was not happy about the activism of Catholic dissidents.[139] One of the leading guardians of Catholic doctrine in these years, the Dominican Father Réginald Garrigou-Lagrange, a close confidant for Pius XII, expressed his displeasure, counseling action against these Catholic objectors.[140]

In the summer of 1942, Maritain, writing from his North American exile, was personally informed of the "disquiet" aroused in French and Roman milieus by "his current ideas."[141] He responded that it would be more appropriate for them to "worry over . . . the Holy Church, which is made vulnerable today by those who would compromise it with the Fascist 'new order' . . . When a Christian has understood that, he has to choose at the price of risks and perils, and not take refuge in a patronizing neutrality." Maritain's anger redoubled in late 1942 and early 1943, when, in response to Allied bombers striking cities in northern Italy, the pope responded swiftly and with strong words, openly warning that attacking Italian cities would turn Catholic opinion against the Allies. When the war was at the pope's doorstep, it seemed, he could find the resolve to speak out.[142]

In the meantime, small Catholic resistance groups were taking matters into their own hands. By 1942 they were active both in occupied territories and in Italy and Germany. Some engaged in active military resistance against Axis forces; others resisted Nazi-Fascism through nonviolent means—for instance, by helping workers who were at risk of deportation to Germany. Intellectuals who had been disseminating anti-Nazi and anti-Fascist tracts for decades received a young cohort of new assistants, and spawned influential clandestine press operations encouraging Catholics to take action against the Axis powers. Still, the resistance was no mass phenomenon and the Catholic resistance was a fringe within the fringe. Robert d'Harcourt, a French Catholic member of the armed resistance movement, noted, "The sociological mass of Catholics is not ready for resistance. Most people don't enjoy living like outlaws, and most don't have the vocation to become martyrs."[143]

Nonetheless, Catholic anti-totalitarian sentiments were certainly on the rise, particularly from early 1943 on. In the summer of 1943 a group of Italian Catholic intellectuals, politicians, and civil society activists gathered in a private home in Rome to draft a clandestine text: *Christian Democracy's Ideas for Reconstruction*. Authored by Alcide De Gasperi, the future leader of the Italian Christian Democratic party, the text called for the creation of a democratic, post-Fascist order and support for a new international oversight mechanism to take the place

Pius XII on a rare venture beyond Vatican City, visiting Roman neighborhoods affected by the August 13 American air raid. Catholic dissidents expressed their frustration that the pope found a strength he had lacked during the entire conflict to clearly denounce acts of aggression. October 15, 1943. Credit: AP Photo of the League of Nations. In the fall of 1944 a number of French Catholic activists adopted their founding manifesto for a new Christian Democratic Party. It demanded the reestablishment of a republican regime and the reconstruction of France in keeping with "the basic principles of Christian civilization." In Germany the Christian Democratic Union was born in the summer of 1945; the organization's founding manifesto urged "all Christian, democratic and social forces to work together to build a new homeland." "Instead of the caricature of a national community created during the Hitler era," the manifesto continued, "we must now have a truly democratic state."[144]

As we will see in Chapter 8, Christian Democracy in the early postwar years was a diverse and contradictory phenomenon. There is no sense in which it was simply the child of the Catholic dissident movement discussed in this chapter. Though some partisans of the movement were inspired and influenced by the figures above, other first-hour Christian Democrats, even as they underwrote democracy, remained under the sway of the "rather undemocratic mentalities of the interwar years."[145] Furthermore, while some Christian Democrats came to the new political movement eager to welcome socialist and communist visions, others emphasized the imperative to fight against socialism and communism. Eventually these discrepancies would come to disturb the pope, who would plot a series of heavy-handed interventions aimed at pushing Christian Democratic Parties to espouse views closer to those of the Holy See.

✿

However, until late 1944, Pius XII paid little heed to the stirrings of the new Christian Democratic movement. Instead, the pope's chief concern was with the growth in Soviet power in Europe. His fears only increased after the battle of Stalingrad and with the uptick in communist activity in Rome and in northern Italy. It was in this context that the pope pushed England and the United States to break with the Russians and conclude a separate peace with Axis powers, insisting that doing so would help Germany deal with the Russian threat.[146] In his wartime conversations with Germany's ambassador to the Vatican, the pope affirmed that if Germany respected the terms of the concordat, then the Vatican would throw its weight behind the German crusade against Russia. In 1944, Pius XII wrote to Cardinal Michael Faulhaber, expressing his view that postwar Germany should include Austria and the Sudeten province of Czechoslovakia because an enlarged Germany was necessary to adequately face off the Soviet menace.[147] As the German ambassador reported to Berlin, "hostility to Bolshevism is, in fact, the most stable component of Vatican foreign policy."[148] In all of these exchanges, the pope spent no ink on explaining, defending, or promoting the Catholic resistance or the emerging Christian Democratic phenomenon.

The pope also held out longer than most the possibility of an Axis victory. Following the humiliating defeat at Stalingrad in February of 1943, the Soviet success in pushing Germany westward in the summer and autumn of 1943, and the Allied invasion of southern Italy in July 1943, it was clear that the Axis was going to lose the war. Nonetheless, the pope kept all lines of communication open, not wanting to hedge his bets. Only in May 1945—when the European war that had begun with Hitler's invasion of Poland ended with Germany's unconditional surrender—did the pope accept the Allied victory.

For the duration of World War II, the papacy and most of the upper hierarchy in Europe had given no strong signals that they were in alignment with anti-Nazi and anti-Fascist Catholic dissidents. Instead, the Holy See had continued to maintain an official position of neutrality, refraining from either publicly excoriating the Axis or praising the Allies. The pope remained rigidly committed to his anticommunist framework, and unwilling to intimate that Nazi-Fascism might be a greater threat to the Church (at least in the short term) than international communism. The papacy proffered silence in response to the slaughter of European Jewry. From 1945 through his death in 1958, Pius XII remained inflexible and unwilling to embrace antiracism, interfaith dialogue, or the idea that the New Europe must be built through the collaboration of people of *all* faiths (and of no faith). Well after the war had ended, the pope remained disinclined to denounce anti-Semitism, and uninterested in discussing the role of Catholics in perpetuating the crimes committed against the Jews during World War II.

Furthermore, in strong contrast to Benedict XV's behavior during World War I, Pius XII did not use his stature as pope to take a clear position on the alternative plans for global governance of the day. Though he spoke vaguely about the need for a new "juridical order," he did not flesh out this idea or explain whether a revised League of Nations would be the way to bring it about.[149] Neither did he explore how, apart from through concordats, states or non-state entities would be compelled to protect human rights.[150] Pius XII's stance on the United States' vision for a postwar Europe was similarly murky. Though he had agreed to work with the United States on a range of different issues, he did not underwrite the Atlantic Charter—but neither did he speak out against it. Similarly, though the pope had personally turned against Nazi Germany, he never clearly articulated his opposition to a potential Nazi New Order or how a papal-led Europe might prevent its resurgence. When in 1942 the Beveridge Report announced a new vision for a postwar order of social rights, the pope was silent. When in 1943–1944 new Christian Democratic parties began issuing their visions for postwar Europe—calling, for instance, for a *révolution par la loi* that would fuse political democracy with social democracy and avoid the extremes of both communism and liberal capitalism—the pope stayed moot. When, even after Allied victory was assured, the United States dropped two devastating atomic bombs on Hiroshima and Nagasaki, inaugurating the era of atomic warfare, the pope did not loudly protest.

The pope's silences and ambiguities had some short-term benefits. By presenting the Vatican as a neutral power, Pius XII was able to maintain relations with both the Axis and the Allies. Through his back-channel diplomacy, he was able to save the city of Rome from heavy destruction and a small number of Jews and Jewish converts to Catholicism from deportation. However, there was no getting around the fact that during the Spanish Civil War and World War II, a great breach had opened up within the Catholic world. Rather than one Catholic internationalist discourse, several now clamored for attention. Some celebrated the interwar concordat revolution; others sternly criticized it. Some advocated for a preservation and radicalization of the Church's interwar crusade against communist internationalism; others called for dialogue, emphasizing that communists and Catholics had more in common than met the eye. Some expressed rage and shame at the Church's interwar goodwill toward dictatorships and Fascism; others saw no need for apologies. Some demanded a reckoning of the Church with its long history of racism and anti-Judaism; others saw this as unessential. All signs indicated that a full-scale confrontation was on the horizon and that the war for the soul of Catholicism was ready to explode on the open stage. Curiously, however, as World War II wound to a close, the tensions receded and the Holy See enjoyed a period of extraordinary—and unexpected—popularity.

8

The Papal Agenda after World War II

All will quickly understand that right now the most important task, more important than any other, is to guarantee a fundamental law of the state for our future generations that is not opposed to moral and religious principles, but rather vigorously inspired by them—nay, that loudly announces them, and pledges to realize those principles to the utmost.

—PIUS XII, OCTOBER 19, 1945

POSTWAR CONDITIONS WERE propitious for the pope. With the implosion of Fascism and Nazism, many agreed that "Christianity [had emerged] as the only practical program for lasting peace and equitable order in our troubled world."[1] Popular piety boomed. The pope basked in the sun of the hour of the Church. He agreed to lend a hand to what Charles de Gaulle called "the great and sacred task of reconstruction."[2] And he welcomed the fact that so many (including Christian Democrats and American diplomats) seemed keen on partnering with the Holy See to place the continent back on its feet.

In 1945 the effects of World War II on the European continent were everywhere visible. The war had wrecked cities, razed towns, dislocated millions, and brutally reduced the continent's population. About 36.5 million Europeans had died between 1939 and 1945 in the war—an historically unprecedented death toll for a conflict lasting just six years. And it was not just soldiers who numbered among the dead, for World War II—which had been a total war—had claimed the lives of at least 19 million noncombatant civilians. Among these, almost

6 million had been Jews, slaughtered solely for the "crime" of being Jewish. Even after the official end of the conflict, suffering hung in the air. Malnutrition and hunger remained realities until well after the conclusion of hostilities. Typhoid, diphtheria, tuberculosis, broncho-pneumonia, typhus, and dysentery were also widespread.[3]

But despite genocide, forced migration, and mass suffering, World War II did not fundamentally transform the Holy See's understanding of itself and its mission in the world. As before the war, concordat di-plomacy and anticommunist mobilization remained central compo-nents of papal diplomacy. To be sure, following the fall of Fascism and Nazism, the papacy understood that it needed to cultivate new allies in pursuit of its old agenda. Already during World War II, the Vatican had taken stock of the growing economic and political importance of the United States as an international actor, and, in strong contrast to the behavior of popes like Benedict XV and Pius XI, did not spurn the newly powerful country; instead, the papacy enlisted it. Well before the launching of the Cold War, Pius XII and papal diplomats in his Curia lobbied hard to get the United States to break its wartime alliance with the Soviet Union, take a position against the expansion of Russian in-fluence in Eastern Europe, and support the undermining of Communist Parties in Western Europe. In the process, the papacy helped convince Europeans—and Americans—that the United States had a crucial role to play in the continent's moral and material reconstruction.

After the war, the papacy also agreed to work with Europe's new Christian Democratic Parties. By this point, Christian Democracy had become a political phenomenon that could not be ignored. In the mid-1940s, from the Netherlands to Belgium, from Germany to Italy, newly founded Christian Democratic Parties swept the polls. Their success was unprecedented, and surprising: most observers had guessed that World War II would swing open the doors to the left, not to a center-right, religiously defined movement. The Vatican showed its willing-ness to partner with the Christian Democrats by placing funds and civil society resources at their disposal. In exchange, the Vatican asked Christian Democrats to reconfirm concordats, embed tight Church–state relations in new postwar constitutions, and make anticommu-nism a core plank in party platforms. Thanks to papal influence, the Christian Democrats not only made concordats central to postwar legal systems; they also launched an all-out attack on communism that long predated the conflict that came to be known as the Cold War and the alignment of politics along two axes, pro-Soviet and pro-American.

As it turned to the United States and to Europe's new Christian Democratic Parties for assistance, the Vatican began to speak a new language that supported the creation of international organizations (including the United Nations), and that accepted the legitimacy of democratic states, on the condition that they define themselves in religious terms, and work in close partnership with the Holy See. Additionally, the pope underwrote an emergent legal-moral language: that of "human rights."[4]

Christian Human Rights

Pius XII's wartime references to human rights had been unsystematic, but it was inescapable that the pope had begun talking about human rights, just as Benedict had joined the national self-determination moment during World War I. Pius XII's wartime human rights talk focused on three elements: the importance of religious rights and their grounding in natural law; the necessity to rein in excessive state power; and the role that international law might play in protecting the rights and dignity of human beings. Ever the international lawyer, Pius XII especially emphasized the third element: that is, the centrality of human rights to the legal ordering of the international community. In three radio addresses broadcast in June 1941 and on Christmas in 1942 and 1944, Pacelli had begun articulating his notion of Christian human rights, when he affirmed that the "juridical order willed by God" brings into being "a definite sphere of rights, immune from all arbitrary attack."[5] Insofar as "natural law has primacy over [political] authority," it "puts limits on [state] sovereignty, and thus protects the rights and liberties of human beings against the excessive power of the state."[6] Reviving the buried anti-totalitarianism of the interwar years, Pacelli further emphasized that "individuals—each and every one—and families have certain rights and liberties which the state must always protect; which it must never violate or sacrifice to a pretended common good." The church defended these rights because it wanted to ensure that "neither the individual nor the family [become] absorbed by the state."[7]

The rights the church protected and guarded were rights upon which no state had the power to infringe, lest it cast itself against God and thus against the entire established order. The particular rights that Pius XII highlighted included the right to worship in public and private, the right to educate children in the faith, the right to private property, the right to marry in the faith, and the right to the priesthood or membership in a religious order. In other words, Pius XII insisted on the distinctly religious meaning of human rights and on the necessary link between natural law, human rights, and "Christian rights." Given this, it is unsurprising that Pius XII believed that to bring about a postwar order characterized by "the preservation of man's God-given rights," it was necessary to have "assurance of . . . the vital interests of the Vatican and of the Catholic Church."[8]

Beginning in 1944, Pacelli yoked his defense of human rights to democracy—and specifically to what he called not the *question*, but the *problem*, of democracy. As the pope saw it, the key problem was that democracy, on its own, was at best value-neutral and a worst a "vague and confused" set of ideas for how to govern. For Europe to truly recover from the cataclysm of the World War, Europeans and non-Europeans alike must erect governments wherein "Christ and his Church" were "the ultimate foundation and directing norm."[9] These governments, the pope asserted, *could* be democratic, but the key point was that they *must* be "based on the immutable principles of natural law and revealed truth," principles that their "spiritually eminent" leaders worked hard to defend. For Europe's future to be one of peace, "the religion of Christ and the Catholic Church must play an essential role in its realization." The new Europe would stand or fall depending on her willingness to embrace "the religion of Christ and the Catholic Church" and companion religious rights.[10] A few Catholic dissidents commented that "efforts to stampede the Roman Church into an explicit approval of democracy" had been "quixotic."[11] Some grumpy American Protestants noted that what Pius XII actually meant by "human rights" was not the rights of all human beings but instead the imperative to protect the Church's privileges, insofar as "only the truth has rights."[12]

Most hailed the Pontiff's sermon and his human rights talk as positive signals of a "modernizing" papacy.[13]

For Pacelli, as for most Americans and Europeans at the time, the emergent language of human rights was not a response to the Holocaust or Jewish suffering in World War II. In some circles, Catholic human rights talk was even taken in a deeply illiberal direction, and used to justify the continued privileging of rights-endowed Christians over others, including Jews.[14] Most often, however, postwar Catholic rights talk simply passed over in silence questions pertaining to Jewish citizens. A May 1945 human rights treaty drafted by a number of prominent European Catholic intellectuals and jurists—including Emmanuel Mounier, Joseph Hours, Jean-Jacques Chevallier, and Georges Cohendy—was typical in that its enthusiasm for "human rights" was not accompanied by any discussion of the recent genocide of European Jewry.[15] Similarly, the pope showed himself unwilling to reckon with the complicity of so many Catholics in the Holocaust and the horrors of World War II. This was true as well for Christian Democratic leaders in numerous Western European countries, who in the early postwar years began to speak out against totalitarian violations of human rights, condemning Nazi Germany and the Soviet Union even as they remained moot on the question of Jewish suffering.[16] Most postwar politicians, as well as the pope, indicated that they agreed with the statement put out by the daily newspaper of Italy's Christian Democratic party on the day of Hitler's death: "We have the strength to forget!," the paper avowed. "Forget as soon as possible!" The consensus was that it was time to stash the past away, move forward, and "govern collectively as though nothing bad had taken place."[17] Only decades later would this dangerous deformation of historical memory be challenged with the rise of "Holocaust consciousness," which threw questions of guilt and culpability—including that of Catholics and the Catholic Church—into sharp relief.[18]

As human rights talk gained followers, the legal apparatus surrounding the protection of minorities—so famously associated with the League of Nations' Minority Treaties after World War I—came undone. A new legal apparatus arose from the ashes of the defunct minority rights regime: one that focused on the defense of the rights of individual human beings rather than on those of a group defined in ethnic, national, or religious terms. This new apparatus was enshrined by the United Nations, the successor organization to the League of Nations, which officially came into existence in October 1945. The United Nations Charter was premised on a commitment to human rights, not minority rights. Agreed upon by representatives of fifty countries in San Francisco at the United Nations Conference on International Organization (April–June 1945), the Charter resolved to "save succeeding generations from the scourge of war" through the foundation of a new intergovernmental organization that would "reaffirm faith in fundamental human rights" and "establish conditions under which justice and respect for the obligations arising from treaties and other sources of international law can be maintained."[19] The new organization also demanded that references to human rights be inserted in the new postwar constitutions of defeated states.[20] The political-legal project after World War I had been the reinvention of borders to conform to imagined nations. But after 1945, Western policy makers (and the pope too) abandoned talk of protecting the rights of European nations. Even though national self-determination had still featured in the 1941 Atlantic Charter, by the mid-1940s this catch-phrase had fallen almost entirely out of use in Western circles, not least because European powers such as Great Britain and France had no interest in giving in to the claims of anticolonial activists and abandoning their empires. (The French Christian Democratic party, the Mouvement Républicain Populaire, was particularly eager to keep the French Empire intact.[21]) The "strange triumph of human rights" over minority rights persisted, despite the fact that the National Association for the Advancement of Colored Peoples (NAACP), led by W. E. B. Du Bois, badgered the new organization to honor the Atlantic Charter's promises; the USSR called upon the United Nations to include mention of national self-determination as a basic human right; and isolated international lawyers—like Raphael Lemkin—emphasized that the lack of minority rights protections was the UN's Achilles' heel.[22]

Just as Pius XII went along with the new human rights language, he also showed his support for the United Nations. Unlike after World War I, when Benedict XV had voiced his opposition to the League, Pius XII applauded the new organization, emphasizing that no one could be more welcoming of the United Nations than the pope.[23] The United Nations was less threatening to the Vatican than the League had been. Crucially, its legal regime was much weaker than its predecessor's. Additionally, unlike the League, the UN's initial actions were not focused on punishing countries responsible for the war, such as Germany and Italy. Finally, the Pontiff's relationship with the United States, which played a central role in getting the new organization off the ground, had changed, and as a result of wartime exchanges (and FDR's campaign on behalf of religious freedom in the Soviet Union), the pope was willing to take a chance and work with the United States. His hope was that in doing so, he would convince the United States to embrace anticommunism and take a stand against the Soviet Union.

Toward the Cold War

After World War II, the pope had good reasons to worry about the rise of the Soviet Union and international communism. Between February and July 1945, the Soviet Union became an occupying power in much of Eastern Europe and the Baltic region. But if the defeat of Nazism had visibly strengthened communist movements across Europe, opposition to communism was also rife, not least because of the Red Army's vicious "liberation" tactics. Thus, Communist Parties could not count on seizing power either through grassroots revolution or through the ballot-box. Across East-Central Europe, cross-party coalitions were formed. The coalitions were united by a shared anti-Fascist program, and across the region new constitutions were adopted that established the legal bases for democracy and recognized human rights and fundamental freedoms. Most countries also instituted sweeping land reforms and expanded public education, old-age pensions, and health insurance. During this same arc of time, Stalin worked to assert communist and Soviet control over East-Central European coalition governments.[24] The pope found the developments deeply worrisome. He emphasized that Eastern Europe faced the serious danger of being deprived of its "God-given rights," and urged postwar leaders to rise to the cause and take decisive action to reduce the influence of the Soviet Union in the region.[25]

But instead of heeding the pontiff's warnings, at the Dumbarton Oaks, Yalta, and Potsdam Conferences in 1944 and 1945, the Allied powers brought the Soviet Union more fully into the fold. At the Yalta Conference of February 1945, Stalin, Churchill, and Roosevelt divided Germany into four occupation zones (American, British, French, and Soviet). Much to the papacy's chagrin, the conference also confirmed Soviet control of Polish Galicia. Finally, the conference vaguely alluded to the principle of internationally controlled free elections in Eastern Europe after the war. In doing so, Yalta seemed to reaffirm the conclusions of an earlier secret conference, held in Moscow in October 1944, when Churchill and Stalin had carved up Europe into Western and Soviet spheres of influence.[26]

As the papacy saw it, Yalta demonstrated that the great powers "were really turning Eastern Europe over to Russian imperialism."[27] Pius XII therefore urged the Catholic hierarchy to respond immediately, asking American Catholics (with whom the papacy now had a closer relationship as a result of the 1930s anticommunist crusade and increased communication in the course of World War II) to get to work and help break apart the wartime coalition between the Soviet Union and the United States. In 1944 the administrative board of the National Catholic Welfare Council—speaking with the consent of the 118 archbishops and bishops of the U.S. Catholic hierarchy—publicly expressed its worries about the Soviet Union via the following widely distributed press statement: "A nation which refuses to accord its own people the full enjoyment of innate human rights (civil and religious) cannot be relied upon to cooperate in the international community."[28] At the United Nations Conference on International Organization in San Francisco in April 1945, which laid the foundation for the future United Nations, consultants from the American Catholic Church lobbied hard to have the UN Charter conform to Pius XII's vision for Christian Europe. The pope and the American Catholic hierarchy were not happy that the Soviet Union was bound to play a major role in the intergovernmental organization, which would be composed of six principal divisions: the General Assembly, the Security Council, the Economic and Social Council, the Secretariat, the International Court of Justice, and the UN Trusteeship Council. In a twin bid to weaken Soviet power, Catholic lobbyists in San Francisco sought to influence the criteria for UN membership and eliminate the Security Council veto. Arguing that Soviet behavior in Eastern Europe ran counter to the principles of "peace-loving nations," they suggested that the country did not deserve a seat at the table.[29]

At the Potsdam Conference, held in occupied Germany from mid-July through early August 1945, the United States appeared to confirm the fact that the Soviet Union had become an occupying power in Central and Eastern Europe over the past five months. Here, the Allies not only agreed to the forced deportation of ethnic Germans from Poland, Czechoslovakia, and Hungary, an act that Pius XII termed "ignominious" and "inhuman" and the German Catholic upper hierarchy called a violation of "God-given natural law" and "human rights." In addition, Potsdam Conference participants agreed to shift Poland's borders to the west to the Oder-Neisse line, which led to the resettlement of Poles in formerly German lands. The Vatican refused to recognize the new borders and redraw diocesan lines; until the 1970s it continued to view the territories as being under German jurisdiction. The *Osservatore Romano* commented that Potsdam had failed to adequately address the pressing issue of Soviet influence in Eastern Europe. After all, thanks to the complicity of the Allied powers, the lands that had been the starting point for the Vatican's recapture of Europe in World War I were now under Stalin's thumb. The Poles, of course, were devastated that the pope had sided "with Germany" and against them.[30]

American bishops followed up on the Potsdam Conference through a lobbying effort aimed at getting the United States to reverse its foreign policy toward the Soviet Union. After their annual meeting, in November 1945, they called on the American government to wake up about the reality of the Soviet Union. They urged the United States to prepare itself for a future war, and choreographed mass protests in numerous cities, calling for the removal of Soviet troops from Eastern Europe. American bishops condemned the Allies' willingness to let Stalin "dig deep inroads" in Europe as he "tirelessly" worked "to grind into dust the blessed freedoms for which our sons have fought, sacrificed, and died." The papal nuncio to France, Monsignor Roncalli (future Pope John XXIII), emphasized it was necessary "to oppose Russian imperialism, and impose . . . a conception of the peace inspired by justice and by Christian principles." Shortly thereafter the pope issued a call to refound a Catholic International that would be capable of fending off Soviet "imperialism" through a genuine "universalist" praxis, and announced that America's war against "the denial of men's civil and religious rights has not ceased." Only by continuing this war would "the heroic death of hundreds of thousands" of soldiers gain meaning, the pope averred.[31]

Meanwhile, between 1944 and 1945 Stalin was consolidating his grip and succeeding in his bid to get communists loyal to the Soviet Union appointed to key ministries across Eastern Europe. Soon enough, the genuine coalitions of the early postwar years had morphed into "bogus coalitions," as Communist Parties seized control of country after country—bringing an end to the brief romance with democratic rule, and putting in place regimes tightly bound to the Soviet Union. The Vatican anticommunist campaign picked up speed. In response to the show trial and imprisonment of the Archbishop Stepinac of Croatia, the papacy highlighted Yugoslav and communist wrongdoing, and encouraged the Holy Office to issue a decree excommunicating all those responsible for the imprisonment and arrest. The Vatican also organized a worldwide press campaign and mass demonstrations. In New York, Pius XII's close ally Cardinal Spellman announced a drive to found an "Archbishop Stepinac High School" to honor the newest martyr to the Catholic cause. Through galvanizing sermons and fundraisers, Spellman was able to raise $4 million in less than year—about $2 million more than was needed.[32]

Just as the capture of Eastern Europe had been a core component of the papacy's countersettlement after World War I, attention to what was under way in Eastern Europe was a centerpiece of early post–World War II papal diplomacy. The Stepinac case was followed by Vatican uproar over the internment and trial of several other high-profile clerics, including Cardinal József Mindszenty, the Primate of Hungary, Cardinal Josef Beran in Czechoslovakia, Cardinal Stefan Wyszynski in Poland, Archbishops Gaspër Thaçi and Vincenc Prennushi in Albania, and Bishop Vincentas Borisevičius in Lithuania. In order to obtain international press attention, papal officials did the opposite of what they had done during the Holocaust: they accelerated the flow of information, sharing reports from priests stationed in East-Central Europe, focusing on the persecutions of the Church in Poland, Hungary,

Romania, the Ukraine, and the Soviet Union. The causes prompted
UN resolutions, which became paradigmatic early cases of the organ-
ization's enforcement of new human rights provisions. In 1947–1948,
Hungary, Bulgaria, and Romania were excluded from the United
Nations.[33]

In February 1948, Romanian party chief Gheorghiu-Dej announced
in a public statement that the Church was one of the few institutional
obstacles to communization. Stalinist elites across the region agreed.
In all but Hungary, Poland, and Bulgaria, religious instruction was
banned, and everywhere except East Germany, the Church lost its control over hospitals, orphanages, and other charitable facilities. In addition, the Czech, Yugoslav, Polish, Hungarian, Romanian, and Albanian
Communist Parties began the process of attempting to convince their
national Catholic churches to break ties with the Vatican. Though they
did not succeed, shortly thereafter both the Polish and the Lithuanian
concordats were abrogated. In Lithuania, the local Communist Party
also began attacking the Church hierarchy and removing hundreds of
clerics from priestly work. In Latvia, Belorussia, and Bulgaria, more
priests were imprisoned and deported, and churches were shut down.
In Estonia, the Catholic Church was also subjected to harsh reprisals. In
Poland the communist regime hesitated a bit longer, but soon enough it
too began curtailing Catholic press organs and discriminating against
believers in its employment practices. In 1949 it began to nationalize
Church-run hospitals, orphanages, and nursing homes. The Polish episcopate responded by making use of the only tools available to it. It
spoke out in the new Catholic language of human rights, condemning
Polish authorities' violations of the innate rights of human beings, and
the deprivation of the rights of Catholics in particular.[34]

In the meantime, in Western Europe, Communist Parties enjoyed
a real heyday. Communism had emerged fortified by the war and the
Resistance, and its prestige was given a boost by the "red" partisans
who had led the fight against Nazi Germany and Fascist forces. Additionally, in a period characterized by mass discontent and economic
dislocation, the communist message on economic redistribution resonated. Finally, Western European Communist Parties were able to
claim ground recently vacated by the papacy, as they revived long-
standing forms of anti-Americanism, and presented themselves as

opposed to the mass influx of American goods and cultural products, and in favor of an alternative model of postwar reconstruction.[35] In the first postwar elections for France's interim Constituent National Assembly, the Communist Party became the single largest party in the country, with over 26 percent of the vote. In Italy, the communists similarly performed well, quickly emerging as the fastest-growing party in Western Europe, with 2.3 million members at its peak.[36] Elsewhere, in countries like Great Britain, Sweden, Denmark, Austria, and Belgium, Socialist, Social-Democratic, and Labor Parties consistently obtained 23 to 48 percent of the vote.[37]

The papacy responded to the electoral success of these parties by undertaking extensive lobbying work, which aimed to compel the United States to deepen its involvement in continental affairs and help prevent the further growth of communism.[38] Well before the launching the United States' June 1947 Marshall Plan of economic aid for European countries, papal lobbyists urged U.S. officials to provide material aid for Western Europe, arguing that destitution bred revolutionism and benefited the communist movement. Beginning in 1947, select papal officials also urged the United States to condone Italy's and Germany's immediate rearmament, in violation of peace treaty terms. Both countries, papal officials noted, stood with the forces of "Christian civilization" and against "totalitarian and tyrannical countries"; thus, "it would seem logical to consider rearming [them] now in spite of [the] peace treaty rather than postponing rearmament until after [the] outbreak of war." The Vatican had supposedly learned, through confidential sources, that the Russians were planning to "invade Italy and surround Vatican State," and then "remove [the] pope to Russia and hold him as a hostage."[39] It was necessary to "make the Americans understand that if communism seizes power, there would be a civil war."[40] In December 1948 Pius XII started speaking publicly in favor of the Christian necessity of defense, emphasizing that Christians needed to guard against the notion that it was crucial to maintain peace at all costs.[41] As he did so, he silenced internal dissenters, like the director of the *Osservatore Romano*, who worried about the pope speaking out too strongly in favor of a militarized Cold War.[42]

Pius XII's conviction that Western Europe needed the United States' protection and assistance to resist the Soviet Union was widely shared by Christian Democratic leaders. As early as December 1947 Alcide De Gasperi, the leader of the Italian Christian Democratic Party, proposed that the United States issue a declaration to remind the public of the United States' "right and duty to intervene wherever Italy's territorial integrity was threatened or the country's current anti-totalitarian democratic government threatened." In early 1948 he applauded when Washington issued a series of National Security Council resolutions that laid out preliminary plans for American military intervention in Italy, in the case of an extralegal communist seizure of power and communist victory at the ballot box.[43] De Gasperi was not the only Christian Democrat to request the United States' greater involvement in the 1940s: leaders of the French MRP party and the German CDU similarly sought out American protection and assistance so as to guard against the threat of a Soviet invasion.[44]

When, with the launching of the Cold War, anticommunism and anti-Sovietism started to become central features of American foreign policy, the papacy and European Christian Democratic Parties rejoiced. Monsignor Tardini, Pius XII's close advisor, noted that the change in American policy toward the Soviet Union was "a logical and well-timed development." The Catholic U.S. secretary of state, James F. Byrnes, asserted that the world was starting to finally heed the pope's long-heralded warning about the Soviet Union. The papal nuncio in Washington patted himself on the back, as did Father Martegani, the editor-in-chief of *Civiltà Cattolica*.[45]

Papal pressure and Christian Democratic urgings were not, of course, alone responsible for the United States' deepening involvement in Europe, the creation of NATO, and the engagement of the United States in a series of proxy wars with the Soviet Union. Religion and religious forces were *a* factor—not *the* factor—in the coming of the Cold War.[46] Nonetheless, the papacy and Christian Democratic parties doubtless had an impact on shifting the understanding of American officials regarding the immediacy of the Soviet threat and on the potential role the United States could play in offsetting that threat. After all, in the early postwar years, American officials had very limited knowledge of European politics and society and were reliant on European powers to supply information and conduct intelligence gathering on their own. Thus, when the pope and Christian

Democrats spoke, American officials—who had few channels of information—listened.

The Concordat Moment, Again

In the early postwar years, the Vatican was confident that it could focus on protecting its interwar prerogatives without worrying about American push-back. Starting in the mid-1940s the pontiff therefore began to call upon Christian Democrats to reinforce Europe's concordatory wall. As Pius XII explained, there was a pressing need for a "more just juridical order . . . that better corresponds to the eternal law of God and is more in conformity with human dignity."[47] Students in institutes of canon law parroted the claims, asserting that concordats were essential to getting Europe back on its feet, in that they would help expedite not just the continent's "juridical reconstruction," but its "cultural, economic, [and] political" life as well.[48] As in the interwar years, the transformation advocated by the Holy See could not take place in just one or two nation-states—it had to be international. As the pope put it: "The world as a whole needs to be rebuilt; the universal order must be reestablished." The time had come "to gather and connect everything in [Christ]: *instaurare omnia in Christo*."[49] For the pope, stuck in the time-loop of the interwar years, *building the new* meant *reestablishing the old.* More specifically, reconstructing Europe meant rebuilding and expanding interwar concordats. As the pope saw things, the reconfirmation of interwar concordats was the prerequisite for any sort of lasting peace.

The project to rebind Western Europe to concordats remained, as before, about building Christian states. The separation of Church and state, papal lobbyists suggested, was nonsensical in the European context: "To say that a State does not have a religion would mean . . . saying it is an Atheist State."[50] Along similar lines, Pius XII emphasized that "there is no example of a people or country which, after having separated itself from the Church and Catholic culture, was ever able to entirely return to it."[51] For the Vatican, this was particularly true in the Italian case. Indeed, papal officials still considered Italy the papacy's crown jewel. They also saw Italy as particularly at risk. With Italy having the largest Communist Party in Western Europe, clerics close to the pope asserted that only the Church could offer the Italian state what it needed to avert left-wing revolution, rebuild itself, and "radically heal."[52]

Starting in 1946, influencing the Italian Constituent Assembly—and hence Italy's new constitution—became a major focus of papal efforts. The Italian elections of June 2, 1946, had given Christian Democracy a lead role in the Assembly. However, the sum of the Socialist and Communist vote (9 million) was still greater than the vote for the Christian Democrats (8 million). (The old Liberals, who garnered, at best, 6 percent of the vote, were no longer a credible threat).[53] The pope was not yet sure whether Christian Democrats were to be entirely trusted, so he pushed the concordat as a useful litmus test—a way to get the Christian Democrats in line.

The pope's hesitation was somewhat warranted in that Christian Democracy—not just in Italy, but across Western Europe—was still working out its identity. In an early phase, Christian Democracy, whose leadership group was dominated by Catholics, held together under one roof a series of individuals espousing contradictory positions: those who made the new party its home included Catholic dissidents calling for radical redistribution and the nationalization of industry (and even a few self-declared "Catholic socialists") and Catholic conservatives interested in restoring old hierarchies and in limiting the power of the state. Through its combination of anti-statism and pro-welfarism, anti-individualism and pro-communitarianism, technocratic common sense and utopianism, the party built broad appeal, even as it drew rather promiscuously on competing strands of Catholic social thought. Though only fringe numbers of Catholics had participated in acts of anti-Fascist and anti-Nazi resistance, Christian Democrats quickly claimed them as their own—and presented themselves as basing their politics on Catholic anti-Fascist and anti-Nazi ideas. At the same time, Christian Democrats freely cited the papacy on everything from Church-state relations to religious anticommunism. In the great jockeying for influence that characterized the 1940s and 1950s, Christian Democrats understood that ideas mattered, and they strove to present Christian Democracy as an intellectually rich party endowed with an attractive "way of seeing, interpreting and changing the world."[54]

Older members of Christian Democratic parties saw their political work as an extension of their religious faith, insofar as Catholicism, for them, was the "spirit and heart of all things," a faith to be applied to all public activities and all aspects of one's life.[55] In lockstep with the papal vision, these Christian Democrats saw themselves as the carriers of a large-scale and rather binding Catholic revolution that was both deep within the soul of each individual, and wide, capable of stretching across the continent, and even the world. "What we need," the founder of the postwar French Christian Democratic movement, Robert Schuman, asserted with characteristic paternalism, is "a team of trained men, ready for the service of the state, apostles of reconciliation and builders of a new world," to carry out "a far-reaching transformation of society" that is not exclusively focused on "a change of policy," but rather on individual conversion—that is, on "changing men."[56] Schuman was not alone: integral beliefs presenting the Christian Democratic project as one aligned with the radical imperative of re-Christianization played a major role in shaping the political and social activism of many postwar Christian Democratic leaders, many of whom had received their political and religious formation in the papacy's Catholic Action youth organizations, where they had been trained to "bring the Kingdom of Christ to earth," celebrate the anti-liberal concordat revolution, and play an active role in the Vatican's anticommunist crusade.[57] For these men, the key danger to be avoided was that of falling into a materialist conception of the world, espoused by liberals, communists, and before them, French revolutionaries, whom they berated as "irresponsible fanatics" and "blind dogmatists."[58]

Other Christian Democrats, however—particularly the younger ones—did not underwrite this vision. They had been heavily influenced by the writings of opponents to the papal international and by the lived practices of the armed Resistance to Nazism and Fascism—a phenomenon that had united in common cause "those who believed in a Heaven and those who didn't," in the words of Louis Aragon's famous wartime poem, *La rose et le réséda*. These activists believed that building a democratic, pluralist Europe would be the key to the continent's future peace. Many welcomed collaboration with socialist, liberal-democratic, and even communist parties, and saw this collaboration as a way to move forward, and build a more just social and economic order.[59] Some called upon Catholics to work with left-wing movements to explore their shared ideological ground, over and against the angry warnings of the *Osservatore Romano*, which fired back that if Catholics entertained deep relations with communists and socialists, "it cannot be said [they] are acting as Catholics."[60] In stark contrast to the Holy See—and in keeping with some of the more radical members of the Catholic left—a small but vocal group of Christian Democrats called for religious freedom and the definition of the state in nonconfessional terms.[61] Having learned the lessons of the interwar years, Christian Democrats in this camp in Italy's Constituent Assembly argued for a founding text that enshrined the principle of "juridical pluralism," by which they meant the protection of both individual and group rights—including the rights of minorities.[62] Furthermore, rather than foregrounding their Catholicism and the project of confessionalizing the state, several Christian Democrats at the Assembly suggested that the new Italian constitution build a shared anti-Fascist identity for the new country. They encouraged communists and socialists to align with this vision.[63]

The Holy See saw what was going on and fretted that the war for the soul of Catholicism was being debated once again. It was time to intervene. As Pius XII put it, Italy was deciding on whether to go the route of "the champions or the destroyers of Christian civilization." In the context, the papacy must push Christian Democracy to build an Italy "on the firm rock of Christianity, on the recognition of the existence of God." An anti-Fascist identity premised on Catholic-socialist and Catholic-communist collaboration simply would not do. To the pope, this sounded like a Popular Front ploy all over again. It could not be allowed to pass.[64]

The pope thus formed a lobby to push the Christian Democrats in the direction he desired. The lobby was composed of Prince don Carlo Pacelli, Pius XII's nephew, who began working "in the name of the Holy Father," in collaboration with "fathers from [the Jesuit journal] *Civiltà* [*Cattolica*]," to ensure that "nothing ends up in the constitution that the Holy See might dislike."[65] The idea was to intervene and make an impact, not least because, according to the apostolic nuncio to Italy (who was still the much-compromised Francesco Borgonini

Duca), "the Christian parliamentarians don't seem very prepared to face the difficulties and problems ahead—and many give the impression of being young novices [*novizietti*]."[66]

As Winston Churchill announced the descent of the Iron Curtain across Europe and the Soviet Union began protesting that the United States was "striving for world supremacy," the new papal lobby got to work. They threatened Christian Democrats that if they failed to act according to Christian precepts, the papacy would throw its weight behind other center-right and even far-right parties.[67] Indeed, as party members knew well, Christian Democracy's success at the polls was due not only to its capacity to exploit the new mood of religious optimism and conquest and position itself against communism, but also to its unique ability to work with the Holy See to exploit the Church's considerable powers in civil society. Particularly in countries like Italy and France, the work of Catholic Action on behalf of Christian Democracy had proved decisive at the polls. It made it relatively cheap and easy to get out the vote, produce electoral propaganda, and raise electoral consciousness, when the party could rely on Catholic devotees (flush with papal funds) to do the heavy lifting. It was a boon that these civil society organizations also had extensive experience in the art of popular mobilization—thanks not least to the training they had received during the papacy's interwar anticommunist crusade. And the fact that Catholic Action had a base among female activists was crucial. The female branches of Catholic Action mobilized extensively on behalf of Christian Democracy early on and increased its appeal for many newly enfranchised Catholic women in Italy, Belgium, and France. Thus, the prospect that Catholic Action might withdraw its support for Christian Democracy was a serious threat.

As a second pressure tactic, papal lobbyists developed an "alternative Constitution," which laid out in detail the papal vision for the ideal founding text. In justifying this move, they suggested that the Christian Democrats had erred in following "the principle of collaboration, and therefore, also, of possible compromise." Instead, the new party should have gone the route of "preparing their own complete Constitution by themselves," without paying any heed to socialist or communist preferences. Papal diplomats also lamented the absence in

Christian Democratic circles of "good canon lawyers" and "theologians," suggesting that their drafting of an alternative Constitution would be a way to repair this lacuna.[68]

The papal lobby's alternative Constitution was significant for what it included and what it excluded. The Constitution called for the full recognition of the Lateran Agreements and "an explicit reaffirmation that the Catholic religion is the religion of the state." Tone-deaf to the rise of a female workforce and the fact that in June 1946 women had just exercised their right to vote for the first time in Italian history, the papal alternative Constitution droned on about the role of men as *pater familias* and the "domestic mission of the woman." The text asserted that public education must be in keeping "with the preexisting rights of families and the superior rights of the Church," adding that it was the duty of the state to provide religious instruction in all public schools. In mid-October 1946, the Holy See encouraged the leading male branch of Italian Catholic Action to draft its own *desiderata*, which included a reference to the "sacred, unitary, and indissoluble quality of marriage," to "the recognition of the parent's right to freely pick schools for their children," and to "the related duty of the state to put private schools on a plane of perfect parity with public ones, both when it comes to their juridical status and in financial terms."[69]

As Christian Democrats in the Constituent Assembly sat down to draft the country's founding text, they were handed these two Vatican texts. This gave them a clear sense of what the original Catholic international wanted to see present in Italy's new constitution. Before 1946 was over, the papal lobby upped its pressure, noting that "the Constitution [must] contain an explicit reference to the Lateran Pacts." "The Pacts," it added, "must be accepted not only as valid on questions of internal politics, but also, in juridical terms, as valid under international law." Through weekly encounters with Christian Democratic politicians, which included blow-by-blow summaries of Constituent Assembly debates and detailed discussions of proposed articles, papal officials advised Christian Democrats to repeatedly and explicitly reference the Lateran Agreements in general, and the concordat in particular. "Stick to the concordat," the lobby admonished, adding that Christian Democrats in the Constituent Assembly must "hew as close as possible, at all times, to the substance of the concordat's phraseology, such that there is no contrast between the Constitution and the concordat." In tandem, papal lobbyists pushed hard for the reconfirmation of marriage as "indissoluble" and the expansion of protections (legal and financial) for Catholic schools.[70]

Christian Democrats responded readily to papal pressure. Some doubtless believed in the importance of the Lateran Agreements, and had been trained from their youth to see the agreements as a sacred text. Others were primarily motivated by utilitarian concerns, calculating that they needed the Holy See's support to consolidate the new party's hold on power. Together, ultramontanist and pragmatic Christian Democrats began to argue that "the concordat is nonnegotiable," and, in close collaboration with the papal lobby, developed a clever stratagem.

As the debates kicked off, the Christian Democrats introduced two proposed articles, both of which would have inserted the concordat into the constitution. The first (then article 7) explicitly claimed that "the relations between the Italian State and the Catholic Church will remain regulated by the Lateran Agreements" and that Catholicism would continue to be "the religion of state." As the lobby hoped, this article would draw the most attention and debate, leaving a second article (article 6), to slide by without much comment. According to article 6, "The norms of international law, such as the current agreement which is still in force between the state and the Church . . . are part of the laws of the state without it being necessary to specify this through a special law. The laws of the state cannot contradict the norms [of international law]." In a private letter, the tactic was explained:

> It is a good idea to *at least propose* [article 7], especially with the aim of distracting attention from the previous article . . . This article [article 6] really contains the cardinal norm: all of the rest could fall, as long as this one stays. It implies: 1) Recognition of the Lateran Agreements ("Agreements still in force"); b) Official recognition of these [the Lateran Agreements] as international law; c) *Automatic* adoption (that is without a need for special executive actions) of the internal law of the State to the previously established concordatory norms; d) *Constitutional* validity of the norms themselves, therefore blocking

the possibility of overturning these norms through ordinary legislative pathways.[71]

In the end, despite concerted opposition from some members of the Constituent Assembly—including the socialists, the *azionisti*, the Republicans, and certain liberals—the gamble paid off, and the Lateran Agreements were recognized as legally valid in the Italian Constitution. Opponents of the Christian Democrats were incensed. As they saw things, the recognition of the Lateran Agreements was a grave mistake: it would "humiliate the state," create a "diarchy of powers and sovereignty," and "insert a foreign body into democracy and deal a mortal blow to the young Italian Republic." One of Italy's most prominent Liberal thinkers, Benedetto Croce, called the insertion of the concordat in the Constitution "an egregious logical error and a juridical scandal." The Socialist paper *L'Avanti* wrote: "Christian Democrats, it's clear, want to transpose, *sic et simpliciter*, the entire concordatory legislation into the Constitution."[72]

It is important to note that despite its big win on the Lateran Agreements, the papal lobby did not obtain all its demands. The proposal to enshrine marriage as indissoluble failed by a margin of three votes (194 to 191), much to the chagrin of Catholic clergy in Italy, who fumed that "the cause of Religion and the Christian Family" had been betrayed. The articles on schooling similarly failed because of internal fractures. The constitutional article that passed the Assembly ultimately asserted equivalence between religious and state schools, but also said that this equivalence could exist only insofar as it did not involve "financial obligations for the State." Though left-wing Christian Democrats were happy with the compromise, the director of the Catholic Action newspaper *Il Quotidiano* seethed that "the battle for the school, as with other liberties, is only just starting now." The *Osservatore Romano* and *Civiltà Cattolica* also came out strongly against the results, attacking those Christian Democrats who had inexplicably failed to show up in the Assembly for the crucial vote. Clashes such as these demonstrated that the partnership between the papacy and Christian Democrats was fragile, and that Christian Democrats sometimes (and increasingly) would, and could, go their own way.

Nonetheless, the Vatican showed itself willing to deliver on its side of the bargain. In the spring of 1948, it heavily intervened in support of Italian Christian Democracy at the polls. Pius XII announced that the choice in the 1948 Italian elections was simple: "Either you are with Christ, or you are against him." Several Cardinals gave sermons with this same theme, and a new branch of Catholic Action, known as the Civic Committees, made Pius XII's Manichean framework the foundation of their massive propaganda work. Presenting the fight against the Popular Front as a fight against revolution and Godlessness, the Civic Committees drew freely on the themes of the interwar anticommunist crusade and on modern-day advertising methods. They distributed short anticommunist films, made and produced by Vatican production agencies, to remote villages; produced posters and pamphlets, highlighting the depravity of communists; and hosted events and debates foregrounding the Catholic anticommunist viewpoint. They played on fears and rumors that Italy—and even Saint Peter's Square—would soon be taken over by the Red Army, should the Christian Democrats lose the elections. They repurposed images from the days of the Spanish Civil War, emphasizing the violence that would surely strike clergy and the laity in the case of a communist victory at the polls. In the early months of 1948, Italy's Catholic Action ranks swelled, reaching well beyond three million activists.[73] The hard work helped seal Christian Democracy's victory on April 18, 1948, when the party won 48 percent of the vote against 31 percent gained by the Popular Front.[74] In a testament to Catholic Action's hard work, the party won most impressively in those regions of Italy where the civil society organization was strongest.[75]

The mass mobilization of 1948 was also aided by the United States' decision to launch a propaganda campaign of its own, which placed a great deal of emphasis on the Marshall Plan and on how America had provided extraordinary wealth and generosity to the Italian people—even as Moscow had shown itself unable to offer Italy significant reconstruction funds and had even prevented its satellites from participating in the Marshall Plan at all.[76] The U.S. campaign for Christian Democracy in 1948 enrolled Italian-American celebrities, like Frank Sinatra and Joe Di Maggio, and it also worked to mobilize Italian-American émigrés to write home to their Italian

Cinema carts bringing papal and Christian Democratic
propaganda to Italy's remote regions. *Iniziativa* 4
(May 1948). Credit: Isacem-Institute for the History of Catholic
Action and the Catholic Movement in Italy Paul VI, Luigi Gedda
Fund, Series Civic Committees

relatives to urge them to vote "for liberty"—that is, for Christian
Democracy.[77]

As debates on the 1948 elections were wrapping up in Italy, a second
papal fight for the concordat was beginning in Germany. The sociopo-
litical context for that fight seemed favorable to the pope. In Germany,
as in Italy, popular religiosity was at an all-time high. Contemporaries
took stock of "a religious revival like none Europe had seen in a hundred years," as the number of regular Catholic churchgoers soared to
above 50 percent of the population. The pope benefited from the mass
perception that the Catholic Church had retained its neutrality during
World War II, and Pius XII was popularly hailed as *Defensor Civitatis*,
the defender of civilization.[78]

Germany's two major Christian parties (the CDU and the Bavarian CSU) enjoyed spectacular success at the polls. Catholics were

Civic Committee poster for the 1948 Italian elections. The caption reads, "And if mommy and daddy don't go vote, we will pee in our beds!" Credit: Isacem-Institute for the History of Catholic Action and the Catholic Movement in Italy Paul VI, Luigi Gedda Fund, Series Civic Committees

disproportionately represented within party leadership, and voted for Christian parties in large numbers, at higher rates than at any other time in German history—including at the end of the Kaiserreich and during the Weimar Republic.[79] The pope was happy to learn that the CDU's first party program heavily emphasized Christian natural law and drew extensively on his June 1945 address, which had defended the Reichskonkordat.[80] German bishops asserted that confessional parties were a way to offset the potential of Soviet expansionism and prevent "the Russians [from] murdering and enslaving those under their rule and suppressing the Roman Catholic Church."[81] The pope and the German hierarchy were reassured by the fact that very early in the CDU's history (by the end of 1945), radical left and Christian socialist tendencies within the party had been suppressed by more moderate and conservative elements.[82] The CDU and CSU also disseminated a convenient history, according to which it was "not the widespread Christian conservative disdain for liberal democracy, Jews, and

The image of St. Peter's is captioned, "Their Dream." The sign on the right
reads, "Piazza Saint Peter the Great." *Rabarbaro*, 20 April 1947. Credit:
Isacem-Institute for the History of Catholic Action and the Catholic Movement in
Italy Paul VI, Luigi Gedda Fund, Series Civic Committees

the legacy of the French Revolution that constituted a 'fertile ground'
in which Nazism was able to take root. Rather, it was secularism,
positivism, value-neutrality, and socialism that were responsible for
the German catastrophe."[83] According to this narrative, the CDU's
members and the German Catholic hierarchy were not only guilt-
free; they had a special role in preventing a new 1933 and in redeeming
postwar Germany, insofar as Catholicism and Nazism were actually
natural enemies.

Following Germany's unconditional surrender in May 1945 and its
division into four occupation zones, Christian Democrats benefited
from the support of the occupying governments in all but the Soviet
zone. This was particularly true in the American zone, where "discrim-
inations *in favor of* Catholics" became the norm, as local authorities
gave distribution privileges and free supplies of hard-to-find printing

Crucified on the hammer and sickle. *Rabarbaro,* 13 April 1947. Credit:
Isacem-Institute for the History of Catholic Action and the Catholic Movement in
Italy Paul VI, Luigi Gedda Fund, Series Civic Committees

paper to a slew of Catholic publicists connected closely with the Christian Democratic parties.[84] The American military governor of Germany, General Lucius Clay, and his political advisor Robert Murphy privileged Catholics not least because they saw Catholicism as a bulwark against the influence of Jewish émigrés in shaping postwar Germany, and against communism and socialism.[85] From the beginning, the occupiers directly involved the Catholic Church in shaping Germany's postwar political life.[86] Tapping contacts in Vatican City and Church dignitaries in the United States, American officials asked for a roster of "German Catholic leaders" to help rebuild Germany and "properly indoctrinate and equip" future generations, and ended up going with a man suggested by Eugenio Pacelli's old friend Cardinal Faulhaber as postwar prime minister of Bavaria: Fritz Schäffer, one of the founders of the CSU, a former leader in the Bavarian People's Party, and a well-known anti-Semite.[87]

As the United States' role in Germany continued to grow—following the stated intention, in September 1946, to keep U.S. troops in Europe indefinitely—the special relationship forged between American occupiers and Church and Christian Democratic dignitaries assumed additional importance. The fact that the Allies exempted all Catholic priests from de-Nazification proceedings, combined with the Church's very limited self-de-Nazification, which resulted only in the defrocking of a handful of priests, reinforced the Church's and the CDU's distorted historiography, according to which Catholicism and Nazism had been opposing trends from the beginning.[88] The message was repeated from the pulpit by many members of the German upper hierarchy, including Clemens August Graf von Galen, bishop of Münster, who stated, "We do not deserve to be considered and handled as guilty parties. We suffered more under the Nazis than others."[89] Adenauer and other leading Christian Democrats similarly were at pains to emphasize how much Catholics had lost under the Nazis.[90] The self-exculpatory statements were part of a larger pattern of Catholic anti-Semitic and anti-Jewish sentiments, which led Catholics to emphasize that Jews did not really deserve full membership in the postwar German polity, either because they had grown "vengeful" and "vindictive" as a result of the war, or because they espoused forms of communist and socialist "materialism" that ran counter to Christian values.[91] A comparable story played out in Austria, where the country's Christian Democratic party (the Austrian People's Party or Österreichische Volkspartei) participated in a similar politics of amnesia, joined by Austrian bishops—who not only willfully neglected to cultivate the memory of the victims of the Nazi movement but also, beginning in the autumn of 1945, urged occupation forces to implement a Christmas amnesty for imprisoned National Socialists.[92]

This climate copiously benefited the Vatican, which was keen on reasserting its role in Central Europe by anchoring the concordat in German and Austrian law at the earliest possible opportunity.[93] The Western occupiers had no objection. Asserting that the Church was "almost [the] only constituted authority" in Germany after the war, both British and American forces on site expressed the desire to avoid any "conflict of jurisdiction" between military government regulations and "the law of [the] Roman Catholic Church, the *Codex Juris Canonici*."[94] They recognized concordats as legally valid, and pushed back against Soviet opposition, arguing that the concordat was a good thing to keep on the books because it was "a bulwark for all religion," not to mention an excellent way to win the local population's loyalty.[95] An American official noted that in Germany it was not advisable to implement "the separation of Church and state, as observed in America." "Some matters upheld in principle in America had to be modified in practice in Germany," particularly as pertained to "the religious situation."[96] However, the occupiers added that they did not have the last word: it would be up to Germany's constituent assembly to decide the fate of the treaty in the longer term.[97] The same was true in Austria, where it took until 1957 for the government to proclaim the 1933 agreement still valid before international law.

In Germany, a pressure campaign mounted, as the pope strove to put the Reichskonkordat back at the center of political debate.[98] He informed his Cardinals that the treaty with Nazi Germany, in the end, had been a terrific treaty—one that "gave Catholics a juridical basis of defense" against an antireligious regime.[99] Pius XII highlighted that the concordat, insofar as it was valid before international law, had a crucial role to play in German reconstruction, because it was up to "international law" to "make secure and defend [the] peace; an international law which recognizes its foundation in that natural law written by God in the conscience of every man, and from which it derives ultimately its binding force."[100] Ergo, Catholics in Germany would do well to protect concordats once again.

The lively debate over the Reichskonkordat kicked off in 1949, following the end of the Berlin blockade and the proclamation of the Federal Republic of Germany, on May 23, 1949. During the drafting of the Federal Republic of Germany's new constitution or Basic Law, in the Parlamentarischer Rat, West Germany's constituent assembly, Germany's largest Christian Democratic party, the CDU, maintained the validity of the treaty, as did Germany's upper hierarchy. Opponents responded that the Reichskonkordat was a dark stain on their country's past. The treaty was an embarrassment to both Germany and the Vatican, they held, in that it had helped the National Socialist regime improve its international image and consolidate its power. Some raised the sticky issue of why the new German state should be protecting the Church when the Church had not sufficiently proven its anti-Nazi credentials.[101] The archbishop of Cologne and chair of the Fulda Bishops' Conference, Joseph Frings, fired back, improbably averring that "the Catholic Church proved itself to be the strongest bulwark against National Socialism," and that Catholics had been Nazism's leading victims.[102]

The papal lobby may have won over German Christian Democrats, but that only meant that the fate of the concordat hinged on Christian Democracy's ability to convince other political parties or at least peel off a few individual votes. Of the 65 voting members in the West German constituent assembly, 27 were Christian Democrats, 27 Socialists, 5 Liberals, and the remainder evenly split between the Communist Party, the German Party, and the Center Party. Unlike in Italy, where the Christian Democratic party was able to win the support of non–Christian Democrats during the Constituent Assembly debates, in Germany the situation proved less favorable. Liberals and Socialists made common cause, thereby handily claiming the majority and shelving the possibility of recognizing the Reichskonkordat in full in Germany's new Basic Law.

Christian Democrats resigned themselves to fighting for piecemeal provisions. In keeping with article 23 of the Reichskonkordat, and under pressure from German bishops, they sought to obtain the "right of the parents" to send children to classrooms where teachers and pupils were of the same confession.[103] Seeking to deliver a measurable win on this hot-button issue, Cardinal Faulhaber asserted that if confessional schools were not preserved, Germany would tumble back into dictatorship. "Every disregard of this legal right and every exaggeration of the power of the state in this field," the Cardinal asserted, "even though it is done in the name of democracy, leads to the degradation of a new state socialism and collectivism."[104] The papacy's apostolic delegate to Germany, Aloisius Muench, echoed the charge, noting that "attempts to abolish the denominational school" constitute "the first step to a totalitarian state."[105] Along similar lines, Bavaria's Catholic Action averred that "the preservation and revival of Christian education is the only effective protection . . . against collectivism and totalitarianism in every form."[106] German bishops leaned on similar overworked arguments as they lobbied the occupying Americans, who agreed that it was necessary to help "establish and maintain the interests and rights of parents and guardians in the field of denominational schools and religious instruction in schools."[107] But despite all the statements in favor of confessional schools, the Christian Democrats again did not win the day.[108]

German Christian Democrats responded to their failures by moving to grant individual German states authority over matters like education and cultural policy, in the hopes that even if the 1933 Reichskonkordat was not recognized, individual states—like Bavaria, Baden, and Prussia—might decide to enforce their own concordats instead.[109] On this key question of regional autonomy, they won. On the ground, local Catholics and members of state-level Christian Democratic parties immediately began doing the work that from their viewpoint the Basic Law had failed to do. In particular, Bavaria—as after World War I—proved a key ally for the pope. Indeed, in the immediate postwar years Pius XII, doubtless drawing on his interwar experiences, had confided in the French ambassador to the Vatican "that Bavaria could be treated as a very coherent entity" in and of itself, and that its independent spirit and history could come in handy during the pursuit of re-Christianization policies.[110]

In Bavaria, Pius XII found an ally in Alois Hundhammer, a long-time proponent of the natural-law revolution and recent co-founder of

the Christian Social Union, who worked overtime to implement a series of "reconfessionalization policies" modeled on interwar concordats.[111] As minister of culture, despite protests and a two-week school
strike in Nuremberg, he succeeded in carrying out a large-scale population transfer along religious lines, which sent Protestant teachers
from Upper Bavaria to Franconia, and Catholic teaching staff from
Franconia to Altbayern. Through his work on the Bavarian Constitutional Assembly and its most important body, the constitutional committee, Hundhammer inserted an antisecular preamble at the start
of Bavaria's postwar constitution. The Christian Democratic bloc in
Bavaria also successfully added articles that gave confessional
schools constitutional priority over other schools, and enshrined confessional and religious education in public schools.[112]

As the Christian Democrats advocated for these measures, they
hammered home the need for a Catholic state grounded in natural law,
emphasizing that secularization violates the world order and that the
Christian-Western tradition was under threat from international communism.[113] Taking stock of how many members of the party were unwilling to abandon the hobbyhorses of the 1920s and 1930s and update
themselves, commentators affirmed their "Ungleichzeitigkeit zur
Moderne"—their asynchrony with the modern. Bavaria in 1917–1918
had been at the cusp of the Catholic revolution to transform law and
culture. In the 1940s and 1950s it continued to cling strongly to its
interwar identity, despite its signs of serious wear.

The Confessional State, Democratic or Not

The Vatican in the mid- to late 1940s showed an impressive aptitude
for remaining the same in changed circumstances. As in the interwar
years, re-Christianizing the state—in Italy, Germany, Austria, and
elsewhere—remained its priority. The extent to which this was true
was born out by the pope's response to antidemocratic Spain in the
1940s and 1950s. Pius XII not only maintained relations with Franco's
dictatorship throughout the 1940s—he actively propped up Spain as a
model for a "Catholic State" done right.

In Spain, following a period of brutal repression, Franco consolidated his rule, and encouraged the drafting of a constitution over the

summer of 1945. Known as the Fuero de los Españoles, the text enumerated a set of rights purportedly recognized by the dictatorial regime. Many promises were a charade (Spain was, for instance, not at all interested in protecting freedom of speech and opinion, despite the text's promises to the contrary), but Pius XII nonetheless asserted that the southern European country was on a right and noble path, and gave his personal benediction to Spain's "Jefe."[114] Papal officials celebrated the Fuero's article 6, according to which the Catholic religion was the religion of state, and only the Catholic Church was allowed to engage in public religious activities—a right no other faith enjoyed.[115] This article would justify sharp restrictions on Spain's Protestant population (which numbered about 30,000) and came under fierce attack in the 1960s, in light of the Conciliar Declaration *Dignitatis humanae* of July 1965.[116] But in the early postwar years, the Holy See and its interlocutors in Spain were happy to see a Constitution that combatted the insidious "spirit of liberalism" and beat back the tendency to separate church and state and obstruct the state's Christianization.[117]

For these reasons and more, the Holy See was happy to defend Spain in the court of international opinion. In 1946 the Vatican vigorously protested the exclusion of Spain from the United Nations. The American Jesuit Edmund Walsh, one of the pioneers of the interwar Catholic anticommunist crusade, ominously warned that "the fate of the Christian order in Spain, and with it the future of the whole world lay in the balance." He added that Spain was "the last bulwark of what remains of the Christian West" and that Stalin's "chief objective" was to knock it down.[118] The London-based *Catholic Times* agreed, arguing that the UN's move ignored "Spain's contribution to the Christian cause" and damaged "that Catholic unity of effort upon which the salvation of the world from the communist menace mainly depends." Other Catholics pushed back. Catholic resistance leader Henri Frenay suggested that if Spain were allowed to join the United Nations, it would be "difficult to present ourselves as champions of liberty [and] outspokenly proclaim the necessity to defend human rights."[119] Luigi Sturzo argued that Spain needed to be kept out, in that the principles of the Atlantic Charter and the statute of the United Nations "needed to be considered ethical and juridical imperatives" that were "to be loyally respected, forever."[120] As John Courtney Murray noted in a memorandum addressed to Monsignor Giovanni Battista Montini, the Vatican's loyalty to Spain got in the way of it being able to "fully and sincerely affirm the human and political values of a democratically organized political society."[121]

But despite objections, the Holy See continued to propose Spain as a model. In 1946, overcoming internal opposition from Europeans opposed to Franco's iron rule over the country, the Vatican agreed to have nondemocratic Spain host the first postwar World Congress of the major transnational Catholic civil society organization, Pax Romana. The Congress was organized by Franco's minister of education, Joaquín Ruiz-Giménez, who in 1948 would become Spain's ambassador to the Vatican and lead negotiator for an impending Spanish-Vatican concordat.[122] The stated purpose of the Congress was to celebrate the fourth centenary of the death of Francisco de Vitoria (1492–1546), the Dominican scholar widely seen as the father of a new "Catholicized" field of international law—which drew heavily on natural law. Cardinal Pizzardo asserted that because "the program of Pax Romana" was "the collaboration with the hierarchy for the extension and defense of the Kingdom of Our Lord Jesus Christ," Vitoria seemed a natural reference point and source of inspiration.[123]

Pax Romana's 1946 World Congress was a lavish display of old-style papal internationalism. The conference was held in Salamanca, the city of Franco's civil war headquarters, and it attracted more than 500 participants. About a dozen ecclesiastical advisors from the Vatican were in attendance, as were delegates from several Latin American countries, most of Western Europe, Britain, and the United States. The final address of the conference, delivered by the British archbishop of Cardiff, Michael McGrath, averred that this World Congress was proof positive that the world understood "that Spain saved Europe during her Civil War, as she did at Lepanto." "On behalf of Catholics throughout the world," the archbishop gushed, directly addressing the Spanish conference organizers, "I want to thank you for having saved Europe; and we thank God that He granted you victory." He vowed that Catholics would "not forget" Spain's valiant "fight against materialism and heresy"—a fight that had great relevance in the context of the simmering Cold War.[124]

The archbishop was not the only person to use the Pax Romana stage to celebrate Spain as a bastion of anticommunist resistance. Throughout the fourteen days of the conference, delegates tirelessly referenced Spain's importance in fighting the Soviet Union. They lamented how little the Western world had learned from the Spanish example. They lambasted Western powers' decisions to work closely with the Soviet Union. They theatrically read aloud from *Divini Redemptoris*. Ignoring the existence of Western and Eastern European coalition governments that depended on dialogue across party lines, Pax Romana delegates emphasized that Marxism was intrinsically perverse and that Catholics were barred from any sort of collaboration or dialogue with communist forces. Finally, delegates celebrated the work of the "Catholic International," which through its "tactical and offensive character" and "militant activism" had opposed the workings of communist internationalism.[125]

Pius XII's last great political-legal project of the 1950s was the conclusion of a concordat with Spain (1953). As the pope saw it, concordat diplomacy was still the key to solving the relationship between Church and state.[126] The Spanish hierarchy helped speed the project along, informing the country's papal nuncio that Spain must continue to act "as the right arm of the Catholic Church, because so much heroism, so many prayers, such martyrdom, could not be wasted."[127] Pius XII, for his part, asserted that the concordat would help crown Spain as a model of Church–state collaboration and anticommunist resistance.[128] "Spain is beautiful," Pius XII announced, not just because of her "blue skies" and "never-ending beaches," but also and more so "because of her fidelity to the Church, [and] her firm devotion to the faith—a faith for which, as she amply demonstrated, she was ready to lay down her life."[129]

The concordat with Spain was the culmination of more than a decade of diplomacy. It affirmed that Catholicism was "the only religion of the Spanish people."[130] It gave the Church the right to conduct its pastoral work freely and to own and manage property. It guaranteed Church control over religious education in both private and public schools, through the choice of religious faculty and religious materials.[131] The Spanish state also agreed to exempt the Church from taxes, and to exempt clergy from military service. It recognized all Church holidays as state holidays and gave ecclesiastical courts final say on questions regarding marriage and annulment. As General Francisco Franco explained, the concordat implied that non-Catholics would still be allowed to practice their religions in private, but not in public, for doing so would conflict with Spain's "Catholic unity." "This tolerance toward other creeds does not mean freedom of propaganda likely to foster religious discrepancies and perturb the sage and unanimous possession of religious truth in this country," Franco noted.[132]

Despite the fact that it was accompanied by a push to limit the rights of other religions, the Spanish concordat of 1953, signed with no prior public debate, was applauded by many Catholic commentators as "the most exemplary accord" signed by Rome.[133] As it had in the 1920s, the papacy argued that individual nation-states would be strengthened by concordats, insofar as "the more deeply a citizen feels himself bound to the eternal foundation of faith and divine law, so much more solid and resistant will be the ties that bind him to the state."[134] Franco hailed the concordat as "the work of a Nation that in all Christianity is justly regarded as the Catholic Nation *por excelencia.*" Spanish Catholic Action characterized it as "a model concordat between the Holy See and a Catholic state in the twentieth century."[135] In these ways and more, the 1953 concordat with Spain was strongly reminiscent of the 1929 Lateran Agreements—which had been similarly fêted even though they elevated the reputation of a dictatorial state and facilitated its entry into the international community. Others saw scant cause for celebration. Commenting on how 1953 was the year, not only of the concordat, but also of a momentous diplomatic agreement with the United States over military bases, an angry Basque political exile stated that Franco had "sold the soul of Spain to the Vatican and her body to the United States!"[136]

※

But had the papacy really claimed the soul not just of Spain but of Western Europe as a whole? Initially, it certainly seemed as though it was doing quite well for itself indeed. The United States, eager to ground its presence in Western Europe and protect itself from the Soviet Union, had agreed to mobilize against the victory of communism at the polls, support Catholic Action movements, and place many of the central themes from the papacy's interwar anticommunist campaign back in circulation. The United States also agreed to back Christian Democratic parties—parties that, with Church support, were able to rise to power in much of Western Europe. Once the Christian Democrats seized power, most appeared willing to do the pope's bidding, and confirm interwar concordats. Both the Christian Democrats and the United States, in turn, participated in a troubling reworking of history, which swept under the rug Vatican involvement in interwar ethno-nationalist movements, and presented the Cold War against communism as the simple continuation of the "hot war" against Nazi-Fascism. How long would the fragile alliance between the United States, Christian Democracy, and the papacy last? How long would it take before the papacy's interwar diplomatic practices would come back to haunt it? As it turned out, the honeymoon of the early postwar years would be short-lived, and the high times of the mid 1940s would quickly give way to years of crisis and profound questioning.

9

History Haunts the Church

It is not easy to be Christian in such times. No one is immune from incurring guilt and blame.

—ERNST-WOLFGANG BÖCKENFÖRDE, 1965

STARTING FROM THE LATE 1940s the Vatican increasingly came under fire—not just from expected quarters, but from within Catholic ranks as well. Through its underwriting of Cold War mythologies, the papacy had aligned itself with a militarized new world order that had shut down the possibilities of fruitful Catholic-socialist and Catholic-communist cooperation. As a result of helping invite the United States to grow its presence in Europe, Pius XII acquired the epithet "Coca-Cola pope"—a booster for American military might and American economic assistance. Further, a new generation of Catholics accused the Holy See of an enduring unwillingness to address its interwar behavior regarding Fascism and Nazism. They questioned its role in the rise and maintenance of European imperialism. And they wondered whether it was time to advance a new vision for Europe—one that depended on the rejection of papal internationalism and revisited some of the key themes of Catholic dissidents of the 1930s and early 1940s.

Troubles started in Poland. From the heart of this interwar Catholic battlefield came a movement pioneered by a new generation of Polish Catholics responding to the papacy's promotion of Cold War anticommunism. They created a so-called Catholic-Socialist International, an organization that was meant to encourage Catholics to see socialists and communists as potential friends and allies. In tandem, in Western Europe, Christian Democratic parties began to forge their own internationalist vision—one separate and distinct from that of the pope. Though the Vatican initially only saw the development of the Catholic-Socialist International as a threat, the growth of a robust Western European Christian Democratic International would pose a greater challenge in the long run. Its existence would weaken the papacy's hold on Catholic civil society structures and embolden a rival brand of political Christianity: one that would withdraw its support form concordats, advocate the separation of church and state, and undermine the papacy's mechanisms for keeping European states in line with Catholic teachings.

Rival Internationalisms and the Splintering of the Catholic Bloc

In 1947, with the founding of the Nouvelles Équipes Internationales (NEI), Western European Christian Democratic parties began to strengthen their transnational connections. In the late 1940s the NEI created its own independent youth organization, which in 1951 was renamed the International Union of Young Christian Democrats. By 1951, the NEI also had an active cultural commission, an East-West commission, and a commission to intensify promotion of European integration. It was working closely with Christian Democrats in Latin America and with some Eastern European Christian Democrats in exile. Additionally, by the late 1940s, prominent postwar European Christian Democrats had begun gathering in secret and unofficial discussion groups known as the "Geneva circles." Like the NEI, the Geneva circles aimed to foster a sense of international mission and unity across national borders. Though figures in regular contact with the Holy See played a role in several of these early gatherings, the Vatican was not their prime initiator, much less the guiding force. Neither was the pope regularly briefed on the content of the conversations.[1]

The new political hegemony of Christian Democratic parties in Western Europe encouraged closer cooperation. In France, Germany, Italy, and Belgium, Christian Democratic parties had emerged as the natural parties of government, and they controlled key ministries, dominating foreign and European policy. Loose ideas of European coop- eration and integration—which had remained largely hypothetical in the interwar years—could now be implemented. Additionally, unlike in the interwar years, both France and Germany were now compara- tively weak countries, and their leaders recognized that in order to re- build strength, they would need to work together rather than at cross purposes. The absence of Eastern European politicians (due to the Cold War) eased potential rivalries. Transnational exchange was also facili- tated by the existence of new venues such as the Council of Europe and the Common Assembly of the European Coal and Steel Community.

Though it would take many years for cooperation to translate into economic and political integration, by the early 1950s it was possible to speak of a Christian Democratic International—that is, of an organ- ization of Christian Democratic parties, led by lay politicians, that met regularly to discuss shared concerns and themes, with an eye toward fostering deeper future cooperation. The Christian Democratic Interna- tional self-consciously operated without clerical oversight and without the direct approval of the pope. Pius XII intentionally remained ex- ternal to developments, limiting himself to campaigning on behalf of Christian Democratic parties and to generic calls for European unity. Heeding the advice of Giovanni Battista Montini (future Pope Paul VI), the pope did not send an observer to the earliest meetings between Christian Democrats fostering transnational cooperation, hoping to avoid "misunderstandings" and the possibility that "the enemies of the Church" would try to discredit Christian Democratic political action.[2]

Had the pope kept a closer watch on the budding Christian Demo- cratic International, he might have seen the movement as more of a threat. This was because even though members of the NEI shared cer- tain baseline anticommunist beliefs, many of them advocated for po- litical Catholicism to move to the left in order to effectively oppose the Soviet Union. At the first NEI congress, for instance, the Domin- ican Father Louis-Joseph Lebret, who would soon play a key role at the Second Vatican Council, urged delegates to convey "a ferment of avant- garde progressiveness." At a later congress, held in Italy in the spring of 1950, Luigi Sturzo celebrated Christian Democracy's root commitments to "liberty" and "the social state" as two essential pillars and conditions for its success in the hegemonic struggle against communism. In keeping with the early *travailliste* (working-class centered) orientation of the French Christian Democratic party, André Collin, leader of the French Mouvement Républicain Populaire, emphasized that Christian Democracy must advance worker-friendly policies and ideologies, and above all refuse to "abandon the laboring masses who place their hopes in us." Furthermore, taking their distance from the pope, Christian Democratic delegates at the NEI congresses recognized the need for cross-confessional alliance building. They pushed back against the notion that Christian Democracy was building a "Vatican" or "Christian Europe."[3] Some Christian Democrats also criticized the rigidity of the emergent Cold War order. They argued that working closely with the United States was a mistake, and that Christian Democrats should instead strive to be a neutral and "third force" in world politics.[4] Pius XII, by contrast, continued to employ Cold War hermeneutics. Just three weeks after the start of the Korean War, he emphasized the perils of pacifism, the threat of communism, and the importance of halting those powers interested in destroying "the sacred rights of the Catholic Church."[5] Additionally, Christian Democratic hesitations notwithstanding, Pius XII emphasized that Vatican Europe was no pipe dream. Waxing lyrical over the possibilities of "powerfully uniting the people of Europe under the flag of the authority of Christ and creating a joyous Christian regime," the pope harkened back to medieval times when "the Holy See was the center and guarantee of this unity and the Roman Pontiff, Prince of the Apostles and Chief of the Church, was seen as the Father of this great Christian family."[6]

As Pius XII saw things, the only way to face the rising tide of communist and socialist internationalism was still, as before, through a Catholic internationalist movement led by the pope. Though Pius XII's tactics did not sit well with all Christian Democrats, it was certainly true that communists and socialists were on the ascendant. Not only was the Labor and Socialist International busy transforming itself into what, beginning in 1951, would be called the Socialist International; in addition, in 1947 Stalin reconstituted the Comintern, rebranding it the Cominform, or Communist Information Bureau. Composed of the Communist Parties of Bulgaria, Czechoslovakia, France, Hungary, Italy, Poland, Romania, the Soviet Union, and Yugoslavia, the Cominform was not just a tool for top-down control of the communist movement. It was also a way for Communist Parties—some of which were enjoying genuine popular support—to trade skills and information.

In response Pius XII fretted, much as he had in the interwar years, about the creeping of Catholics toward these two movements. It was at this point that the Vatican received word of a new Catholic organization getting off the ground in Poland. Dziś i Jutro (Today and Tomorrow), named after its eponymous journal, was founded by an infamous interwar right-wing Fascist, Bolesław Piasecki, just after World War II. By the late 1940s, in the wake of Germany's division, the organization had settled on its goal: building what it called a "Catholic-Socialist International." The movement's partisans—who soon included Catholics not just in Poland but also in France, Italy, East Germany, Czechoslovakia, and Hungary—made pleas for peace and claimed that Catholics and socialists were not at the antipodes. They protested Germany's division and remilitarization and the rallying of Western Europeans to the "bloc" mentality imposed by the Cold War, proposing to bring Catholics sympathetic to socialism under one shared roof.

Much to the pope's chagrin, Dziś i Jutro (known since 1952 as PAX) not only articulated its "pro-peace" anti-Germanism in self-avowedly Catholic lingo; the organization also was careful to present itself as a friend of Polish Stalinism. Thus, throughout the entire postwar decade the organization did not protest the antireligious practices in the Soviet bloc. It was also one of the only Catholic organizations not to be suppressed by the government.[7] Against the backdrop of antireligious actions by the governments of the Soviet Union, Hungary, Czechoslovakia, Poland, and Romania—the incarceration of leading ecclesiastics, the expulsion of the last apostolic nuncio in Eastern Europe, and the attack on national Catholic Action organizations —Dziś i Jutro stayed mum.[8] And though the work of Dziś i Jutro activists was theirs alone (Poland's new communist leaders neither directed the work, nor fully understood it), this did not spare them from the papacy's wrath. By the late 1940s, following the Cominform's call for cooperation with Catholics "who want peace and defense of their vital interests [and] seek cooperation and unity with the non-Catholic workers' movement," Pius XII requested the surveillance of Catholic progressive milieus sympathetic to the Polish movement in France and Belgium.[9] In the early 1950s, the Holy Office would begin the official process of censure, and by 1955 it had condemned Dziś i Jutro's flagship journal and a collection of essays by the movement's founder.

By this point, however, several Western European Catholics had already joined with Polish activists to express their openness to a Communist-led peace movement. Spearheaded by the Stockholm Appeal, this movement called for a complete ban on nuclear weapons and the unity of "all humanity" around peace, irrespective of "political or religious opinions." In response, Pius XII publicly chided "pacifist efforts or propaganda originating from those who deny all belief in God" as "always very dubious."[10] The *Osservatore Romano*, for its part, asserted that the Soviets could not speak of peace, for everywhere they went, they made war. In a historic first, the Vatican daily went so far as to accuse the Soviet Union of having started World War II.[11]

In tandem, the papacy became more anxious that Western European Christian Democratic parties were not doing enough to counter insurgents in their own ranks. Why was Christian Democracy not cracking down on those members of the party advocating open dialogue with communists across the Iron Curtain? And why had Christian Democrats not yet spearheaded a large-scale anti-Soviet front within Western Europe, leaving that job instead to a host of Catholic civil society organizations and to groups covertly funded by Washington? Lambasting Western European Christian Democrats for their slow action to fight communism and left-wing Catholic tendencies, the Vatican expressed a growing frustration with a Christian Democratic movement unwilling to do its bidding.

As was the case after World War I, the papacy's expectations for Italy were particularly high. Following the pope's heavy involvement in the 1948 Italian elections, in February 1949 Eugenio Pacelli sat down with the Italian Christian Democratic leader, Alcide De Gasperi. The purpose of the encounter, for the pope, was to use the occasion of the twentieth anniversary of the Lateran Pacts to send the Christian Democrat a warning: De Gasperi must promise to launch a no-holds-barred campaign against communism, or risk losing Vatican support. Indeed, De Gasperi's baseline allegiance to an anti-Fascist ideology that held open the possibility of Catholic-communist cooperation, the pope suggested, was out of step with the times and not an acceptable stance, given the present conditions of the Cold War. Italian bishops similarly encouraged their Christian Democratic interlocutors to abandon what they considered the naive era of dialogue with communism and accept that "communism continues to represent the most horrible enemy for souls and for the Church."[12] Pius XII personally asked a prominent Christian Democrat, Mario Cingolani, to inform De Gasperi, "You need to act with more decision, and be stronger."[13]

As papal diplomats counseled, Christian Democracy must build an ambitious anticommunist front, composed of a range of right-wing parties and groups.[14] Members of the Roman Curia believed that Christian Democrats were creating a "curtain of smoke that hides from view the danger that Bolshevism embodies." The problem, they said, had been long in the making: after all, the partisans of the "anti-Franco campaign," who had entered the ranks of Christian Democracy, had been disorienting Catholic minds since the late 1930s. If Christian Democracy took a hard-line position against international communism, then it would finally be able to seize its historic role.[15]

As members of the Roman Curia counseled, part and parcel of Christian Democracy's hard turn against communism should involve the decision to work in even closer partnership with the United States, by joining with the United States in the North Atlantic Treaty Organization. When the papacy's back-channel campaign in favor of Christian Democratic support for NATO was leaked to the press, the Italian Communist Party's leader, Palmiro Togliatti, penned an article entitled "God and the Atlantic Pact." The piece skewered the Vatican for "granting new legitimacy to the criminal plans of [American] imperialists" under the pretext of seeking "to destroy atheism and exterminate those who 'hate God.'"[16] At the third conference of the Cominform, Togliatti cranked up the volume, encouraging Catholics to break free from "the policy of the leading circles of the Church, who are allies of imperialism and reaction and enemies of social process."[17]

Though few Catholics heeded the words of the Italian Communist party leader, Pius XII decided that the time was ripe for the Holy Office to issue an admonitory decree. Papal insiders declared that doing so would help "open the eyes of the progressive Christian groups that have been collaborating with the Communists."[18] Released on July 1, 1949, the text affirmed that the time had come to shut down those "vain efforts to try to reach an agreement between communism and Christianity." It also barred Catholics from collaborating with Communist Parties or other communist organizations in any form. If they did, they would be punished, up to and including through excommunication. As *Civiltà Cattolica* emphasized, the Holy Office decree definitively "expelled" communism, identifying communism as the Church's "multiform" and "irreducible enemy."[19] Catholicism and communism, as in the good old days, were cast as sworn enemies once again.

If the July 1949 decree sounded like a relic of the 1930s, that is because it was. The first draft of the decree had been penned in the late 1930s by the Holy Office. Then, under papal orders, the Holy Office paused, in the wait-and-see atmosphere of World War II. Only in the mid-1940s, under Pius XII's orders, was work on the decree resumed. The text had been finished for quite some time when, in the summer of 1949, the pope finally decided to make it public.[20] The document sought to reaffirm the centrality of anticommunism to Catholic identity politics, and to compel Christian Democrats and Catholics across Europe to definitively break with a politics of pluralism and underwrite the new Atlantic geography of power. "Because the forces of evil now have a bloc," *Civiltà Cattolica* explained, Catholics must have one too. "One bloc," the journal wrote, "can be countered only through the [existence of the] other bloc."[21] CIA agents applauded, noting that the decree was a "very powerful factor in the East-West struggle" and that it "brought into open and basic conflict . . . the two most powerful organizations for moving men to act on behalf of doctrine": namely, the Communist International and the Holy See.[22] In Latin America the faithful were walked through the decree by a pamphlet entitled *Let's Define Ourselves! Are We Catholics or Communists?*[23] The European Left saw the Holy Office pronouncement as a good organizing opportunity. In Italy, it marked the starting point for a campaign for the full-scale abrogation of the Italian concordat, in the name of European "secularism."[24]

In the short term, the 1949 decree did not lead to the repeal of Europe's concordats—but neither did it consolidate an anticommunist Catholic bloc. Within a year of its issuance, the Polish Church and the Hungarian Church had entered into formal agreements with local communist regimes, independent of any Vatican intervention, and without papal approval. To add insult to injury, the Polish agreement was none other than a concordat—and, more troublingly for the pope, "the first concordat concluded over the head of the Secretariat of State, and without its influence," as a contemporary observer noted.[25] In Western Europe too, the Holy Office's 1949 decree deepened the splintering of Catholic ranks, rather than healing rifts and leading to a rallying around the pope. Leftist Catholics openly sympathetic with socialism and communism, already marginalized, engaged more openly in anti-papal rhetoric, and won new followers.[26] Moderate French and Belgian Christian Democrats, who supported what was known as the "worker-priest movement," which encouraged proselytism in working-class and communist neighborhoods, began to take their distance from the papacy. (In 1953 Pius XII would ban the worker-priest movement on account of its willingness to reach across the Catholic-communist divide.[27]) The decree also led to a break at the highest ranks of the central government of the Roman Catholic Church. Those members of the upper hierarchy who in the 1940s had supported a politics of dialogue—and even favored cross-party coalition governments as a key factor for Europe's stabilization—suddenly found themselves demoted and under attack.[28] Only a handful of those who remained dared to criticize the decree and the new propensity of the Holy See to "start seeing nothing but excommunicated people, everywhere."[29]

The Vatican's 1949 decree marked the opening salvo of a battle to push Western European Christian Democrats farther to the right.[30] As *Civiltà Cattolica* emphasized, waffling in the center was no longer an option "in the present parliamentary situation."[31] Starting from the early 1950s, papal lobbyists thus began to target Italian Christian Democrats, encouraging them to forge an anticommunist front with monarchist and Fascist parties. The alliance building should begin in the upcoming 1952 civic elections in Rome. In what papal officials dubbed the "Sturzo Operation," they encouraged neo-Fascist, monarchist, and Christian Democratic candidates to appear on the same unified electoral list. Luigi Sturzo was chosen as the man to play a leading role: it was he who would announce the idea of creating a broad anticommunist front—a man, that is, "whom no one could accuse of having sympathies for Fascism or a distaste for democracy."[32] Associating

Sturzo with the plan would mean that hesitant Christian Democrats might change their position, because the recommendation would be coming straight from one of Italy's most famous Catholic anti-Fascists. Should the Christian Democrats consent to take part in the Operation, papal lobbyists noted, they would have a chance to prove that they were ready to "courageously and resolutely demonstrate their Christian convictions."[33] Sturzo, concerned about the global rise of the communist movement, let himself be pulled into the drama. As the Sicilian cleric noted, it was time for the Christian Democratic party to show that it was ready to resist "every totalitarian trap and every subversion of a regime of democracy and liberty."[34]

Surprisingly, the Italian Christian Democratic party decided to resist papal pressure. Thanks to the rise of the independent Christian Democratic International, the early 1950s were not the mid-1940s, and now leading Christian Democrats felt they could afford to cross swords with the papacy. In 1952 Alcide De Gasperi, at his party's national congress, not only rejected attempts to move the party to the right and turn it into the leader of an "intransigent anticommunist" movement; he explained that it was high time for Christian Democracy to take a position against the "highest ecclesiastical circles" and against all Catholics who historically had been "so easily drawn to dictatorships and conservative ideas." The Sturzo Operation should be roundly rejected as a terrible idea that, if realized, would manifest as a "grave catastrophe."[35] Within the year, over and against continued clerical attempts to cast the Christian Democrats as an arm of the Catholic Church and a means through which to achieve Italy's full confessionalization, De Gasperi reaffirmed the secularism of his party.[36] The idea that Christian Democracy would doubtless assist the papacy in its long-standing battle against secularization was no longer guaranteed.

✿

The relationship between Catholics and the universal Roman Catholic Church was not just experiencing problems in Italy. Similar contrasts were emerging in Germany and France as well..

When, starting from the late 1940s and early 1950s, Pius XII began to promote the necessity of anti-Russian military defense systems, growing numbers of French Catholics called upon their brethren to reconstitute themselves as a neutral bloc, just as they had during the Spanish Civil War. Prominent figures like Étienne Gilson, for instance, urged fellow Catholics to distance themselves from the United States and the North Atlantic Treaty Organization. NATO, they argued, was a tool of American imperialist power—not a way to keep Europe safe.[37] On the pages of journals like *La vie intellectuelle, Paroisse universitaire,* and *Esprit,* French Catholics expressed concerns about the role of the papacy in perpetuating a climate of war rather than one of peace. Commentators affirmed that the "Coca-Cola pope" had helped build a "Vatican Europe"—a new configuration of geopolitical continental affairs that paved the way for American imperialism and advanced a clerical, conservative, and antimodern agenda.[38] The Catholics criticizing the papacy's role in rebranding Europe were coming from right and left, and included prominent intellectuals like Edmond Michelet, Marcel Prélot, and Louis Terrenoire, and top-flight politicians like Vincent Auriol (president of the French Republic) and Joseph Hours, a founder of the Mouvement Républicain Populaire.[39] As many of these critics argued, rather than falling in line with an American-led and Vatican-backed bipolar order, Europeans must commit to a "third way," neither communist nor capitalist.

The papacy replied by employing euphemistic language and issuing blanket paternalistic statements. As Pius XII emphasized, he stood with the United States because he was in favor of "opening toward the world community."[40] Father Ottaviani, from his post in the Holy Office, urged the laity to get into line with the pope's views—despite a growing demand from below to give both bishops and the laity greater say in setting the papacy's priorities.[41] Pius XII stated that the role of the laity was to "collaborate in the work of the episcopacy"—not chart its own course.[42] "It is necessary that the laity is and remain under the authority, the direction, and the vigilance of those who by divine mandate received the charge to lead the Church of Christ," the pope chided his wayward flock.[43] In a speech on the 85th anniversary of the founding of the Catholic Action youth organization in Italy, the pope resorted to heavily militarized language to emphasize the dangers of disunity. "All Catholic Action," he said, "must be a unified front against the enemy, strong and impermeable as a battalion ready for war." Underlining the importance of the papacy's central leadership, he added: "Remember that a battalion cannot be orderly . . . if it lacks unity of command: for this, we strongly exhort you and all Catholic forces to let yourselves be guided in your apostolic work by he who the Holy Spirit has placed in the position to lead the Church of God."[44]

Though France did, at last, sign on to NATO, its membership would be much-contested and relatively short-lived.[45] In 1954, in another sign of disunity, the French National Assembly voted against ratifying the European Defense Community by a vote of 319 to 264. The pope was furious, and blamed the splintering of the Catholic vote for the results.[46] *Civiltà Cattolica*, for its part, lambasted Catholic internationalists for their inability to join hands and combat communist evil.[47] But many Catholic leaders did not flinch. Referencing the need to think beyond the Cold War (and interwar) Catholic-communist binary, a series of high-profile figures—including, to name only a few, the leader of Christian Democracy in Germany, Konrad Adenauer; the prominent German Catholic theologian Marcel Reding; and Florence's Left Catholic mayor, Giorgio La Pira—planned reconciliation trips to Moscow.[48] La Pira even attempted to organize a world conference that would have brought communists and Catholics together in common dialogue. His efforts were immediately shut down by the Holy See as "inopportune, given the present circumstances."[49] One of Germany's leading national newspapers caught wind of the developments and came out against the papacy—and in favor of a "shift toward coexistence."[50] On November 1, 1954, the highest-ranking supporter of dialogue and an opponent of the papacy's hard-line anticommunist positions was ousted from Rome, after which time the pope refused to grant the exiled cleric a single audience.[51] Pius XII justified his response, asserting that he was simply doing what was needed to preserve his title as "defender of the freedoms of the Church" and "defender of Christianity."[52] In sermon after sermon, he reiterated the core components of the 1949 decree, reminding his listeners that all forms of "encounter" or "discussion" with communists were strictly prohibited.[53] In February 1956 the director of the *Osservatore Romano* penned a prickly article reminding Catholics that even in the wake of Khrushchev's de-Stalinization speech (February 1956), discussion with communists remained impossible.[54] The more things changed, the more they seemed to stay the same.

Nonetheless, the ground under the Vatican was shifting. Its relationship with the United States was being suddenly thrown in question because of a series of recent developments, including the decision of the U.S. Supreme Court to affirm the separation of Church and state, and the wave of anti-Catholic sentiment that was sweeping the United States, in the context of a debate over the rights of private and parochial schools.[55] During the same period, an anticommunist religious front led by the United States government spectacularly failed, largely because of a strong surge in American Protestant anti-Catholicism, which manifested in American Protestant Churches objecting to joining in an anticommunist front with the pope.[56] Frightened by the threats he was receiving on a weekly basis regarding his ties to "anti-American" Rome, Myron Taylor in January 1950 resigned as Truman's personal representative to the pope. Therein Pius XII lost a crucial point of contact with the American president. Regular diplomatic relations between the Holy See and the United States would not be reestablished until 1984, during the presidency of Ronald Reagan.

Papal officers took the departure of Truman's personal representative from Rome as a personal affront—not least because it came on the heels of the declaration of the 1950 Holy Year and undermined the fiction of a Cold War West led by two closely allied powers.[57] At the same time, the break with the Americans provided an opportunity for the Vatican to rebut the charge that it had been a booster for American hegemony in Europe. Thus, from 1950 on, the pope revived a previously suppressed anti-Americanism. As Pius XII now affirmed, the United States' position in the Cold War was hypocritical: the great power, despite all its anticommunist talk, seemed uninterested in bringing down the Iron Curtain. Impervious to the persecutions and rights violations underway in the Eastern bloc, the United States was taking no serious action. Perhaps, the pope bitterly suggested, the United States was more interested in *realpolitik* and the profit motive than in upholding the principles of Christian morality.[58] The Vatican, papal diplomats noted, stood alone in its "prophetic" denunciation of the Soviet Union. The United States was a false leader.[59] In a radio message to the world, the pope denounced American materialism, American hypermodernity (which "reduced society to automatization"), and several other shortcomings of that part of the world "that loves to call itself the 'free world.'" As the pope sarcastically noted, the so-called free world in fact was beginning to pose a fundamental threat to freedom, in that it was doing nothing to counter the growing numbers of people on its soil who stood against the Church, which was the only true guarantor of "authentic liberty."[60]

In the mid-1950s, the pope took a step further, presenting the United States as a dangerous opponent of Catholic internationalism. The United States "denied the transcendent," and instead sought to reduce and resolve everything through man-made techniques and technologies, running roughshod over "the primacy of the spiritual."[61] The materialist craze, the pope asserted, had pushed an expanding and poorly regulated Hollywood film industry to profit from the depiction of "exciting, insidious, and corrupting" scenes devoid of any educational or religious content—scenes that showed humanity's dark side without exploring or explaining its capacity to redeem itself.[62] And when it came to the letter of the law, the new U.S.-led international legal community had made a grave mistake in not placing more emphasis on natural law. In so doing, it had undermined the possibility for "all peace-making action" and "international reconciliation." "Natural law," Pius XII argued, "is the common and solid foundation of all law, the universal language necessary for all understanding" and that which gives "international law" its binding, "obligatory character." For this reason, the recognition of natural law was the necessary prerequisite in the "prevention of conflicts" and the building of a genuine peace.[63] Ten years later, in his 1955 Christmas sermon, Pius XII also came out strongly against the horrors of atomic war and the United States' use of the atom bomb. Catholic youth activists, particularly outside of Europe, enthusiastically picked up on the new version of papal anti-Americanism, while older members of the European left wondered why the pope had been silent all these years.[64]

In keeping with its new-and-old anti-Americanism, the 1950s Vatican—as it had in the interwar years—took a hard stance against Protestantism and interconfessional dialogue. Coming out strongly against Protestant proselytism in southern Europe, the pope argued that in Catholic-majority states, "error" (in the form of non-Catholic religions) had no rights and that therefore Protestant activism must be curtailed.[65] He elaborated in an audience with American journalists visiting Rome, "It is obvious and fundamental to observe that man, endowed by his Creator with freedom of choice between good and evil, is not thereby given the right to choose evil; but he is privileged freely to choose the good, which is his duty, and thus merit the eternal reward reserved for him by God."[66] The pope's defenders further claimed that limiting the rights of non-Catholic religions was a behavior "in conformity with the doctrine of the Church."[67] Indeed, they explained that the poisonous export of the "Anglo-Saxon" model of "subjective individualism and indifferentism" had led Catholics to conclude that complete religious freedom was demanded "by the exigencies of modern times."[68] Shortly thereafter, the Holy Office issued a decree banning interconfessional dialogue.[69] Dissenters fired back in defense of liberty and against the confessionalization of the state as a dangerous anachronism. Citing Maritain as their guide, growing numbers of Catholic theologians began to reference the need for Catholic pluralism and a true religious freedom that opened the way for *all* faiths to have a role in the public sphere.[70]

The papacy was unmoved. The Holy Office successfully pulled from publication an edited book on Catholic understandings of religious freedom, and drafted extended attacks on the calls for religious freedom put forward by figures like Jacques Maritain, Yves Congar, Jacques Leclercq, and John Courtney Murray.[71] In March 1953, in a speech at the Lateran University, Cardinal Ottaviani, pro-secretary of the Holy Office, condemned the "liberalization thesis" and spoke in favor of "the Catholic state."[72] Within the year, the Holy Office had issued a formal statement declaring the Catholic confessional state "an ideal to which organized political society is universally obliged" and condemning "full religious liberty."[73]

In another sign that history was haunting the Holy See, *Civiltà Cattolica* suddenly decided to issue a deeply critical review of Jacques Maritain's work *Integral Humanism.* The mid-1950s review condemned not just the 1936 book but also the "radical Catholic" and "contemporary progressivist wing" that had flourished as a result of Maritain's thinking—a wing that was at once unwilling to defend the West from Bolshevism and eager to engage communists and other non-Catholics ("those furthest from Christian truth") in dialogue. As the journal's editor-in-chief irately put it, Maritain and his "progressivist" allies "believed themselves to be the evangelical progenitors of a new society . . . whereas in reality, contemporary society, with its aberrant attitudes, penetrates [the progressivist] and conquers him, models him in its image, and absorbs him, removing from him all his positive and benevolent attempts to further grow Christianity in the world." In the same issue, Father Messineo celebrated a second classic from the interwar years: Henri Massis's *L'Occident et son destin*, originally published in 1927. Massis's uncompromising Catholicism, and his call to defend the West against the atheistic East, had "tragic contemporary relevance," the Jesuit father noted.[74] Nearly thirty years had passed since the publication of Massis's text, but the Jesuit journal nonetheless decided that the most expedient way to make its point about the direction of European Catholicism and European Catholic politics was to take a giant step backward to the interwar battle for the soul of Catholicism.

The Shock of the Global

None of the Vatican's interwar orthodoxies were safe in the storm-swept 1950s. Starting in 1947 and then with increasing vigor beginning in the early 1950s, a new generation of border-crossing Catholic third-world intellectuals began coming out strongly against the papacy's long-standing hesitance to criticize European imperialism. After all, a revolution was under way: in just two decades after the end of World War II, nearly all of Europe's colonies in Africa and Asia gained independence, in what one scholar has called "one of the most dramatic processes of political emancipation in world history."[75]

Pius XII had, like his predecessor, stressed the importance of developing indigenous clergy and of not imposing "European cultural models" on "new nations, proud of their own sometimes ancient cultures." However, he at the same time did not come out strongly in favor of the wave of anticolonialism sweeping much of the world.[76] Furthermore, the papacy tacitly underwrote French colonial ambitions in Vietnam when it recognized the so-called Associated State of Vietnam, which the French had proclaimed in 1949, following three brutal years of war against the Viet Minh. Papal officials also welcomed the new French-appointed emperor, Bao Dai, to Rome for an audience with the pope, and framed the key question in Vietnam as one, not of independence from colonial rule, but of curtailing the spread of communist influence. (The Viet Minh were aided after 1949 by China's new communist government, which Pius XII sternly criticized in his 1958 encyclical, *Ad Apostolorum Principis: On Communism in China*.) The situation effectively blinded the papacy to the growing numbers of anticolonial Catholics in Vietnam, and his statements and actions made life infinitely more difficult for Catholics on the ground, in that the Viet Minh became more hostile to Catholics following Pius XII's pronouncements.[77]

The urgings of the anticolonialist movement grew more insistent. In 1950, in his conversation-changing *Discours sur le colonialisme*, the Martinican poet and political activist Aimé Césaire accused the Church of colluding in the oppression of colonial peoples. In 1953 the bishops of Madagascar prepared the ground for Catholic anticolonialist discourse by affirming that it was a real mistake to argue that embracing decolonization was tantamount to embracing communism.[78] Then a group of African Catholic students based in France got the church hierarchy's attention through a movement in favor of decolonization. On the pages of the French-based *Présence Africaine*, scholar-activists like Alioune Diop and Léopold Senghor called upon the Church to respect African culture, discipline racist European missionaries in Africa, and get behind the decolonization wave. They established ties with European Catholic youth organizations, most of which had favored colonialization and defended the "civilizing mission" through the early- to mid-1950s. On the heels of France's loss of Indochina and the start of the Algerian War, however, the opinions of these lay Catholics began to shift—a transformation Catholic organizations populated by non-European students and intellectuals were only too happy to speed along.[79] But high-ranking European clergy and missionary societies based in territories on the threshold of independence continued to resist calls for independence. In Cameroon, for instance, the upper hierarchy cast doubt on the "moral steadfastness and spiritual earnestness" of the territory's Christians, claiming that only through Western involvement could the lot of African subjects improve. These figures even deployed the language of human rights in their attempts to undermine the cause of anticolonial activists through their lobbying of international institutions, such as the United Nations.[80]

In response, anticolonial activists, such as those gathered within the French Union of Catholic African Students, cranked up the volume. The Franco-African group—whose numbers were growing every year, not least because the number of African students in France had doubled between 1949 and 1960—became active in print campaigns and conferences.[81] Their request was loud and bold: it was time, they said, for the central government of the Roman Catholic Church and "the highest Catholic authorities," to issue a clear condemnation of the "sin" of colonialism. Through a ninety-page booklet, *The Catholic Hierarchy and Colonial Ethics*, they compiled cherry-picked speeches and texts by Catholic clergy between 1880 and 1954, in a bid to convince both French and African Catholics that Catholic teachings actually opposed colonialism. In a lecture in Paris in the same year delivered by the organization's main clerical protector, Father Joseph Michel, the enterprising African Catholic students sent the message that France had a "duty to decolonize." Father Michel affirmed that Catholic anticolonialism had deep roots, that Catholic social teachings mandated decolonization, and that colonization had almost never led to the well-being or development of colonized people.[82] Though in 1954 Pius XII had announced that colonized peoples had the right to seek freedom, the Catholic students' views were considerably more radical, presenting decolonization not as acceptable but as necessary, in view of the toxic "accomplishments" of European imperialism over the course of the last several centuries.

Conservatives in the French Church were troubled by the new movement. Monsignor Marcel Lefebvre, the pope's delegate in French sub-Saharan Africa, condemned the students and their clerical defenders for their "extreme" views, while Father Joseph-Vincent Ducatillon, the provincial superior of the Dominican order in France, defended a "theology of colonization," through reference to Francisco de Vitoria. Arguing that peoples and goods had the right to circulate freely, Ducattillon noted that colonization should be understood as the right to circulate for the betterment of all peoples. "Colonial expansion" was best "defined as the need of abundant and evolving peoples, brimming with vitality, to spread, to swarm, to pour out, to find spaces and new countries where they can exercise their spirit of adventure and enterprise," all the while respecting the dignity of local inhabitants and ensuring that "nothing should be unjustly taken from them." Cardinal Feltin, the archbishop of Paris, expressed milder views, but nonetheless positioned himself against the African students too. He asserted that the Church was interested in the fate of Africans and African Catholicism, but also that it did not endorse anticolonial revolution. "Exaggerations," he said, could fuel extremism, and this was something the Church opposed: in place of revolution, the Church favored "change that transforms hearts and minds bit by bit, so men can become brothers."[83] How exactly the cleric sought to translate this vague recommendation into practice in the context of raging anticolonial and neocolonial wars was unclear.

The African students and their supporters in France did not relent. In 1956, as anticolonial movements in sub-Saharan Africa were on the rise, the African students helped promote a booklet written by a group of African priests, entitled *Des prêtres noirs s'interrogent* (Black priests are wondering). The text condemned missionary activism in Africa, highlighting in particular the inability of European missionaries to understand or treat local populations with respect. In the same year, the African students held their first annual convention at Pau, where they issued a loud call for decolonization and African autonomy. "We affirm our attachment to the natural right of African peoples to self-determination," they announced. "Rather than diminishing this attachment, our faith reinforces it, because it aims at the liberation and the spiritual blossoming of man." At a time when the majority of French people were ambivalent about the just-won independence of Tunisia and Morocco and opposed Algerian self-rule, the students reaffirmed the "duty to decolonize" for all countries, including Algeria. The following year they held their second annual convention in Rome, where they targeted several members of the Vatican hierarchy for lobbying. In a speech on behalf of African students and attended by the secretary of Propaganda Fide, Pietro Cardinal Sigismondi, the leading spokesperson of the African students called on "religious authorities" to support the cause of decolonization. "The Church," he said, "which has taken the part of the weak over and over again for centuries, must be an active presence at the side of colonized peoples

at this decisive moment." "Should not the church take a solemn position against colonialism?"[84]

The same weekend that the African students convened in Rome,
the pope released his answer to the charge of being imperial Europe's
handmaiden. The encyclical, *Fidei Donum*, was drafted with the help
of Monsignor Lefebvre. Though milder than Lefebvre's tirades, the text
was certainly no ringing endorsement of decolonization. In keeping
with earlier statements issued by Benedict XV and Pius XI, it emphasized that European missionaries should prepare for decolonization by
training indigenous clergy.[85] At the same time, the text celebrated the
European civilizing mission, much as Pius XII had in his 1955 Christmas
message, which had urged colonial peoples to credit "Europe . . . for
their advancement," adding that without European influence, "they
might have been drawn by a blind nationalism to plunge into chaos or
slavery."[86] In keeping with this, the encyclical stressed that despite
the growing numbers of African clergy, native clergy alone would not
be sufficient to bring about the continent's re-Christianization.
Thus, Pius XII called upon bishops from around the world to redouble
their efforts to send missions and funds to Africa. Further eschewing
the explicit question of decolonization, the encyclical emphasized
that sometimes achieving independence too quickly could harm a nation rather than help it. Finally, the pope discussed at length the manifold threats to newly independent nations, particularly communism
and Americanization.[87] The African students were disappointed, but
unsurprised: they knew that change from on high would come neither
easily nor quickly.

Meanwhile several European Christian Democrats began to slowly
come around to the positions of anticolonial activists. In 1960 the Nouvelles Équipes Internationales chose as the theme of its annual conference "Christian Democracy and the Third World." The conference
resolution called for a world development fund and respect for the economic sovereignty of independent nations. It also cautioned the United
States and the Soviet Union against trying to assert their influence on
newly decolonized countries. The following year the NEI conference
took a radical step forward. In its concluding documents, members of
this emergent Christian Democratic International proclaimed the right
of all peoples to national self-determination, in keeping with the princi-

ples laid out long ago in the 1941 Atlantic Charter, and, before that, those of Benedict XV and Pius XI in the interwar years.[88] Pius XII was still unwilling to go this route, but the new organization seemed ready to strike out a new course and, in the words of a leading Italian Christian Democrat, embrace the "profound transformation in the balance of global power since the Second World War." "We certainly can no longer assert that there are some peoples that make history and others that merely experience it: the democratic conscience of the world would rebel against this view."[89]

Speaking in concert with the African students who since the 1950s had been calling for equality, dignity, and independence for colonized peoples, many young Catholics and Christian Democrats in Europe joined anticolonial student movements in the 1960s, helping spawn a distinctive new Catholic third-worldism.[90] Pax Romana, which in the early postwar years had hewed close to the pope and celebrated Franco's Spain, took the turn as well. Starting from the 1960s the organization, which was still principally composed of European Catholic students and postgraduates, put the fate of the "third world" at the center of its work. At its annual 1968 congress, for instance, Pax Romana focused on how to repair the imbalances of wealth and power created by centuries of imperialism, inviting César Chávez as the keynote speaker.[91] By the 1970s the "Nodding Negro" *(Nickneger)* donation boxes in churches, which portrayed a mute and powerless bobbing black figure, had become offensive: young clerics and Catholic activists were interested in empowering individuals from the former colonies, not presenting them as disembodied subjects of pity and charity.[92]

Anti-Semitism and the Holocaust

One last issue emerged to the fore for the papacy in the 1950s and early 1960s: the question of Catholic complicity in the Holocaust. Tensions began in Germany, with a legal and scholarly debate over the validity of the Reichskonkordat. The debate flared up in 1949 during the Basic Law discussions, and again in 1953 during a controversy over private schools in Baden-Württemberg. In 1955–1957, the Reichskonkordat battle ended up before the Constitutional Court.[93] Mainstream German Catholic organizations mobilized to defend the treaty, penning scholarly analyses of its history.[94] Many younger German Catholics, however, objected, emphasizing that the re-search German Catholic scholars leaned on to defend the Reichskon-kordat's validity was rushed and spotty. Others, more pointedly, won-dered why the Church was not willing to engage with the core objection of critics—that is, that the Holy See could and should have done more to counter Nazism's rise to power.[95]

In 1957 the debates came to a head when a young Catholic legal scholar by the name of Ernst-Wolfgang Böckenförde unveiled a searing and multipart critique of Church-state relations. On the heels of the CDU's landslide victory in the 1957 federal election, Böckenförde penned his attack on the pages of a prestigious Catholic journal, *Hochland*. Böckenförde's article criticized the tight links between Christian Democracy and the Church, and the shaky intellectual foun-dations for that partnership. In particular, the scholar took aim at what he saw as the Church's slavish and dangerous adherence to natural law, which he presented as a core component of the CDU-Church alliance.

Böckenförde explained that by subscribing to the doctrine of natural law, the CDU and the papacy had set as their end-goal the creation of an ahistorical political order based on natural-law theory. What mattered for this agenda was to achieve a Christian state, wherein the Church would retain and expand its institutional privileges. This end-goal mortally endangered democracy itself, because it meant that the Church did not endow democracy with any independent normative worth; in-stead, it would accept any form of government—including dictator-ship—so long as that government espoused principles derived from natural law and promised to build a Christian state.[96] Böckenförde thus urged the Church to reject its narrow reliance on natural legal frameworks, and adopt a true democratic and pluralist ethos—one that integrated and embraced the legacy of 1789.[97] A number of com-mentators agreed, including the prominent Austrian public intel-lectual and jurist Hans Kelsen.[98] In the next issue of *Hochland*, the assistant to the Münster bishop, Hermann-Joseph Spital, rebuked Böck-enförde and his supporters, reaffirming the centrality of natural legal teachings.[99]

Unfazed, Böckenförde extended his thinking in a second article, which explored the enthusiasm with which many members of the

Catholic Church had welcomed Nazism in 1933. Entitled "German Catholicism in the Year 1933," the searing piece argued that Hitler's
willingness to embrace concordat diplomacy, coupled with the Church's
long-standing aversion to democracy and liberalism, had contributed
to Nazism's success. To make his case, the young Catholic lawyer drew
on newly published sources documenting clerical relations with the
National Socialist German Workers' Party.[100] Böckenförde suggested
that the Roman Catholic Church and authoritarian regimes may have
shared an affinity that had been hereto left unexplored. He provoca-
tively asked: "Can one seriously say that the positions and political
principles that led to the errors of 1933 are overcome in German Catholicism today?"[101] In 1963 Rolf Hochhuth's play *The Deputy* once
again placed the question of papal complicity in Nazism's crimes at
the center of Germany's political debate. Defenders of the papacy sprang
into action, but the controversy had clearly left its mark.[102]

✦

As the *affaires* of the 1950s and early 1960s rained down on the papacy,
they elicited differing responses. In the case of Catholic socialism, Pius
XII condemned; when it came to the charge of Catholic philo-Nazism,
he denied. The birth of the Christian Democratic International, he
largely ignored. Regarding the debate over imperialism and the role of
the Catholic Church, the pope did what he could to kick the can down
the road. By the time African students visited Rome in the mid-1950s
to push for radical change, a physically and psychically exhausted Pius
XII had been diagnosed with cancer and was facing death. Interwar
Catholic internationalism—which Eugenio Pacelli had defended
throughout his life, and which had enjoyed a resurgence after 1945—
was suddenly under fire from all sides. Tormented by the question of
how the supranational church would survive "in this world of Communism, Americanism, and [anticolonial] nationalism," in 1957 the
forlorn pope affirmed that the Church was like a "lost wayfarer,"
making its way "through the darkness, a darkness almost of death."[103]
Could the Church find its way, and face its aggressors? Dipping into
fatalistic pessimism, Pius XII answered in the negative: "It seems that
every effort is useless . . . It's not possible to find the way, and words
get lost as the tempest rages."[104] In the Vatican pavilion at the 1958

Catholic internationalism is frozen in time. Children visit the ghostlike status of Pope Pius XII, at the Vatican pavilion at the Brussels world fair on October 6, 1958. Pius XII was gravely ill at the time and would die on October 9, 1958. Source: AP Photo

World's Fair, even the large white statue carved to honor Pius XII appeared evanescent—more ghostly than majestic.

When he rose to the Throne of St. Peter in 1958, Pius XII's successor, John XXIII (Angelo Giuseppe Roncalli), faced a choice: he could keep the Vatican the same in new circumstances, or he could address some of the papacy's critics. The new pope chose the latter route, and announced that the time had come for an *aggiornamento*—a "bringing up to date" of the Church's teachings, preachings, and practices. As soon as he assumed office, Roncalli began issuing messages that did not aim to direct European political life—something Christian Democrats picked up on immediately.[105] Additionally, John XXIII convened an Ecumenical Council, the highest decision-making body in the Roman Catholic Church. When he embarked on the Second Vatican Council project, the new pope understood that it was necessary to escape from elements of Pius XII's reign, but he was not interested is using the Council to help mediate the Church's dignified retreat from the modern world. Instead, he hoped that the Council would help the Church preserve many of its core teachings and forms of rule, all the while appeasing those Catholics demanding change.

What happened at the Council surprised both John XXIII and his successor, Paul VI. Instead of proceeding according to plan, the Council became a raucous and rude debate over the soul of Catholicism.[106] It was a battle that had raged since the 1930s, and never before had it been staged so publicly. Many of the bishops at the Council, in fact, did not reaffirm papal orthodoxies codified in the years since World War I; instead, they asked whether the time had come to revise the Church's relations with the laity and the state, rethink the knotty issue of religious freedom, and develop a new approach to decolonization and the non-European world. None of these issues had been laid out in advance by John XXIII or Paul VI as key points of discussion. They came, instead, from across the Catholic world, and were foisted upon the Vatican from below.

10

The Upending of Catholic Internationalism

> The Church must change—rejuvenate herself, renew herself, in order to maintain through change her fundamental identity.
>
> —JEAN GUITTON, 1976

At vatican ii, the papacy was confronted with the shock of the global. At any given moment in St. Peter's, 2,100 to 2,200 bishops were present, hailing from 116 countries. There were about 400 accredited theologians in attendance as well, as well as hundreds of nonaccredited members of the general public. Scores of newspaper reporters in Rome helped make the Council front-page news in scores of countries. For these reasons, historian John O'Malley has playfully called the Second Vatican Council "the biggest meeting in the history of the world."[1]

The Council lasted for three years and resulted in the publishing of sixteen authoritative texts, many of which challenged the legacy of Catholic internationalism. The all-powerful role of the pope and the Curia would be limited by the procedures of the Council itself, for it was the job of the bishops (not the Curia) to examine and determine the Church's decrees.[2] The bishops who decided the direction of the conversation were more diverse than they had ever been before.[3] The new balance of power meant that although Italian bishops still far outnumbered clerics from any other single nation (they constituted 14 percent of the 2,594 bishops present), even if they joined with their conservative fellow Spanish bishops (thus reaching a total of 17.4 percent), they could still be easily outnumbered by one of several voting blocs, such as that of Latin American bishops (who constituted about 22 percent of voting bishops), or that of African and Asian bishops (also at 22 percent).[4]

By the end of the Second Vatican Council, the bishops at Vatican II had swept away at least sixty-seven early preparatory documents, which were "couched in the condemnatory language" familiar to clerics from texts like the Syllabus of Errors.[5] Instead, they had settled on sixteen constitutions, decrees, and declarations that were more positive in tone. The texts were living proof that the war for the soul of Catholicism was not over. For even though the texts all engaged with the recent challenges to the legacy of Catholic internationalism, they were shot through with contradictions and inconsistencies. They celebrated natural law and hailed antinomianism; defended both religious freedom and the idea that the Church alone possessed access to absolute truth; advocated religious tolerance alongside a call to proselytize and convert non-Catholics; and eschewed a defense of the Church's right to intervene in political affairs, while also not clearly rejecting that position. Furthermore, despite hundreds of petitions and the speeches of as many clerics and counselors, it was decided that in order to avoid controversy, no single document would be drafted detailing the Church's views on communism and communist states. For these reasons, Vatican II is best seen as a testament to ongoing quarrels, not a wholesale resolution of them.[6]

Of the Council's sixteen texts, four in particular are useful hermeneutics, which point to how Vatican II transformed interwar Catholic internationalism, even as it left that task unfinished. *Lumen Gentium* (the Dogmatic Constitution of the Church), *Dignitatis Humanae* (the Declaration on Religious Freedom), *Nostra aetate* (the Declaration on the Relation of the Church to Non-Christian Religions), and *Gaudium et spes* (the Pastoral Constitution on the Church in the Modern World) all addressed crisis points of the 1950s: Church-state relations; religious freedom and Catholic anti-Semitism; and the relationship between the still quite Eurocentric Holy See and the non-Western Catholic world. Though the four texts did not resolve these crisis points, they were milestones along the way. But "milestones," as the historian Charles Cohen reminds us, "do not move; they only demarcate a point left behind *en route*."[7]

Addressing Crisis Points

Lumen Gentium (on the Dogmatic Constitution of the Church) was the Church's belated response to charges that the pope and the Curia had too much power to determine the direction of the Roman Catholic Church and that the structure of the Church overall was excessively hierarchical and even authoritarian. In keeping with the demands made by Catholic theological and lay movements since the 1930s, the encyclical increased the power of both bishops and the laity. Through the phrase "people of God," it signaled that all elements of the Church were fully fledged participants in its life.[8] Additionally, *Lumen Gentium* specified that the pope should no longer be seen as an absolute monarch; instead, the council of bishops was henceforth to be considered a "college" within the Church, and "the subject of supreme and full power over the universal Church."[9] The changes were not without contestation. When 322 members of the Council (most of whom were from Italy, Spain, Ireland, and Portugal) voted against the use of the word "college" and the increased power bestowed upon bishops, a "Preliminary Note of Explanation" was added. The note effectively dialed back some of *Lumen Gentium*'s most radical claims, reaffirming that the college of bishops was headed by the Roman Pontiff, and that it exercises its authority only with the assent of the pope.[10]

Taking two steps forward and one step back, *Lumen Gentium* also addressed another crisis point of the 1930s through the 1950s: the question of Church-state relations. The text made the revolutionary claim that the Church should no longer be seen as the only locus of grace in the world, asserting that "many elements of sanctification and of truth are found outside its visible confines." At the same time, *Lumen Gentium* affirmed that the Church was "the pillar and mainstay of the truth" (in the singular, not in the plural), and seemed to deny rights to those who were unwilling to embrace Catholic truths, asserting that those who "knowing that the Catholic Church was made necessary by Christ, would refuse to enter or to remain in it, [can] not be saved."[11] In sum, the idea that the Church was interested in perpetuating a thick understanding of religious freedom (various roads lead to the truth; people of many faiths can be saved) was undermined by the claim that ultimately there exists only one truth (Catholicism) and only one road to salvation (the Roman Catholic Church).

※

The uneasy coexistence of apparently contradictory positions was also a feature of *Dignitatis Humanae* (the Declaration on Religious Freedom) and *Nostra Aetate* (the Declaration on the Relation of the Church to Non-Christian Religions). Both texts are generally read as further signs of the Church's liberalization. Overturning a core precept of papal internationalism, *Dignitatis Humanae* steered clear of making an argument for confessional states. An earlier draft of the text had done this quite explicitly, asserting that the state must "provide the moral, intellectual, and social conditions in which people can more easily come to the divine truth." "In order to protect its subjects from the seduction of error and to preserve the nation in unity of faith," the draft stated, the state had the duty "to prohibit false worship and to prevent the spread of false ideas that cause people to depart from the true God and the true Church."[12]

The final version of *Dignitatis Humanae* eschewed this verbiage. The text asserts that religious liberty is grounded in the essential dignity of every human being, and that religious liberty is best understood as "the right to seek the truth without coercion," insofar as no human being is "to be forced to act in a manner contrary to his conscience."[13] So far, so good: this definition of religious liberty as the "individual's right to choose" had already been articulated in several settings (including the United Nations) and hewed close to a transatlantic Cold War language of religious freedom, which emphasized the right of individuals to form their own belief systems.[14] To this understanding of religious freedom, the text added the idea that the state's core responsibility toward its citizens was to protect their religious freedom. It was not permissible, therefore, for states to repudiate religion, or prohibit its exercise, because states, the document affirmed, were legitimate only insofar as they adhered to Catholic teachings ("It is through adherence to the Catholic Church that temporal polities receive their perfection as human societies.") In addition, *Dignitatis Humanae* asserted that the state must nurture and foster religious education (as concordats had long taught, and Christian Democrats had recently re-affirmed). The encyclical then added a final wrinkle: though human beings are free to choose the truth, they are morally obliged to embrace the truth of the Catholic faith once they encounter and recognize it. This is because, the text underscored, Catholicism is best understood as the only true religion.[15] *Dignitatis Humanae* was thus a mix of old and new, for even as it asserted that the Church could tolerate inter-confessional exchange, it stated that as a matter of principle, it could never accept the idea that Catholicism was just one faith among several. Catholic triumphalism was, it seemed, compatible with religious freedom.

Nostra Aetate, the Declaration on the Relation of the Church to Non-Christian Religions, similarly quilted together old and new. It applied the new teachings on religious freedom to the Church's relations with Buddhism, Hinduism, Islam, and Judaism. The chapter on Judaism—despite its scant length (fifteen sentences)—broke considerable ground: in the same years that the papacy was urging the publication of a select portion of the Vatican's archive from the World War II years, and scrapping the mention of "perfidious Jews" from the Good Friday liturgy,[16] *Nostra Aetate* invalidated theological anti-Semitism by emphasizing that "the Jews should not be presented as rejected or accursed by God, as if this followed from the Holy Scriptures." It recognized the continued holiness of the Jewish people, explaining that Christ's "passion cannot be charged against the Jews, without distinction, then alive, nor against the Jews of today." Finally, it condemned racism in sharp tones.[17] As the bishops noted, the Jews deserved special attention because of "the historical context: six million Jewish dead . . . If the Council, taking place twenty years after these facts, remains silent about them, then it would inevitably evoke the reaction expressed by Hochhuth in his play *The Deputy.*"[18]

But even as it introduced important innovations, *Nostra Aetate* did not put non-Christian interlocutors on an equal playing field. Buddhism, Hinduism, and Islam were applauded principally insofar as elements of these religions resonated with Catholic teachings. As one scholar has recently charged, "In *Nostra Aetate,* the 'rays' found outside of the church must always emanate from and reflect the familiar contours of the 'sun' that is Christ."[19] The text was, in other words, inscribed with a tension between affirming religious freedom and the importance of dialogue and "asserting the supremacy of Christianity—Catholic Christianity—over all other religions."[20] Its positions were more conservative than those of several interwar and early postwar Catholic dissidents, who called for full parity between all religious faiths and did not insist on using Catholicism as the yardstick for assessing the worth of other religious traditions.

The last key text of Vatican II—*Gaudium et Spes* (Pastoral Constitution on the Church in the Modern World)—tackled a final pressing issue raised by many Catholics in the 1950s: the relationship of the Holy See and the Western world to the decolonizing non-Western world. The text was, like its Vatican II companions, both revolutionary and cautious. Though it did not take a clear position against imperialism, *Gaudium et Spes* urged Catholics to diminish the possibility of a World War III by fostering the economic development of poorer regions of the world and opening dialogue with peoples of all nations, races, and religions.[21] Additionally, *Gaudium et Spes* blamed the United States for its unwillingness to fight global poverty and for its role in perpetuating the arms race.[22] Over and against Cold War orthodoxies, the Pastoral Constitution, in a passage written by the archbishop of Vienna, Franz König, actually suggested that Catholics and communists would benefit from opening up lines communication.[23]

Gaudium et Spes was innovative in one last crucial respect as well: it quietly rejected concordat diplomacy. The text asserted that Catholics must be ready and willing to repudiate the concordat project, should "it become clear that their use will cast doubt on the sincerity of [the Church's] witness or [if] new ways of life demand new methods." Instead, Catholics must show their commitment to a more genuine universalism by taking part in existing international instruments. Catholics, the text averred, must participate in the United Nations, a "universal" organization already "endowed with the power to safeguard on the behalf of all security, regard for justice, and respect for rights." It was through *these* instruments—not concordats—that Catholics could realize the kingdom of Christ on earth.[24]

Gaudium et Spes was groundbreaking in its call upon Catholics to refuse confessionally exclusive internationalism, embrace the Global South, and reject American hegemony and Cold War orthodoxies. However, it did not roundly criticize the European imperial project. This was not entirely surprising, in that the text's leading author was the Dominican Father Louis-Joseph Lebret.[25] Lebret was a cleric who had never explicitly renounced European imperialism, and who continued to defend the importance of Europe's playing a "civilizing role" in the third world. Indeed, Lebret was concerned about the rise of American hegemony, and convinced that Europe should continue its "civilizing mission" in the so-called third world without American assistance.

In 1955 Lebret had begun advocating that the Church break away from the United States and work in partnership with Western European states to combat poverty in the decolonizing third world.[26] In 1958, on the eve of Pius XII's death, Lebret hammered home these themes through a best-selling book entitled *The Suicide or Survival of the West?* The book condemned Western Europe's decision to embrace the "illusory" solutions proposed by the "self-interested" United States after 1945. Far from being the world's liberator, the United States sought to "exercise an imperialism without limits on the world," much like "Adolf Hitler, [who] in *Mein Kampf* had expressed the implacable logic of the necessity of Germany to dominate the world." As a result of its exploitative and disingenuous behavior, the United States had impoverished the third world, and America itself had become "hated almost everywhere." Taking a page from Saint Paul's oft-quoted wake-up call in Ephesians 5:14, Lebret noted, "It is really the time to say to the West: 'Awake, you who sleep.'"[27]

As the Dominican father saw it, European Catholics must break their partnership with the United States and forge an "international bridge of solidarity" with antipoverty activists in the third world.[28] True to this vision, the Dominican priest founded an institute that brought together economists and theorists, the Institut international de recherche et de formation en vue du développement harmonisé (IRFED). IRFED was not simply a home for Catholic intellectuals; it was a meeting ground for experts, technocrats, and planners who traveled to countries in Latin America, North and West Africa, the Middle East, and Southeast Asia. IRFED's members played a leading role at the

United Nations, speaking before international bodies like the UN's Food and Agriculture Organization and UNESCO. In 1964 its members—including Lebret himself—helped found UNCTAD, the United Nations Conference on Trade and Development. As the Dominican Father noted, it was imperative for Catholics to take part in UN activities: "It seems crucial that an antimaterialist, Catholic-inspired, spirit be brought there . . . Otherwise, the seats will doubtless be seized by an ill-assorted group of technicians lacking a clear doctrine on the question of what grounds human beings, society, and civilization."[29] The task of Catholics was to guarantee that existing internationalist instruments not be captured by materialist and antireligious elements.

From Anathema to Dialogue

Lebret's centrality to Vatican II, proves, yet again, the ambiguous quality of the Council as a whole. For even when it came to the burning question of decolonization, Vatican II's symbol of the new papal approach to Africa and the third world was a figure who had not explicitly turned against imperialism. At the same time, the papacy's shift toward Catholic third-worldism did not go uncontested in Europe's conservative Catholic strongholds. At the Second Vatican Council and thereafter, many European clerics condemned the Holy See for its concentration on the economic problems of developing countries at a time when "the most obtrusive social phenomena of the moment are surely the continuing and demonic successes of the communists, of which [the papacy] makes scant mention."[30] The critics had a point: for apart from the passing statement in *Gaudium et Spes* regarding the desirability of Catholic–communist dialogue, Vatican II said nothing on communism or communist internationalism. This silence was all the more deafening given how much attention communism had garnered in the previous forty years of Vatican history.

Since the preparatory commissions for Vatican II, several clerics had been clamoring for communism's official discussion at the Council. They petitioned, sending in letters from Italy, Spain, and Latin America. However, John XXIII deflected their requests, asserting that because he wanted the Orthodox churches present at the Council, including an official discussion and "schema" on communism was a bad idea, as this would likely alienate them. For a period the issue was dropped. But it returned a few years later, when the Council met for its last session. In the autumn of 1965, more than 400 Council clergymen sent in a petition demanding that Schema 13 (the Council document concerned with the church in the modern world) also address the "problem of communism."[31] This was necessary, they said, so that the Council would not in retrospect be accused of silence, "as, for example, today, surely unjustly, Pius XII [is accused] regarding the victims of Nazism."[32] More than a third of the 435 signatories of the petition were from Italy and Spain—two of the countries most active in the Vatican's interwar and postwar anticommunist crusade.[33] But once again the proposal was shot down: the more global character of the bishopric at Vatican II allowed for the de-centering of a position that, as it turned out, was desired only by a minority of predominantly European Catholic clergy.[34]

To be sure, both John XXIII and Paul VI did "do something" about communism, but it was not what the clerics wanted. While Vatican II was under way, John XXIII issued his final encyclical, *Pacem in Terris*. This was the first encyclical in papal history addressed to all peoples rather than just Catholics. In this text the pope strongly defended papal neutrality in the Cold War, calling for nuclear nonproliferation and condemning the arms race pursued by both the United States and the Soviet Union—an arms race that in the context of the 1962 Cuban missile crisis had brought the world to the brink of atomic war. The text was deeply discomfiting for many clerics who had come of age during the Church's interwar anticommunist crusade.

As the Second Vatican Council was wrapping up, in 1965, Paul VI tapped the archbishop of Vienna, Franz König, the cleric who had played an important role in drafting the section of *Gaudium et Spes* encouraging dialogue with communism, to help create a new papal Secretariat, entitled the Secretariat for Non-Believers. The name was likely intended to bring to mind the Secretariat on Atheism of the interwar years, but as a way to signal change rather than continuity. As Archbishop König asserted in 1966, the new Secretariat was uninterested in issuing a condemnation of communism. In direct contrast to its predecessor, "the Secretariat for Non-Believers does not intend to

A globalizing church charts a new course. A cleric reads the front page of
the Vatican newspaper, *l'Osservatore Romano*, at a Vatican City newspaper
stand on April 11, 1963, the day John Paul XXIII issued the encyclical
Pacem in Terris. Source: AP Photo

promote or prepare any battle against atheism," the cleric averred.[35]
Instead, the institution would go the route of direct dialogue—a
choice that would have been anathema for the Jesuits heading up the
old Secretariat. At the new Secretariat's first international congress
in April 1965, more than 200 theologians and intellectuals came together to discuss the theme "Christianity and Marxism today."[36] For
the next few years of activity, the institution supported several ongoing
dialogue initiatives, including the Paulus-Gesellshaft of Munich and
the work of French Catholic intellectuals like Jean-Yves Calvez and
Dominique Dubarle. A new cohort of Jesuit priests (no longer under
the watchful eye of the former Superior General Włodzimierz
Ledóchowski, who had died in 1942) participated in the movement,
through their studies of the intellectual affinities between Catholicism

and communism.[37] They were spurred on to do so by the new Superior General of the Jesuits, the Belgian Father Jean-Baptiste Janssens, who as early as 1949 had called on the Jesuits to commit their energies toward solving the "social question" and ensure that the Jesuits no longer appear "to be allied with the rich and the capitalists."[38] Those dissidents of the 1930s and 1940s who were still alive and active applauded the new spirit of Catholic–communist dialogue ushered in by the newborn Secretariat for Non-Believers.[39] So did non-Catholics. Louis Althusser, one of the leaders of the French Left in the 1960s, later recalled that it was after Vatican II, "in large part through the Catholic organizations, that I came into contact . . . with Marxism."[40]

In September 1964, on the eve of the founding of the new Secretariat, Pope John XXIII concluded the first written agreement of the Vatican with a Communist government in forty-two years. The Hungarian agreement jump-started negotiations between the papacy and other Eastern European communist countries in the mid 1960s.[41] In March of the same year, Pope Paul VI, in keeping with John's line, met with a delegation of German Social Democrats at the Vatican, much to the dismay of old-guard Christian Democrats.[42] For though the papacy's new *Ostpolitik* was in keeping with some trends within the Catholic world, it was jarring for members who had lived through the papacy's anticommunist crusade. The sixty-nine-year-old conservative German Christian Democrat Heinrich Krone wondered, "What is going on in the Vatican? . . . The political struggle against the danger of world communism is weakened by this new direction."[43] Konrad Adenauer, for his part, blamed the pope for taking the wind out of the sails of Western anticommunist movements and strengthening European Communist parties, and repeatedly expressed the hope that the Vatican would revert to its old anticommunist ways.[44]

But these disgruntled Catholics would not have their way: Within three years a car with a red hammer-and-sickle pendant would enter the Damascus Court of the Vatican and deposit a Soviet head of state for an audience with the pope. For the first time in fifty years, talks with the Soviet Union were happening once again. And this was no blast back to the 1920s: by 1967 the thrust of papal diplomacy had fundamentally changed. Classic concordatory policy was no longer a model for the pope. Catholic and communist observers quickly caught wind of the epochal shift. Palmiro Togliatti, the secretary of the Italian Communist party, as well as a flurry of Russian-language publications concurred: a new era was dawning.[45]

In 1971, in an apparent sanctioning of the new turn, Pope Paul VI issued his most radical text to date on Catholic–communist relations. The apostolic letter's title, *Octogesima Adveniens*—"The Approaching Eightieth"—referred to the eightieth anniversary of the landmark social encyclical *Rerum Novarum*, which had been followed up forty years later by Pius XI's *Quadragesimo Anno*. The text was miles apart from *Rerum Novarum*'s harsh condemnation of socialism, and *Quadragesimo Anno*'s lambasting of the essential link between socialism, liberalism, and communism. Neither did it present communism as the most dangerous ideology on the planet, as *Divini Redemptoris* had. By contrast, *Octogesima Adveniens* urged more attention to what it called the "new proletarians" living in urban ghettos and in underdeveloped regions, focusing in particular on the plight of women and young people. It spoke out against the idea that Catholic social doctrine could apply to all places and peoples, and that it could provide an answer to all the world's problems. In fact, the Church could not "put forward a solution that has universal validity." To this, Paul added that there were promising indications of Catholic–communist dialogue. And more: the pope even asserted that Marxism was a working tool that some could find useful in their quest to fight capitalism and achieve greater social justice in the world.[46] Church spokesman Bishop Agostino Toniolo explained at a news conference that whereas *Rerum Novarum* had contained a blanket condemnation of socialism and *Quadragesimo Anno* of communism, Pope Paul's letter did not pass "global judgment."[47] In place of establishing a stark divide between Catholicism and other internationalist ideologies, it called for dialogue and understanding.

In the meantime, an extraordinary transformation was under way in Western Europe. In Italy, Austria, and Germany the Christian Democrats had decided to open to the left. In Italy, under the leadership of Aldo Moro, Christian Democracy was forging an electoral alliance with the socialists. In Austria, the Christian Democratic Party was entering into what would be a long-lived Grand Coalition with the Social Democratic Party. The German CDU also participated in several state-level Grand Coalitions in the 1950s, and in 1966 it kicked off a federal-level coalition with the Socialist Party that would last until 1969. The response of the clergy to these developments was muted. In a historic first, bishops and upper clergy in these countries stopped instructing the faithful on how to vote, affirming their commitment to nonintervention in political matters, in a tip of the hat to Vatican II.[48]

The coalitions of the 1960s were ground-shaking. The idea that Catholics were in the business of building a specifically Christian international order through legal and cultural activism had been the centerpiece of papal internationalism after World War I. According to the papal mandate, collaboration and cooperation with liberals, socialists, and communists was strictly forbidden. Now everything seemed different. Growing numbers of activists were encouraging cross-party, interfaith, and cross-national dialogue. In addition, holding up texts like *Gaudium et Spes* as a flag, they called for a shift from the "Catholic world" to the world as a whole. In the process, the very idea that Catholics had a proud alternative way of conceptualizing and practicing internationalism seemed to be fading away. So did the notion that the Church would ever countenance ethno-nationalist and exclusivist visions of Catholicism again.

If a papal diplomat had fallen asleep in 1935 and reawakened thirty years later, he would have been shocked by the changes surrounding him. By 1965 the internal structure of the Roman Catholic Church had been democratized, with a much-reduced role for the pope as an actual and imagined center of decision making. Overturning centuries of bigotry, the Vatican had challenged the long history of Catholic anti-Semitism and anti-Judaism and put forward a new conception of religious freedom that seemed more in tune with the spirit of the times. Despite the long shadow of the Church's anticommunist crusade, the central government of the Roman Catholic Church had opened up relations with the Eastern bloc and encouraged the faithful to seek dialogue and mutual cooperation with the communist "other." Responding to the growing anxieties about the Church's participation in a global Cold War, the papacy had also revisited a buried tradition of anti-Americanism, and presented itself as a neutral power interested, above all, in peace.

After Vatican II and Christian Democracy's opening to the left, global Catholicism and the Catholic Church would never be the same. The 1960s Church had addressed many of the nagging questions that lay and dissident Catholics had been raising for decades. The Vatican hoped that its responses would not only appease critics but bring about a boom in European Catholicism and a renewed explosion of the faith. Instead, ironically, the opposite happened. Western Christendom imploded, in a manner that was both sudden and unexpected.

Epilogue

One among Many

"THE CHURCH IS EUROPE: and Europe is The Church," Hilaire Belloc proclaimed in 1920.[1] A devout Catholic who had spent several months in his early thirties in a walking pilgrimage from Central France to Rome, the Anglo-French writer believed that the Roman Catholic Church after World War I had won the battle for re-Christianizing the continent. But by the 1970s Belloc's contention that the European continent was a continent of the Church no longer rang true. Western Christendom was greatly weakened, and the core components of the papacy's activism in the twentieth century—concordat diplomacy and anticommunist crusading—no longer had robust defenders.

In many senses, papal internationalism had created the conditions for its own unmaking. At the height of the Great War, fear of the imagined secular Europe-to-come had spurred the papacy to undertake a novel course of action and throw its weight behind a diplomacy of state-to-state treaties recognized under international law. Through concordat diplomacy, the papacy was able to present itself as the maker of an alternative peace settlement that was neither Wilsonian nor Leninist but Christian. In the shadow of the Paris peace settlement that brought the Great War to a close and the explosion of left-wing radicalism following the Bolshevik Revolution, the Vatican sold con-

310

cordats as tools for counterrevolutionary consolidation. These treaties, papal diplomats emphasized, could assert control over rebellious peripheries and resistant populations. They could fortify imagined communities united by bonds of faith and culture. And they could drastically weaken the appeal of liberal, socialist, and communist political parties.[2]

Concordat diplomacy worked. By the early 1930s the pope had signed more than a dozen treaties with a range of insurgent forces, mainly on the radical right. He had also reacquired a state of his own, his coffers were flush with funds, and he had become an important force in European family law, educational policy, and youth activism. By the eve of World War II, the pope had also gained international renown for an anticommunist crusade, which made use of modern media to foreground a message presenting Rome's Catholic International as the only convincing response to Moscow's Communist International, or Comintern. In addition to giving Europe's everyday citizens the tools they needed to carry out re-Christianization on the ground, the papacy's anticommunist campaign sanctioned the use of violence against the communist enemy and instituted elaborate mechanisms that policed the boundaries of official Catholicism and silenced dissident voices.

Midcentury papal diplomacy was antidemocratic through and through. Its practices fostered the birth of new movements that would ultimately undermine it. In the 1920s and 1930s, new connections between lay Catholics led to the birth of a dissident movement that encouraged an alternative mode of religious internationalism. Partisans of this movement were highly critical of the papacy's partnership with authoritarian and right-wing states. They worried that an excessive concern with protecting the rights of Catholic citizens and the Catholic Church had caused the pope to legitimize dangerous political movements. Catholic dissidents also objected to the papacy's hard-line anticommunist agitation, particularly when the metaphorical war against communism began claiming real lives, during the Spanish Civil War and the Nazi invasion of the Soviet Union.

Initially the Vatican responded to its objectors by sticking to its old course. Just like after World War I, when the papacy had played a crucial role in legitimizing the nation-state as a political form and in strengthening its legal and social appeal, after World War II the papacy did so again. The pope now saw the nation-state as a vector for the expansion of his international agenda, not a handicap to it. Thus, he embraced the nationalist motifs employed by the Christian Democratic political parties that showed themselves eager to hush up the Vatican's dealings with Nazi and Fascist movements and recognize interwar concordats as legally binding. He encouraged the launching of a global Cold War that made anticommunism a necessary condition of full national participation. And he participated in the process of "rescuing the European nation-state," precisely at a time when that nation-state was coming under fire, on account of the toxic nationalisms of the interwar years and the rise of decolonization.

However, starting in the early 1950s, the dissident Catholic movement gained new followers. They confronted the Holy See on its marriage of convenience with Nazi and Fascist parties. They spoke out loudly against European imperialism, calling on the pope to do the same. They forged bonds with socialist movements and directly challenged the core premises of the nascent Cold War. They began cultivating transnational connections and building border-crossing institutions of their own, independent from papal oversight. They encouraged Christian Democrats to bow out of their partnerships with the pope.

If Catholic internationalism had created the conditions for its own unmaking, in the 1960s it completed the process. Through the Second Vatican Council and subsequent decisions, the papacy responded to its objectors. It accepted decolonization. It took its distance from the concordat imperative. It embraced democracy and human rights. It denounced racism, neo-Fascism, and anti-Semitism. It suspended decades of anticommunist activism and opened talks with the Soviet Union and countries in the Eastern bloc.

The changes came too late. In the 1960s the Church's presence in European civil society, particularly among youth, dropped precipitously. In parts of Germany, Catholic youth groups lost more than 59 percent of their members in just over a decade; in Italy, Catholic Action's membership fell by half in just five years (from 3.3 million in 1965 to 1.65 million in 1970).[3] In tandem, the traditional social markers of Catholicism—Church attendance, baptisms, and religious marriages—declined, as

Europeans called into question centuries-old norms pertaining to birth control, child-rearing, and gender relations. Buoyed by the battles of the 1950s and eager to follow their electorate, Western European state leaders also began to rebel against the practice of partnering with the Holy See.

In response to the social and political changes under way, in July 1968 Pope Paul VI issued *Humanae vitae*. Many lay Catholics in Eastern Europe and the decolonizing world welcomed the encyclical, which rejected artificial contraception and reaffirmed the sanctity of life and marriage. A flurry of Catholics in Western Europe rushed to denounce it, however. They were incensed that Paul VI, the "progressive pope," would use his encyclical to reaffirm (not revise) traditional Catholic teachings on sex and the family—and that he would do so just as the women's movement was asserting itself and student uprisings were ricocheting from Rome to Prague.[4]

In Germany, the movement to overturn traditional Catholic teachings on sex and sexuality took off immediately, and the Vatican was forced to recognize that it could not count on German Catholics to follow its teachings. From a 1971 poll on whether women should have the right to terminate a pregnancy, the pope learned that 51 percent of German Catholic women said yes, no further questions asked; 70 percent said yes if extenuating social or economic circumstances existed; and 80 percent said yes where a high probability existed that the child would be born with serious mental or physical disabilities.[5] In response, leaders in the German Catholic Church doubled down, defending *Humanae vitae* in sermons and print publications. Establishing a parallel between abortion in the 1970s and euthanasia in Nazi Germany, Cardinal Joseph Höffner of Cologne announced, "It is only a small step from legalized abortion to sterilization and from there to the elimination of 'unworthy life.'"[6] A few years later, the largest official festival of Roman Catholic laity in Central Europe, the Katholikentag, took as its motto the fight against reform and against "socio-liberal" attempts to de-Christianize marriage and family policy. The German Jesuit priest Karl Rahner, a leader in Vatican II, wrote that if the German Church continued down its current path, it would become "a historically and socially meaningless sect."[7] By the mid-1970s, West Germany had enacted new legislation that allowed women to assert and exercise the right to an abortion.[8] In tandem, the CDU entered the political opposition for the first time since the first postwar elections. Many commentators concluded that the Catholic Church had not played its cards well, alienating potential Christian Democratic voters and causing them to switch sides.

Italy also witnessed a rebellion from below, as lay Catholics protested *Humanae vitae*'s ban on divorce. In November 1969, a coalition of deputies in Parliament affirmed that all Italians should be able to divorce by civil procedures, and that the process should be simple and not cumbersome. They then mustered the votes to legalize divorce and challenge the religious definition of marriage imposed by the Lateran Agreements. Subsequently, the Vatican, the Christian Democrats, and a small neo-Fascist party (the Movimento Sociale Italiano) organized a mass mobilization, calling for a popular referendum to overturn the 1969 Divorce Law. Held in May 1974, the referendum became a vote on the role of the Vatican in Italian politics and society. Slogans at rallies in favor of the Law asserted, "Say Yes to Divorce—Sign Against the Concordat"; "Referendum *or* Reverendum?"; "Vote Divorce, Block the Roman Rota"; and "No to the Clerical Dictatorship."

The referendum results shocked the Holy See. Despite its large-scale mobilization against the new legislation, a clear majority (59.1 percent) of Italians voted in favor of keeping the 1969 Divorce Law in place. In private Paul VI fretted that the Italian Church had made a mistake in helping organize the protests: the Church, he said, had "called upon Italians to engage in a useless act of heroism" and had shown itself to be badly out of step with the spirit of the times. The pope further noted that the referendum had "mortally wounded" the concordat, showing that "the new conditions of social life and ecclesiastical thought" made the interwar text out-of-date.[9] The head of the Italian Episcopal Conference agreed, noting that the time had come for the Holy See to "show that it was in agreement with the political, cultural, and religious pluralism of modern society."[10] True, the results of recent debates around birth control and marriage had been shocking, but without that shock, the Vatican would have "never had a clear idea of the current situation" and of the burning "need to revise the concordat."[11]

The point had been recently driven home by a controversy in Rome, when the city's Prefect had appealed to article 1 of the Italian Concordat (on Rome's "sacred character") to justify his push to ban the

The papacy's position on divorce and its control over marriage policy met with rising challenges in Italy in the 1960s and 1970s. Pro-divorce and anti-papacy demonstration, Rome, Piazza Navona, June 7, 1969. Credit: Alamy Photo

performance of Rolf Hochhuth's play *The Deputy* in the capital city. This act—which was widely interpreted as an attempt to curtail freedom of speech and to silence any discussion of Catholic complicity in the Holocaust relations—raised a firestorm of protest. Within less than two years, the Italian Chamber of Deputies (with Christian Democratic support) had approved a motion to create a Commission to revise the concordat.[12] Over the course of the late 1960s and early 1970s, the Commission hammered out a proposal for a revised treaty, which recommended eliminating the confessional character of the Italian state. The proposal called for a clearer separation of Church and state when it came to family law and education; and in partial response to a 1977 movement to abrogate the Lateran Agreements in their entirety, it introduced the principle of religious freedom, explicitly stating that all religions must be placed on equal footing.[13] Seven drafts later, the final agreement was reached. On February 18, 1984, the new concordat was signed into law.

Italy's new prime minister, the socialist Bettino Craxi, hailed the new treaty as "a grand agreement enshrining freedom": freedom of the church, freedom of the state, and the freedom of Italians to choose Catholicism, other religions, or no religion, as their own.[14] The 1984 concordat comprised 14 articles in place of the original 45. Unlike its predecessor, it eliminated the confessional character of the Italian state, removed reference to the "sacred character" of the city of Rome, and scaled back the role of the Vatican in domains like family law and education. The papacy was still granted "full freedom to engage in its pastoral mission," and religious instruction would still be provided in schools, but it would no longer be obligatory. Furthermore, clergy were from now on not allowed to stand trial before separate courts of law, and bishops would not be asked to swear loyalty to the Italian state. The funding provided to the Vatican by the Italian state was scaled back, though not eliminated.[15] "The [1984] agreement constitutes a prototype for the postconciliar concordatory conventions," the Vatican secretary of state under Pope Francis, Pietro Parolin, later noted. It "affirms that the political community and the Church are independent and autonomous from one another," rather than intimately interconnected, as had been the case prior.[16]

The concordatory revolution was not limited to Italy. In Spain, too, conversations about revising the country's concordat picked up in the mid-1960s, amid calls for complete religious liberty and the elimination of the Church's special privileges.[17] Spanish clergy organized a Joint Assembly of Bishops and Priests in 1971, with the aim of "examin[ing] in depth the signs of the times." In preparation for the meeting, the clergy were polled, and in response to the question "Do you agree with the position of the Spanish Church in regard to social and political matters?," 62 percent of the clergy said they had little or no agreement with the Church. Among clergy under forty years of age, that response jumped to 85 percent. Another question asked clergy if they viewed the existing "system of Church–state relations" in Spain negatively or positively. Sixty-six percent of total clergy viewed it negatively, as did 85 percent of young priests. At the Assembly itself, these young priests demanded an end to "official Catholicism" and voted in favor of a resolution that called for the revision of the 1953 concordat as "necessary and urgent." Similar sentiments were reaffirmed at the

1973 Bishops' Conference, which resulted in a second statement in support of revising the treaty.[18] The editors of Spain's left-wing Catholic journal *Vida Nueva* commented, "[The concordat] was destined to endure through all the centuries. Seventeen years have passed and today those exemplary agreements are leaking water from all sides."[19]

Shortly after Franco's death on November 20, 1975, the new agreement was signed. It renounced two key provisions of the earlier agreement that had helped cement Church–state ties: the government's right to block the nomination of bishops, and several of the papacy's juridical privileges.[20] Albeit not as groundbreaking as the 1984 Italian concordat, the new Spanish text nonetheless constituted a minor revolution. In 1978 Spain's democratic constitution completed what the new Spanish concordat had begun. It ended the confessional identification of church and state, explicitly declaring that "no confession will have a state character."[21] The new constitution also created a clear distinction between private and public education, and allowed for a civil divorce procedure.[22] Thus the institutional grounding of the separation of Church and state was the firmest it had been in the past thirty years.

The Vatican's response to these developments has been conflicted. Following the death of Pope Paul VI and the appointment of John Paul II (Karol Józef Wojtyła) in 1978, the central government of the Roman Catholic Church received an influx of new bishops critical of the Second Vatican Council and its legacy. Though these figures begrudgingly accepted trends under way in central and southern Europe, they were also eager to restore papal anticommunism and overturn the new mantra of East–West dialogue. Thus, along with John Paul II (who was born and raised in Poland, and the first non-Italian pope in 455 years), they reverted to Cold War orthodoxies. They encouraged the papacy to play an active role in supporting anticommunist dissident movements and take credit for the fall of the Berlin Wall and the dissolution of the Soviet bloc. Despite decades of attack on concordat diplomacy, they spurred the papacy to return to the concordat and conclude treaties with post-Soviet Latvia, Lithuania, Estonia, and newly unified Germany.[23]

The new-and-old treaties emphasized that in matters pertaining to education, family law, and the organization of civil society, church and state must work closely together. They called on the state to "guarantee that the education of children and young people will take into account . . . Christian values and ethics," and promised to protect the "inalienable right of parents to the religious education of their children in schools." As with the concordats of the interwar years, they asserted, "The curriculum for teaching the Catholic religion, as well as the textbooks used, shall be determined by the ecclesiastical authority and shall be made known to the relevant civil authorities." Even the defense of the 1917 Code of Canon Law was unapologetically back in use. For instance, in the new Polish concordats article 10, on marriage, it specified: "Preparation for the celebration of marriage according to Canon Law shall involve instructing the spouses on the indissolubility of Canon Law marriage and on the legal provisions of Polish law concerning the effects of marriage."[24] Additionally, the new concordats provided for the financial support of the Church by the state. In these respects and more, the post-1989 concordats were strange relics of the interwar years, out of date and yet perfectly at home in the restorationist post–Cold War climate.

Nostalgia for Hilaire Belloc's Europe was visible in the practices of Pope Benedict XVI (Joseph Aloisius Ratzinger), as well. Ratzinger was a Bavarian theologian who in the 1980s had played a crucial role in policing the writings of Catholics sympathetic to socialism and communism as Prefect of the Congregation for the Doctrine of the Faith (the former Holy Office). Taking the name Benedict XVI in a tip of the hat to Benedict XV, the father of the new Catholic diplomacy born during World War I, Benedict XVI worked to put the pope back on the pedestal he had stepped off as a result of Vatican II. He reaffirmed the role of the Curia in internal decision-making and resurrected the old Latin Mass, despite objections that doing so made Catholic teachings inaccessible to everyday people. Benedict XVI crossed swords with religious orders whom he accused of spending too much time focusing on the poor and too little on defending Catholic teachings on marriage, abortion, and sexuality. He got himself into trouble with comments

on the limits of interfaith dialogue, offensive statements about the
Muslim religion, and the decision to lift the excommunication of a
famous bishop known as a Holocaust denier.[25] Finally, Benedict applauded the decision by the European Court of Human Rights to keep
crucifixes in Italian public schools, despite objections that doing so
would violate "confessional neutrality" and the principle of state
secularism.

Following the 2013 election of Pope Francis I (Jorge Mario Bergoglio),
the tug of war between fans and critics of Catholic internationalism
continued. Since coming to office, Francis has voiced his criticisms of
post–World War I papal diplomacy and spoken in favor of Vatican II,
intimating that he sees his aim as getting the Council's reformist
agenda fully implemented in the life of the Church. In October of
2018, he canonized one of the figures most associated with the Second
Vatican Council: Pope Paul VI. Francis has also condemned centuries of European imperialism and the papacy's complicity therein. In
the face of a right-wing Polish Catholic political movement that
criminalized discussion of Polish involvement in the Holocaust, he has
affirmed that all countries have the duty to fight anti-Semitism and
keep the memory of the Holocaust alive.[26] In addition, in keeping with
the precepts of encyclicals like *Populorum Progressio*, Francis has
called for more attention to poverty and economic inequality. Aligning
himself with the papal détente of the 1960s and 1970s, Francis has
suggested that communists "think like Christians" on these and other
topics. For this, he has received a great deal of attention from conservative Catholics, who have accused him of being a "closet communist"
and have taken great pains to document Francis's supposed connections
with communist individuals, ideas, and organizations.[27]

The past, it seems, does not pass. Despite the decline of global communism since the 1970s, the specter of the religious Cold War—and
its articulation of a politics of absolutes—still haunts our present. Despite the fact that the concordat moment is long gone, bits and pieces
of the 1917 Code of Canon Law remain embedded in European legislation. Despite the fact that the separation of Church and state has been
recognized as an important principle on the European continent, the

Catholic Church—to the exclusion of other religious institutions—
still earns part of its keep through funds supplied by European states. It
still enjoys preferential treatment in European courts of law.

Catholic internationalism is the Vatican's most enduring legacy—its
signal contribution to the short twentieth century. For good or ill,
starting in a pronounced way after World War I, the Church recast
itself as a political actor capable of contending with rival political actors for the soul of Europe. It crafted peace settlements; it took control
of international legal instruments. In the process, the papacy used a
range of techniques to break down the distinction between a public
secular sphere and a private religious one, maligning political forces
that sought to challenge its work. Still today, the European continent
remains not-quite-secular. And the political dictates of the central government of the Roman Catholic Church—on everything from capitalism
to climate change, and from Donald Trump to the Syrian refugee crisis—
still capture the public's imagination, shape voting patterns, and make
front-page news. Against the wishes of the past century's secularists, the
pope—a *sui generis* sovereign—still wields a megaphone and commands
a following. Though the Vatican is neither a nation-state nor a corporation, it remains a political actor of great force.[28]

Abbreviations

AACI	Archive of Italian Catholic Action, Istituto Paolo VI, Rome
AAF	Archives de l'Académie Française, Paris
AAS	*Acta Apostolicae Sedis*
ACC	*Civiltà Cattolica* Archive, Rome
ACDF	Archivio della Congregazione per la Dottrina della Fede
ACS	Central Archives of the State, Rome
ADSS	*Actes et documents du Saint-Siège relatifs à la Seconde Guerre Mondiale*
A.E.S.	Affari Ecclesiastici Straordinari
ALS	Archivio Luigi Sturzo, Rome
ARSI	Roman Archives of the Jesuit Order, Rome
ASV	Vatican Secret Archives, Rome
BVP	Bayerische Volkspartei
DDI	*Documenti diplomatici italiani*
DGPS	Direzione Generale Pubblica Sicurezza
DPP	Divisione Polizia Politica
FDRL	FDR Presidential Library and Museum, Hyde Park, NY
FRUS	*Papers Relating to the Foreign Relations of the United States*
IfZG	Institut für Zeitgeshichte, Munich
JESCOM	Jesuit Center for Social Communication

LdR	*Lettres de Rome*
MAE	French Ministry of Foreign Affairs Archives, Paris
MCP	Ministero della Cultura Popolare
MI	Italian Interior Ministry
MKK	*Bayerischer Kurier*
NARA	National Archives and Records Administration, Archive II, College Park, MD
NCWC	National Catholic Welfare Conference Archives, Catholic University of America, Washington, DC
PPF	President's Personal File
PSF	President's Secretary's File

Notes

INTRODUCTION: ON THE BRINK OF A NEW ERA

1. Woodrow Wilson, "War Message to Congress," delivered at the Joint Session of the Two Houses of Congress, April 2, 1917. U.S. 65th Congress, 1st session, Senate document 5.

2. Eugenio Pacelli to Pietro Gasparri, June 6, 1918. Vatican Secret Archives, Rome (hereafter cited as ASV), Affari Ecclesiastici Straordinari (hereafter cited as A.E.S.), Germania, 1917–1919, pos. 1664, fasc. 873, f. 30.

3. Eugenio Pacelli to Pietro Gasparri, Munich, December 20, 1918. ASV, A.E.S., Baviera, terzo periodo. 1918–1921, pos. 67, ff. 15–18.

4. Clifford Geertz, "Local Knowledge: Fact and Law in Comparative Perspective," in his *Local Knowledge: Further Essays in Interpretive Anthropology* (New York: Basic Books, 1983), 167–234, at 232.

5. Studies on the papacy and the Soviet Union have offered important insights but failed to study the workings of the papal anticommunist campaign in any detail. See Philippe Chenaux, *L'Église catholique et le communisme en Europe (1917–1989): De Lénine à Jean-Paul II* (Paris: Éditions du Cerf, 2010); Peter C. Kent, *The Lonely Cold War of Pope Pius XII: The Roman Catholic Church and the Division of Europe, 1943–1950* (Montreal: McGill-Queen's University Press, 2002); and Laura Pettinaroli, *La Politique russe du Saint-Siège (1905–1939)* (Rome: École française de Rome, 2015).

6. *Lettres de Rome*, 1, no. 1 (May 1935): 1, Roman Archives of the Jesuit Order (ARSI), Jesuit Center for Social Communication (hereafter cited as JESCOM), the Private Library of Father Ledóchowski.

7. Stephen J. Brown, "Catholic Internationalism," *Studies: An Irish Quarterly Review* 14, no. 55 (1925): 476–479.

8. For the de-privatization of religion more broadly, see José Casanova, *Public Religions in the Modern World* (Chicago: University of Chicago Press, 1994).

9. Talal Asad, *Formations of the Secular: Christianity, Islam, Modernity* (Stanford, CA: Stanford University Press, 2003); Saba Mahmood, *Religious Difference in a Secular Age: A Minority Report* (Princeton, NJ: Princeton University Press, 2015); Samuel Moyn, *Christian Human Rights* (Philadelphia: University of Pennsylvania Press, 2015); Elayne Oliphant, "The Crucifix as a Symbol of Secular Europe: The Surprising Semiotics of the European Court of Human Rights," *Anthropology Today* 28, no. 2 (2012): 10–12; Mayanthi L. Fernando, *The Republic Unsettled: Muslim French and the Contradictions of Secularism* (Durham, NC: Duke University Press, 2014).

10. See David Blackbourn, *Marpingen: Apparitions of the Virgin Mary in Nineteenth-Century Germany* (New York: Knopf, 1993); Ruth Harris, *Lourdes: Body and Spirit in the Secular Age* (London: Allen Lane, 1999); Thomas Kselman, *Miracles and Prophecies in Nineteenth-Century France* (New Brunswick, NJ: Rutgers University Press, 1983); Robert Orsi, *The Madonna of 115th Street: Faith and Community in Italian Harlem, 1880–1950* (New Haven, CT: Yale University Press, 1985); and Jonathan Sperber, *Popular Catholicism in Nineteenth-Century Germany* (Princeton, NJ: Princeton University Press, 1984).

11. Tom Buchanan and Martin Conway, eds., *Political Catholicism in Europe, 1918–1965* (Oxford: Oxford University Press, 1996); James Chappel, *Catholic Modern: The Challenge of Totalitarianism and the Remaking of the Church* (Cambridge, MA: Harvard University Press, 2018); John Connelly, *From Enemy to Brother: The Revolution in Catholic Teaching on the Jews* (Cambridge, MA: Harvard University Press, 2012); Martin Conway, *Catholic Politics in Europe, 1918–1945* (London: Routledge, 2017); Marco Duranti, *The Conservative Human Rights Revolution: European Identity, Transnational Politics and the Origins of the European Convention* (Oxford: Oxford University Press, 2017); Elizabeth Foster, *Faith in Empire: Religion, Politics, and Colonial Rule in French Senegal, 1880–1940* (Stanford, CA: Stanford University Press, 2013); Foster, *African Catholic: Decolonization and the Transformation of the Church* (Cambridge, MA: Harvard University Press, 2019); Emmanuel Gerard and Gerd-Rainer Horn, eds., *Left Catholicism, 1943–1955: Catholics and Society in Western Europe at the Point of Liberation* (Leuven: Leuven University Press, 2001); Stefanos Geroulanos, *An Atheism That Is Not Humanist Emerges in French Thought* (Stanford, CA: Stanford University Press, 2010); Udi Greenberg, *The Weimar Century: German Émigrés and the Ideological Foundations of the Cold War* (Princeton, NJ: Princeton University Press, 2014); Carlo Ivernizzi-Accetti, *What Is Christian Democracy? The Forgotten Ideology* (Cambridge: Cambridge University Press, forthcoming); Wolfram Kaiser, *Christian Democracy and the Origins of the European Union* (Cambridge: Cambridge University Press, 2007); Piotr Kosicki, *Catholics on the Barricades: Poland, France, and "Revolution," 1891–1956* (New Haven, CT: Yale University Press, 2018); Piotr Kosicki and Sławomir Łukasiewicz, eds., *Christian Democracy across the Iron Curtain* (London: Palgrave Macmillan, 2018); John McGreevey, *American Jesuits and the World: How an Embattled Religious Order*

Made Modern Catholicism Global (Princeton, NJ: Princeton University Press, 2016); Paul Misner, *Catholic Labor Movements in Europe: Social Thought and Action, 1914–1965* (Washington, DC: Catholic University of America, 2015); Maria Mitchell, *The Origins of Christian Democracy: Politics and Confession in Modern Germany* (Ann Arbor: University of Michigan Press, 2012); Renato Moro, *La formazione della classe dirigente cattolica* (Bologna: Il Mulino, 1979); Moyn, *Christian Human Rights*; Camille Robcis, "Catholics, the 'Theory of Gender,' and the Turn to the Human in France: A New Dreyfus Affair?," *Journal of Modern History* 87, no. 4 (December 2015): 892–923; Mark Ruff, *The Battle for the Catholic Past in Germany, 1945–1980* (Cambridge: Cambridge University Press, 2017); Ruff, *The Wayward Flock: Catholic Youth in Postwar West Germany, 1945–1965* (Chapel Hill: University of North Carolina Press, 2005); Stephen Schloesser, *Jazz Age Catholicism: Mystic Modernism in Postwar Paris* (Toronto: University of Toronto Press, 2005); Sarah Shortall, *Soldiers of God in a Secular World: The Politics of Catholic Theology in Twentieth-Century France* (Cambridge, MA: Harvard University Press, forthcoming); Noah Benezra Strote, *Lions and Lambs: Conflict in Weimar and the Creation of Post-Nazi Germany* (New Haven, CT: Yale University Press, 2017); Kimba Allie Tichenor, *Religious Crisis and Civic Transformation: How Conflicts over Gender and Sexuality Changed the West German Catholic Church* (Waltham, MA: Brandeis University Press, 2016); Peter Van Kemseke, *Towards an Era of Development: The Globalization of Socialism and Christian Democracy, 1945–1965* (Leuven: Leuven University Press, 2006); Susan B. Whitney, *Mobilizing Youth: Communists and Catholics in Interwar France* (Durham, NC: Duke University Press, 2009); Albert Wu, *From Christ to Confucius: German Missionaries, Chinese Christians and the Globalization of Christianity, 1860–1950* (New Haven, CT: Yale University Press, 2016); and Ernest P. Young, *Ecclesiastical Colony: China's Catholic Church and the French Religious Protectorate* (Oxford: Oxford University Press, 2013).

12. See Cemil Aydin, *The Politics of Anti-Westernism in Asia: Visions of World Order in Pan-Islamic and Pan-Asian Thought* (New York: Columbia University Press, 2007); Doris L. Bergen, *Twisted Cross: The German Christian Movement in the Third Reich* (Chapel Hill: University of North Carolina Press, 1996); Abigail Green, *Moses Montefiore: Jewish Liberator, Imperial Hero* (Cambridge, MA: Harvard University Press, 2012); Abigail Green and Vincent Viaene, eds., *Religious Internationals in the Modern World* (Basingstoke, UK: Palgrave, 2012); Susannah Heschel, *The Aryan Jesus: Christian Theologians and the Bible in Nazi Germany* (Princeton, NJ: Princeton University Press, 2008); David A. Hollinger, *Protestants Abroad: How Missionaries Tried to Change the World but Changed America* (Princeton, NJ: Princeton University Press, 2017); Richard Steigmann-Gall, *The Holy Reich: Nazi Conceptions of Christianity, 1919–1945* (Cambridge: Cambridge University Press, 2003); Michael G. Thompson, *For God and Globe: Christian Internationalism in the United States between the Great War*

and the Cold War (Ithaca, NY: Cornell University Press, 2015); Yuri Slez-kine, *The Jewish Century* (Princeton, NJ: Princeton University Press, 2004); and Sarah Abrevaya Stein, *Extraterritorial Dreams: European Citizenship, Sephardi Jews, and the Ottoman Twentieth Century* (Chicago: University of Chicago Press, 2016).

13. Some important exceptions to this rule include Fabrice Bouthillon, *La naissance de la Mardité: Une théologie politique à l'age totalitaire: Pie XI (1922–1939)* (Strasbourg: Presses universitaires, 2002); Daniele Menozzi and Renato Moro, *Cattolicesimo e totalitarismo: Chiese e culture religiose tra le due guerre mondiali* (Brescia: Morcelliana, 2004); John Pollard, *Money and the Rise of the Modern Papacy: Financing the Vatican, 1850–1950* (Cambridge: Cambridge University Press, 2004); and Pollard, *The Papacy in the Age of Totalitarianism, 1914–1958* (Oxford: Oxford University Press, 2014). These works differ from my own in that they tend to present the papacy as reacting to secular movements and ultimately losing ground against them. They do not dedicate much attention to showing how the papacy developed its own proactive strategy, which dialogued with secular movements and leaned on concepts like international law, self-determination, human rights, and democracy. The core thematic of "internationalism" (as a papal practice, strategy, and goal) is also absent from the above-referenced works.

14. Charles Maier, *Recasting Bourgeois Europe: Stabilization in France, Germany and Italy in the Decade after World War I* (Princeton, NJ: Princeton University Press, 1975), 594. The importance of trans-war continuities in understanding Europe post-1945 has been highlighted more recently by several scholars, including Chappel, *Catholic Modern*; Patricia Clavin, *Securing the World Economy: The Reinvention of the League of Nations, 1920–1946* (Oxford: Oxford University Press, 2013); Greenberg, *The Weimar Century*; Jan-Werner Müller, *Contesting Democracy: Political Ideas in Twentieth-Century Europe* (New Haven, CT: Yale University Press, 2014); Philip Nord, *France's New Deal: From the Thirties to the Postwar Era* (Princeton, NJ: Princeton University Press, 2012); Quinn Slobodian, *Globalists: The End of Empire and the Birth of Neoliberalism* (Cambridge, MA: Harvard University Press, 2018); Adam Tooze, *The Deluge: The Great War, America and the Remaking of the Global Order, 1916–1931* (New York: Penguin House, 2014); and Strote, *Lions and Lambs*.

15. See Alan Milward, *The European Rescue of the Nation-State* (London: Taylor and Francis, 1999); and A.W. Brian Simpson, *Human Rights and the End of Empire: Britain and the Genesis of the European Convention* (Oxford: Oxford University Press, 2004).

16. Well-known interventions in the long-standing debate over the papacy's relationship to Fascism and Nazism include Frank J. Coppa, "Between Morality and Diplomacy: The Vatican's 'Silence' during the Holocaust," *Journal of Church and State* 50, no. 3 (Summer 2008): 541–568; John Cornwell, *Hitler's Pope: The Secret History of Pius XII* (New York: Penguin Books, 1999); Peter Godman, *Hitler and the Vatican: Inside the Secret Archives That Reveal*

the New Story of the Nazis and the Church (New York: Free Press, 2004); Daniel Goldhagen, *A Moral Reckoning: The Role of the Church in the Holocaust and Its Unfulfilled Duty of Repair* (New York: Vintage Books, 2013); Jacques Kornberg, *The Pope's Dilemma: Pius XII Faces Atrocities and Genocide in the Second World War* (Toronto: University of Toronto Press, 2015); Guenter Lewy, *The Catholic Church and Nazi Germany* (Boulder, CO: Da Capo Press, 2000 [1964]); Michael Phayer, *The Catholic Church and the Holocaust* (Bloomington: Indiana University Press, 2000); and José M. Sánchez, *Pius XII and the Holocaust: Understanding the Controversy* (Washington, DC: Catholic University of America Press, 2002). Important recent additions to the literature on papal–Fascist and papal–Nazi relations include Lucia Ceci, *The Vatican and Mussolini's Italy* (Boston: Brill, 2016); Emma Fattorini, *Hitler, Mussolini, and the Vatican: Pope Pius XI and the Speech That Was Never Made*, trans. Carl Ispen (Malden, MA: Polity Press, 2011); David Kertzer, *The Pope and Mussolini: The Secret History of Pius XI and the Rise of Fascism in Europe* (New York: Random House, 2014); Robert Ventresca, *Soldier of Christ: The Life of Pope Pius XII* (Cambridge, MA: Harvard University Press, 2013); and Hubert Wolf, *Pope and Devil: The Vatican's Archives and the Third Reich*, trans. Kenneth Kronenberg (Cambridge, MA: Harvard University Press, 2010).

17. For versions of the argument from necessity, see, *inter alia*, Fattorini, *Hitler, Mussolini, and the Vatican*; John Pollard, *The Vatican and Italian Fascism, 1929–1932: A Study in Conflict* (Cambridge: Cambridge University Press, 1985); Ventresca, *Soldier of Christ*; and Wolf, *Pope and Devil*. For arguments about the identity of views, see Bouthillon, *La Naissance*; Ceci, *The Vatican and Mussolini's Italy*; Derek Hastings, *Catholicism and the Roots of Nazism: Religious Identity and National Socialism* (Oxford: Oxford University Press, 2011); and Menozzi and Moro, *Cattolicesimo e totalitarismo*; Andrea Riccardi, ed., *Pio XII* (Bari: Laterza, 1985).

18. Through their detailed analyses of how Catholic clerics and lay activists in Germany interfaced with Nazism, scholars such as Lauren Faulkner Rossi, Kevin Spicer, and Todd Weir have emphasized the importance of anticommunism as a force that drew Catholics into the Nazi orbit. See Lauren Faulkner Rossi, *Wehrmacht Priests: Catholicism and the Nazi War of Annihilation* (Cambridge, MA: Harvard University Press, 2015); Kevin Spicer, *Hitler's Priests: Catholic Clergy and National Socialism* (DeKalb: Northern Illinois University Press, 2008); Todd Weir, "The Christian Front against Godlessness: Anti-Secularism and the Demise of the Weimar Republic, 1928–1933," *Past and Present* 229, no. 1 (2015): 201–238; Weir, "A European Culture War in the Twentieth Century? Anti-Catholicism and Anti-Bolshevism between Moscow, Berlin and the Vatican, 1922 to 1933," *Journal of Religious History* 39, no. 2 (2015): 280–306.

19. Eugenio Pacelli, *Gesammelte Reden: Erster Apostolischer Nuntius beim Deutschen Reich* (Berlin: Buchverlag Germania, 1930), 26.

CHAPTER 1 ▪ THE THREAT OF A SECULAR ORDER

Epigraph: Matthias Erzberger, *Parere sul miglior modo di risolvere la Questione Romana* (n.p.: n.p., 1920), 7.

Unless otherwise noted, all translations are my own.

1. The Grand Masonic Master Ferrari, in a circular of December 1916, as quoted in Matthias Erzberger, *Souvenirs de guerre* (Paris: Payot, 1921), 169.
2. See Emma Fattorini, *Germania e Santa Sede: Le nunziature di Pacelli tra la grande guerra e la repubblica di Weimar* (Bologna: Il Mulino, 1992), 18; Alberto Monticone, "Benedetto XV e la Germania," in *Benedetto XV e la pace—1918*, ed. Giorgio Rumi (Brescia: Morcelliana, 1990), 9–19; John Pollard, *The Papacy in the Age of Totalitarianism, 1914–1958* (Oxford: Oxford University Press, 2014), 38–39; and Jean-Marc Ticchi, "Fondements et modalités de l'impartialité du Saint-Siège pendant la Première guerre mondiale," *Relations internationales* 160 (January–March 2015): 39–51.
3. Klaus Epstein, "Erzberger's Position in the Zentrumsstreit before World War I," *Catholic Historical Review* 44, no. 1 (April 1958): 1–16, at 1–6.
4. Monsignor Giacomo Della Chiesa to Secretary of State Merry Del Val, May 24, 1910. ASV, Segreteria di Stato, 1910, rubrica 12, fasc. 6, ff. 209–212; and Monsignor Giacomo Della Chiesa to Secretary of State Merry Del Val, December 16, 1910. ASV, Segreteria di Stato, 1910, rubrica 80, fasc. 1, pp. 10–12. As cited in Antonio Scottà, *Giacomo Della Chiesa, arcivescovo di Bologna (1908–1914)* (Soveria Mannelli: Rubbettino 2002), 340.
5. Erzberger, *Souvenirs de guerre*, 60.
6. See Tullio Aesecher, *Un confine per il papa: Problematiche territoriali nella Questione Romana e confine dello Stato della Città del Vaticano* (Rome: Bardi Editore, 2009), 30–33; Carlotta Benedetti, "Le Carte Erzberger," *Collectanea Archivi Vaticani: Dall'Archivio Segreto Vaticano—Miscellanea di testi, saggi e inventari*, 96, no. 7 (Vatican City: Archivio Segreto Vaticano, 2014): 3–102, at 8 and 30; Hubert Wolf, "Matthias Erzberger, Nuntius Pacelli und der Vatikan. Oder: Warum der Kirchenstaat nicht nach Liechtenstein verlegt wurde," in *Matthias Erzberger: Ein Demokrat in Zeiten des Hasses* (Karlsruhe: G. Braun, 2013), 251–270. For Erzberger's own reports, see his *Souvenirs de guerre*.
7. ASV, Carte Erzberger, 4, fasc. 11, ff. 27–30, 86–89,111–112; ibid., 1, fasc. 1, ff. 207–208, 342–346. As quoted in Benedetti, "Le Carte Erzberger," at 32, 34. Also see Erzberger, *Souvenirs de guerre*, 31–32, 161.
8. As reported by Jean Jules Jusserand, dispatch no. 581, and the British ambassador to Paris, September 4, 1915, French Ministry of Foreign Affairs Archives, Paris, *Paix 1914-1920*, vol. 2. Cited in Annie Lacroix-Riz, *Le Vatican, Europe et le Reich: De la Première Guerre mondiale à la guerre froide, 1914–1945* (Paris: Armand Colin, Nouvelle édition refondue, 2010), 527.
9. On how Woodrow Wilson's religious beliefs shaped his political actions, see Barry Hankins, *Woodrow Wilson: Ruling Elder, Spiritual President* (Ox-

ford: Oxford University Press, 2016); and Cara Lea Burnidge, *A Peaceful Conquest: Woodrow Wilson, Religion, and the New World Order* (Chicago: University of Chicago Press, 2016).

10. Woodrow Wilson, "Address of the President of the United States Delivered at a Joint Session of the Two Houses of Congress, April 2, 1917," U.S. Department of State, *Foreign Relations of the United States* (hereafter cited as *FRUS*), *1917, Supplement 1, The World War*, ed. Joseph V. Fuller (Washington, DC: U.S. Govt. Printing Office, 1931), 194–203.

11. Jean-Louis Jadoulle, *Chrétiens modernes?* (Louvain-la-Neuve : Academia-Bruylant/Presses universitaires de Louvain, 2006), 5:770–784.

12. See Claude Fohlen, "Catholicisme américain et catholicisme européen: La convergence de l'Américanisme," *Revue d'histoire moderne et contemporaine* 34 (1987): 215–230; and Scott Appleby, *Church and Age Unite! The Modernist Impulse in American Catholicism* (South Bend, IN: University of Notre Dame Press, 1992).

13. Pope Leo XIII, *Longinqua Oceani* (January 6, 1895), available online at http://w2.vatican.va/content/leo-xiii/en/encyclicals/documents/hf_l-xiii _enc_06011895_longinqua.html.

14. Pope Leo XIII, *Testem benevolentiae nostrae* (January 22, 1899), available online at https://w2.vatican.va/content/leo-xiii/la/letters/documents/hf_l -xiii_let_18990122_testem-benevolentiae.html. Also see Pope Leo XIII, *Sapientiae Christianae* (January 10, 1890), available online at http://w2.vatican .va/content/leo-xiii/en/encyclicals/documents/hf_l-xiii_enc_10011890 _sapientiae-christianae.html.

15. For the horrified reaction of the powerful Vatican secretary of state, see, e.g., Pietro Gasparri, *Diario*, II, 65, April 7, 1917. Also see Pope Benedict XV, speech before the "Opera della preservazione della Fede," November 22, 1915; *Ad Beatissimi Apostolorum*; "I discorsi degli statisti alleati e l'appello di pace del Papa," *Civiltà Cattolica*, February 2, 1918, 194; and numerous *Osservatore Romano* articles: January 19, 1919; February 14, 1919; June 12, 1920.

16. Eugenio Pacelli to Pietro Gasparri, Munich, September 6, 1917, ASV, A.E.S., Stati Ecclesiastici, 1914–1921, pos. 1317, fasc.470, vol. 4, f. 242; and Pacelli to Gasparri, Munich, December 20, 1918, ASV, A.E.S., Baviera, terzo periodo, 1918–1921, pos. 67, ff. 15–18. For Pacelli's message, which included Wilson's texts in English and German, see ASV, Arch. Nunz. Monaco 410, fasc. 4, f. 16.

17. L.C. [Luigi Capalti], "Il Messaggio del Presidente Wilson al Congresso," *Osservatore Romano*, April 5, 1917.

18. ASV, A.E.S., Germania 415, June–July 1918 binder. As cited in Fattorini, *Germania e Santa Sede*, 91–92.

19. "Cose Italiane," *Civiltà Cattolica*, March 16, 1918.

20. Matthias Erzberger, "La lotta di Wilson contro la pace," May 28, 1918, ASV, A.E.S., Germania, 1917–1919, pos. 1664, fasc. 873, ff. 42, 43–45. Erzberger's analysis is also included as an addendum to Eugenio Pacelli's letter to Gasparri, June 6, 1918, ASV, A.E.S., Germania, 1917–1919, pos. 1664, fasc. 873, f. 30.

21. On the Committee of Public Information and the debates it generated within the United States, see Sarah Ellen Graham, *Culture and Propaganda: The Progressive Origins of American Public Diplomacy, 1936–1953* (London: Routledge, 2015).

22. J. Michael Hogan, *Woodrow Wilson's Western Tour: Rhetoric, Public Opinion, and the League of Nations* (College Station: Texas A&M University Press, 2006); Daniela Rossi, *Woodrow Wilson and the American Myth in Italy: Culture, Diplomacy, and War Propaganda* (Cambridge, MA: Harvard University Press, 2008).

23. As cited in Friedrich Ritter von Lama, *Die Friedensvermittlung Papst Benedikt XV und ihre Vereitlung durch den deutschen Reichskanzler Michaelis: Eine historisch-kritische Untersuchung* (Munich: J. Kösel and F. Pustet, 1932), 32–33.

24. Ibid., 2–75.

25. Benedict XV, *Ad Beatissimi Apostolorum* (November 1, 1914), §11, available online at http://w2.vatican.va/content/benedict-xv/en/encyclicals/documents/hf_ben-xv_enc_01111914_ad-beatissimi-apostolorum.html.

26. The Bern representative, Monsignor Marchetti-Selvaggiani, is quoted in Philipp Scheidemann, *Papst, Kaiser und Sozialdemokratie in ihren Friedensbemühungen im Sommer 1917* (Berlin: Verlag für Sozialwissenschaft, 1921), 21; and in Arno J. Mayer, *Wilson vs. Lenin: Political Origins of the New Diplomacy, 1917–1918* (Cleveland: World Publishing Co., 1969), 232.

27. Leipzig *Freie Presse*, September 1, 1917, as cited in John L. Snell, "Benedict XV, Wilson, Michaelis, and German Socialism," *Catholic Historical Review* 37, no. 2 (July 1951): 151–178, at 158.

28. *Germania*, August 16, 1917.

29. See the telegrams to the pope from the chancellor of the German Empire, Theobald von Bethmann-Hollweg, and the emperor of the Austro-Hungarian Empire, Karl I, dated September 28, 1917. In *FRUS, Supplement, the World War, 1917* (Washington, DC: U.S. Govt. Printing Office, 1917), 217–220. For Matthias Erzberger's decision to bring the papal peace plan before the Reichstag, see Erzberger, *Souvenirs de guerre*, 41–49; and Charles Seymour, *The Intimate Papers of Colonel House* (New York: Houghton Mifflin, 1926), 1:150–151. On Spain's endorsement of the plan, see Spanish ambassador Juan Riaño to the U.S. Secretary of State, Washington, December 27, 1916, In *FRUS, Supplement, the World War, 1916* (Washington, DC: U.S. Govt. Printing Office, 1916), 118.

30. Secretary of State to the Diplomatic Representatives in Allied Countries, Washington, DC, August 18, 1917, in *FRUS 1917*, supplement 2, *The World War*, 165.

31. Colonel House to President Woodrow Wilson, Magnolia, Massachusetts, August 17 and 19, 1917, as reprinted in Seymour, *The Intimate Papers*, 3:156–158.

32. The letter was sent to the Holy See via the British Foreign Office because Washington and the Vatican had no direct diplomatic ties. See Secretary of State to the Ambassador in Great Britain, Washington, DC, August 27 1917. As reprinted in *FRUS 1917*, supplement 2, *The World War*, 117–179.

33. The Ambassador in Great Britain (Page) to the Secretary of State, London, August 30, 1917; and the Ambassador in France (Sharp) to the Secretary of State, Paris, August 31, 1917; both as reprinted in *FRUS* 1917, supplement 2, *The World War*, 181–182.

34. ASV, Stati Ecclesiastici, VI 216/XIII; ASV, Stati Ecclesiastici, VI 216/XIII; both as cited in Fattorini, *Germania e Santa Sede*, 64–65.

35. As noted in Enrico Serra, "La nota del primo agosto 1917 e il governo italiano: Qualche osservazione," in Rumi, *Benedetto XV e la pace, 1914–1918*, 61; John Pollard, *Benedict XV (1914–1922) and the Pursuit of Peace* (London: Geoffrey Chapman, 1999),128; and Mayer, *Wilson vs. Lenin*, 354.

36. Alfred Loisy to Alfred Fawkes, ca. October 1917, cited in Alfred Fawkes, "The Papacy and the Modern State," *Harvard Theological Review* 11 (1918): 376–394, at 376.

37. Eugenio Pacelli to Pietro Gasparri, Munich, December 20, 1918, ASV, A.E.S., Baviera, terzo period, 1918–1921, pos. 67, ff. 15–18.

38. "I discorsi degli statisti belligeranti e l'appello di pace del Papa," *Civiltà Cattolica*, February 16, 1918, 289–329, at 303.

39. To my knowledge, no monograph on this important educational institution exists. For some discussion of the Academy's importance and role, see David Alvarez, "The Professionalization of the Papal Diplomatic Service, 1909–1967," *Catholic Historical Review* 75, no. 2 (April 1989): 233–248; Maria Pia Donato, "Accademie e accademismi in una capitale particolare: Il caso di Roma, secoli XVIII–XIX," *Mélanges de l'École française de Rome: Italie et Méditerranée* 111, no. 1 (1999): 415–430; and Roberto Regoli, "Merry Del Val e l'Accademia dei Nobili Ecclesiastici," *Archivio della Società romana di storia patria* 139 (2016): 145–163. For contemporary accounts, see Ferdinando Procaccini di Montescaglioso, *La Pontificia accademia dei nobili ecclesiastici: Memoria storica* (Rome: A. Befani, 1889); and Adolfo Giobbio, *Lezioni di diplomazia ecclesiastica dettate nella Pontificia Accademia dei nobili ecclesiastici* (Rome: Tipografia vaticana, 1899–1904).

40. George Smith Walter, "International Law," in *The Catholic Encyclopedia: An International Work of Reference on the Constitution, Doctrine, Discipline, and History of the Catholic Church*, vol. 9 (New York: Encyclopedia Press, 1914), 76.

41. James Lorimer, *Institutes of International Law: A Treatise of the Jural Relations of Separate Political Communities* (Edinburgh: Blackwood, 1883), 1:117, as cited in Martti Koskenniemi, *The Gentle Civilizer of Nations: The Rise and Fall of International Law, 1870–1960* (Cambridge: Cambridge University Press, 2004), 65. For similar sentiments, see, e.g., Johann Caspar Bluntschli, "Das römische Papsttum und das Völkerrecht," in *Gesammelte kleine Schriften* (Nördlingen: C. H. Beck'sche buchhandlung, 1879–1881), 248–255.

42. See James Muldoon, "The Contribution of the Medieval Canon Lawyers to the Formation of International Law," *Traditio* 28 (1972): 483–497; Claude Prudhomme, "L'Académie pontificale ecclésiastique et le service du Saint-Siège," *Mélanges de l'école française de Rome*, 116, no. 1 (2004): 61–89; Karl

Shoemaker, "World War I, Self-Determination, and the Legacies of Medieval Jurisprudence," *Uluslararasi Suçlar ve Tarih* 15 (2014): 59–75.

43. Joseph Adam Gustav Hergenröther, *Catholic Church and Christian State* (London: Burns and Oates, 1876), 369. Hergenröther's original 1873 German-language edition of this work was translated into Italian in 1877–1878. Also see Paul Pradier-Fodéré, *Traité de droit international* (Paris: Pedone-Lauriel, 1885).

44. Hergenröther, *Catholic Church*, 369.

45. The booklet, *La séparation de l'Église et de l'État en France. Exposé et documents* (Rome: n.p, 1905), was authored by Pietro Gasparri and Eugenio Pacelli, among others.

46. Canon 218. On how the *Codes Iuris Canonici* definitively strengthened the pope's power, see Constant Van De Wiel, *History of Canon Law* (Leuven: Peeters, 1992).

47. Charles P. Sherman, "A Brief History of Imperial Roman Canon Law," *California Law Review* 7, no. 2 (January 1919): 93–104.

48. The full text of the Code of Canon Law is reprinted in Edward N. Peters, ed., *1917 Pio-Benedictine Code of Canon Law* (San Francisco: Ignatius Press, 2001).

49. The only scholar to pay due attention to the content of the Code is Carlo Fantappiè. His various works on the subject include *Chiesa romana e modernità giuridica* (Milan: Giuffrè, 2008); "Alle origini della codificazione pio-benedettina: Nuovi sviluppi delle teorie canonistiche sotto il pontificato di Leone XIII," *Quaderni fiorentini per la storia del pensiero giuridico moderno* 25 (1996): 346–407; and "Gl'inizi della codificazione pio-benedettina alla luce di nuovi documenti," *Il diritto ecclesiastico* 113 (2002): 16–82.

50. Anton Maria Bettanini, "Pio XII insegnante di diplomazia nella Pontificia Accademia ecclesiastica: Ricordi di un accademico," in *La Pontificia Accademia ecclesiastica, 1701–1951* (Vatican City: Tipografia della Poliglotta Vaticana, 1951), 71–74, at 74. Pacelli drew up his tract with the encouragement of the newly minted cardinal Pietro Gasparri, who was secretary of state under Pope Benedict XV from 1914.

51. For instance, the investiture strife was settled by the first concordat in Church history, the 1122 Concordat of Worms; the violent persecution of the Church in Poland was settled by the Concordat of Poland (ratified in 1289), the Concordat with Sardinia cleared up a debate surrounding ecclesiastical nominations (in 1727), and the concordat of 1801 temporarily settled the tormented relations between the French state and the Catholic Church.

52. ASV, A.E.S., Stati Ecclesiastici 157, Voto di Mgr. Pacelli. Pacelli's February 1916 votum is reprinted and discussed in Romeo Astorri, "Diritto comune e normativa concordataria: Uno scritto inedito di mons. Pacelli sulla 'decadenza' degli accordi tra Chiesa e Stato," *Storia contemporanea* 4, no. 22 (1991): 685–701.

53. Eugenio Pacelli, *La personalità e la territorialità delle leggi specialmente nel diritto canonico: Studio storico-giuridico* (Rome: Tipografia Poliglotta Vaticana, 1912); Pacelli to Gasparri, May 2, 1921, ASV, A.E.S., Germania 504. As cited in Fattorini, *Germania e Santa Sede*, 213.

54. Paul Parsy, *Les Concordats récents, 1914–1935: Histoire, analyse, règles communes* (Paris: J. Gabalda, 1936), ii; and G. Lampis, "Il Concordato tra la Santa Sede e lo Stato Lituano," *Rivista di Diritto Pubblico* 21 (1929): 227.
55. See, for instance, article 16 of the *Concordato Stipulato fra la Santa Sede ed il Governo di Serbia* (Rome: Tipografia dell'Unione Editrice, 1915), 8–9.
56. This language was a direct response to the fact that many states had broken diplomatic relations with the pope following the loss of the Papal States and the lack of clarity under the law of the pope's status. See Josef L. Kunz, "The Status of the Holy See in International Law," *American Journal of International Law* 46, no. 2 (1952): 308–314.
57. As was true in so many other respects in the 1910s, Eastern European countries were the places where the Vatican and Europe's Great Powers tried out their plans for reordering international affairs. On this phenomenon, see Matthew Frank, *Making Minorities History: Population Transfer in Twentieth-Century Europe* (Oxford: Oxford University Press, 2017), chaps. 1 and 2; Carole Fink, *Defending the Rights of Others: The Great Powers, the Jews, and International Minority Protection, 1878–1938* (Cambridge: Cambridge University Press, 2004); Holly Case, *Between States: The Transylvanian Question and the European Idea during World War II* (Stanford, CA: Stanford University Press, 2009), introduction and chap. 1; Gerry Simpson, *Great Powers and Outlaw States: Unequal Sovereigns in the International Legal Order* (Cambridge: Cambridge University Press, 2004); and Natasha Wheatley, *The Temporal Life of States: Sovereignty at the Eclipse of Empire* (forthcoming).

CHAPTER 2 ■ A NEW CATHOLIC DIPLOMACY

Epigraph: R. P. Yves de la Brière, *Études et paix* (Paris: Flammarion, 1932), 603.

1. As cited in Neal Pease, *Rome's Most Faithful Daughter: The Catholic Church and Independent Poland, 1914–1939* (Athens, OH: Ohio University Press, 2009), 31.
2. Martin Kitchen, *The Silent Dictatorship: The Politics of the German High Command under Hindenburg and Ludendorff, 1916–1918* (London: Croom Helm, 1976), 183.
3. The phrase "sword and plow" is Hindenburg's. See John Wheeler-Bennett, *Wooden Titan: Hindenburg in Twenty Years of German History, 1914–1934* (New York: William Morrow, 1936), 126.
4. Cited in Fritz Fischer, *Griff nach der Weltmacht: Die Kriegszielpolitik des Kaiserlichen Deutschland, 1914–18* (Düsseldorf: Droste, 1961), 299–300, as cited in Adam Tooze, *The Deluge: The Great War, America, and the Remaking of the Global Order, 1916–1931* (New York: Penguin Books, 2014), 114.
5. On German anxieties about American influence in Russia and the Far East—and the plan to create a Russo-Japanese-German alliance to block its spread—see General Alfred von Tirpitz, *Erinnerungen* (Leipzig: V. Hase und Koehler, 1919). According to Gustav Stresemann, the only way for Germany to face the power of American industry would be for it to consolidate a bloc

of 150 million consumers in Eastern and Central Europe. For more on the long life of these ideas, see Stephen G. Gross, *Export Empire: German Soft Power in Southeastern Europe, 1890–1945* (Cambridge: Cambridge University Press, 2016).

6. The phrase "a firm and permanent alliance" is from the Taryba's declaration of December 11, 1917. See Vejas Gabriel Liulevicius, *War Land on the Eastern Front: Culture, National Identity and German Occupation in World War I* (Cambridge: Cambridge University Press, 2000), 96, 202–204.

7. Liulevicius, *War Land on the Eastern Front*, 205–206.

8. Pacelli to Gasparri, "Sul deputato Erzberger: confidenziale e personale," Munich, October 22, 1917, ASV, Stati Ecclesiastici, Germania 371. Pacelli expressed similar ideas in a second letter to Gasparri, dated May 27, 1918, ASV, Stati Ecclesiastici, Germania 371.

9. Pacelli to Erzberger, July 13, 1917, ASV, Carte Erzberger 4, fasc. 7, ff. 236–237.

10. Klaus Epstein, *Matthias Erzberger and the Dilemma of German Democracy* (Princeton, NJ: Princeton University Press, 1959), 219–220, 237.

11. On this, see Jeremy Smith, *The Bolsheviks and the National Question, 1917–1923* (London: Macmillan, 1999), 8–20; Arno Mayer, *Wilson vs. Lenin: Political Origins of the New Diplomacy, 1917–1918* (Cleveland: World, 1964), 248, 298–303; and Erez Manela, *The Wilsonian Moment: Self-Determination and the International Origins of Anticolonial Nationalism* (Oxford: Oxford University Press, 2007), 37.

12. Pacelli to Gasparri, "Sul deputato Erzberger."

13. *The Papers of Woodrow Wilson*, ed. Arthur S. Link (Princeton, NJ: Princeton University Press, 1966–1994), 45:197; 48:96–97, 205–206, 435–438; 45:537–538; 46:323.

14. Vladimir Lenin, "Sotsialisticheskaia revoliutsiia i parvo natsii na samoopredelenie," as cited in Robert A. Jones, *The Soviet Concept of "Limited Sovereignty" from Lenin to Gorbachev* (Basingstoke: Macmillan, 1990), 40–41.

15. Two months later, the Bolsheviks issued a second declaration, which gave the right of self-determination only to "toiling and exploited people," not to all nationalities. In tandem, the Russian Soviet Federative Socialist Republic refused to recognize the independence of a series of new nation-states, including Lithuania (which declared independence in December 1917), Transcaucasia (February 1918), Estonia (May 1918), and Latvia (November 1918). In 1920, Stalin further qualified Bolshevik support for the principle of self-determination by arguing that border regions seceding from Russia would become enslaved by imperialism, thus making the demand for secession "counterrevolutionary."

16. Niels Thorsen, *The Political Thought of Woodrow Wilson* (Princeton, NJ: Princeton University Press, 1988), 164–166, 174–180.

17. See Allen Lynch, "Woodrow Wilson and the Principle of 'National Self-Determination': A Reconsideration," *Review of International Studies* 28, no. 2 (April 2002): 419–436, at 422, 424, 425; Victor S. Mamatey, *The United States and East Central Europe, 1914–1918: A Study in Wilsonian Diplomacy and Propaganda* (Princeton, NJ: Princeton University Press, 1957);

Ronald Steel, "Prologue-1919–1945–1989," in *The Treaty of Versailles: A Reassessment after 75 Years*, ed. Manfred F. Boemeke, Gerald D. Feldman, and Elisabeth Glase (Cambridge: Cambridge University Press, 1998), 25; and Klaus Schwabe, *Woodrow Wilson, Revolutionary Germany, and Peacemaking, 1918–1919*, trans. Rita and Robert Kimber (Chapel Hill: University of North Carolina Press, 1985), 173.

18. Robert Lansing is quoted in Whittle Johnston, "Reflections on Wilson and the Problems of World Peace," in *Woodrow Wilson and a Revolutionary World*, ed. Arthur S. Link (Chapel Hill: University of North Carolina Press, 1982), 207.

19. For scholarship emphasizing Wilson's realism and diplomatic savvy in the use of the phrase, see Charles Seymour, "Woodrow Wilson and Self-Determination in the Tyrol," *Virginia Quarterly Review* 38, no. 4 (1962); David F. Trask, *The United States in the Supreme War Council: American War Aims and Inter-Allied Strategy, 1917–1918* (Middletown, CT: Wesleyan University Press, 1961); and Lawrence E. Gelfand, "The American Mission to Negotiate Peace," in Manfred F. Boemeke, Gerald D. Feldman, and Elisabeth Glaser, eds., *The Treaty of Versailles: A Reassessment after 75 Years* (Cambridge: Cambridge University Press, 1998).

20. Matthias Erzberger, "Il messaggio di Wilson al congresso dell'11 febbraio, e la sua accoglienza in Germania," February 18, 1918, enclosed by Pacelli in a message to Gasparri dated February 22, 1918, ASV, A.E.S., Stati Ecclesiastici, 1914–1921, pos. 1317, fasc. 470, vol. 11, ff. 261–267.

21. Cardinal Gasparri to Roman Dmowski, autumn 1916, in Władysław Studnicki, *"Polityka polska i odbudowa państwa* (Warsaw: skł. gł. w Księgarni Hoesicka, 1925), 208, as cited in Hansjakob Stehle, *The Eastern Politics of the Vatican, 1917–1979* (Athens, OH: Ohio University Press, 1981), 19.

22. "Nazionalismo e amor di patria secondo la dottrina cattolica," *Civiltà Cattolica*, January 16, 1915. Also see Charles Loiseau, "La politique du Saint-Siège en Europe centrale (1919–1936)—II," *Le monde slave* 14, no. 1 (1937): 103–104.

23. Pope Benedict XV first articulated these views in the landmark July 28, 1915, apostolic exhortation, "Allorché fummo chiamati," as reprinted in *Acta Apostolicae Sedis* (hereafter cited as *AAS*) (Rome: Typis Polyglottis Vaticanis, 1915), 7:365–368.

24. As cited in Orio Giacchi, "La recente politica della Santa Sede nell'Europa nord-orientale," *Rassegna di politica internazionale* 8 (1936): 25.

25. *AAS* (1921), 13:521.

26. Achille Ratti to William Warner Bishop, Librarian of the University of Michigan, Warsaw, June 12, 1919, as cited in Oscar Halecki, "The Place of Częstochowa in Poland's Millennium," *Catholic Historical Review* 52, no. 4 (January 1967): 494–508, at 506.

27. Of 27 million Poles, 75 percent (22 million) were Catholics. See *Statesman's Yearbook, 1930*, 1192, as cited in John Pollard, *The Papacy in the Age of Totalitarianism, 1914–1958* (Oxford: Oxford University Press, 2014), 223.

28. Rom Landau, *Piłsudski and Poland* (New York: Dial Press, 1929), 20.
29. Neal Pease, "The Marshal and the Almighty: Piłsudski and Religion," *Polish Review* 56 (2011): 47–56, at 47, 50.
30. Krzysztof Jeżyna, "Działalność społeczno-polityczna w Akcji Katolickiej," *Roczniki Teologiczne* 44, no. 3 (1997): 107–124, at 113. I thank Piotr Puchalski for his invaluable help in identifying and translating this and other Polish materials used in this chapter.
31. Ratti to Hoover, Rome, May 15, 1922, ASV, A.E.S., Pontificia Commissione Pro Russia, sc. 73, fasc. 334, p. 72.
32. Konrad Sadkowski, "From Ethnic Borderland to Catholic Fatherland: The Church, Christian Orthodox, and State Administration in the Chelm Region, 1918–1939," *Slavic Review* 57, no. 4 (Winter 1998): 813–839, at 839.
33. Cardinal August Hlond, *"O chrześcijańskie zasady życia państwowego"* (Gniezno, April 23, 1932), in *Na straży sumienia narodu: Wybór pism i przemówień* (Warsaw: Ad Astra, 1999), 55–56, 69, as quoted in Brian A. Porter-Szücs, *Faith and Fatherland: Catholicism, Modernity, and Poland* (New York: Oxford University Press, 2011), 173.
34. Stanislav Holubec and Gavin Rae, "A Conservative Convergence? The Differences and Similarities of the Conservative Right in the Czech Republic and Poland," *Contemporary Politics* 16, no. 2 (June 2010): 189–207, at 194.
35. Pease, *Rome's Most Faithful Daughter*, 67–68.
36. Ibid., 156, 167.
37. Ibid., 59.
38. The Holy See followed the Danzig question closely. See, e.g., ASV, Segreteria di Stato, A.E.S., Baviera, 1922–1939, pos. 625, f. 141.
39. Carlo A. Jemolo, *Church and State in Italy, 1850–1950* (Oxford: Blackwell, 1960), 168.
40. As cited in Giancarlo Zizola, *Il Conclave: Storia e segreto* (Rome: Newton, 1993), 202–203. However, as a relatively unknown quantity, Ratti had not been anyone's first pick; he was viewed instead as an acceptable compromise candidate when the Cardinals were unable to pick between Merry Del Val and Pietro Gasparri.
41. Józef Pelczar, *Wezwanie do pracy nad duchownem odrodzeniem się narodu polskiego* (Krakow: Self-published, 1915), 2, as quoted in Porter-Szücs, *Faith and Fatherland*, 172.
42. Pease, *Rome's Most Faithful Daughter*, 68, 71.
43. *Gazeta Świąteczna: Wychodzi raz na tydzień przed każdą niedzielą*, second Sunday issue, February 1925.
44. "Konkordat," *Orzeł Biały: Tygodnik, wychodzi na każdą niedzielę*, April 19, 1925.
45. Pease, "Poland and the Holy See, 1918–1935," *Slavic Review* 50, no. 3 (Fall 1991): 521–530, at 525.
46. Father Rosa, "La guerra fratricida in Italia e il 'grido di pace' del Papa," *Civiltà Cattolica*, August 19, 1922; Giuseppe Angelini, "Responsabilità?," *Osservatore Romano*, May 15, 1919. The latter article was actually written by Gas-

parri, as documented in his *Memorie*. See *Il cardinal Gasparri e la questione romana (con brani delle memorie inedited)*, ed. G. Spadolini (Florence: Le Monnier, 1972), 227–231.

47. "Le vie dei popoli," *Osservatore Romano*, October 30, 1920.

48. "Dove sono i responsabili?," *Osservatore Romano*, November 6, 1919. For similar sentiments, see also "Un'altra illusione," *Osservatore Romano*, November 9, 1919; and "L'irresponsibilità della guerra e della pace falsa," *Osservatore Romano*, November 22, 1919.

49. Angelini, "Di chi la colpa?," *Osservatore Romano*, March 18, 1920.

50. See Renato Moro, "L'opinione cattolica su pace e guerra durante il fascismo," in *Chiesa e guerra: Dalla "benedizione delle armi" alla "Pacem in terris,"* ed. Mimmo Franzinelli and Riccardo Bottoni (Bologna: Il Mulino, 2005), 221–319; and Giuseppe M. Croce, "Le Saint-Siège et la Conférence de la paix (1919): Diplomatie d'Église et diplomaties d'État," *Mélanges de l'école française de Rome* (1997): 793–823.

51. Mark Mazower, *Governing the World: The Rise and Fall of an Idea* (London: Penguin, 2013), 186.

52. See Susan Pedersen, *The Guardians: The League of Nations and the Crisis of Empire* (Oxford: Oxford University Press, 2017).

53. "Il problema internazionale," *Civiltà Cattolica*, June 5, 1926, as cited in Renato Moro, "Religione del trascendente e religioni politiche: Il cattolicesimo italiano di fronte alla sacralizzazione fascista della politica," *Mondo Contemporaneo* 1, no. 1 (2005): 9–67, at 15.

54. ASV, Segreteria di Stato, Austria, pos. 465, b. 28, f. 1919.

55. Angelini, "Di chi la colpa?" These ideas were repeated by numerous articles in the *Osservatore Romano*, particularly in the summer of 1920. See, e.g., "L'uomo propone . . . ," *Osservatore Romano*, August 22, 1920; and "È possibile la pace," *Osservatore Romano*, August 25, 1920. After Angelini, the next director of the newspaper, Giuseppe Dalla Torre, published several articles on this theme under his own name as well; see, e.g., his "Pace vittoriosa e pace di riconciliazione," *Osservatore Romano*, August 1, 1920; and "La nuova politica di pace," *Osservatore Romano*, August 28, 1920.

56. B. M. (Battista Montini), "Per il 29 Giugno: Petro Salutem," *La Fionda*, June 21, 1919, as reprinted in Pope Paul VI, *Scritti giovanili*, ed. Cesare Trebeschi (Brescia: Queriniana, 1979), 125.

57. The article (without additional references) is quoted in Janek Wasserman, *Black Vienna: The Radical Right in the Red City, 1918–1938* (Ithaca, NY: Cornell University Press, 2014), 24.

58. Dalla Torre to Gasparri, November 17, 1919, ASV, A.E.S., Stati ecclesiastici, pos. 1443, b. 587, f. 96441.

59. See Matthew Gavin Frank, *Making Minorities History: Population Transfer in Twentieth-Century Europe* (Oxford: Oxford University Press, 2017); Carole Fink, *Defending the Rights of Others* (Cambridge: Cambridge University Press, 2004); and Volker Prott, *The Politics of Self-Determination: Remaking Territories and National Identities in Europe, 1917–1923* (Oxford: Oxford University Press, 2016).

60. Bruce Cronin, *Institutions for the Common Good: International Protection Regimes* (Cambridge: Cambridge University Press, 2003), 79.

61. Hans Aufricht, "On Relative Sovereignty: Part II," *Cornell Law Quarterly* 30, no. 3 (1945): 342, as cited in Natasha Wheatley, "New Subjects in International Law and Order," in *Internationalisms: A Twentieth-Century History*, ed. Glenda Sluga and Patricia Clavin (Cambridge: Cambridge University Press, 2017), 265–286, at 274.

62. Henry Morgenthau, "The Jews in Poland and My Meetings with Paderewski, Piłsudski, and Dmowski: Extracts from an Article on Poland," *The World's Work* 43 (1922): 617–630, at 626.

63. Raymond L. Buell, "France and the Vatican," *Political Science Quarterly* 36 (1921): 30–50.

64. "Memorandum of M. Paderewski," in "The Council of Four: Minutes of Meetings, May 24 to June 28, 1919," in *FRUS, The Paris Peace Conference* (Washington, DC: U.S. Government Printing Office, 1919), 6:535.

65. "Atti della S. Sede. Allocuzione di S. S. Benedetto XV nel Concistoro tenuto il 13 giugno 1921," *AAS* (1921), 13:281–289, at 284.

66. Aide-mémoire to the League of Nations, June 4, 1922, archives of the Catholic University of America, National Catholic Welfare Conference, Office of the General Secretary, box 18, file 44, as cited in Adriano Ercole Ciani, "The Vatican, American Catholics and the Struggle for Palestine, 1917–1958: A Study of Cold War Roman Catholic Transnationalism" (PhD diss., University of Western Ontario, 2011), 38.

67. Pope Benedict XV, allocution to the College of Cardinals, March 10, 1919. For a broader discussion of the papacy's reactions to the Balfour Declaration, see Andrej Kreutz, *Vatican Policy on the Palestinian–Israeli Conflict: The Struggle for the Holy Land* (New York: Greenwood Press, 1990), 41–42; Ciani, "The Vatican," 38–39; and Sergio I. Minerbi, *The Vatican and Zionism: Conflict in the Holy Land, 1895–1925* (Oxford: Oxford University Press, 1990).

68. As referenced in Pease, *Rome's Most Faith Daughter*, 35ff.

69. *Gazeta Świąteczna: Wychodzi raz na tydzień przed każdą niedzielą*, May 1920.

70. See M. B. Biskupski, "The Origins of a Relationship: The United States and Poland, 1914–1921," *Polish Review* 54, no. 2 (2009): 147–158; and Neal Pease, *Poland, the United States, and the Stabilization of Europe, 1919–1933* (Oxford: Oxford University Press, 1986).

71. *FRUS* 1922, 2:870–872, 873–874.

72. As cited in Mamatey, *United States and East Central Europe*, 174, 310.

73. Trygve Throntveit, "The Fable of the Fourteen Points: Woodrow Wilson and National Self-Determination," *Diplomatic History* 35 (2011): 445–481.

74. See, e.g., "Przegląd spraw bieżących. Polityka zagraniczna," *Przegląd Narodowy*, August–September 1920.

75. Jarosław Sozańskim, *International Legal Status of Lithuania, Latvia, and Estonia in the Years 1918–1994* (Riga: Poligräfists, 1995), 71.

76. Vello Salo, "The Catholic Church in Estonia, 1919–2001," *Catholic Historical Review* 88, no. 2 (April 2002): 281–293.

77. Heinrich August Winkler and Stewart Spencer, *The Age of Catastrophe: A History of the West, 1915–1945* (New Haven, CT: Yale University Press, 2015), 147.

78. "Latvija un vatikans," *Valdības Vēstnesi,* July 4, 1921. The same announcement was reprinted in German Latvian in *Latvijas Sargs,* July 3, 1921. I thank Indra Ekmanis for her research assistance in identifying and translating these articles.

79. *FRUS* 1922, 2:873–874.

80. "Katoļu wirsgana baznicas leetā," *Tautas Balss,* December 10, 1921.

81. Giacchi, "La Recente Politica della S. Sede."

82. "Waj tas taisniba?," *Latvijas Vēstnesis,* November 29, 1921.

83. "Atskaņas," *Latvijas Sargs,* October 16, 1921. For similar sentiments, see "Laikrakztu apskats," *Liepājas Avīze,* June 9, 1921; "Diplomatijas triumfs: Jezuiti," *Svari,* October 14, 1921; and "Sekcija," *Valdības Vēstnesis,* June 18, 1921.

84. "Latvijas Pāvests," *Svari,* October 28, 1921. For more satirical poetry about the concordat, see "Diplomatijas triumfs," *Svari,* October 14, 1921.

85. Petras Klimas, *Le développement de L'État lithuanien à partir de l'année 1915 jusqu'à la formation du gouvernement provisoire au mois de novembre 1918* (Paris: Langlois, 1919), 258; Gregor Rutenberg, *Die baltischen Staaten und das Völkerrecht* (Riga: Verlag der Buchhandlung G. Loefler, 1928), 152; Juozas Prunskis, *Comparative Law, Ecclesiastical and Civil, in the Lithuanian Concordat* (Washington, DC: Catholic University of American Press, 1945), 24.

86. Kęstutis Kazimieras Girnius, "Nationalism and the Catholic Church in Lithuania," in *Religion and Nationalism in Soviet and East European Politics,* ed. Pedro Ramet (Durham, NC: Duke Press Policy Studies, 1984), 82–103, at 82.

87. On the contested status of this city in the interwar years, see Theodore Weeks, *Vilnius between Nations, 1795–2000* (DeKalb: Northern Illinois University Press, 2005), esp. chap. 4; and Alfred Senn, *The Great Powers, Lithuania and the Vilna Question, 1920–1928* (Leiden: Brill, 1966).

88. Alfonsas Eidintas, *Antanas Smetona and His Lithuania: From the National Liberation Movement to an Authoritarian Regime, 1893–1940* (Leiden: Brill, 2015), 150, 194.

89. Ibid., 150, 194, 252.

90. Giacchi, "La Recente Politica della S. Sede," 23–24, 29.

91. Karel Skalický, "The Vicissitudes of the Catholic Church in Czechoslovakia, 1918–1988," in *Czechoslovakia: Crossroads and Crises, 1918–88,* ed. Norman Stone and Eduard Stouhal (London: Macmillan, 1992), 297–324, at 298; Holubec and Rae, "A Conservative Convergence?," 193–194; John O. Crane, "Church and State in Czechoslovakia," *Slavonic Review* 6, no. 17 (December 1927): 364–378, at 371; and Pollard, *The Papacy in the Age of Totalitarianism,* 84.

92. Peter Kent, "The 'Proferred Gift': Abortive Yugoslav Concordat of 1935–37," in *Decisions and Diplomacy: Essays in Twentieth-Century International History,* ed. Dick Richardson and Glyn Stone (London: Routledge, 1995), 111–130, at 125, 127; Ceslas Novak and Thomas Gilby, "The Second Adriatic Concordat," *New Blackfriars* 18, no. 210 (September 1937): 692–694.

93. See, e.g., Felice M. Cappello, *I diritti e i privilege tollerati o concessi dalla Santa Sede ai governi civili* (Rome: Civiltà Cattolica, 1921); Francesco Guglielmo Savagnone, *Il diritto ecclesiastico del dopo Guerra e la conciliazione tra stato e chiesa* (Palermo: G. Castiglia, 1921); Aristarco Fasulo, *Il primato papale nella storia e nel pensiero italiano* (Rome: Bilychnis, 1924); Francesco Ruffini, *Corso di diritto ecclesiastico italiano: La libertà religiosa come diritto pubblico subiettivo* (Turin: Fratelli Bocca Editori, 1924).

94. For this protection, see the following articles of concordats: Latvia (art. 10); Italy (art. 35), Bavaria (art. 9), Romania (art. 19), German Reich (art. 25), Austria (art. 6).

95. This was the case with the following articles of concordats: Bavaria (art. 9), Lithuania (art. 13), Romania (art. 19), Germany (art. 25).

96. For this protection, see the following articles of concordats: Latvia (art. 11), Poland (art. 13), Lithuania (art. 13), Italy (art. 39), Romania (art. 16), Prussia (art. 12), Baden (art. 9), Germany (art. 20), Austria (art. 5).

97. The phrase is from a published text emitted by the Prussian episcopate to protest school reforms, Bavaria, June 28, 1924. As quoted in Fattorini, *Germania e Santa Sede*, 154.

98. For this protection, see the following articles of concordats: Bavaria (art. 2), Poland (art. 10), Lithuania (art. 10), Italian (art. 29), Romania (art. 17), Baden (art. 5,1), German Reich (art. 15), Austria (art. 10).

99. Take, for instance, the 1801 concordat with France, which affirmed: "No Bull, brief, decree, mandate, provision, nor any other dispatch from the Court of Rome, even if it deals with very particular things, can be received, published, printed, or otherwise produced without the authorization of the Government."

100. This exact wording was present in the *Concordato Stipulato fra la Santa Sede ed il Governo di Serbia* (Rome: Tipografia dell'Unione Editrice, 1915), art. 12, p. 8. This was also the case for the Yugoslav, Italian, Austrian, and Lithuanian concordats; in these years, Latvia and Poland also recognized as much under common law.

101. This was the case for the Serbian, Italian, and Austrian concordats.

102. This was true for the Serbian concordat.

103. This prohibition was laid out expressly in the Latvian, Polish, Lithuanian, and Italian agreements.

104. Art. 5 of the concordat with Serbia, for instance, noted that the archbishop and the bishop would receive yearly salaries from the state, plus a guaranteed pension.

105. Clergy are exempt from military service and certain civil functions in the following concordats: Latvia (art. 9), Poland (art. 5), Lithuania (art. 5), Italy (Lateran Agreement, art. 10). Clergy are tried and punished by a separate penal system, and not by lay courts: Latvia (art. 17), Lithuania (art. 19), Poland (art. 22).

106. See Canons 121, 122, 123, 614, 1553, and my discussion of the 1917 Code of Canon Law.

107. Joseph Prunskis, *Comparative Law, Ecclesiastical and Civil, in the Lithu-anian Concordat* (Washington, DC: Catholic University of American Press, 1945), 26. Also see Arnaldo Bertola, "Attività concordataria e codifi-cazione del diritto della Chiesa," *Archivio Giuridico* 111 (1934): 174; and Yves de la Brière, "La Renaissance contemporaine du droit canonique dans plusiers législations séculières grâce aux divers concordats du pontificat de Pie XI," *Revue de Droit International et de Législation Comparée* 16 (1935): 217–218.

108. R. P. Yves de la Brière, *Études* (1930): 603.

109. S. Goyeneche, "De Pii PP. XI operositate legifera," *Apollinaris* 12 (1939): 489. For similar sentiments, see Nikolaus Hilling, "Die Gesetzgebung des Pius XI," *Archiv für katholisches Kirchenrecht* 119 (1939): 309–351, and 120 (1940): 4–32; and Max Bierbaum, *Das Konkordat in Kultur: Politik und Recht* (Freiburg im Breisgau: Herder und Co., 1928), 4.

110. Pius XI, *Ubi arcano Dei* (December 23, 1922), §64. Available online at http://w2 .vatican.va/content/pius-xi/en/encyclicals/documents/hf_p-xi_enc _19221223_ubi-arcano-dei-consilio.html.

CHAPTER 3 ▪ PAPAL OFFICIALS BUILD LOCAL BRIDGES

Epigraph: Giuseppe Angelini, "Sulla fine di un anno memorabile," *Osservatore Romano*, January 1, 1919; Angelini, "O Wilson o Lenin," *Osservatore Romano*, January 13, 1919.

1. Pope Leo XIII, *Quod Apostolici Muneris* (December 28, 1878), as reprinted in *Pope Leo XIII: His Life and Letters: From Recent and Authentic Sources*, ed. James F. Talbot (Boston: Martin Garrison and Co., 1886), 111–120, at 111–112.

2. Pope Leo XIII, *Humanum Genus* (April 20, 1884), §27, available online at http://w2.vatican.va/content/leo-xiii/en/encyclicals/documents/hf_l-xiii _enc_18840420_humanum-genus.html.

3. James Joll, *The Second International, 1889–1914* (London: Weidenfeld and Nicolson, 1968), 1; Donald Sassoon, *One Hundred Years of Socialism: The West European Left in the Twentieth Century* (New York: New Press, 1996), 27.

4. As cited in Geoff Eley, *Forging Democracy: The History of the Left in Europe* (Oxford: Oxford University Press, 2002), 152.

5. Rosa Luxemburg, "Our Program and the Political Situation" (December 31, 1918), as reprinted in *Selected Political Writings of Rosa Luxemburg*, ed. Dick Howard (New York: Grove Press, 1974). Available online at the Lux-emburg Internet Archive, https://www.marxists.org/archive/luxemburg /1918/12/31.htm.

6. Sassoon, *One Hundred Years of Socialism*, 42–43; Eley, *Forging Democracy*, 153.

7. A compilation of all papal encyclicals that deal with communism and socialism can be found in Giovanni Battista Guzzetti, *Cristianesimo e*

marxismo, vol. 4, *Chiesa, comunismo, e socialismo* (Milan: Istituto sociale ambrosiano, 1961).

8. The decree of January 23, 1918, was entitled, "On the Separation of Church from State and School from Church." It was in line with Lenin's frequently articulated notion that "the socialist proletariat [demands] the full separation of the church from the state," so as to "bring an end to [Russia's] shameful and cursed past, wherein the church was enserfed to the state, and the people were enserfed to the state church." V. I. Lenin, "Socialism and Religion" (1905), in *Lenin Collected Works* (Moscow: Progress, 1965), 10:83–87.

9. See Victoria Smolkin, *A Sacred Space Is Never Empty: A History of Soviet Atheism* (Princeton, NJ: Princeton University Press, 2018), chap. 1.

10. *Civiltà Cattolica*, December 17, 1923.

11. Edmund Walsh notes of meeting with Father Ledóchowski, March 9, 1922, ASV, A.E.S., quarto periodo, Russia, pos. 659, fasc. 40.

12. "Bolscevismo russo e bolscevismo tedesco," *Osservatore Romano*, January 16, 1919.

13. In late June 1918, Gasparri formally named Ratti provisional apostolic visitor to Russia. Gasparri to Ratti, June 30, 1918, ASV, Archive of Mons. Ratti, 1918–1921, fasc. 191, ff. 202–203.

14. As cited in Ernesto Buonaiuti, *La Chiesa e il comunismo* (Milan: Bompiani, 1945), 13.

15. Hansjakob Stehle, *Eastern Politics of the Vatican, 1917–1979* (Athens, OH: Ohio University Press, 1981), 19–20.

16. Pietro Gasparri, "Memorie: Polonia," n.d., ASV, A.E.S., Stati Ecclesiastici, pos. 515, fasc. 530, ff. 30–31.

17. "Papież Pius Jedenasty," *Orzeł Biały : Tygodnik, wychodzi na każdą niedzielę*, April 19, 1925.

18. As cited in Marisa Patulli Trythall, "Pius XI and American Pragmatism," *Pius XI and America: Proceedings of the Brown University Conference*, ed. Charles R. Gallagher, David I. Kertzer, and Alberto Melloni (Berlin: LIT Verlag, 2012), 25–86, at 53. Also see James J. Zatko, "The Vatican and Famine Relief in Russia," *Slavonic and East European Review* 42, no. 98 (December 1963): 54–63.

19. For more on this period in Vatican–Soviet relations, see G. M. Croce, "Santa Sede e Russia Sovietica alla Conferenza di Genova," *Cristianesimo nella Storia* 23, no. 2 (2002): 345–365; Laurent Koelliker, "La perception de la Russie par le Pape Benoît XV: Aspects politiques, diplomatiques et religieux," and Piero Doria, "La documentazione vaticana sui rapporti Santa Sede-Russia," in *Santa Sede—Russia da Leone XIII a Pio XI: Atti del secondo Simposio organizzato dal Pontificio Comitato di Scienze Storiche e dall'Istitute di Storia Universale dell'Accademia Russa delle Scienze*, ed. Massimiliano Valente (Vatican City: Libreria Editrice Vaticana, 2006), 17–49, 50–99; and Laura Pettinaroli, *La politique russe du Saint-Siège, 1905–1939* (Rome: École française de Rome, 2015).

20. ASV, A.E.S., Pontificia Commissione Pro Russia, sc. 73, fasc. 334, ff. 70–71.

21. ASV, Carte Erzberger 3, fasc. 6, f. 155.

22. Otto Ritter letter of November 12, 1916, Bayerisches Hauptstaatarchiv, MA 94522, as cited in Jörg Zedler, *Bayern und der Vatikan: Eine politische Biographie des letzten bayerischen Gesandten am Heiligen Stuhl Otto von Ritter (1909–1934)* (Paderborn: Schöningh, 2013), 320. For similar themes, see Stewart A. Stehlin, *Weimar and the Vatican, 1919–1933: German-Vatican Diplomatic Relations in the Interwar Years* (Princeton, NJ: Princeton University Press, 1983), 384.

23. Matthias Erzberger, *La Ligue des peuples: Les conditions e la paix mondiale* (Lausanne: Librairie Nouvelle, 1919), 215. Also see Erzberger's texts on Wilson prepared for Pacelli of October 15 and 25, 1918, ASV, A.E.S., Germania 438. In the autumn of 1918, Erzberger was working hard to have all majoritarian political parties in Germany—including, of course, the Center Party—back the creation of the League of Nations. For more information, see Emma Fattorini, *Germania e Santa Sede: Le Nunziature di Pacelli fra la Grande Guerra e la Repubblica di Weimar* (Bologna: Il Mulino, 1992), 65, 81–82; and Klaus Epstein, *Matthias Erzberger and the Dilemma of German Democracy* (New York: H. Fertig, 1971), 279.

24. The statistics are compiled in Hubert Wolf, "Matthias Erzberger, Nuntius Pacelli und der Vatikan: Oder, Warum der Kirchenstaat nicht nach Liechtenstein verlegt wurde," in *Matthias Erzberger: Ein Demokrat in Zeiten des Hasses*, ed. Boris Barth (Karlsruhe: Braun, 2013), 134–157, at 140.

25. On Bavarian Catholicism more broadly, see Derek Hastings, *Catholicism and the Roots of Nazism: Religious Identity and National Socialism* (Oxford: Oxford University Press, 2015), 20–45.

26. Michael von Faulhaber, *Waffen des Lichtes: Gesammelte Kriegsreden* (Freiburg im Breisgau: Herder, 1918), 132. On von Faulhaber, see Mary Alice Gallin, "The Cardinal and the State: Faulhaber and the Third Reich," *Journal of Church and State* 12 (1970): 385–404; and Ludwig Volk, *Der bayerische Episkopat und der Nationalsozialismus, 1930–4* (Mainz: Matthias Grünewald, 1966), 5–7. For more on how German Catholics "shared in the national upsurge of patriotic feeling and, as the war continued, came to believe that its requirements would bring opportunities for the full integration of Catholics into German society," see Ellen Lovell Evans, *The German Center Party, 1870–1933: A Study in Political Catholicism* (Carbondale: Southern Illinois University Press, 1981), 203.

27. Eugenio Pacelli, *Gesammelte Reden: Erster Apostolischer Nuntius beim Deutschen Reich* (Berlin: Buchverlag Germania, 1930), 26.

28. Anthony Read, *The World on Fire: 1919 and the Battle with Bolshevism* (London: Pimlico, 2009), 36.

29. Fattorini, *Germania e Santa Sede*, 97.

30. Eliza Ablovatski, "The 1919 Central European Revolutions and the Judeo-Bolshevik Myth," *European Review of History* 17, no. 3 (June 2010): 473–489, at 476.

31. Pacelli to Gasparri, "Sulle cause della catastrofe della Germania," November 15, 1918, ASV, A.E.S., Germania 1918–1919, pos. 1665, fasc. 878, ff. 16–18.

32. See Pacelli to Gasparri, Rorschach, November 26, 1918, ASV, A.E.S., Bavaria 1918–1920, pos. 62, fasc. 40, f. 2.

33. Zedler, *Bayern und der Vatikan*, 327.

34. Eugenio Pacelli to Francesco Pacelli, December 6, 1919, Pacelli family archives. Cited in Andrea Tornielli, *Pio XII: Eugenio Pacelli: un uomo sul trono di Pietro* (Milan: Mondadori, 2009), 111–112.

35. As Pacelli saw it, German politicians (Erzberger included) had "largely underestimated" the extraordinary importance of the United States. Too many had assumed that American military intervention was "an American-style bluff, and that the United States, so far away and so little prepared for war, would not have been able to represent a serious threat or overcome the invincible German power." Pacelli to Gasparri, "Sulle cause della catastrofe della Germania."

36. Schioppa to Gasparri, Munich, December 20, 1918. ASV, A.E.S., Baviera, 1918–1921, pos. 67, fasc. 42, ff.15–17.

37. On Catholic attitudes toward the Eisner regime, see Rudolf Kanzler, *Bayerns Kampf gegen den Bolschewismus Geschichte der bayerischen Einwohnerwehren* (Munich: Parcus, 1931), 13–16; Bernhard Grau, *Kurt Eisner: 1867–1919* (Munich: C. H. Beck, 2017), chap. 8; Werner Blessing, "Kirchenglocken für Eisner? Zum Weltanschauungskampf in der Revolution von 1918/19 in Bayern," *Jahrbuch für fränkische Landesforschung* 53 (1992): 403–420.

38. "Der Jude als Minister-präsident," *Bayerischer Kurier* (henceforth *MKK*), November 25, 1918. Even mainstream Catholic papers—like the official diocesan weekly *Münchener Katholische Kirchenzeitung,* and the leading organ of the Catholic Center Party, *Germania*—used anti-Semitic tropes to highlight Eisner's Jewishness. So did other prominent Catholic conservative papers in Munich, like the *Allgemeine Rundschau* and the *Historisch-politische Blätter.* For summaries of how German Catholic papers saw the Eisner-led revolution, see Lorenzo Schioppa to Pietro Gasparri, November 28, 1918, ASV, A.E.S., Germania 1918–1019, pos. 1665, fasc. 878, ff. 241–271.

39. *Amtsblatt*, December 20, 1918; February 27, 1919; and January 31, 1919. Referenced in Hastings, *Catholicism*, 48–49.

40. Pacelli to Gasparri, ASV, A.E.S., Baviera, 1918–1921, pos. 67, fasc. 42, f. 4. Pacelli repeated the same condemnation of Eisner as a criminal and a "Galician Jew" in his letter to Gasparri of November 20, 1918. Ibid., pos. 45, fasc. 36, f. 26.

41. Pacelli to Gasparri, ASV, A.E.S., Baviera, 1918–1921, pos.67, fasc.42, f. 3.

42. On Catholic anti-Semitism in Poland, see Brian Porter-Szücs, *Faith and Fatherland: Catholicism, Modernity and Poland* (Oxford: Oxford University Press, 2011); Porter-Szücs, "Antisemitism and the Search for a Catholic Modernity," in *Antisemitism and Its Opponents in Modern Poland*, ed. Robert Blobaum (Ithaca, NY: Cornell University Press, 2005), 103–123; and Ronald Modras, *The Catholic Church and Antisemitism in Poland, 1933–1939* (Chur, Switzerland: Harwood Academic, 1994) On Catholic anti-Semitism in France, see Vicki Caron, "Catholic Political Mobilization and Antisemitic

Violence in Fin de Siècle France: The Case of the Union Nationale," *Journal of Modern History* 81, no. 2 (June 2009): 294–346; and Caron, "Catholics and the Rhetoric of Antisemitic Violence in fin-de-siècle France," in Nemes and Unowsky, *Sites of European Antisemitism*, 36–60. On Italy, see Simon Levis Sullam, "Per una storia dell'antisemitismo cattolico in Italia," in *Cristiani d'Italia: Chiese, società, Stato (1861–2011)*, ed. Alberto Melloni (Rome: Istituto della Enciclopedia Italiana, 2011), 1:461–470; Giovanni Miccoli, "Antiebraismo, antisemitismo: Un nesso fluttuante," and Renato Moro, "Propagandisti cattolici del razzismo antisemita in Italia," both in *Les racines chrétiennes de l'antisémitisme politique*, ed. Catherine Brice (Rome: École Française de Rome, 2003), 3–23, 275–345; and Moro, "Le premesse dell'atteggiamento cattolico di fronte alla legislazione razziale fascista: Cattolici ed ebrei nell'Italia degli anni venti (1919–1932)," *Storia contemporanea* 19, no. 6 (December 1988): 1013–1119. On Hungarian Catholic anti-Semitism, see Paul Hanebrink, *In Defense of Christian Hungary: Religion, Nationalism, and Antisemitism, 1890–1944* (Ithaca, NY: Cornell University Press, 2006); and Marsha L. Rozenblit, "'Christian Europe' and National Identity in Interwar Hungary," in *Constructing Nationalities in East Central Europe*, ed. Pieter M. Judson and Marsha L. Rozenblit (New York: Berghahn Books, 2005), 192–202.

43. Christian Rank, *Föderalismus und Republikkritik: Bayerische Volkspartei, Politik der Eigenstaatlichkeit und der Umgang mit der Weimarer Demokratie in der Ära Held (1924–1933)* (Regensburg: Regensburg St. Katherinenspital, 2016); Klaus Rose, *Zwischen Königlich Bayerischen und brauner Diktatur: Die Bayerische Volkspartei in der Donaustadt Vilshofen, 1918–1933* (Vilshofen: Kultur- und Geschichtsverein Vilshofen, 2013).

44. On the Revolution and the repression that followed, see Allan Mitchell, *Revolution in Bavaria, 1918–9: The Eisner Regime and the Soviet Republic* (Princeton, NJ: Princeton University Press, 2015).

45. "Münchener, seid dankbar!," *MKK*, May 11, 1919.

46. Heim to Pacelli, February 24, 1920, ASV, A.E.S., Baviera, 1918–1921, pos. 67, fasc. 43, ff. 75–79.

47. Pacelli to Gasparri, May 6, 1919, ASV, A.E.S., Baviera, 1918–1921, ff. 44–52.

48. Pacelli to Gasparri, 18 August 1920. ASV, Arch. Nunz. Berlino 92, fasc.4, ff. 5–8.

49. On the conspiracy theory of Judeo-Bolshevism, see István Deák, "Jews and Communism: The Hungarian Case," and Dan Diner and Jonathan Frankel, "Jews and Communism: The Utopian Temptation," both in *Dark Times, Dire Decisions: Jews and Communism*, ed. Jonathan Frankel (Oxford: Oxford University Press, 2004), 38–61, 3–12; André Gerrits, *The Myth of Jewish Communism: A Historical Interpretation* (Brussels: Peter Lang, 2009); Paul Hanebrink, *A Specter Haunting Europe: The Myth of Judeo-Bolshevism* (Cambridge, MA: Harvard University Press, 2018); and William O. McCagg Jr., "Jews in Revolutions: The Hungarian Experience," *Journal of Social History* 6, no. 1 (1972): 78–105.

50. Pacelli to Gasparri, Munich, April 30, 1919, ASV, A.E.S., Baviera, 1918–1920, pos. 67, fasc. 42, ff. 42–45.

51. Pacelli to Gasparri, Munich, April 18, 1919. ASV, A.E.S., Baviera, 1918–1920, pos. 62, fasc. 40, ff. 36–38, at 36–37.

52. "Niederlage der Sozialdemokratie in Bayern," *Allgemeine Rundschau*, June 28, 1919; "Kommunismus?," *MKK*, June 1, 1919, as cited in Hastings, *Catholicism*, 51–52.

53. Cécile Tormay, *An Outlaw's Diary* (New York: McBride, 1923–1924), 1:9.

54. Teodoro Valfré di Bonzo to Gasparri, Vienna, April 15, 1919, ASV, A.E.S., Austria Ungheria, 1918–1920, pos. 1340, fasc. 532, ff. 92–94.

55. This is the central argument in Ablovatski, "The 1919 Central European Revolutions," 473.

56. Eley, *Forging Democracy*, 179–182.

57. "Manifesto of the Communist International to the Proletariat of the Entire World," March 6, 1919, in *The Communist International, 1919–1943: Documents*, ed. Jane Degras (Oxford: Oxford University Press, 1956), 1:47.

58. Sassoon, *One Hundred Years of Socialism*, 33–35.

59. At the Comintern's founding congress, only delegates from Germany, Hungary, the Baltic, and Eastern Europe represented really-existing Communist parties; the others present spoke for parts of the world where there were hardly any communist organizations at all. Eley, *Forging Democracy*, 180–181.

60. *Allgemeine Rundschau*, June 26, 1926. Catholics aligned with this view included Theodore Steinbüchel, Werner Becker, Carl Muth, and Walter Dirks.

61. Siegfried Landshut and Jacob Peter Mayer, eds., *Karl Marx: Der historische Materialismus: Die Frühschriften* (Leipzig: Alfred Kröner, 1932). See Terrell Carver and Daniel Blank, *A Political History of the Editions of Marx and Engel's German Ideology Manuscripts* (New York: Palgrave Macmillan, 2014), introduction; and James Chappel, *Catholic Modern: The Challenge of Totalitarianism and the Remaking of the Church* (Cambridge, MA: Harvard University Press, 2018), 174ff.

62. Pacelli to Gasparri, Munich, August 18, 1920, ASV, Arch. Nunz. Berlino 92, fasc.4, ff. 5–8.

63. Schioppa to Gasparri, Munich, March 19, 1920, ASV, A.E.S., Germania, 1918–1920, pos. 1640, fasc. 866, ff. 1r–20v.

64. Pacelli to Gasparri, Munich, April 12, 1919, ASV, A.E.S., Baviera, 1918–1921, pos. 67, fasc. 43, ff. 42; and Pacelli to Gasparri, "Sulla situazione politica," Munich, March 28, 1919, ASV, Arch. Nunz. Monaco 395, fasc.1, f. 59.

65. Pacelli to Gasparri, Munich, August 18, 1920, ASV, Arch. Nunz. Berlino 92, fasc.4, ff. 5–8.

66. Heim to Pacelli, February 24, 1920, ASV, Arch. Nunz. Berlino 92, fasc.4, ff. 5–8.

67. Pacelli to Gasparri, February 5, 1921. ASV, A.E.S., Germania 504. As reprinted in Fattorini, *Germania e Santa Sede*, appendix, 360–366.

68. Pacelli to Gasparri, Munich, August 18, 1920, ASV, Arch. Nunz. Berlino 92, fasc.4, ff. 5–8.

69. Heim to Pacelli, February 24, 1920.

70. Berlin wanted the Holy See's support in keeping the potential or already lost territories of the Rhineland and Upper Silesia. Again, Pacelli used this to his benefit. As he instructed Gasparri in the spring of 1921: "I know that the German government is extremely nervous about the Saar question. I would beg Your Excellency to let the government wallow in this healthy state of fear." Pacelli to Gasparri, May 2, 1921, ASV, A.E.S., Germania 504. As cited in Fattorini, *Germania e Santa Sede*, 213.

71. Among other things, Pacelli delayed moving his headquarters from Munich to Berlin as long as he possibly could, so as to emphasize (as was indeed the case) that his primary loyalties were to Bavaria.

72. Zedler, *Bayern und der Vatikan*, 442.

CHAPTER 4   ■   THE FASCIST TEMPTATION

Epigraph: The report of Gasparri's chat with the Belgian Ambassador can be found in N. E. Beyens, *Quatre ans à Rome, 1921–1926: Fin du pontificat de Benoît XV, Pie XI, les débuts du fascisme* (Paris: Plon, 1934), 136–137.

1. Giorgio Candeloro, *Storia dell'Italia moderna: La prima guerra mondiale, il dopoguerra, l'avvento del fascismo* (Milan: Feltrinelli, 1996), 8: 281.

2. "Cose Italiane," *La Civiltà Cattolica* (1920): 3:554–556; and *L'Osservatore Romano*, September 3, 15, 18, and 22, 1920. As cited in Zunino, "L'atteggiamento dei cattolici di fronte all'occupazione delle fabbriche," *Rivista di Storia Contemporanea* (1973): 186–215, at 187–189.

3. Pietro Gasparri to the Archbishop of Benevento, Alessio Ascalesi, and to the Archbishop of Conza, Carmine Cesarano, November 1919, ASV, Segr. Stat, 1919, rubrica 80, fasc. unico, ff. 126–127.

4. See Francesco Margiotta Broglio, *Italia e Santa Sede dalla grande guerra alla Conciliazione: Aspetti politici e giuridici* (Bari: Laterza, 1966); and Roberto Pertici, *Chiesa e Stato in Italia dalla grande guerra al nuovo concordato (1914–1984)* (Bologna: Il Mulino, 2009).

5. For more on the tepid attitudes of the Holy See toward the Popular Party, see Giovanni Miccoli, *Fra mito della cristianità e secolarizzazione* (Casale Monferrato: Marietti, 1985), 85; Giovanni Sale, "Il Partito Popolare Italiano fra tattica elettorale intransigente e aconfessionalismo," *La Civiltà Cattolica*, 154 (2003): 117–129; Pietro Scoppola, "Per una valutazione del popolarismo," *Quaderni di cultura e storia sociale* 2, no. 5 (1953): 185–198; Antonio Scornajenghi, "Santa Sede e il Partito Popolare Italiano alla vigilia delle elezioni politiche del 1919," *Rivista di storia della Chiesa in Italia* 59, no. 1 (January–June 2005): 73–85; and Gabriele De Rosa, *Il Partito Popolare Italiano* (Bari: Laterza, 1996).

6. Letter of Gasparri to the Bishop of Bergamo, L. M. Marelli, March 8, 1919, ASV, Segr. Stat, 1919, rubrica 80, fasc. unico, ff. 15–16.

7. Pastoral letter of Cardinal Tommaso Pio Boggiani, as reprinted in *L'azione cattolica e il Partito Popolare* (Genoa: Tipografia arcivescovile, 1920), 22–23, 25.

8. April 1921 report of the police inspector of the Province of Rovigo, as cited in Michael Ebner, *Ordinary Violence in Mussolini's Italy* (Cambridge: Cambridge University Press, 2011), 23.

9. As referenced in Francesco Coppola, *La rivoluzione fascista e la politica mondiale* (Rome: Edizioni di Politica, 1923), 11.

10. The citation is from the June 1919 founding program of the Fascist movement, reprinted in Renato De Felice, *Mussolini il rivoluzionario* (Turin: Einaudi, 2005), 742–743. For more on early Catholic interpretations of Fascism, see G. Baget Bozzo, "Il fascismo e l'evoluzione del pensiero politico cattolico," *Storia contemporanea* 4 (1974): 671–700; P. G. Zunino, *Interpretazione e memoria del fascismo. Gli anni del regime* (Rome: Laterza, 1991), 143ff.

11. The first citation comes from Benito Mussolini, "Tra il vecchio e il nuovo: Navigare necesse," *Il Popolo d'Italia*, January 1, 1920; the second from Benito Mussolini, *Opera omnia* (Florence: La Fenice, 1951–1980), 15:125; the third from Camera dei Deputati, *Atti Parlamentari*, Legislatura 26, *Discussioni*, June 21, 1921, 97. See Lucia Ceci, *The Vatican and Mussolini's Italy* (Boston: Brill, 2016), 60–61.

12. See Emilio Gentile, *Il culto del littorio: La sacralizzazione della politica nell'Italia fascista* (Rome: Laterza, 1993), 142–143, and id., *Le religioni della politica: Fra democrazie e totalitarismi* (Rome: Laterza, 2007), 145–146.

13. Archbishop of Milan (Achille Ratti), "Homily Held in the Cathedral on September 8," *Rivista Diocesana* 24 (1921): 330, as cited in Luigi Salvatorelli, *Pio XI e la sua eredità pontificale* (Turin: Einaudi, 1939), 54.

14. A. C. Jemolo, "Pio XI e la nuova situazione politica del papato," *Nuova Antologia* (February 16, 1922): 379.

15. The interview with Gasparri is reprinted in "Le fascisme et le Vatican," *Le Journal*, November 11, 1922; the report of Gasparri's chat with the Belgian ambassador is in Beyens, *Quatre ans à Rome*, 136–137.

16. Gasparri's letter to Italian bishops, dated October 2, 1922, is cited in Liliana Ferrari, *Una storia Azione cattolica: Gli ordinamenti statutari da Pio XI a Pio XII* (Genoa: Marietti, 1989), 31.

17. See, e.g., Maffeo Pantaleoni, "Plutocrazie e bolscevismo giudaico sgretolano il fascismo," *Vita italiana* (July 1921); and Pantaleoni, *Bolscevismo italiano* (Bari: Laterza, 1922).

18. Pius XI, *Ubi Arcano Dei Consilio* (December 23, 1922), §§7, 10–15, and 48. Available online at https://w2.vatican.va/content/pius-xi/en/encyclicals/documents/hf_p-xi_enc_19221223_ubi-arcano-dei-consilio.html.

19. Ibid., §§45, 46, 48, 54, and 58.

20. Ibid., §46.

21. *Documenti diplomatici italiani* (hereafter cited as *DDI*) (Rome: Istituto poligrafico dello stato, 1970), ser. 7, vol. 4, no. 308.

22. The men who were asked to step out of the limelight included Roberto Farinacci, Aldo Oviglio, and, to a lesser extent, Giovanni Gentile.

23. The 1926 letter is cited in Alfredo Canavero, "De Gasperi, Gemelli, e i clerico-fascisti," *Nuova Antologia* (January–March 2009): 349–361, at 354. For more on these themes, see Richard A. Webster, *Cross and the Fasces: Chris-*

tian Democracy and Fascism in Italy (Stanford, CA: Stanford University Press, 1960), 153–161. See also Gabriele Turi, "Il progetto dell'Enciclopedia italiana: l'organizzazione del consenso fra gli intellettuali," *Studi storici* 13, no. 1 (1972): 93–152, at 144–148.

24. [G. Busnelli], *"L'Enciclopedia Italiana," La Civiltà Cattolica* 4 (1929): 536. For more, see Gabriele Turi, "Ideologia e cultura del fascismo nello specchio dell'Enciclopedia italiana," *Studi storici* 20, no. 1 (1979): 157–211.

25. The text of the law (officially known as the Royal Decree of October 1, 1923, no. 2185) is reproduced in Howard Rosario Marraro, *Nationalism in Italian Education* (New York: Italian Digest and News Service, 1927), 109–110.

26. For context, see Tracy Koon, *Believe, Obey, Fight: Political Socialization of Youth in Fascist Italy, 1922–1943* (Chapel Hill: University of North Carolina Press, 2012), 55; for Gentile's own justification, see Koon, *Fascismo al governo della scuola: Discorsi e interviste,* ed. Ferruccio Emilio Boffi (Palermo: Remo Sandron, 1924).

27. For the Catholic reaction to the Gentile reform, see "L'insegnamento religioso nella scuola: Propositi del Governo e spropositi dei liberali," *Civiltà Cattolica,* February 8, 1923; Benedetto Croce, "Cultura e vita morale," *La Critica,* July 20, 1923, 253–256; Giovanni Gentile, *La riforma della scuola in Italia* (Florence: Lettere, 1989), 136. See also Luciano Pazzaglia, "Consensi e reserve nei giudizi dei cattolici sulla Gentile (1922–1924)," *Quaderni del Centri Studi C. Trabucco* 7 (1985): 35–114; Gabriele Turi, *Giovanni Gentile: Una Biografia* (Florence: Giunti, 1995), 319–325; and Giovanni Battista Guzzetti, *Il movimento cattolico italiano dall'unità ad oggi* (Naples: Dehoniane, 1980), 379–391.

28. Pope Pius XI, *Discorsi di Pio XI,* ed. Domenico Bertetto (Vatican City: Libreria Editrice Vaticana, 1985), 6–7.

29. Fascist surgical violence quote in Benito Mussolini, "La morale," *Popolo d'Italia,* April 19, 1921; Mussolini refers to Fascist violence as "child's play" in "Continuando," *Popolo d'Italia,* August 6, 1922. As cited in Ebner, *Ordinary Violence,* 42.

30. Paolo Spriano, *Storia del Partito comunista italiano* (Turin: Einaudi, 1969), 2: 262–303.

31. Antonio Gramsci to Giulia Schucht, June 22, 1924, in Antonio Gramsci, *Lettere, 1908–1926,* ed. Sergio Caprioglio (Turin: Einaudi, 1992), 356–357. Gramsci and the Communist Party did not join the Aventinian opposition to the Fascist takeover.

32. Mussolini, *Opera Omnia,* 21:238.

33. Filippo Maria Tinti, *Sionismo e Cattolicismo* (Bari: Società Tipografica Pugliese, 1926).

34. [E. Rosa], "La parte dei cattolici nelle presenti lotte dei partiti politici in Italia," *La Civiltà Cattolica,* August 7, 1924, as cited in Renato Moro, "Religione del trascendente e relgioni politiche: Il cattolicesimo italiano di fronte alla sacralizzazione fascista della politica," *Mondo contemporaneo* 1 (2005): 9–67, at 14.

35. See Brunella Dalla Casa, *Attentato al duce: Le molte sortie del caso Zamboni* (Bologna: Il Mulino, 2000).

36. Pius XI, as cited in Pierre Milza and Serge Bernstein, *Storia del fascismo* (Milan: Rizzoli, 2004); "Un nuovo esecrabile attentato contro l'on: Mussolini," *L'Osservatore Romano*, November 2–3, 1926, as cited in Ceci, *Vatican and Mussolini's Italy*, 113.

37. Paolo Spriano, *Storia del Partito comunista italiano*, vol. 2 (Turin: G. Einaudi, 1969), 18–122; Alistair Davidson, *Antonio Gramsci: Towards an Intellectual Biography* (Leiden: Brill, 1977), 260.

38. Moro, "Religione del trascendente," 16.

39. Tonino Fabbri, *Fascismo e bolscevismo: Le relazioni nei documenti diplomatici italo-russi* (Padova: Libreria universitaria edizioni, 2013), 65ff.

40. Benito Mussolini, "Dottrina politica e sociale," *Enciclopedia Treccani*, vol. 14.

41. Joseph Henri Ledit, *Diario di una spedizione in Russia* (1926), Archivio del Pontificio Istituto Orientale, as cited in Vincenzo Poggi, *Per la storia del Pontificio Istituto Orientale: Saggi sull'istituzione, i suoi uomini e l'Oriente Cristiano* (Rome: Pontificio Istituto Orientale, 2000), 286.

42. Pacelli to Gasparri, Berlin, June 14, 1927, ASV, A.E.S., Pro Russia (quarto periodo), 1924–1941, sc. 13, fasc. 83, ff. 11–2. For the expression of similar sentiments by Pacelli, see, e.g., D'Herbigny, "Voto del relatore"; and Pacelli to Cardinal Luigi Sincero, president of the Pro Russia Commission, Rorschach, November 11, 1927, ASV, A.E.S., Pro Russia (quarto periodo), 1924–1941, sc. 13, fasc. 83, ff. 34–35.

43. Michel D'Herbigny, "Voto del relatore sulla lettera di Sua Ecc. Rev.ma Mons. Eugenio Pacelli," June 14, 1927, ASV, A.E.S., Pro Russia (quarto periodo), 1924–1941, sc. 13, fasc. 83, f. 14.

44. ARSI, Tacchi Venturi, b. 8, fasc. 446, Tacchi Venturi to Gasparri, December 1, 1926, as cited in David Kertzer, *The Pope and Mussolini: The Secret History of Pius XI and the Rise of Fascism in Europe* (New York: Random House, 2014), 427.

45. Daniel Peris, "The 1929 Congress of the Godless," *Europe-Asia Studies* 43, no. 4 (1991): 711–732.

46. As cited in Daniel Peris, *Storming the Heavens: The Soviet League of the Militant Godless* (Ithaca, NY: Cornell University Press, 1998), 127n34.

47. See Glennys Young, *Power and the Sacred in Revolutionary Russia: Religious Activists in the Village* (University Park: Pennsylvania State University Press, 1997); and Lynn Viola, *Peasant Rebels under Stalin: Collectivization and the Culture of Peasant Resistance* (Oxford: Oxford University Press, 1999), 57–60.

48. For more on the antireligious campaigns of the 1920s, see Paul Froese, *The Plot to Kill God: Findings from the Soviet Experiment in Secularization* (Berkeley: University of California Press, 2008); William B. Husband, *"Godless Communists": Atheism and Society in Soviet Russia, 1917–1932* (DeKalb: Northern Illinois University Press, 2000); James Thrower, *Marxist-Leninist "Scientific Atheism" and the Study of Religion and Atheism in the USSR* (Berlin: Walter de Gruyter, 1983); and David E. Powell, *Antireligious Propaganda in the Soviet Union: A Study in Mass Persuasion* (Cambridge: MIT Press, 1975).

49. Letter from Pius XI to Cardinal Basilio Pompilj, *Osservatore Romano*, February 9, 1930. For drafts of the letter, see "Progetto di lettera del Santo Padre all'Emm. Signor Cardinal Vicario," early 1930, ASV, A.E.S., Pro Russia (quarto periodo), 1924–1941, sc. 13, fasc. 84, ff. 44–45.

50. As cited in Daniel Gorman, *The Emergence of International Society in the 1920s* (Cambridge: Cambridge University Press, 2014), 1. For more on this phenomenon, see David Armstrong, Lorna Lloyd, and John Redmond, *International Organization in World Politics* (London: Palgrave Macmillan, 2005), 16–33; Patricia Clavin and Glenda Sluga, eds., *Internationalisms: A Twentieth-Century History* (Cambridge: Cambridge University Press, 2016); Akira Iriye, *Global Community: The Rise of International Organizations in the Making of the Contemporary World* (Berkeley: University of California Press, 2002), 20–30; Daniel Laqua, "Democratic Politics and the League of Nations: The Labour and Socialist International as Protagonist of Interwar Internationalism," *Contemporary European History* 24 (2015): 175–192; and Laqua, ed., *Internationalism Reconfigured: Transnational Ideas and Movements between the World Wars* (London: Tauris, 2011).

51. As cited in Gorman, *Emergence of International Society*, 47.

52. For a recent analysis, see Oona Hathaway and Scott Shapiro, *The Internationalists: How a Radical Plan to Outlaw War Remade the World* (New York: Simon and Schuster, 2017).

53. Zara S. Steiner, *The Lights That Failed: European International History, 1919–1933* (Oxford: Oxford University Press, 2005), 344.

54. John Pollard, *The Papacy in the Age of Totalitarianism, 1914–1958* (Oxford: Oxford University Press, 2014), 204–206.

55. James F. McMillan, "France," in *Political Catholicism in Europe, 1918–1965* (Oxford: Clarendon Press, 1996), 34–68, at 42.

56. Oscar L. Arnal, *Ambivalent Alliance: The Catholic Church and the French Action, 1899–1939* (Pittsburgh: University of Pittsburgh Press, 1985), 117.

57. Gustav Streseman, "Nobel Lecture: The New Germany," June 29, 1927. Reprinted online at http://www.nobelprize.org/nobel_prizes/peace/laureates/1926/stresemann-lecture.html.

58. "Luci ed ombre sul problema europeo," *Civiltà Cattolica*, February 7, 1930.

59. Monsignor Besson, Bishop of Lausanne, to Gasparri, December 19, 1926, and Gasparri to Monsignor Serena, secretary of the Apostolic Nunziature in Bern, December 4, 1926. For the former: ASV, A.E.S., Stati ecclesiastici, P391, P.O. 272 P35 / 27. For the latter: ASV, A.E.S., Stati ecclesiastici, P391, P.O. F272, P2846 / 26. As cited in Americo Miranda, *Santa Sede e Società delle Nazioni* (Rome: Studium, 2013), 148–149.

60. Antonio Mattiazzo, "Le internazionali cattoliche: Origini e programmi," in *Genesi della coscienza internazionalista nei cattolici tra '800 e '900* (Padua: Libreria editrice gregoriana, 1983): 59–168, at 111; Etienne Fouilloux, *Les catholiques et l'unité chrétienne du XIXe au XXe siècle* (Paris: Le Centurion, 1982), 411.

61. For "fourth Rome" quote, see Katerina Clark, *Moscow, the Fourth Rome: Stalinism, Cosmopolitanism, and the Evolution of Soviet Culture, 1931–41* (Cambridge, MA: Harvard University Press, 2011), 2. On Communist

354   NOTES TO PAGES 111–113

internationalism and its intersection with broader trends, see Cemil Aydin, *The Politics of Anti-Westernism* (New York: Columbia University Press, 2007); Fernando Claudín, *The Communist Movement from Comintern to Cominform: Part One, The Crisis of the Communist International*, trans. Brian Pearce (New York: Monthly Review Press, 1967), 159–166; Manu Goswami, "Colonial Internationalisms and Imaginary Futures," *American Historical Review* 117, no. 5 (2012): 1461–1485; Francine Hirsch, Lisa Kirschenbaum, Tim Rees, and Andre Thorpe, eds., *International Communism and the Communist International, 1919–1943* (Manchester: Manchester University Press, 1998); Lisa A. Kirschenbaum, *International Communism and the Spanish Civil War: Solidarity and Suspicion* (Cambridge: Cambridge University Press, 2015); Erez Manela, *The Wilsonian Moment: Self-Determination and the International Origins of Anticolonial Nationalism* (Oxford: Oxford University Press, 2007); Kevin McDermott and Jeremy Agnew, *The Comintern: A History of International Communism from Lenin to Stalin* (New York: St. Martin's Press, 1997), 81–119; and Ali Raza, Franziska Roy, and Benjamin Zachariah, eds., *The Internationalist Moment: South Asia, Worlds and World Views, 1917–1939* (New Delhi: Sage, 2014).

62. "Luci ed ombre sul problema europeo," *Civiltà Cattolica*, February 7, 1930.

63. See P. S. Gupta, *A Short History of the All-Indian Trade Union, 1920–1947* (New Delhi, AITUC, 1980), 118ff; Carolien Stolte, "Trade Unions on Trial: The Impact of the Meerut Conspiracy Case on Trade Union Internationalism, 1929–32," *Studies of South Asia, Africa and the Middle East* 33, no. 3 (2013): 345–359.

64. For more on these movements, see Michelle Louro, "Rethinking Nehru's Internationalism: The League Against Imperialism and Anti-Imperial Networks, 1927–1936," *Third Frame: Literature, Culture and Society* 2, no. 3 (September 2009): 79–94; Fredrik Petersson, *Willi Münzenberg, the League Against Imperialism, and the Comintern, 1925–1933* (Lewiston, NY: Queenston Press, 2013); Michael Goebel, *Anti-Imperial Metropolis: Interwar Paris and the Seeds of Third World Nationalism* (Cambridge: Cambridge University Press, 2015), 189–194; Jonathan Derrick, *Africa's Agitators: Militant Anti-Colonialism in Africa and the West, 1918–1939* (New York: Oxford University Press), 235ff; and Jennifer Anne Boittin, *Colonial Metropolis: The Urban Grounds of Anti-Imperialism and Feminism in Interwar Paris* (Lincoln: University of Nebraska Press, 2015).

65. Fabrice Bouthillon, *La naissance de la Mardité: Une théologie politique à l'âge totalitaire, Pie XI (1922–1939)* (Strasbourg: Presses universitaires de Strasbourg, 2002), 215.

66. The phrase is Oscar Arnal's, in his *Ambivalent Alliance: The Catholic Church and the Action Française, 1899–1939* (Pittsburg: University of Pittsburg Press, 1985), 117.

67. Letter of the Archbishop of Salisburg, Mons. Sigismund Waitz, to Eugenio Pacelli, May 1935, ASV, A.E.S., Austria IV, fasc.14, f. 72r.

68. Pius XI, Allocution to the Secret Consistory regarding Catholic Action, Vatican City, December 20, 1926, as reprinted in *Pio XI e l'Azione Cattolica*,

ed. A. M. Cavagna (Rome: Ferrari, 1928), 61–63. Also see Pius XI's condemnation of Action Française, which was also intended to send a message to Polish and Italian Catholics. The condemnation was printed in the *Osservatore Romano* on December 21, 1926. For more, see Peter J. Bernardi, *Maurice Blondel, Social Catholicism, and French Action: The Clash over the Church's Role in Society during the Modernist Era* (Washington, DC: Catholic University of America Press, 2009); and Eugen Weber, *French Action: Royalism and Reaction in Twentieth Century France* (Paris: Hachette, 1990), chap. 13.

69. Mariano Cordovani, "L'autorità sociale nella dottrina cattolica," in *Atti della XI sessione delle 'Settimane sociali d'Italia' (Torino, settembre 1924)* (Milan:Vita e Pensiero, 1924), 53–70; Cordovani, *Cattolicesimo ed Idealismo* (Milan: Vita e Pensiero, 1928), 229.

70. "'Funzione educativa' e 'carattere etico' dello Stato," *Civiltà Cattolica* 3 (1922): 142.

71. Luigi Sturzo, "Spirito e realtà," *La rivoluzione liberale*, January 22, 1924.

72. "Principii di dottrina cattolica circa lo Stato e la convivenza civile," *Civiltà Cattolica*, January 15, 1927, as cited in Moro, "Religione del trascendente," 17, 19.

73. Pius XI letter to Cardinal Gasparri, *Civiltà Cattolica*, January 24, 1927.

74. *DDI*, ser. 7, vol. 4, no. 308, as cited in Kertzer, *Pope and Mussolini*, 99.

75. Edoardo Bressan, "Mito di uno Stato cattolico e realtà del regime: Per una lettura dell'*Osservatore Romano* alla vigilia della Conciliazione," *Nuova rivista storica* 64 (1980): 81–128; and G. Baget Bozzo, "Il fascismo e l'evoluzione del pensiero politico cattolico," *Storia contemporanea* 4 (1974): 671–677.

76. Three interlinked agreements composed the pacts: a concordat, a conciliation treaty, and a financial treaty. The pacts were concluded on February 11, 1929. In the Chamber, they were discussed on May 10, 1929, and they were approved four days later by the overwhelming majority of 357 in favor and only 2 against. The Senate was equally quick to ratify: after a debate in late May, 316 voted for and 6 against. Two weeks later, on June 7, 1929, the final ratifications took place.

77. Francesco Pacelli, *Diario della Conciliazione con verbali e appendice di documenti*, ed. Michele Maccarrone (Vatican City: Libreria Editrice Vaticana, 1959), 21.

78. The full Italian-language text is reprinted in *Trattato e concordato fra la Santa Sede e l'Italia, ed allegati e disposizioni relative* (Rome: Istituto poligrafico dello stato, 1929).

79. John Pollard, *Money and the Rise of the Modern Papacy: Financing the Vatican, 1850–1950* (Cambridge: Cambridge University Press, 2005), 148.

80. Egilberto Martire speech to the Italian Parliament, as cited in Pollard, *Vatican and Italian Fascism*, 75.

81. P. A. Vermeersch, "L'attualità dell'enciclica," *Studium* 5–6 (1931).

82. *Osservatore Romano*, February 12, 1929.

83. "Le nuove finalità dell'Azione Cattolica nel discorso del Presidente Generale Comm. Luigi Colombo," *Azione giovanile*, March 17, 1929, as cited in Moro, "Religione del trascendente," 19.

84. Tacchi Venturi to Gasparri, Rome, February 21, 1929, ASV, A.E.S., pos. 630a, fasc. 63, ff. 88–89; and ACS, Segreteria Particolare Duce, Carteggio Riservato, b. 68, Rome, February 17, 1929. Cited in Kertzer, *Pope and Mussolini*, 118. For more on the view that the Fascists and the Church must work together to stop Freemasons and anticlericals from committing "acts of brigandage" in Italy, see Pacelli, Udienze notes for November 16, 1930, ASV, A.E.S., Stati Ecclesiastici, 1930–1938, pos. 430a P.O., fasc. 340, f. 56.

85. DDI, 7, vol. 10 (proofs), May 29, 1931. As cited in John Pollard, *The Vatican and Italian Fascism, 1929–32: A Study in Conflict* (Cambridge: Cambridge University Press, 1985), 108.

86. My position here is closest to that of John Pollard and Frank J. Coppa, "Mussolini and the Concordat of 1929," in *Controversial Concordats: The Vatican's Relations with Napoleon, Mussolini, and Hitler* (Washington, DC: Catholic University of America Press, 2012), 81.

87. "Christian restoration," in "Preparazione elettorale," *La Civiltà Cattolica*, April 6, 1929; "Italy Has Been Remade Catholic" in Adriano Bernareggi, "Chiesa e Stato (I vari aspetti del problema)," *Studium* 8–9 (1929); on the promise of the concordat, see Editorial Board, "11 Febbraio 1929," *Studium* 2 (1929); and Editorial Board, "La fine dell'anticlericalismo," *Studium* 3 (1929); Thomas B. Morgan, *A Reporter at the Papal Court: A Narrative of the Reign of Pope Pius XI* (New York: Longmans, Green and Co., 1937), 177; on the "end of statolatry," see N.P.F., "Valutazione storica del concordato," *Studium* 3 (1929).

88. Yves Simon to Jacques Maritain, June 12, 1940, and Simon to Maritain, November 6, 1941, as cited by John Hellman, "The Anti-Democratic Impulse in Catholicism: Jacques Maritain, Yves Simon, and Charles de Gaulle during World War II," *Journal of Church and State* 33, no. 3 (Summer 1991): 453–471, at 457, 459.

89. Pier Giorgio Zunino, *La Questione Cattolica nella sinistra italiana* (Bologna: Il Mulino, 1977), 243–244.

90. Miglioli interview with *Le Monde*, as reprinted in "Fascismo e Vaticano," *L'Italia del Popolo*, May 9, 1929. Sturzo is cited in Pollard, *Vatican and Italian Fascism*, 55, 180.

91. See Alcide De Gasparri to Simone Weber, February 26, 1929, in *Lettere sul Concordato* (Brescia: Morcelliana, 1970), 64, 78.

92. As cited in Stefano Catini, *Sturzo, l'uomo degli altri* (Rome: Edizioni Nuova Cultura, 2016), 79.

93. Pius XI, "Alla Federazione francese dei sindacati cristiani" (1931), in *Discorsi di Pio XI*, ed. Domenico Bertetto (Turin: Società editrice internazionale, 1960), 3:811.

94. "Relazione fiduciaria da Milano del 7 May 1935," as cited in Renato Moro, *La formazione della classe dirigente cattolica* (Bologna: Il Mulino, 1979), 486.

CHAPTER 5 ▪ LAUNCHING THE ANTICOMMUNIST CRUSADE

Epigraph: *Lettres de Rome* (hereafter cited as *LdR*) 1, no. 1 (May 1935): 1. Stored in ARSI, JESCOM, the Private Library of Father Ledóchowski, *LdR*, vol. 1 (1935).

1. A. James Gregor, *Italian Fascism and Developmental Dictatorship* (Princeton, NJ: Princeton University Press, 2016), 153.
2. Hans Fallada, *E adesso pover'uomo?*, trans. Bruno Revel (Palermo: Sellerio, 2008), 220–221.
3. Harold George Nicolson, *Peacemaking, 1919* (Berlin: S. Fischer, 1933), 108; Adam Tooze, *The Deluge: The Great War, America and the Remaking of the Global Order, 1916–1931* (New York: Penguin Books, 2015), 487, 516.
4. As cited in John Pollard, *Money and the Rise of the Modern Papacy: Financing the Vatican, 1850–1950* (Cambridge: Cambridge University Press, 2004), 150, 157.
5. From Domenico Tardini's report of his February 3, 1934, Audience with Pope Pius XI, as cited in C. F. Casula, *Domenico Tardini (1888–1961): L'azione della Santa Sede nella crisi fra le due guerre* (Rome: Studium, 1988), 292–293.
6. Nogara archives, Nogara's diary, entry for February 15, 1932, as cited in Pollard, *Money*, 165.
7. Father Martin Gillet, "Le impressioni americane," *Memorie Domenicane: Rassegna di Letteratura, Storia, Arte* (March–April 1931): 138–143.
8. Ernst Jünger, *Der Arbeiter: Herrschaft und Gestalt* (Berlin: Klett-Cotta, 2014), 92. Also see Jünger, *Der gefährliche Augenblick*, ed. Ferdinand Bucholtz (Berlin: Junker und Dünnhaupt, 1931); and *Die veränderte Welt*, ed. by Edmund Schultz (Breslau: W. G. Korn, 1933).
9. Letter from Father Friedrich Muckermann, SJ, to Eugenio Pacelli, Münster, April 29, 1931, ASV, Segr. Stato, 1931, rubr. 362, fasc. 3, ff. 197–199.
10. On the German bishops' reaction, see Paul Misner, *Catholic Labor Movements in Europe* (Washington, DC: Catholic University of America, 2015), 172.
11. See Walter Z. Laqueur, *Young Germany: A History of the German Youth Movement* (New Brunswick, NJ: Transaction Books, 1962); and Robert A. Krieg, "A Precursor's Life and Work," in *Romano Guardini: Proclaiming the Sacred in a Modern World*, ed. Robert A. Krieg (Chicago: Archdiocese of Chicago Liturgy Training Publications, 1995).
12. Letter of Dr. Pfeiffer to President of Italian Catholic Action, Kosice, May 1930. Archive of Italian Catholic Action, Istituto Paolo VI, Unione Popolare, Miscellaneo, b. 63, fasc.4, f. 100.
13. 1921 Manifesto, as reprinted in *Manifeste der Jugend* (Düsseldorf: Verlag Haus Altenberg, 1958).
14. Bluette [? handwriting difficult to decipher] to Gasparri, Paris, April 23, 1923. ASV, A.E.S. *Stati Ecclesiastici* (4th period), 1922–1934, pos. 293 P.O., fasc.19, f. 48. Also see Konrad Algermissen, *Die gottlosenbewegung der Gegenwart und ihre Überwindung* (Hannover: Joseph Giesel, 1933).
15. Dr. Pfeiffer to President of Italian Catholic Action, May 1930.

16. For more detail, see Herbert Gottwald, "Volksverein für das katholische Deutschland," in *Lexikon zur Parteiengeschichte: Die bürgerlichen und kleinbürgerlichen Parteien und Verbände in Deutschland, 1789–1945*, ed. Dieter Fricke (Köln: Paul-Rugenstein, 1985), 436, 460; Todd Weir, "The Christian Front against Godlessness: Anti-Secularism and the Demise of the Weimar Republic, 1928–1933," *Past and Present* 229, no. 1 (2015): 201–238; and Pettinaroli, *La politique russe*, 936.

17. Eugenio Pacelli, *Die Lage der Kirche in Deutschland 1929*, ed. Hubert Wolf and Klaus Unterburger (Paderborn: Schöningh, 2006), 173, 179.

18. Count Casimiro Ledóchowski, "Promemoria sulla situazione politico-religiosa dell'Europa," June 1931, ASV, A.E.S., *Stati Ecclesiastici* (quarto periodo), 1930–1932, pos. 317 P.O., fasc. 100, ff. 27–34.

19. Michel D'Herbigny, preparatory notes, and "Ex audientia Ssmi" notes, May 8, 1931, ASV, A.E.S., Pro Russia (quarto periodo), 1924–1935, pos. Scatola 4, fasc. 27, f. 28.

20. For a detailed analysis of how "crisis of civilization" talk pervaded the Catholic world in these years, see Renato Moro, *La formazione della classe dirigente cattolica, 1929–1937* (Bologna: Il Mulino, 1979).

21. Letter of Ledóchowski to d'Herbigny, Rome, December 6, 1931, ASV, A.E.S., *Pro Russia* (quarto periodo), 1924–1935, pos. Scatola 4, fasc. 27, ff. 82–83.

22. D'Herbigny's summary of a recent audience with Pius XI, May 8, 1931, ASV, A.E.S., *Pro Russia* (quarto periodo), 1924–1935, sc. 4, fasc. 27, f. 28.

23. Archive of Italian Catholic Action, Istituto Paolo VI, Rome (hereafter cited as AACI), Archivio della Presidenza della FUCI, b. "Materiale 1931 / 35," f. "Circolari Ufficio Centrale, 1931 / 35."

24. ASV, Nunziatura Italia 120, fasc. 10, Russia, fol. 12, Nuncio Borgongini-Duca to Pacelli, February 25, 1930, as cited in Todd Weir, "A European Culture War in the Twentieth Century? Anti-Catholicism and Anti-Bolshevism between Moscow, Berlin, and the Vatican, 1922–1933," *Journal of Religious History* 24, no. 1 (2014): 16.

25. Dépêche 296 de Fontenay, Rome, October 11, 1930, Archives of the French Finance and Foreign Economic Affairs Ministry, vol. 32, bk. 2. As cited in Fabrice Bouthillon, *La naissance de la mardité: Une théologie politique à l'âge totalitaire* (Strasbourg: Presses universitaires de Strasbourg, 2002), 215.

26. See, e.g., Eugenio Pacelli, Udienze notes for January 21, 1931, ASV, A.E.S., Stati Ecclesiastici, 1930–1938, pos. 430a, P.O., fasc. 341, ff. 22; and Pacelli's Udienze notes, September 3, 1934, ASV, A.E.S., Stati Ecclesiastici, 1930–1938, pos.430b P.O., fasc. 361, f. 110.

27. ARSI, Ledóchowski, b. 1008, fasc. 1013, f. 319; Summary of 1931 Ledóchowski audiences with the pope, ASV, Prefettura Casa Pont., Udienze b.15–16.

28. "I 'besbosniki' in Germania," *Osservatore Romano*, April 11, 1931, ASV, A.E.S., Pro Russia (quarto periodo), 1924–1935, pos. Scatola 4, fasc. 27, f. 27.

29. Fiduciario #42 [Umberto Benigni], "Albania e Jugoslavia, cioè il gesuita d'Herbigny," Rome, January 26, 1930, Central Archives of the State, Rome (hereafter cited as ACS), Interior Ministry (MI), Direzione Generale Pubblica Sicurezza (DGPS), Divisione Polizia Politica (DPP), fascicoli personali, b. 386, fasc. D'Arbigny [*sic*] [d'Herbigny].

30. Letter of Card Bertram to Orsenigo, Breslau, February 27, 1933, Archivio della Congregazione per la Dottrina della Fede (hereafter cited as ACDF), R.V. 1933, n. 15, ff. 6–11.

31. Letter of Cardinal Schulte, Archbishop of Cologne, to Orsenigo, February 28, 1933, ACDF, R.V. 1933, n. 15, ff.14–16.

32. Konrad Algermissen, who was active in the *Volksverein*, is warmly referred to Pizzardo in 1937 by Mons. Luigi Hudal as an "an excellent expert on the Godlessness movement." Note of Luigi Hudal to Pizzardo, March 10, 1937, ASV, A.E.S., Stati Ecclesiastici, 1936–1938, pos. 533 P.O., fasc. 556, f. 100. For more information, see the letter of Cardinal Schulte, Archbishop of Cologne, to Cesare Orsenigo, Cologne, February 28, 1933, ACDF, R.V. 1933, n. 15, f. 15.

33. The organization's leader, Oswald von Nell-Breuning, was a Jesuit who is widely credited with being the most important intellectual influence on the encyclical. On this, see Noah Benezra Strote, *Lions and Lambs: Conflict in Weimar and the Creation of Post-Nazi Germany* (New Haven, CT: Yale University Press, 2017), 58ff.

34. David W. Southern, *John LaFarge and the Limits of Catholic Interracialism, 1911–1963* (Baton Rouge: Louisiana State University Press, 1996), 216.

35. "I 'besbosniki in Germania," *Osservatore Romano*, April 11, 1931.

36. Pope Pius XI, *Quadragesimo Anno* (May 15, 1931), §§3, 88. Available online at http://w2.vatican.va/content/pius-xi/en/encyclicals/documents/hf_p-xi_enc_19310515_quadragesimo-anno.html.

37. Ibid., §§46, 55, and 120.

38. Ibid., §§71, 117, 118, and 120.

39. By this point, the Fascist project to re-domesticate Italian women was already well under way: In 1921, the year before the Fascists came to power, 5 million women had been employed outside the home and there were 9.3 million housewives in Italy; by 1931, 3.9 million women worked outside the home, and there were 11.3 million housewives. Piero Meldini, *Sposa e Madre Esemplare: Ideologia e Politica Della Donna e Della Famiglia durante il Fascismo* (Florence: Guaraldi Editore, 1975), 73. Also see Victoria De Grazia, *How Fascism Ruled Women* (Berkeley: University of California Press, 1993).

40. Pius XI, *Quadragesimo Anno*, §§112, 121, 122. Note: Much this dramatic wording was repeated almost verbatim in a draft encyclical, *Divinum Mandatum*, that was never published. See encyclical draft, September 10, 1932, ASV, Epis. Ad Princ. Positiones et minutae, 1930–1932, b. 168, fasc. 23, ff. 1–12.

41. Ibid., §§36, 91–95, 112, and 122.

42. Both Catholics and Fascists were confused on this key point. Some argued that *Quadragesimo Anno* was anti-statist and anti-Fascist, while others saw the text as a ringing endorsement of Fascist corporatism. Perhaps Pius XI intended it this way, in the hope that both Fascist censors and Catholic anti-Fascists would see what they wished to see in the text. Without a doubt, the Fascist regime was happy that the encyclical could be read as a celebration of Fascist corporatism, and worked to stamp out any sites of Catholic dialogue that might come to contrary conclusions. For instance, the Fascist authorities

banned a planned 1935 Social Week on the topic of corporatism and the
"crisis of capitalism" when they learned that Father Gustave Desbuquois,
who had put forward an anti-statist and anti-Fascist reading of *Quadragesimo
Anno*, had been invited to participate in the event. Father Desbuquois to
Ledóchowski, Vanves, April 5, 1935, ARSI, Ledóchowski 1016, fasc. 5, d.
553; addendum to the letter of Igino Righetti to Ledóchowski, Rome,
March 15, 1935, ARSI, Ledóchowski 1016, fasc. "Settimana sociale italiana
1935," f. 553.

43. Letter from Muckermann, SJ, to Pacelli, Münster, April 29, 1931, ASV, Segr.
Stato, 1931, rubr. 362, fasc. 3, ff. 197–199.

44. The phrase is from Sergio Paronetto's review of Callisto Giavazzi, "La distribuzione della ricchezza," *Studium* 5 (1933): 314. In response to the worry
that the Catholic critique of capitalism was receding, a younger generation
of activists in Italian Catholic Action started elaborating a strong critique
of their own, which combined an attack on the contradictions of liberal
economics (drawn from Marx, Luxemburg, and Sombart, whose *Modern
Capitalism* was translated into Italian in 1925), with a moral critique of capitalism imbued with anti-Protestant discourse (Troeltsch's *Protestantism
in the Formation of the Modern World* was translated in Italian 1929, and
Weber's *The Protestant Ethic and the Spirit of Capitalism* was translated in
1931). Some key early texts emerging from this moment include Amintore
Fanfani's *Le origini dello spirito capitalistico in Italia* (Milan: Vita e pensiero, 1933), his *Cattolicesimo e protestantesimo nella formazione storica
del capitalismo* (Milan: Vita e pensiero, 1934), and Callisto Giavazzi, *La
distribuzione della ricchezza* (Rome: Istituto cattolico di attività sociali,
1933).

45. Letter of Ledóchowski to Ottaviani, Rome, May 16, 1931, ASV, Secr. Stato
1931, rubr. 1, fasc. 3; Letter of Dott Barone Raitz r. Krentz to Tipografia Vaticana, Rome, May 19, 1931. ASV, Segr. Stato 1931, rubr. 1, fasc. 3.

46. Letter of Archbishop and Cardinal Hayes to Pacelli, New York, June 10, 1932,
ASV, Segr. Stato 1932, rubr. 1, fasc. 4, f. 25.

47. Letter from J. M. Tinz (?) to Tacchi Venturi, January 27, 1931, stored in ARSI,
JESCOM 1038 (De comm. Atheo, 1933–1943), fasc. "Comm.Propaganda."

48. Ibid.

49. See, e.g., Peter C. Kent, *The Lonely Cold War of Pope Pius XII: The Roman
Catholic Church and the Division of Europe, 1943–1950* (Montreal: McGill-
Queen's University Press, 2002); Jonathan Luxmoore, *The Vatican and the
Red Flag: The Struggle for the Soul of Eastern Europe* (London: G. Chapman,
1999); Paul Philip Mariani, *Church Militant: Bishop Kung and Catholic Re-
sistance in Communist Shanghai* (Cambridge, MA: Harvard University
Press, 2011); Michael Phayer, *Pius XII, the Holocaust and the Cold War*
(Bloomington: Indiana University Press, 2008); and Anthony Rhodes, *The
Vatican in the Age of the Cold War, 1945–1980* (Norwich, UK: Michael Rus-
sell, 1992).

50. See, e.g., Philippe Chenaux, *L'Église catholique et le communisme en Europe (1917–1989)* (Paris: Cerf, 2009); Laura Pettinaroli, *La politique russe du
Saint-Siége (1905–1939)* (Rome: École française de Rome, 2015); and Hansjakob

Stehle, *Eastern Politics of the Vatican, 1917–1979*, trans. Sandra Smith (Athens, OH: Ohio University Press, 1981).

51. Edoardo Bressan, "*L'Osservatore Romano* e le relazioni internazionali della Santa Sede, 1917–1922," *in Benedetto XV e la Pace*, ed. Giorgio Rumi (Brescia: Morcelliana, 1990), 234.

52. April 14, 1932, circular letter, ASV, A.E.S., Stati Ecclesiastici (quarto periodo), 1932–1942, pos. 474 P.O., fasc. 475, ff. 28f. The countries to which the circular was sent included Austria, Argentina, Albania, Australia, the Belgian Congo, Belgium, Brazil, Bolivia, Bulgaria, Canada, Chile, China Colombia, Cuba, Czechoslovakia, France, Haiti, Hungary, Indochina, Iraq, Iran, Ireland, Japan, Kenya, Latvia, Lithuania, Libya, the Netherlands, Peru, Philippines, Poland, Portugal, Romania, South Africa, Switzerland, Syria, Turkey, Venezuela, and Yugoslavia. The highways and byways of Vatican information dispersal are outlined in Cardinal Pacelli's note accompanying the April 14, 1932, circular letter.

53. Ibid.

54. In 1930 the Centro had changed its name to Associación Anticomunista Internacional. See Michel Caillat, Mauro Cerutti, Jean-François Fayet, and Jorge Gajardo, "Les archives de l'Entente internationale anticommunist de Théodore Aubert," *Matériaux pour l'histoire de notre temps* 73 (January–March, 2004): 25–31.

55. Ledóchowski, "On Catholic Action in Spain: A Letter Addressed to the Provincials of Spain," Rome, May 9, 1933, as reprinted in Ledóchowski, *Selected Writings of Father Ledóchowski* (Chicago: Loyola University Press, 1945), 619–620.

56. The Swiss *Entente Internationale contre la Troisième Internationale* and the French journal *Unitas* received the most attention from the papacy. Letter from Lodygensky and Nicolski to d'Herbigny, Geneva, July 10, 1933, ASV, A.E.S., Pro Russia (quarto periodo) 1924–1935, pos. sc. 4, fasc. 29, ff. 50–52; Ledit, "Documenta," April 1935, stored in JESCOM, the Private Library of Father Ledóchowski, *LdR* 1 (1935): 6.

57. See Pacelli, Udienze notes for January 16, 1931, ASV, A.E.S., Stati Ecclesiastici, 1930–1938, pos. 430a P.O., fasc. 341, f. 16. Also see letter from Lodygensky and Nicolski to d'Herbigny, Geneva, July 10, 1933, ibid.

58. Pacelli, Udienze notes for January 16, 1931.

59. Letter from Guido Pescari to Aubert, Rome, December 20, 1932; letter of December 30, 1933; and letter from Giobbe to Aubert, December 21 1934; all ASV, A.E.S., Pro Russia (quarto periodo), 1922–1937, pos. sc. 45, fasc. 265, ff. 44, 49, 52.

60. Derek Hastings, *Catholicism and the Roots of Nazism: Religious Identity and National Socialism* (Oxford: Oxford University Press, 2010).

61. Pacelli to Gasparri, May 1, 1924, ASV, Archivio della Nunziatura di Monaco, vol. 396, fasc. 7, f. 79, as cited in Hubert Wolf, *Pope and Devil: The Vatican's Archives and the Third Reich* (Cambridge, MA: Harvard University Press, 2010), 135.

62. "Il Partito di Hitler condannato dall'autorità ecclesiastica," *Osservatore Romano*, October 11, 1930.

63. Konrad Heiden, *A History of National Socialism*, vol. 2 (New York: Routledge, 2010 [1934]), chap. 7.

64. As testified by the Centrum representative in Rome, Baron Edmund von Frentz, in December 1931. Cited in Jutta Bohn, *Das Verhältnis zwischen katholischer Kirche und faschistischem Staat in Italien und die Rezeption in deutschen Zentrumskreisen (1922–1933)* (Frankfurt am Main: Peter Lang, 1992), 201.

65. See Cesare Orsenigo to Pacelli, December 29, 1930, ASV, A.E.S., Germania (quarto periodo), pos. 621, fasc. 138, ff. 19–20; and Pacelli's notes on his Udienze al Corpo Diplomatico, December 2, 1933, ASV, A.E.S., Stati Ecclesiastici (quarto periodo), 1933–1940, pos. 430b P.O., fasc. 360, f. 42.

66. Günter Neliba, *Wilhelm Frick: Der Legalist des Unrechtsstaates—Eine Biographie* (Paderborn: Schöningh, 1992), 57–62.

67. "La persecuzione in Spagna e la reazione della coscienza cattolica," *Bollettino ufficiale della Azione Cattolica Italiana* (November–December 1932): 384–386.

68. Enrico Rosa, "Vita Ecclesiae," *Studium* 8–9 (1934).

69. Letter from Muckermann, SJ, to Pacelli, Münster, April 29, 1931, ASV, Segr. Stato, 1931, rubr. 362, fasc. 3, ff. 197–199. For more on this perception of the Second Spanish Republic, see Paul Preston, *The Spanish Holocaust* (London: HarperCollins, 2008), 3–33.

70. Letter from Muckermann, SJ, to Pacelli, Münster, April 29, 1931.

71. See Stadtarchiv Mönchengladbach, Algermissen Papers, no. 15/7/5. As cited in Todd Weir, "The Christian Front against Godlessness: Anti-Secularism and the Demise of the Weimar Republic, 1928–1933," *Past and Present* 229 (November 2015): 14.

72. Letter from Bishop Wilhem Berning to Nunzio Orsenigo, Osnabrück, January 5, 1932, ASV, A.E.S., Pro Russia (quarto periodo), 1924–1935, pos. Scatola 4, fasc. 27, f. 60.

73. Pacelli's audience with Pius XI of March 27, 1933, reporting on a recent meeting with Groenesteyn. ASV, A.E.S., Stati Ecclesiastici (quarto periodo), pos. 430, fasc. 359, f. 82, as cited in Wolf, *Pope and Devil*, 164–165.

74. Pacelli audience with Prince Albrecht of Bavaria, March 28, 1933, ASV, A.E.S., Stati Ecclesiastici (quarto periodo), pos. 430, fasc. 359, ff. 82–83.

75. As cited in Frank McDonough, *Hitler and the Rise of the Nazi Party* (New York: Taylor and Francis, 2012), 99.

76. Letter of Pizzardo sending Orsenigo's report to Pro Russia Commission, Vatican, February 2, 1933, "Registri-Lettere in arrivo," ASV, A.E.S., Pro Russia (quarto periodo), 1930–1940, pos. Scatola 43, fasc. 248, f. 57.

77. Letter of Pacelli to Orsenigo and Vassallo di Torregrossa of February 20, 1933, as referenced in the letter of Pacelli to Sbarretti, Vatican, March 29, 1933, ACDF, R.V. 1933, n. 15, f. 1.

78. Letter of Cardinal Faulhaber to Torregrossa, Munich, March 5, 1933, ACDF, R.V. 1933, n. 15, ff. 41–42.

79. Letter of Orsenigo to Pacelli, Berlin, March 7, 1933, ACDF, R.V. 1933, n. 15, ff. 3–4.

80. Audience of March 4, 1933, ASV, A.E.S., Stati Ecclesiastici, quarto period, pos. 430, fasc. 359, fol. 66, as cited in Wolf, *Pope and Devil*, 158.

81. *Encyclopedia of the Third Reich*, ed. Christian Zentner and Friedemann Bedürftig (New York: Da Capo Press, 1997), 237.

82. Audience of March 4, 1933, ASV, A.E.S., Stati Ecclesiastici, quarto period, pos. 430a, fasc. 348, f. 3, as reprinted in Ludwig Volk, *Das Reichskonkordat vom 20. Juli 1933* (Mainz: Matthias-Grünewald-Verlag, 1972), 65, note 24.

83. Charles-Roux to Paul-Boncour, dated March 7, 1933, as reprinted in Volk, *Das Reichskonkordat*, note 25.

84. Faulhaber to the Bavarian episcopate, March 24, 1933, in Bernhard Stasiewski, ed., *Akten deutscher Bischöfe über die Lage der Kirche, 1933–1945*, vol. 1, *1933–1934* (Mainz: Matthias Grünewald-Verlag, 1968), 16–18.

85. Faulhaber's memorandum, undated [mid-March 1933], ASV, A.E.S., Germania (quarto periodo), pos. 643, fasc. 159, ff. 119–121, as cited in Wolf, *Pope and Devil*, 165.

86. Hitler's declaration upon introducing the Enabling Act in Parliament on March 23, 1933, as reprinted in Hubert Gruber, *Katholische Kirche und Nationalsozialismus, 1930–1945: Ein Bericht in Quellen* (Paderborn: Schöningh, 2006), 34.

87. For more on this episode, see Eugene Jones, "Franz von Papen, Catholic Conservatives, and the Establishment of the Third Reich, 1933–1934," *Journal of Modern History* 83 (June 2011): 272–318.

88. Memorandum 6781 from Apostolic Nuncio to Germany Cesare Orsenigo, Berlin, March 26, 1933, to Eugenio Cardinal Pacelli, Secretary of State, Rome, A.E.S., Germania, 1933–1945, "Episcopacy and National Socialism," pos. 621, fasc. 139, RG 76.001M: Selected Records from the Vatican Archives, 1865–1939, United States Holocaust Memorial Museum, Washington, DC, quoted in Suzanne Brown-Fleming, "'May Your Holiness Act in the Interest of Protecting Those Who Remain Morally Thinking People': Vatican Responses to Antisemitism, 1933," Search and Research Lectures and Papers, International Institute for Holocaust Research, Yad Vashem: World Holocaust Remembrance Center, 2017.

89. Audience with Pacelli of March 25, 1933, ASV, A.E.S., Stati Ecclesiastici (quarto periodo), pos. 430a, fasc. 348, f. 15, as cited in Wolf, *Pope and Devil*, 165.

90. The announcement by the German bishops about their stance toward National Socialism, dated March 28, 1933, can be found in Gruber, *Katholische Kirche und Nationalsozialismus*, 39.

91. April 1, 1933, Udienza Pacelli with Ratti, ASV, A.E.S., Stati Ecclesiastici, 1930–1938, pos. 430a P.O., fasc. 348, ff. 21f.

92. Orsenigo to Pacelli, April 8, 1933, ASV, A.E.S., Germania (quarto periodo), pos. 645, fasc. 162, ff. 13–14; Orsenigo to Pacelli, December 8, 1930, ASV, A.E.S., Germania (quarto periodo), pos. 621, fasc. 138, ff. 19–20; Pacelli's audience with Pius XI of March 27, 1933, reporting on a recent meeting with Groenesteyn, ASV, A.E.S., Germania (quarto periodo), pos. 430, fasc. 359, f. 82.

93. Cardinal Sincero's views on D'Herbigny, as reported by Pizzardo, Rome, October 19, 1931, ACS, MI, DGPS, DPP, Fascicoli personali, ser. B, b. 19, fasc. "Pizzardo monsignore," f. 102.

94. Ledóchowski to Pius XI, Rome, December 5, 1931, and letter of Ledóchowski to Ottaviani, Rome, March 29, 1934, both ARSI, Registro-Epistolae ad Romanam Curiam, 1930–1934, ff. 117, 410.

95. D'Herbigny, preparatory notes, and "Ex audientia Ssmi" notes, May 8, 1931, ASV, A.E.S., Pro Russia (quarto periodo), 1924–1935, pos. Scatola 4, fasc. 27, f. 28.

96. AAS, 26:139 (1934), as cited by Ledóchowski, "On the Need of Vigorously Opposing Modern Atheism: A Letter Addressed to the Whole Society," Rome, April 27, 1934, in Selected Writings of Father Ledóchowski (Chicago: American Assistancy of the Society of Jesus, 1945), 601–606.

97. AACI, "Relazione documentata confidenziale riservata alla persona di S.E. Rev.ma il signor Cardinale Luigi Lavitrano presidente della Commissione Cardinalizia per l'A.C.I.," Rome, August 12, 1942, PG XV, b. 2.

98. On the many services performed by Ledóchowski for the pope, see Giuliano Cassiani Ingoni, Padre Włodzimierzo Ledóchowski, XXVI Generale della Compagnia di Gesù, 1866–1942 (Rome: La Civiltà Cattolica, 1945), 108–123; and Giorgio Petracchi, "I gesuiti e il comunismo tra le due guerre," in La Chiesa cattolica e il totalitarismo, ed. Vincenzo Ferrone (Florence: L. S. Olschki, 2004), 123–124. On Ledóchowski's personality, see the contemporary reports of men who knew him well, including Ingoni, Padre Włodzimierzo Ledóchowski, 129–130; Friedrich Muckermann, Im Kampf zwischen zwei Epochen: Lebenserinnerungen (Mainz: Matthias-Grünewald, 1973), 635–636; ARSI, Ledóchowski 1025, fasc. "Testimonianze dagli Stati Uniti," sf. 335, Lord, Daniel, SJ St. Louis, September 29, 1943; and ARSI, Ledóchowski, 1025/8, fasc. 321, letter of Father Paul de Chastoney, SJ, Sondico, February 14, 1943.

99. The earliest planning document located is the letter of Joseph-Henri Ledit to Włodzimierz Ledóchowski, Rome (Pont. In. Orientalium Studiorum), January 8, 1933, ARSI, JESCOM 1038 (De comm. Atheo, 1933–1943), fasc. "Secretar. AntiCom. Rome."

100. As cited in Timothy H. Sherwood, The Preaching of Archbishop Fulton J. Sheen: The Gospel Meets the Cold War (Lanham, MD: Lexington Books, 2011), 56, n. 34.

101. Edmund Walsh, SJ, "The Catholic Church in Present-Day Russia," speech delivered at the American Historical Association annual meeting, Minneapolis, December 29, 1931, 1–38, stored in ARSI, Library, Comunismo Varia (I).

102. Ibid.

103. March 1935 note, ASV, A.E.S., Pro Russia (quarto periodo), sc. 38, fasc. 223, f. 61.

104. LdR 1, no. 6 (October 1935): 4, stored in JESCOM, the Private Library of Father Ledóchowski, LdR 1 (1935).

105. LdR 1, no. 1 (May 1935): 1.

106. Much of this had already been laid out in the planning documents. See, e.g., Ledóchowski to "The provincials of the American Assistancy and Canada: Directions to accompany letter on communism," Rome, April 17, 1934, ARSI, JESCOM 1038 (De comm. Atheo, 1933–1943), fasc. "Defensio contra Comm."

107. See *L'Osservatore Romano*, August 22, 1927.

108. D'Herbigny, preparatory notes, and "Ex audientia Ssmi" notes, May 8, 1931, ASV, A.E.S., Pro Russia (quarto periodo), 1924–1935, pos. Scatola 4, fasc. 27, f. 28.

109. "Parole lette dal compagno D. Achille Ratti durante la S. Messa cantata," in *Il corso del MDCCCLXXIX (Seminario di Milano) al Sacro Monte sopra Varese nel giorno VII giugno MCMIV dopo XXV anni di sacerdozio* (Milan: I Sacri Monti, 1904), 24.

110. Victoria De Grazia, *The Culture of Consent: Mass Organization of Leisure in Fascist Italy* (Cambridge: Cambridge University Press, 1981), 155.

111. According to article 6b of the Lateran Treaty, "Vatican City will build in its territory an autonomous radiotelegraphic and radiotelephonic station." According to article 6c, the Italian state would contribute 500,000 lire to the functioning of this station, while the remainder of the funds would be supplied by Vatican state itself.

112. Livia Bornigia, "Italian Broadcasting, Radio Vaticana and the Roman Catholic Church, 1910–1945" (PhD diss., University of Leicester, 2007), 115. The leading recent history of Vatican Radio is Raffaella Perin, *La radio del papa: Propaganda e diplomazia nella seconda guerra mondiale* (Milan: Il Mulino, 2017). Also see Marilyn J. Matelski, *Vatican Radio: Propagation by the Airwaves* (Westport, CT: Praeger, 1995).

113. Pope Pius XI, *Divini Illius Magistri* (December 31, 1929), §90. Available online at http://w2.vatican.va/content/pius-xi/en/encyclicals/documents /hf_p-xi_enc_31121929_divini-illius-magistri.html.

114. Bornigia, "Italian Broadcasting," 6.

115. Marconi's inaugural speech is quoted in Fernando Bea, *Qui Radio Vaticana: Mezzo secolo della radio del papa* (Vatican City: Edizioni radio vaticana, 1981), 44.

116. *L'Osservatore Romano*, February 12, 1931. For similar sentiments, see *L'Osservatore Romano*, February 14, 1931.

117. ASV, Segr Stato 1931, rubr. 1, fasc. 3.

118. Forges Davanzati, *La Tribuna*, February 14, 1931; *La Gazzetta Del Popolo*, February 14, 1931, as cited in Bea, *Qui Radio Vaticana*, 46, 51–52.

119. In 1935 the Ministry of Press and Propaganda forbade Italians to listen to any "foreign radio stations" other than Vatican Radio.

120. Bornigia, "Italian Broadcasting," 159.

121. Cesare Orsenigo to Pacelli, Berlin, January 29, 1933, ASV, A.E.S., SE4, 1932–1942, pos. 474 P.O., fasc. 477, ff. 3–5; Pacelli to Soccorsi, SJ, Vatican, April 24, 1936, ASV, A.E.S., SE4, 1936–1938, pos. 533 P.O., fasc. 556, f. 5; Circular 1478/36, from Pacelli, Vatican, April 30, 1936, ASV, A.E.S., SE4,

1936–1938, pos. 533 P.O., fasc. 556, ff. 29–30; and ACS, MI, DGPS, DPP, b. 44, fasc. C11/48 Germania Polizia.

122. De Grazia, *The Culture of Consent*, 155.

123. Letter from D'Herbigny to Monsieur Georges Goyau, Vatican, July 11, 1932, ASV, A.E.S. Pro Russia 1921–1944 (quarto periodo), pos. Scatola 37, fasc. 215, f. 73.

124. Letter from Reynold de Cressier to Bordeaux, Fribourg (Switzerland), January 19, 1933, ASV, A.E.S., Pro Russia (quarto periodo), pos. Scatola 37, fasc. 216, ff. 50–51.

125. Carlo Bo, "Letteratura come vita," *Il Frontespizio*, September 1938; Egidio Cabianca, "Ha ragione Bontempelli," *Studium* 7–8 (1933), as cited in Jorge Dagnino, *Faith and Fascism: Catholic Intellectuals in Italy, 1925–1943* (London: Palgrave Macmillan, 2017), 139.

126. Pope Pius XI, *Casti Connubii* (December 31, 1930), §45. Available online at https://w2.vatican.va/content/pius-xi/en/encyclicals/documents/hf_p-xi _enc_19301231_casti-connubii.html.

127. Letter from D'Herbigny to Monsieur Georges Goyau, Vatican, July 11, 1932, ASV, A.E.S., Pro Russia (quarto periodo), pos. Scatola 37, fasc. 215, f. 73.

128. Letter of Henri Bordeaux to Goyau, Paris, September 17, 1932, ASV, A.E.S., Pro Russia (quarto periodo), pos. Scatola 37, fasc. 216, f. 18. Goyau's many works include *L'Église libre dans l'Europe libre* (Paris: Perrin, 1920), *La pensée religieuse de Joseph de Maistre* (Paris: Perrin, 1921), *Orientations catholiques* (Paris: Perrin, 1925), and *Dieu chez les Soviets* (Paris: Flammarion, 1929). On Bordeaux's respect for Mussolini (whom he had personally met), see Archives de l'Académie Française, Paris (hereafter cited as AAF), Registre des procès-verbaux, December 27, 1934.

129. Undated business card-letter from Baudrillart to Goyau, AAF, Fonds Goyau, 7 AP 1, correspondance Mgr Baudrillart; and letter from Castelnau to Goyau, Paris, July 19, 1921, AAF, 7 AP 5, correspondance Gen. Castelnau.

130. Letter from D'Herbigny to Monsieur Georges Goyau, July 11, 1932, ASV, A.E.S., Pro Russia (quarto periodo), pos. Scatola 37, fasc. 215, f. 73; letter of d'Herbigny to Baudrillart, September 29, 1932, ASV, A.E.S., Pro Russia (quarto periodo), pos. Scatola 37, fasc. 216, f. 19.

131. D'Herbigny to Baudrillart, September 29, 1932.

132. Draft of letter from D'Herbigny to Goyau, eventually sent on August 26, 1932, ASV, A.E.S., Pro Russia (quarto periodo), pos. Scatola 37, fasc. 215, ff. 79–82. Emphasis in the original.

133. Letter of Henri Bordeaux to Georges Goyau (to be communicated to the pope), Paris, September 17, 1932, ASV, A.E.S., Pro Russia (quarto periodo), pos. Scatola 37, fasc. 216, f. 18.

134. Letter of d'Herbigny to Bordeaux (with copy to Goyau), Vatican, September 29, 1932, ASV, A.E.S., Pro Russia (quarto periodo), pos. Scatola 37, fasc. 216, ff. 24–28.

135. Susan Rubin Suleiman, *Authoritarian Fictions: The Ideological Novel as a Literary Genre* (Princeton, NJ: Princeton University Press, 1992).

136. Letter from Baudrillart to d'Herbigny, Paris, March 27, 1936, ASV, A.E.S., Pro Russia (quarto periodo), pos. Scatola 37, fasc. 216, f. 72.

137. Baudrillart, "Concours de Romans sur le Bolchevisme," Paris, March 21, 1934, ASV, A.E.S., Pro Russia (quarto periodo), pos. Scatola 37, fasc. 216, f. 81

138. Letter from Baudrillart to d'Herbigny, Paris, March 27, 1936, ASV, A.E.S., Pro Russia (quarto periodo), pos. Scatola 37, fasc. 216, f. 72.

139. The novel was eventually published in Germany. Alja Rachmanova, *Die Fabrik der Neuen Menchen* (Berlin: Deutsche Buchgemeinschaft, 1937).

140. Ibid., 62.

141. Bordeaux, "Rapport du concours de romans sur le bolchévisme organisé par l'Académie d'Education et d'Entr'aide sociales," Paris, November 28, 1935, ASV, A.E.S., Pro Russia (quarto periodo), pos. Scatola 37, fasc. 217, ff. 9–17.

142. Letter from d'Herbigny to Baudrillart, Rome, February 14, 1936, ASV, A.E.S., Pro Russia (quarto periodo), pos. Scatola 37, fasc. 217, f. 6.

143. Erik von Kühnelk-Leddhin, *Jesuiten, Spiesser, Bolschewicken* (Salzburg: Salzburg Pustet, 1933).

144. Ibid., 81.

145. John LaFarge, "Christian Front to Combat Communism," *America* 55 (September 5, 1936): 108–110; LaFarge, *Communism and the Catholic Answer* (New York: America Press, 1936).

146. Johannes Schwarte, *Gustav Gundlach, SJ (1892–1963): Massgeblicher Repräsentant der katholischen Soziallehre während der Pontifikate Pius' XI und Pius' XII* (Munich: F. Schöningh, 1975), 29–32.

147. Letter of Cardinal Faulhaber to Torregrossa, Munich, March 5, 1933, ACDF, R.V. 1933, n. 15, ff. 41–42.

148. "Nos Lettres se spécialisent de plus en plus dans l'étude du communisme, laissant de côté les athées d'autres tendances." In "Pour la paix, ou pour la . . . 'lutte finale'?," *LdR* 1, no. 7 (November 1935): 1.

149. *LdR* 1, no. 1 (May 1935): 14–15.

150. Ross Hoffman, *Rome Diary,* August 7, 1936. As cited in Patrick Allitt, *Catholic Converts: British and American Intellectuals Turn to Rome* (Ithaca, NY: Cornell University Press, 2000), 222.

151. Ledóchowski, "On Furthering the Fight against Atheism: A Letter Addressed to the Whole Society," June 19, 1936, in *Selected Writings of Father Ledóchowski,* 608–614.

152. ARSI, JESCOM 1038, DcA, fasc. SAR.

153. P. Tacchi Venturi to A. Bocchini, December 10, 1934, ACS, Polizia di stato, A1, 1937, b. 37, fasc. "Ledit."

154. As cited in Father Ledit's obituary of Ledóchowski, written between December 14, 1942, and January 31, 1943, ARSI, JESCOM, Ledochówski, "Varia ad eius Vitam," n. 1025 / 355.

155. Ibid.

156. Pope Pius XI, *Vigilanti Cura* (June 29, 1936). Available online at http://w2 .vatican.va/content/pius-xi/en/encyclicals/documents/hf_p-xi_enc_29061936 _vigilanti-cura.html.

CHAPTER 6 ▪ CATHOLIC ANTI-FASCISM, SILENCED

Epigraph: Yves Simon to Jacques Maritain, June 12, 1940, as cited by John Hellman, "The Anti-Democratic Impulse in Catholicism: Jacques Maritain, Yves Simon, and Charles de Gaulle during World War II," *Journal of Church and State* 33, no. 3 (Summer 1991): 453–471, at 457 and 459.

1. Pope Pius XI, *Rappresentanti in Terra* (December 31, 1929), as reprinted and translated in *Catholic Educational Review* 28 (March 1930): 129–164.
2. Letter of Pius XI to Cardinal Schuster, as reprinted in the *Osservatore Romano*, April 26, 1931.
3. Pope Pius XI, *Non Abbiamo Bisogno* (June 29, 1931). Available at https://w2 .vatican.va/content/pius-xi/en/encyclicals/documents/hf_p-xi_enc _29061931_non-abbiamo-bisogno.html.
4. See *La Civiltà Cattolica* 3 (1931): 115–117.
5. Pacelli's Udienza with Pius XI, August 19, 1931, ASV, A.E.S., *Stati Ecclesiastici*, 1930–1938, pos. 430a P.O., fasc. 343, f. 49.
6. Pacelli's audience with Pius XI of July 6, 1931, ASV, A.E.S., *Stati Ecclesiastici*, 1930–1938, pos. 430a P.O., fasc. 343, f. 3.
7. Suzanne Brown-Fleming, "Love Thy Neighbor? Catholic Responses to the First Anti-Jewish Laws," unpublished paper, Fifth Annual Summer Workshop for Holocaust Scholars, Yad Vashem, Jerusalem, July 9–12, 2012.
8. Carl Schmitt, "Die Wendung zum Totalen Staat," *Europäische Revue* 7 (1931): 241–250. Gustav Gundlach, "Zur Arbeitsdienstpflicht," *Stimmen der Zeit* 124 (1932–1933): 56–59.
9. Letter from Father Anton Scharnagl, Munich, to Eugenio Cardinal Pacelli, Secretary of State, Rome, April 18, 1933, ASV, A.E.S., Germania 1933–1945, Hitler's Chancellery 1933–1945, pos. 643, fasc. 157, RG 76.001M: Selected Records from the Vatican Archives, 1865–1939, United States Holocaust Memorial Museum, Washington, DC. As cited in Brown-Fleming, "Love Thy Neighbor?" On Italy, see Emilio Gentile, "New Idols: Catholicism in the Face of Fascist Totalitarianism," *Journal of Modern Italian Studies* 11, no. 2 (2006): 143–170; and Jan Nelis, "The Clerical Response to a Totalitarian Political Religion: *La Civiltà Cattolica* and Italian Fascism," *Journal of Contemporary History* 46, no. 2 (April 2011): 245–270.
10. Canonical proceedings against German theologians expressing their support for the theory of the Nazi "total state," such as Karl Eschweiler and Hans Barion, seemed to signal that Catholic anti-totalitarianism was here to stay, as did the condemnation of the leading Fascist theorist of the "total state," Giovanni Gentile. See Robert Krieg, *Catholic Theologians in Nazi Germany* (New York: Continuum, 2004), 50; Elena Cavalcanti, "Appunti sull'ecclesiologia tra il 1924 e il 1939," in *Cattolici e fascisti in Umbria, 1922–1945*, ed. Alberto Monticone (Bologna: Il Mulino, 1978), 168–169; Gabriele Turi, *Giovanni Gentile: Una biografia* (Florence: Giunti, 1995); and Guido Verucci, *Idealisti all'indice: Croce, Gentile e la condanna del Sant'Uffizio* (Rome: Laterza, 2006).

11. "Voto del P. Gillet, Consultore," in "Nazionalismo, razzismo, stato totalitario," Suprema Sacra Congregazione del S. Offizio, April 1936, pp. 1–3, ACDF, S.O., Rerum Variarum 1934, n. 29, f. 4.

12. Letter of Alois Hudal to Domenico Sbarretti, October 7, 1934, in "Nazionalismo, razzismo, stato totalitario," Suprema Sacra Congregazione del S. Offizio, April 1936, pp. 1–3, ACDF, S.O., Rerum Variarum 1934, n. 29, f. 3.

13. May 1, 1935, draft, as stored in "Elenchus Propositionum de Nationalismo, Stirpis cultu, Totalismo," ACDF, S.O., Rerum Variarum 1934, n. 29.

14. "Voto" of March 17, 1935, as stored in "Elenchus Propositionum de Nationalismo, Stirpis cultu, Totalismo," ACDF, S.O., Rerum Variarum 1934, n. 29.

15. May 1, 1935, draft.

16. "Voto" of March 17, 1935.

17. For more on how the papacy celebrated this definition of rights, see Dan Edelstein, On the Spirit of Rights (Chicago: University of Chicago Press, 2018), conclusion.

18. Hewing close to Catholic tradition, the Syllabus explicitly refrained from condemning Nazi-Fascism for its violation of the right of religious freedom—a right that, after all, popes had long condemned as "insane" whenever they saw it mentioned. As will be explored in subsequent chapters, this position, like so many others, would change only in the 1960s, under the influence of Catholic dissidents.

19. May 1, 1935, draft, in "Nazionalismo, razzismo, stato totalitario," Suprema Sacra Congregazione del S. Offizio, April 1936, pp. 1–3, ACDF, S.O., Rerum Variarum 1934, n. 29, f. 3.

20. "Le decisioni del settimo Congresso mondiale dell'Internazionale comunista," sent to Pius XI on November 13, 1935, ASV, A.E.S. Pro Russia (quarto periodo), 1921–1944, sc. 37, fasc. 218, ff. 62–63.

21. LdR 1, no. 6 (Oct 1935): 1. Stored in JESCOM, the Private Library of Father Ledóchowski, Lettres de Rome, vol.1 (1935).

22. Guido Gonella, "L'attività sovversiva dell'Internazionale comunista," Osservatore Romano, August 23, 1935.

23. Paul Preston, The Spanish Civil War: Reaction, Revolution, and Revenge (London: Routledge, 2007 [1986]), 82.

24. "Intervención comunista en los asuntos de España," addendum to report "Avances y estado actual del comunismo en España," March 28, 1936, ASV, A.E.S., Stati Ecclesiastici (quarto periodo) 1932–1942, pos. 474 P.O., fasc. 481, ff. 110–111, p. 60, re: 967 circular.

25. ARSI, Ledóchowski, b. 1008, fasc. 1013, f. 319.

26. Ledit, "Documenta," June 1935, ARSI, JESCOM, the Private Library of Father Ledóchowski, Lettres de Rome, vol. 1 (1935), 4.

27. Pacelli circular of February 20, 1936, ASV, A.E.S., Stati Ecclesiastici, 1932–1942, pos. 474 P.O., fasc. 480, ff. 15–16.

28. Hugh Thomas, The Spanish Civil War (New York: Modern Library, 1961), 93.

29. As cited in Preston, The Spanish Civil War, 217.

30. See, e.g., Cardinal Gomá, *Un cardenal español y los católicos vascos: La consciencia Cristiana ante la Guerra de la Península Ibérica* (Bilbao: Minerva, 1937), and his *Le problème basque* (Paris: B. Grasset, 1938).

31. "Nota d'archivio circa la venuta di una commissione di baschi," undated and unsigned, ASV, Arch Nunz Parigi (quarto periodo), b. 609, fasc. 849, f. 21.

32. ASV, A.E.S., Stati Ecclesiastici (quarto periodo), 1935, pos. 530 P.O., fasc. 552, f. 57.

33. *La Croix*, April 15, 1936, Pacelli's letter to the Assembly, bearing the same date, is also reprinted in *La Documentation catholique*, June 13, 1936, bk. 35, cols. 1478–1479. See *Lettres de Rome* (May 1936): 111–112.

34. Paul Christophe, *1936: Les catholiques et le Front populaire* (Paris: Les éditions ouvrières, 1986), 43.

35. Marc Sherer, *Catholics and Communists* (Paris: Cerf, 1936), as quoted in "Section de Jeunesse de l'U.I.L.F.C.," May 15, 1937, ASV, A.E.S., Stati Ecclesiastici (quarto periodo), 1936–1937, pos. 535 P.O., fasc. 558, ff. 78–79.

36. Ledóchowski to Pius XI, April 1, 1936, and Ledóchowski to Pius XI, February 24, 1937, ASV, A.E.S., Stati Ecclesiastici, pos. 548, fasc. 577, f. *Enciclica Divini Redemptoris*.

37. Maurice Thorez, spring 1936, as quoted in Jean Grandmougin, *Histoire vivante du Front populaire, 1934–1939* (Paris: Albin Michel, 1966), 164–166. On Catholic responses to the *main tendue*, see John Hellman, "Vichy Background: Political Alternatives for French Catholics in the Nineteen-Thirties," *Journal of Modern History* 49, no. (March 1977): D1111–D1144.

38. Marcel Dupont, "Réflexions sur les grèves," *Terre Nouvelle* (July 1936), as cited in Daniel L. Lewis, "Emmanuel Mounier and the Politics of Moral Revolution: Aspects of Political Crises in French Liberal Catholicism, 1935–1938," *Catholic Historical Review* 56, no. 2 (July 1970): 266–290, at 285.

39. Pius XI's speech is reprinted in "Il più grande pericolo," *Bollettino Ufficiale dell'Azione Cattolica* (June 1936): 21.

40. Pius XI, "Per l'inaugurazione dell'esposizione mondiale della stampa cattolica," speech of May 12, 1936, Rome, in *Discorsi di Pio XI*, ed. Domenico Bertetto (Vatican City: Libreria Editrice Vaticana, 1985), 3:487–488. Emphasis mine.

41. *Osservatore Romano*, June 3, 1936.

42. ARSI, JESCOM 1038 (De comm. Atheo, 1933–1943), fasc. "Communismus: S.D.A. Conventus Romae habitus 10–12/5/1936."

43. "Voto del P. Gillet, Consultore," in "Nazionalismo, razzismo, stato totalitario," April 1936, pp. 1–3, ACDF, S.O., Rerum Variarum 1934, n. 29, f. 4; and "Voto del Mons. Tardini, Consultore," in "Nazionalismo, razzismo, stato totalitario," April 20, 1936, pp. 6–11, ACDF, S.O., Rerum Variarum 1934, n. 29, f. 4.

44. Pierre Lucius, *Révolutions du XXème siècle* (Paris: Payot,1934), 85; Jacques de Broze, "Essai sur la notion d'état," *Revue du XXème siècle* 2 (1935):15–23, 180–191. As cited in James Chappel, "The Catholic Origins of Totalitarianism Theory," *Modern Intellectual History* 8, no. 3 (2011): 561–590, at 583.

45. Joseph Ledit, "Nota d'Ufficio," in "Nazionalismo, razzismo, stato totalitario," Suprema Sacra Congregazione del S. Offizio, July 1936, pp. 1–7, ACDF, S.O., Rerum Variarum 1934, n. 29, f. 9.

46. Preston, *The Spanish Civil War*, 89.

47. By the end of the civil war in 1939, about 6,000 Spanish clergy had been killed. See Maria Thomas, "Disputing the Public Sphere: Anticlerical Violence, Conflict, and the Sacred Heart of Jesus, April 1931—July 1936," *Cuadernos de Historia Contemporánea* 33 (2011): 49–69; and Antonio Montero Moreno, *Historia de la persecución religiosa en España, 1936–1939* (Madrid: Biblioteca de Autores Cristianos, 1961).

48. C.V. (Cesco Vian), "La nostra responsabilità," *Azione fucina*, July 26, 1936.

49. "Minaccia e realtà," *Bollettino Ufficiale dell'Azione Cattolica* (August 1936): 169–171.

50. "Intervención comunista en los asuntos de España," addendum to report "Avances y estado actual del comunismo en España," March 28, 1936, ASV, A.E.S., Stati Ecclesiastici (quarto periodo) 1932–1942, pos. 474 P.O., fasc. 481, ff. 110–111, p. 60, re: 967 circular.

51. To the Spanish Embassy at the Holy See, July 31, 1936, ASV, A.E.S. Spagna (quarto periodo) 1936–1939, pos. 895 P.O., fasc. 285, f. 9.

52. "La Santa Sede e la situazione religiosa in Spagna," *Osservatore Romano*, August 10–11, 1936. The article was written by Eugenio Pacelli and rubber-stamped by Pius XI.

53. Stanley Payne, *Spanish Catholicism: An Historical Overview* (Madison: University of Wisconsin Press, 1984), 172.

54. As cited in Emilio Silva and Santiago Macías, *Las fosas de Franco: Los republicanos que el dictador dejó en las cunetas* (Madrid: Temas de Hoy, 2003), 131.

55. Emilio Mola speech, as reprinted in Fernando Díaz-Plaja, *La guerra de España en sus documentos: El siglo XX. La Guerra (1936–9)* (Madrid: Faro, 1963), 189–191.

56. Hilari M. Raguer, *Gunpowder and Incense: The Catholic Church and the Spanish Civil War* (London: Routledge, 2012), 49.

57. Ledóchowski text of Vatican Radio broadcast, sent to Pius XI, Rome, August 26, 1936, ARSI, Registro—Epistolae, Apud Curiae Romanae, 1935–1937, f. 252.

58. Cardinal Isidro Gomá, *Iglesia, Estado y Movimiento Nacional* (Madrid: Edic. del Movimiento, 1963), 21–23.

59. Father P. J. Mendendez-Reigada, OP, "La guerra nacional Española ante la moral y el derecho," *La Ciencia Tomista* 56 (1937): 40–57.

60. The first to use the term "crusade" was Bishop Pla y Deniel, in a pastoral letter of late September 1936 entitled "Las dos ciudades." The next famous usage of the term was by Cardinal Gomá, in his pastoral letter "El caso de España," of November 1936. For Bishop Pla y Deniel's pastoral, see Moreno, *Historia de la persecución*, 688–708; for Gomá's, see *Por Dios y por España: Pastorales, instrucciones, y articulos* (Barcelona: R. Casulleras, 1940), 17–39.

61. Norman B. Cooper, *Catholicism and the Franco Regime* (Beverly Hills, CA: Sage, 1975), 11.

62. Dal Superiore Generale dei Teatrini, September 11, 1936, ASV, A.E.S., Spagna (quarto periodo) 1936–1939, pos. 895 PO, fasc. 285, f. 51.

63. Henri Massis and Robert Brasillach, *The Cadets of the Alcazar* (New York: Paulist Press, 1937), 61, as cited in James Chappel, *Catholic Modern: The Challenge of Totalitarianism and the Remaking of the Church* (Cambridge, MA: Harvard University Press, 2018), 100.

64. Dal Superiore Generale dei Teatrini, September 11, 1936.

65. Georges Bidault, "Le martyre de Guernica," *L'Aube* (April 30–May 1, 1937): 1; editorial, "Croisades," *Sept* (September 18, 1936): 1; General de Castelnau, "L'année nouvelle," *France Catholique,* December 12, 1936, 1.

66. *Osservatore Romano*, January 8, 1937.

67. Alfred Ancel, *La philosophie religieuse du parti communiste: Dogme et morale communistes* (Paris: [n.p.], 1936); *The Pope on the Spanish Terror* (London: Catholic Truth Society, 1936); Cardinal Gomá, *The Martyrdom of Spain* (Dublin: J. Duffy for the Irish Christian Front, 1936).

68. Arnd Bauerkämper, "Transnational Fascism: Cross-Border Relations between Regimes and Movements in Europe, 1922–1939," *East Central Europe* 37 (2010): 214–246, esp. 230–233; Philip Morgan, *Fascism in Europe, 1919–1945* (London: Routledge, 2007), 167ff; Roger Griffin, "Europe for the Europeans: Fascist Myths of the European New Order," in *A Fascist Century*, ed. Matthew Feldman (London: Palgrave Macmillan, 2008), 132–180, at 150.

69. Catholic periodicals that argued that the Spanish Civil War was part of the Soviet plot for global revolution included *America, Catholic Action, Catholic Mind, Catholic Digest, Catholic World, Columbia, Commonweal,* and *Sign*. For an overview of the American Catholic response to the Spanish Civil War, see Michael E. Chapman, *Arguing Americanism: Franco Lobbyists, Roosevelt's Foreign Policy and the Spanish Civil War* (Kent, OH: Kent State University Press, 2011), 1–35, 156–184; and George Q. Flynn, *Roosevelt and Romanism: Catholics and American Diplomacy, 1937–1945* (Westport, CT: Greenwood Press, 1976), 33–52.

70. Norman Thomas, interview, May 14, 1938, Columbia University Oral History Project, as cited in Flynn, *Roosevelt and Romanism,* 43.

71. Julián Casanova, *The Spanish Republic and Civil War* (Cambridge: Cambridge University Press, 2010), 225.

72. Ottaviani's notes from his November 19, 1936, audience with the pope, ACDF, ACTA C.G. 1936.

73. Concha Herrera Murube of the Falange's *Sección Femenina*, in a letter to the Italian Fascist Party Secretary, October 30, 1936, ACS, Ministero della Cultura Popolare (hereafter cited as MCP), Direzione Generale Pubblica Sicurezza, box 204. As cited in Toni Morant I Ariño, "Spanish Fascist Women's Transnational Relations during the Second World War: Between Ideology and Realpolitik," *Journal of Contemporary History* (forthcoming).

74. "Dilata post publicatoinem Enciclicae quae est in praeparatione," March 17, 1937, ACDF, ACTA C.G. 1937.

75. Hubert Wolf, *Pope and Devil: The Vatican's Archives and the Third Reich*, trans. Kenneth Kronenberg (Cambridge, MA: Harvard University Press, 2010), 265.

76. The point is also made by Peter Godman, *Hitler and the Vatican: Inside the Secret Archives That Reveal the New Story of the Nazis and the Church* (New York: Free Press, 2004), 146.

77. In *Mit brennender Sorge*, there was no mention of terms like "battle," "fight," and "armed"—which, by contrast, played a leading role *Divini Redemptoris*. The word "blood" appeared twice, but in both cases the context was a mention of Nazi "myths of race and blood." In other words, there were no references to blood spilt in the context of battle.

78. Frank J. Coppa, *The Papacy, the Jews and the Holocaust* (Washington, DC: Catholic University of America, 2011), 163.

79. Pius XI, *Mit brennender Sorge* (March 14, 1937), §§3, 5, 8, 10, 13, 19, 22, 29, 30, 31. Available at http://w2.vatican.va/content/pius-xi/en/encyclicals /documents/hf_p-xi_enc_14031937_mit-brennender-sorge.html.

80. Pius XI, *Divini Redemptoris* (March 19, 1937), §§5, 7, 9, 11. Available at https://w2.vatican.va/content/pius-xi/en/encyclicals/documents/hf_p-xi _enc_19370319_divini-redemptoris.html.

81. "De Communismo," in "Nazionalismo, razzismo, stato totalitario," Suprema Sacra Congregazione del S. Offizio, March 1937, pp. 13–22, ACDF, S.O., Rerum Variarum 1934, n. 29, f. 16.

82. *Divini Redemptoris*, §§10, 11, 27–28, 30, 50.

83. Ibid., §§17, 20, 22, 27–28, 33, 35–36, 46, 50.

84. Ibid., §§2, 15, 17, 19, 22, 55, 57, 66.

85. Ibid., §§73, 77–79.

86. Ibid., §64.

87. Renata Keller, *Mexico's Cold War: Cuba, the United States, and the Legacy of the Mexican Revolution* (Cambridge: Cambridge University Press, 2017), 35. Also see Barry Carr, *Marxism and Communism in Twentieth-Century Mexico* (Lincoln: University of Nebraska Press, 1992), 16–31.

88. See David Raby, "La 'Educación socialista' en México," *Cuadernos Políticos* 29 (1981): 75–82. Regarding resource nationalization, by 1938 Cárdenas's project had resulted in the expropriation and redistribution of more than six million acres of U.S.-owned property in Mexico, and the nationalization of Mexico's petroleum sector. See John J. Dwyer, *The Agrarian Dispute: The Expropriation of American-Owned Rural Land in Postrevolutionary Mexico* (Durham, NC: Duke University Press, 2008); and Jonathan C. Brown, *Oil and Revolution in Mexico* (Berkeley: University of California Press, 1993). On transatlantic opposition to Cárdenas, see Brígida von Mentz, Verena Radkau, Daniela Spenser, and Ricardo Pérez Montfort, *Los empresarios alemanes, el Tercer Reich y la oposición de derecho a Cárdenas* (Mexico: Ediciones de la Casa Chata, 1988).

89. Father Alba, "Pro Memoria," March 1936, underlining in the original, ARSI, Registro-Allegata, Epistolae ad Romanam Curiam, nn. 1–100, 1934–1938, ff. 303–312.

90. David Green, *The Containment of Latin America: A History of the Myths and Realities of the Good Neighbor Policy* (Chicago: Quadrangle, 1971); Fredrick B. Pike, *FDR's Good Neighbor Policy: Sixty Years of Generally Gentle Chaos* (Austin: University of Texas Press, 1995); and Greg Grandin, *Empire's Workshop: Latin America, the United States, and the Rise of the New Imperialism* (New York: Metropolitan Books, 2006).

91. November 6, 1936, memorandum for Pacelli, signed by Gerardo, Busto, Castiello, and Pablo Arámburu, ASV, A.E.S., Messico (quarto periodo), 1936, pos. 590, fasc. 388, f. 32.

92. Letter to Pacelli from Gerardo, Bishop of Chiapas, New York, November 8, 1936, underlining, most likely by Pacelli, in the original, ASV, A.E.S., Messico (quarto periodo), 1936, pos. 590, fasc. 388, ff. 17–20.

93. Jean Meyer, *De una revolución a la otra: México en la historia* (Mexico City: El Colegio de México, Centro de Estudios Históricos, 2013), 503–505.

94. Letter from Ledóchowski to Pizzardo, March 9, 1937, ASV, A.E.S., Messico (quarto periodo), pos. 591, fasc. 388, ff. 62–63, as cited in Stephen J. C. Andes, *The Vatican and Catholic Activism in Mexico and Chile: The Politics of Transnational Catholicism, 1920–1940* (Oxford: Oxford University Press, 2014), 172.

95. Pius XI, *Firmissimam Constantiam* (March 28, 1937), §26–27. Available at http://w2.vatican.va/content/pius-xi/en/encyclicals/documents/hf_p-xi _enc_19370328_firmissimam-constantiam.html.

96. ASV, A.E.S. Messico (quarto periodo), 1937, pos. 591 P.O., fasc. 388, f. 58.

97. Enrico De Rosa, "L'Enclica sul Messico e l'opera della restaurazione sociale," *Civiltà cattolica*, May 19.

98. Letter from Archbishop Ruíz to Pizzardo, San Antonio, Texas, April 24, 1937, ASV, A.E.S., Messico (quarto periodo), 1937, pos. 591 P.O., fasc. 389, f. 3.

99. Letter of Amleto Cicognani, U.S. Nunzio, to Pizzardo, March 29–30, 1937, ASV, A.E.S. Messico (quarto periodo), 1937, pos. 591 P.O., fasc. 389, ff. 89–90.

100. Ledit, March 9, 1938, *De Secretariatu Defensionis Contra Communismum Atheisticum* (Rome: Typis Pontificiae Universitatis Gregorianae, 1938); Jonathan P. Herzog, *The Spiritual-Industrial Complex: America's Religious Battle against Communism in the Early Cold War* (Oxford: Oxford University Press, 2014), 56.

101. Letter, Ledóchowski to Tardini, Rome, January 11, 1939, ARSI, Registro-Epistolae ad Romanam Curiam, 1938–1945, f. 43.

102. Herzog, *The Spiritual-Industrial Complex*, 56–59.

103. As cited in Peter McDonough, *Men Astutely Trained: A History of the Jesuits in the American Century* (New York: Free Press, 1992), 69.

104. Catholic anticommunists in the United States also promptly integrated the Vatican's new version of anti-totalitarianism. Thus, for instance, in a 1937 convention focusing on the ills of communism, Archbishop McNicholas of Cleveland, Ohio, informed his audience of more than 10,000 that communism usurped freedom and replaced it with "national totalitarianism." David J. Endres, *American Crusade: Catholic Youth in the World Mission Movement* (Eugene, OR: Pickwick, 2010), 101.

105. "Words, too," is a direct quote from Reinhart Koselleck, "Einleitung," in *Geschichtliche Grundbegriffe* (Stuttgart: Klett-Cotta, 1992), 1: xiii–xxviii.
106. Dominic Tierney, *FDR and the Spanish Civil War: Neutrality and Commitment in the Struggle That Divided America* (Durham, NC: Duke University Press, 2007), 75–135.
107. "U.S. People & Freedom. The New York Group," *People & Freedom* 63 (1944): 4.

CHAPTER 7 ▪ THE WAR FOR THE SOUL OF CATHOLICISM

Epigraph: Jean Grenier, *Essai sur l'esprit d'orthodoxie* (Paris: Gallimard, 1938), 13–16.
1. Members of this movement included Luigi Sturzo, Emmanuel Mounier, Jean Grenier, Yves Simon, Paul Vignaux, Alfredo Mendizábal, Joan B. Roca i Caball, Gallegos Rocafull, Alberto Onaindía, Ricardo Marín, and Jean Tarragó (better known by his pseudonym Victor Montserrat). Many of them read and wrote for periodicals like *Abendland, Hochland, Germania, La cité chrétienne, Politique, Temps Présent, l'Aube,* and *Bulletin Catholique International.*
2. For a general discussion, see Gerd-Rainer Horn, *Western European Liberation Theology: The First Wave (1924–1959)* (Oxford: Oxford University Press, 2008); and Gerd-Rainer Horn and Emmanuel Gerard, eds., *Left Catholicism: Catholics and Society in Western Europe at the Point of Liberation* (Leuven: Leuven University Press, 2001). On the Spanish side of the story, see Daniel Arasa, *Católicos del bando rojo* (Barcelona: Styria, DL, 2009); *La guerra española y los católicos* (Buenos Aires: Publicaciones de Patronato Hispano-Argentino de Cultura, 1942); and Luisa Marco Sola, "El factor Cristiano: Católicos y sacerdotes antifranquistas en los medios republicanos," *El Argonauta Español* 7 (2010). On French Catholics, see Lucio Pala, *I cattolici francesi e la Guerra di Spagna* (Urbino: Argalìa, 1974); David Wingeate Pike, *Les français et la guerre d'Espagne (1936–1939)* (Paris: Presses universitaires de France, 1975); and Herbert R. Southworth, *Guernica! Guernica!* (Berkeley: University of California Press, 1977). For a broader discussion, with references to the role of Catholic anti-Fascists throughout, see the special issue on transnational anti-Fascism, *Contemporary European History* 25, no. 4 (November 2016).
3. Luigi Sturzo, "Spirito e realtà," *La rivoluzione liberale,* January 22, 1924.
4. Francesco Piva and Francesco Malgeri, *Vita di Luigi Sturzo* (Rome: Cinque lune, 1972), 295.
5. For the expression of similar sentiments by Sturzo, see Sturzo, *Miscellanea londinese* (Bologna: Zanichelli, 1965–1974), 3:124ff.
6. "Extremely sad" and "unjust war" quote in Sturzo to Father Bozzetti, July 26, 1936, Archivio Luigi Sturzo (hereafter cited as ALS), Rome, f. 85, A., c. 4; "The tragedy of Abyssinia," from Sturzo to Vaussard, ALS, f. 22, A., c. 4. As cited in Alessardo Fruci, *Diritto e Stato nel pensiero di Luigi Sturzo* (Rome: Nuova cultura, 2012), 80. For an expression of similar sentiments, see Sturzo, *Miscellanea londinese* (Bologna: Zanichelli, 1965–1974), 3:124ff.

7. See Sturzo, *Articles a "El Matí," 1929–1936* (Barcelona: F. Camps-Clotilde Parellada / Partit Popular Europeu 1992); and also two journal issues— *Estampa* (September 15, 1934) and *El Liberal* (July 6, 1937)—for explicit discussions of Sturzo's influence in Spain.

8. Sturzo to Sugranyes de Franch, February 18, 1937, in R. Sugranyes de Franch, *Militant per la justícia. Memoriès dialogades amb el pare Hilari Raguer* (Barcelona: Proa, 1998), 61–62.

9. Gallegos Rocafull, "Las razones de una actitud católica," *La Vanguardia de Barcelona*, December 10, 1936, republished as "Por qué estoy al lado del pueblo: Las razones de una actitud católica," *La Mañana* (December 11, 1936). The same article was also republished in Barcelona's *La Noche* and in the Mexican newspaper *El Nacional.*

10. *El mundo católico y la carta colectiva del episcopado español* (Burgos: Ediciones Rayfe, 1938), 21, 69–70.

11. Jacques Maritain, "De la guerre sainte," *La Nouvelle Revue Française* (July 1, 1937): 21–37.

12. Letter from Jacques Maritain to Charles Journet, March 13, 1936, as cited in Daniele Lorenzini, *Jacques Maritain e i diritti umani: Fra totalitarismo, antisemitismo e democrazia* (Brescia: Morcelliana, 2012), 92.

13. Mounier, "Réponse à notre ami Semprun," *Esprit* (May 1938): 247. Quoted in Daniel L. Lewis, "Emmanuel Mounier and the Politics of Moral Revolution: Aspects of Political Crises in French Liberal Catholicism, 1935–1938," *Catholic Historical Review* 56, no. 2 (July 1970): 266–290, at 288.

14. Grenier, *Essai sur l'esprit d'orthodoxie*, 13–16.

15. Maritain to Charles Journet, November 17, 1936, as reprinted in Guy Boissard, *Quelle neutralité face à l'horreur: Le courage de Charles Journet* (Saint-Maurice: Saint-Augustin, 2000), 46.

16. J. -M de Semprum Gurrea, "Après les élections en Espagne," *Esprit* (April 1936): 135; José Berganin, "Espagne victorieuse de soi," *Esprit* (June 1, 1937): 500; and "Guernica," *Esprit* (May 1937): 327. As cited in Oscar Arnal, "Stillborn Alliance: Catholic Divisions in the Face of the Main Tendue," *Journal of Modern History* 51, no. 1 (March, 1979): 1001–1028, at 1023.

17. James McMillan, "France," in *Political Catholicism in Europe, 1918–1965*, ed. Tom Buchanan and Martin Conway (Oxford: Oxford University Press, 1996), 50–51.

18. Henri Fereol, "Libres opinions," *Jeune-Republique*, May 9, 1937, 3; Roger Lardenois, "L'Espagne republicaine a faim," *Jeune-République*, April 24, 1938, 1. As cited in Arnal, "Stillborn Alliance," 1010, 1023.

19. Hugo García, "La propaganda exterior de la República durante la Guerra Civil: Origen, éxitos y miserias de los servicios de París," *Mélanges de la Casa de Velázquez* 39, no. 1 (2009): 215–240; Luisa Marco Sola, "La Oficina de Propaganda Católica de París: Propaganda cristiana antifascista para la II República durante la Guerra Civil española (1936–1939)," *Historia del Presente* 18 (2011): 149–160.

20. Luisa Marco Sola traces how this repeatedly took place with articles from *Esprit*, which were translated and republished in Spanish newspapers like

La Vanguardia de Barcelona and *La Mañana,* which was published in the providence of Jaén, just north of Granada. See Sola, "El factor Cristiano."

21. Thomas E. Blantz, *George N. Shuster: On the Side of the Truth* (Notre Dame, IN: University of Notre Dame Press, 1993), 84–87.

22. See Maritain, "De la guerre sainte," which became the preface to Alfred Mendizábal's *Aux origines d'une tragédie* (Paris: Desclée de Brouwer, 1937).

23. Reprinted in *La paix civile* (boletín del Comité), no.1, December 1937. As cited in Hilari Raguer, *Gunpowder and Incense: The Catholic Church and the Spanish Civil War* (London: Routledge, 2012), 214.

24. Catholic defenders of Franco fired back with manifestos of their own, such as the *Manifiesto de adhesión de los intelectuales franceses a Franco,* or through books such as the *La persécution religieuse en Espagne* (Paris: Plon, 1937), written by Joan Estelrich, who lost his friendship with Maritain and Mauriac immediately after its publication.

25. Maritain, *Religion et culture* (1930), reprinted in *Oeuvres Complètes* (Paris: Éditions Saint-Paul, 1982–), 4:193–255; Maritain, *Du régime temporel et de la liberté* (1933), reprinted in *Oeuvres Complètes,* 5:319–515; and Maritain, *Integral Humanism: Temporal and Spiritual Problems of a New Christendom* (Notre Dame, IN: University of Notre Dame Press, 1973), 167–168.

26. Maritain, *Integral Humanism,* 163–164, 166, 179, 209.

27. Henri de Lubac, "Le pouvoir de l'Église en matière temporelle," *Revue de Sciences Religieuses* 12 (1932): 329–354.

28. Maritain, *Integral Humanism,* 33, 39, 168.

29. See, e.g., Ignacio G. Menéndez-Reigada, "Acerca de la 'guerra santa,' contestación a M. J. Maritain," *La Ciencia Tomista* 58 (1937): 356–374; and Antonio José Gutierrez, *Sentido y causas de la tragedia española* (Madrid: San Sebastian, 1942), 101–107, 134–143, 177–189.

30. See Paolo Pombeni, *Socialismo e cristianesimo: 1815–1975* (Brescia: Queriniana, 1977), 76; and Lucio Pala, *I cattolici francesi e la guerra di Spagna* (Urbino: Argalia, 1974), 54–74.

31. N. A. Berdyaev, review of *Essai sur l'esprit d'orthodoxie,* by Jean Grenier, *Put'* 57 (August–October 1938): 84–86, as cited in Toby Garfitt, "Jean Grenier and the 'Spirit of Orthodoxy,'" in *God's Mirror: Renewal and Engagement in French Catholic Intellectual Culture in the Twentieth Century,* ed. Katherine Davies and Toby Garfitt (New York: Fordham University Press, 2015), 88–103.

32. See Étienne Fouilloux, *Une église en quête de liberté: La pensée catholique française entre modernisme et Vatican II (1914–1962)* (Paris: Desclée de Brouwer, 2006), 113. More broadly, see Pietro Doria, "Jacques Maritain e la Guerra Civile Spagnola nella documentazione dell'Archivio Segreto Vaticano, 1936–1939," in *Notes et documents* 34, no. 13 (2009): 38–68.

33. ARSI, Assistentia Hispanica 1013, "De Rebus Hispaniae (1936–1939) Bellum Civile."

34. Letter from Valeri to Pizzardo, Paris, March 24, 1937, ASV, A.E.S., Stati Ecclesiastici (quarto periodo), 1926–1939, pos. 378 P.O., fasc. 261, ff. 82–83. For

similar themes, see Bernadot to Maglione, May 29, 1936, ASV, A.E.S., Francia (quarto periodo), 1936–1939, pos. 797 P.O., fasc. 351, ff. 61–67.

35. Letter of Ledóchowski to Reverendo in Ct Padre P.X. ("A tutti i provinciali d'Italia"), Rome, November 25, 1936, ARSI, JESCOM 1038 (De comm. Atheo, 1933–1943), fasc. "Defensio contra Comm."

36. "Au jour le jour: L'ennemi," *L'Action Française,* December 26, 1936, ASV, Archivio della Nunziatura Apostolica in Parigi, b. 602, fasc. 774, f. 14.

37. "Resoluta," June 30, 1936, ACDF, ACTA C.G. 1936.

38. John Connelly, *From Enemy to Brother: The Revolution in Catholic Teaching on the Jews, 1933–1965* (Cambridge, MA: Harvard University Press, 2012), 49.

39. As cited in Igor Lukes, *Czechoslovakia between Stalin and Hitler: The Diplomacy of Edvard Beneš in the 1930s* (New York: Oxford University Press, 1996), 211.

40. See Georges Passelecq and Bernard Suchecky, *The Hidden Encyclical of Pius XI,* trans. Steven Rendall (New York: Harcourt Brace, 1997).

41. J. M. Oesterreicher to K. Thieme, January 6, 1939, Thieme Papers, Institut für Zeitgeshichte (hereafter cited as IfZG), Munich, Germany, ED 163 / 40, as cited in Connelly, *From Enemy to Brother,* 98.

42. Luigi Sturzo, *Politica e morale* (1938), in Sturzo, *Politica e morale (1938)— Coscienza e politica (1953)* (Bologna: Zanichelli: 1972), 139, as cited in Lucia Ceci, *The Vatican and Mussolini's Italy* (Boston: Brill, 2016), 237. For more on Sturzo's critique of anti-Semitism, see Eugenio Guccione, "Razzismo e antisemitismo nelle analisi di Luigi Sturzo," *Storia e Politica* 2 (2010): 30–38.

43. Connelly, *From Enemy to Brother,* 99.

44. Note on Pius XI stored within a Fascist secret police file on Giuseppe Pizzardo, dated Rome, December 25, 1937, ACS, MI, Direzione Generale Pubblica Sicurezza, DPP, Fascicoli personali, ser. B, b. 19, fasc. "Pizzardo monsignore," f. 31.

45. Renato Moro, *La Chiesa e la sterminio degli ebrei* (Bologna: Il Mulino, 2009), 92.

46. Letter of Gustav Gundlach to John LaFarge, October 16, 1938, as cited in Moro, *La Chiesa,* 91–92.

47. See Giovanni Miccoli, *I dilemma e i silenzi di Pio XII: Vaticano, Seconda guerra mondiale, e Shoah* (Milan: Rizzoli, 2007), 454; Michael Phayer, *The Catholic Church and the Holocaust, 1930–1965* (Bloomington: Indiana University Press, 2002), 44.

48. The point is made in Martin Conway, "Catholic Politics or Christian Democracy? The Evolution of Interwar Political Catholicism: A Comment," *in Christian Democracy in 20th-Century Europe,* ed. Michael Gehler, Wolfram Kaiser, and Helmut Wohnout (Vienna: Böhlau Verlag, 2001), 294–312, at 300–301, with reference to Jean Chélini and Joël Benoît d'Onorio, eds., *Pie XII et la cité: La pensée et l'action politiques de Pie XII* (Aix-en-Provence: Presses universitaires d'Aix-Marseille, 1988); Oliver Logan, "Pius XII: *Romanità,* prophecy and charisma," *Modern Italy* 3, no. 2 (1998): 237–247; and John

Boyer, "Catholics, Christians and the Challenges of Democracy: The Heritage of the Nineteenth Century," in Gehler et al., *Christian Democracy in 20th-Century Europe*, 23–59.

49. Father Ledit's memories of Ledóchowski, undated manuscript, ARSI, JESCOM, Ledochówski, "Varia ad eius Vitam" n. 1025/355.

50. Pope Pius XII, "Con Immenso Gozo," radio message to Catholics in Spain, April 16, 1939. The speech was delivered after the victory of General Franco in the Spanish Civil War, April 14, 1939.

51. Oesterreicher to Thieme, May 1, 1939, IfZG, ED, 163/59. As cited in Connelly, *From Enemy to Brother*, 159.

52. Letters of August 26 and 29, 1939, in *Journet-Maritain: Correspondence*, ed. Pierre Mamie and Georges Cottier (Paris: Éditions Saint-Paul, 1997), 2:876–877, as cited in Connelly, *From Enemy to Brother*, 148.

53. Emmanuel Mounier, "Sur les décombres du communisme," *Esprit* (March 1940); P.L.L. [Landsberg], "Les faussaires," *Esprit* (January 1940).

54. Gabriele De Rosa, *Luigi Sturzo e la democrazia europea* (Bari: Laterza, 1990), 22.

55. *Discorsi e Radiomessaggi di Sua Santità Pio XII* (Vatican City: Tipografia poliglotta vaticana, 1960), 1:305–307.

56. *Actes et documents du Saint-Siège relatifs à la Seconde Guerre Mondiale* (henceforth *ADSS*), 1:386 (doc. 257). Notes of Monsignor Tardini following Pius XII's meeting with Ribbentrop, Vatican City, March 11, 1940.

57. *ADSS*, 1:249 (doc. 131). Notes of Monsignor Tardini, following a meeting with the Ambassador of Spain to the Holy See, Vatican City, August 26, 1939.

58. Timothy Snyder, *Bloodlands: Europe between Hitler and Stalin* (New York: Basic Books, 2010), 21.

59. As cited in Richard C. Lucas, *The Forgotten Holocaust: The Poles under Foreign Occupation, 1939–1944* (New York: Hippocrene Press, 2013), 1–3.

60. Tony Judt, *Postwar: A History of Europe since 1945* (New York: Penguin Books, 2005), 18.

61. Guenther Lewy, *Catholic Church and Nazi Germany* (Boulder, CO: Da Capo Press, 2001), 227; Bohdan Wytwycky, *The Other Holocaust* (Washington, DC: Novak Report of the New Ethnicity, 1982), 51; Phayer, *Catholic Church and the Holocaust*, 21.

62. August Hlond, report of April 1940, as reprinted in Hlond, *The Persecution of the Catholic Church in German-Occupied Poland: Reports* (New York: Longmans Green, 1991), 79–86.

63. Foreign Minister Daladier to Ambassador Charles-Roux, Paris, September 29, 1939, *ADSS*, 3:85–86.

64. See David J. Alvarez and Robert A. Graham, *Nothing Sacred: Nazi Espionage against the Vatican, 1939–1945* (London: Frank Cass, 1997), 25–33; and Owen Chadwick, *Britain and the Vatican* (Cambridge: Cambridge University Press, 2011), 86–98.

65. Eleanor Roosevelt, *The Autobiography of Eleanor Roosevelt* (New York: Da Capo Press, 1992), 209–212.

66. *Discorsi e Radiomessaggi di Sua Santità Pio XII*, 1:435–445.

67. Pius XII, *Summi pontificatus* (October 20, 1939), §§52, 58, 75. Available on-line at http://w2.vatican.va/content/pius-xii/en/encyclicals/documents/hf_p -xii_enc_20101939_summi-pontificatus.html.

68. Pius XII, Christmas broadcast, December 25, 1939, as reprinted in *Discorsi e Radiomessaggi*, 1:422, 438.

69. Phayer, *Catholic Church and the Holocaust*, 26.

70. See Robert Ventresca, *Soldier of Christ: The Life of Pope Pius XII* (Cambridge, MA: Harvard University Press, 2013), 181ff; Phayer, *Catholic Church and the Holocaust*, 22–23; Lukas, *Forgotten Holocaust*, 16.

71. Pius XII, *Summi pontificatus*, §17.

72. Francesco Pellegrino, "L'enciclica *Summi Pontificatus* e le sue ripercussioni nella stampa mondiale," *La Civiltà Cattolica* 91, no. 2 (1940): 17–19.

73. Pius XII, speech at the Palazzo Quirinale in Rome, December 28, 1939, in *Discorsi e Radiomessaggi di Sua Santità Pio XII*, 1:455–456.

74. Pius XII, Allocution *Hereux est pour Nous*, October 18, 1939, as reprinted in *AAS* 31 (1939): 611.

75. Pius XII's December 24, 1939, allocution to the College of Cardinals is re-printed and translated in *The Pope's Five Peace Points: Allocution to the Col-lege of Cardinals by His Holiness Pope Pius XII on December 24th, 1939* (London: Catholic Truth Society, 1941), 9.

76. Martin Conway, introduction to *Political Catholicism in Europe, 1918–1965*, ed. Tom Buchanan and Martin Conway (Oxford: Oxford University Press, 1996); 26–27; John Hellman, *Emmanuel Mounier and the New Cath-olic Left, 1930–1950* (Toronto: University of Toronto Press, 1981), 188–220; and Hellman, *The Knight-Monks of Vichy France: Uriage, 1940–1945* (Mon-treal: McGill-Queen's University Press, 1993).

77. Léon Papeleux, *Les silences de Pie XII* (Brussels: Vokaer, 1980), 66.

78. Wolfram Kaiser, *Christian Democracy and the Origins of the European Union* (Cambridge: Cambridge University Press, 2007), 138–139, 144.

79. See Martin Conway, "Legacies of Exile: The Exile Governments in London during World War II and the Politics of Postwar Europe," in *Europe in Exile: European Refugee Communities in Britain, 1939–1945*, ed. Martin Conway and José Gotovitch (Oxford: Berghahn Books, 2001), 255–274.

80. "A New League of Nations Now: Proposal Endorsed by International Chris-tian Democratic Union," *People & Freedom* 46 (1943): 3. Maritain is quoted in Pierre Guillen, "Plans by Exiles from France," in *Plans for European Union in Great Britain and in Exile, 1939–1945*, ed. Walter Lipgens (Berlin: De Gruyter, 1985), 303.

81. The manifesto was first published in New York by the Maison française in 1942. This copy is reprinted in Maritain, *Oeuvres Complètes*, 7:1214–1229. It was then translated and reprinted as "In the Face of the World's Crisis: A Manifesto by European Catholics Sojourning in America," *Commonweal*, August 12, 1942, 415–421. *The Dublin Review* (October–December 1942), *The Sword of the Spirit* (1943), *Nova et Vetera* (1942), and *Cahiers du témoignage chrétien* (August and December, 1943) all published the manifesto as well. Sturzo initially refused to sign the manifesto, because he believed it was too critical of liberalism and not critical enough of the Church and its support

of Nazi-Fascist regimes. See Sturzo to Maritain, March 6, 1942, as cited in Or Rosenboim, *The Emergence of Globalism: Visions of World Order in Britain and the United States, 1939–1950* (Princeton, NJ: Princeton University Press, 2018), 264.

82. Jacques Maritain, "Christian Humanism," *Fortune*, April 1942; Maritain, *Christianity and Democracy* (1944; New York: Scribner, 1950). For more on Maritain and human rights, see Lorenzini, *Dai diritti della persona ai diritti dell'uomo.*

83. Confidential report to Dr. Fry and Mrs. Stanley, from M. Rapaport, J. L. Brown of Foreign Language Section on May 7, 1942, file 3, box 18, Jacques Maritain Papers, Maritain Institute, University of Notre Dame. As cited in John McGreevy, *Catholicism and American Freedom* (New York: W. W. Norton, 2002), 202.

84. Kaiser, *Christian Democracy*, 153. By 1943 many of the same Catholics who had celebrated the Atlantic Charter were concerned about the inclusion of the Soviet Union and the fact that Great Powers were being granted veto powers.

85. *Völkischer Beobachter*, August 30, 1941, as cited in Toni Morant I Ariño, "Spanish Fascist Women's Transnational Relations during the Second World War: Between Ideology and Realpolitik," *Journal of Contemporary History* (forthcoming).

86. Valentina Pisanty, *La difesa della razza: Antologia, 1938–1943* (Milan: Bompiani, 2006); Jeffrey Herf, *The Jewish Enemy: Nazi Propaganda during World War I and the Holocaust* (Cambridge, MA: Harvard University Press, 2006); and Lorna Waddington, *Hitler's Crusade: Bolshevism and the Myth of International Jewish Conspiracy* (London: Tauris, 2007).

87. For instance, in September 1941 the newspaper *Y*, for female Falangists, published a color map of Europe in a two-page spread, showing the main victories of the Axis powers, with arrows drawn from all the countries participating in the "European crusade against Bolshevism" pointing to the heart of the USSR. *Y*, September 1941. As cited in Ariño, "Spanish Fascist Women's Transnational Relations."

88. Mimmo Franzinelli, *Il riarmo dello spirit: I cappellani militari nella seconda guerra mondiale* (Treviso: Pagus, 1991), 105ff.

89. Alberto Casella, *Natale Legionario (Fronte Russo)*, collana "vita legionaria," no. 3, Radiotrasmissione effettuata il 10 febbraio 1942 per il XIX annual di fondazione della miliza, p. 17. Also see Mario Parodi, *Il bolscevismo contro Dio, contro la famiglia* (Rome: Filipponi Brunetto, 1941). As cited in Marla Stone, "The Changing Face of the Enemy," *Constellations*, 15, no. 3 (September 2008): 332–350; and in Stone, "Italian Fascism's Soviet Enemy and the Propaganda of Hate, 1941–1943," *Journal of Hate Studies: Hate and Political Discourse*, 10 (2012): 73–98, at 80.

90. Gordon Zahn, *German Catholics and Hitler's Wars* (New York: Shed and Ward, 1962); Heinrich Missalla, *Für Gott, Führer und Vaterland: Die Verstrickung der katholischen Seelsorge in Hitlers Krieg* (Munich: Kösel, 1999); Guenter Lewy, *The Catholic Church and Nazi Germany* (Boulder, CO: Da Capo Press, 2001), 249.

91. Giovanni Papini, *Questa guerra* (1941 edition), as referenced in Lucia Ceci, *Vatican and Mussolini's Italy*, 268.

92. Jacques Delperrié de Bayac, *Histoire de la Milice* (Paris: Fayard, 1996), 580–581.

93. *Y*, September 1941, as cited in Ariño, "Spanish Fascist Women's Transnational Relations."

94. Centro Cattolico Cinematografico, *Segnalazioni Cinematografiche* 13 (1940–1941): 42.

95. Simona Colarizi, *L'opinione degli italiani sotto il regime* (Rome: Laterza, 2000), 360–361; Italo Garzia, *Pio XII e l'Italia nella seconda guerra mondiale* (Brescia: Morcelliana, 1988), 199.

96. *ADSS*, 5:8–13.

97. Ceci, *Vatican and Mussolini's Italy*, 276.

98. *ADSS*, 5: doc. 151, Notes of Monsignor Tardini of Pius XII's conversation with Attolico, November 27, 1941.

99. Bernardo Attolico to Ciano, September 16, 1941, *DDI* 9, no. 7: 580ff (doc. 570).

100. Note of Tardini, September 5, 1941, *ADSS*, 5:182–184 (doc. 62).

101. *ADSS*, 5:208, 229, 272.

102. For Hitler's views, see "Internationaler Militärgerichtschof," [Nuremberg Trial], vol. 38, 1086–1094, doc. 221; for the Wehrmacht orders, see Lationa counselor Fischer's note of December 4, 1941. As cited in Hansjakob Stehle, *Eastern Politics of the Vatican, 1917–1979* (Athens, OH: Ohio University Press, 1981), 217–218.

103. The article appeared on the front page of *Pravda* on September 8, 1941, and was translated by Father Leopold Braun in his letter to Myron Taylor, Moscow, October 3, 1941. FDR Presidential Library and Museum, Hyde Park, NY (hereafter cited as FDRL), President's Secretary's File (hereafter cited as PSF), box 51, "Diplomatic Correspondence: Vatican: Taylor, Myron C., 1941."

104. Pedro Ramet, "Interplay of Religious and Nationalities Policy," in *Religion and Nationalism in Soviet and East European Politics*, ed. Pedro Ramet (Durham, NC: Duke University Press, 1984), 20.

105. Roosevelt's Navy and Total Defense Day Address, October 27, 1941, in *The Public Papers and Addresses of Franklin D. Roosevelt* (New York: Harper, 1941), 440.

106. Tardini's private response to Roosevelt, as reprinted in *ADSS*, 5: doc. no. 74. As cited in Stehle, *Eastern Politics of the Vatican*, 210.

107. Letter of Father Leopold Braun to Myron Taylor, Moscow, October 3, 1941, FDRL, PSF, box 51, "Diplomatic Correspondence: Vatican: Taylor, Myron C., 1941."

108. Monsignor Fulton J. Sheen, "Soviet Russia May Be Helped but Russia Must Be Reformed," *America*, October 18, 1941, 35, as cited in David S. Foglesong, *America's Secret War against Bolshevism: U.S. Intervention in the Russian Civil War, 1917–1920* (Chapel Hill: University of North Carolina Press, 1995), 88.

109. Fulton J. Sheen, *Philosophies at War* (New York: Charles Scribner's Sons, 1943), 8–9; Cardinal Spellman, "Radio Address," March 22, 1942, sent to

FDR and stored in FDRL, President's Personal File (hereafter cited as PPF) 4404, folder "Spellman, Archbishop Francis J., 1936–1942" (from which the second citation is drawn). For similar themes, also see John A. Ryan and Francis J. Boland, *Catholic Principles of Politics* (New York: MacMillan, 1940); and Cardinal Spellman, "Baccalaureate Address," p. 2, FDRL, PPF 4404, folder "Spellman, Archbishop Francis J., 1936–1942."

110. Timothy Snyder, "Holocaust: The Ignored Reality," *New York Review of Books*, July 16, 2009.

111. Quote from Serrano in the Falangist newspaper *Arriba*, June 25, 1941.

112. Jan T. Gross, *Neighbors: The Destruction of the Jewish Community in Jedwabne, Poland* (Princeton, NJ: Princeton University Press, 2001), 123.

113. Andrej Angrick, *The "Final Solution" in Riga: Exploitation and Annihilation, 1941–1944* (New York: Berghahn Books, 2012), 66–76.

114. Anton Weiss-Wendt, *Murder without Hatred: Estonians and the Holocaust* (Syracuse, NY: Syracuse University Press, 2009), 39, 40, 45, 90, 94–105.

115. Leni Yahil, *The Holocaust: The Fate of European Jewry, 1932–1945* (New York: Oxford University Press, 1987), 282–283.

116. For how the law impacted Algerian Jews, see Ethan B. Katz, *The Burdens of Brotherhood: Jews and Muslims from North Africa to France* (Cambridge, MA: Harvard University Press, 2015).

117. *ADSS*, 2: doc. 406, Le métropolite de Léopol des Ruthenes Szeptyckyj au pape Pius XII, August 29–31, 1942.

118. Phayer, *Catholic Church and the Holocaust*, 48.

119. *ADSS*, 3: doc. 241; and 4: doc. 257. As cited in Stehle, *Eastern Politics*, 216.

120. *ADSS*, 8: doc. 493.

121. John Pollard, *The Papacy in the Age of Totalitarianism, 1914–1958* (Oxford: Oxford University Press, 2014), 333.

122. Pius XII, address to the College of Cardinals, June 2, 1943.

123. *ADSS*, 7: "La Saint Siège et la Guerra Mondiale, novembre 1942–1 décembre 1943"; doc. 71, Pius XII radiomessage, December 24, 1942.

124. Phayer, *Catholic Church and the Holocaust*, 49; Saul Friedländer, *Nazi Germany and the Jews* (London: Phoenix, 2008), 75.

125. Giovanni Miccoli, "La Santa Sede nella seconda guerra mondiale," in *Fra mito della cristianità e secolarizzazione*, ed. Giovanni Miccoli (Casale Monferrato: Marietti, 1985), 131–337, at 226.

126. Kevin Spicer, *Hitler's Priests: Catholic Clergy and National Socialism* (DeKalb: Northern Illinois University Press, 2008), 199.

127. Giovanni Miccoli, *I dilemmi e i silenzi di Pio XII. Vaticano, seconda guerra mondiale e Shoah* (Milan: Rizzoli, 2007), 399–400.

128. Mario Barbera, "La questione dei giudei in Ungheria," *La Civiltà Cattolica* 89 (1938): 146–153.

129. Ventresca, *Soldier of Christ*, 179–180, 211–215.

130. Harold Tittman, "The Position of the Vatican in the Present Conflict," Memorandum no. 85, June 16, 1942; and Memorandum no. 86, June 23, 1942. National Archives and Records Administration, Archive II, College

Park, Maryland, Myron Taylor Papers. As cited in Phayer, *Catholic Church and the Holocaust*, 24, 27.

131. Vincent A. McCormick, SJ, diary entry, as cited in Ventresca, *Soldier of Christ*, 190.

132. Robert E. Lucey, "A Worldwide Attack on Man," *Voice for Human Rights* 1, no. 2 (September 1940): 7, as cited in Samuel Moyn, *The Last Utopia: Human Rights in History* (Cambridge, MA: Harvard University Press, 2012), 51.

133. Henri de Lubac, *Résistance chrétienne à l'antisemitisme: Souvenirs, 1940–1944* (Paris: Fayard, 1988).

134. Pierre Chaillet, "Le sens de notre témoignage," in *Cahiers du témoignage chrétien* 6–7, special issue: *Antisémites* (April–May 1942), as cited in Sylvie Bernay, "La propagande antisémite contre les protestations épiscopales de l'été 1942," *Revue d'Histoire de la Shoah*, 1 (2013): 245–271, at 245. Between 1941 and 1945, Pierre Chaillet, Gaston Fessard, Stanislaus Fumet, Henri de Lubac, Georges Bernanos, Yves de Montcheuil, and Jean Lacroix wrote for the journal. Jacques Maritain was one of its editors.

135. See Jacques Maritain, *A Christian Looks at the Jewish Question* (New York: Longmans, Green and Co., 1939), 1, 4, 6, 10.

136. Maritain, "Qui est mon prochain?," *La vie intellectuelle* (August 1939); Maritain, "The Achievement of Cooperation among Men of Different Creeds," *Journal of Religion* 21 (1941): 364–372; and Maritain, "Who Is My Neighbor?," in *Ransoming the Time* (New York: Scribner's, 1941), 115–140.

137. Aliza Luft, "Shifting Stances: How French Bishops Defected from Support for the Anti-Semitic Vichy Regime to Save Jews during the Holocaust" (PhD diss., University of Wisconsin–Madison, 2016), 20; J. M. Mayeur, "Les Églises devant la persecution des Juifs en France," in *La France et la question juive 1940–1944: Actes du Colloque du Centre de documentation juive contemporaine (10–12 mars 1979)* (Paris: S. Messinger, 1981), 150ff.

138. See Miccoli, "La Santa Sede," 324–326; Miccoli, *I dilemma e i silenzi*, 391–399.

139. See *Journet-Maritain Correspondance* (Fribourg: Saint-Augustin, 1998), 3:52–53.

140. On Garrigou-Lagrange, see Michael Kerlin, "Reginald Garrigou-Lagrange: Defending the Faith from *Pascendi dominici gregis* to *Humani Generis*," *US Catholic Historian* 25, no. 1 (2007): 97–113.

141. Charles Blanchet, "Jacques Maritain, 1940–1944: Le refus de la défaite et ses relations avec le général De Gaulle," in *Cahiers Jacques Maritain* 16 (April 1988): 42, as cited in John Hellman, "The Anti-Democratic Impulse in Catholicism: Jacques Maritain, Yves Simon, and Charles de Gaulle during World War II," *Journal of Church and State* 33, no. 3 (Summer 1991): 453–471, at 465.

142. Maritain to "une religieuse," June 3, 1942, reprinted in *Cahiers Jacques Maritain* 16 (April 1988): 93, as cited in Hellman, "The Anti-Democratic Impulse," 466.

143. Robert d'Harcourt, *Catholiques d'Allemagne* (Paris: Plon, 1938), 10, as cited in Renée Bédarida, *Les catholiques dans la guerre, 1939–1945: Entre Vichy et la Résistance* (Paris: Hachette, 1998), 118.

144. "Idee ricostruttive della Democrazia Cristiana (Rome, 1943)," in *Storia della Democrazia Cristiana*, ed. Francesco Malgeri (Rome: Edizioni Cinque Lune, 1987), 1:389–393; Wolfgang Treue, *Deutsche Parteiprogramme seit 1861* (Zurich: Musterschmidt-Verlag-Göttingen, 1968), 4:188–191.

145. Martin Conway, "The Evolution of Inter-War Political Catholicism: A Comment," in Gehler et al., *Christian Democracy in 20th-Century Europe*, 308–309.

146. Phayer, *Catholic Church and the Holocaust*, 58.

147. Papeleux, *Les silences*, 68–69.

148. Saul Friedländer, *Pius XII and the Third Reich: A Documentation* (New York: Knopf, 1966), 195.

149. See Pius XII, "Allocuzione natalizia al sacro collegio e alla prelature romana," *La Civiltà Cattolica* 92, no. 1 (1941): 3–13; Pius XII, "Pacificazione e ordine interno delle nazioni nel messaggio natalizio di Pio XII," *La Civiltà Cattolica* 94, no. 1 (1943): 65–78.

150. Pius XII, "Radiomessaggio nel cinquantesimo anniversario della *Rerum Novarum*," *La Civiltà Cattolica* 92, no. 2 (1941): 401–411.

CHAPTER 8 ▪ THE PAPAL AGENDA AFTER WORLD WAR II

Epigraph: Letter from Pius XII to the *Settimane sociale dei cattolici italiani*, October 19, 1945, reprinted in *AAS*, 37:274.

1. Carlos Romulo, "Natural Law and International Law," *University of Notre Dame Natural Law Institute Proceedings* 3 (1949): 121, 126, as cited in Samuel Moyn, *Christian Human Rights* (Philadelphia: University of Pennsylvania Press, 2015), 92.

2. "L'Exposition de la Reconstruction," *Revue Urbanisme* 109 (1946): 132–133. Charles de Gaulle's words hung over entrance of the Gare des Invalides during the Première Exposition de la Reconstruction during the winter of 1945–1946.

3. Tony Judt, *Postwar: A History of Europe since 1945* (New York: Penguin Books, 2005), 17, 20.

4. Marco Duranti, *The Conservative Human Rights Revolution: European Identity, Transnational Politics, and the Origins of the European Convention* (Oxford: Oxford University Press, 2017); and Rosario Forlenza, "The Politics of the *Abendland*: Christian Democracy and the Idea of Europe after the Second World War," *Contemporary European History* 26, no. 2 (May 2017): 261–286.

5. The citations are drawn from Pius XII, "The Anniversary of Rerum Novarum," speech in St. Peter's Square, June 1, 1941; and Pius XII, Christmas address, 1942, as reprinted in *The Major Addresses of Pope Pius XII*, ed. Vincent A. Yzermans (St. Paul: North Central, 1961), 2:31, 61. In the June 1941 address, Pius XII called for an international bill acknowledging the rights of the human person.

6. Guido Gonella, *Principi di un ordine sociale: Nota ai messaggi di S.S. Pio XII* (Vatican City: Civitas, 1944), 108.

7. Pius XII, "The Modern State" (speech before the delegates of the International Congress of Administrative Sciences, Rome, 5 August 1950), as reprinted in *The Major Addresses of PopePope Pius XII,* 1:140–141.

8. Ibid.

9. Pius XII, "Democracy and a Lasting Peace," December 24, 1944, §19, as reprinted in *Discorsi e radiomessaggi di Sua Santità* (Vatican City: Tipografia poliglotta vaticana, 1960), 4:237, 241, 243.

10. Ibid., §§39, 4, 44, 82.

11. Special Collections Research Center, University of Chicago, Adler papers, box 29.

12. W. E. Garrison, "Democratic Rights in the Roman Catholic Tradition," *Church History* 15, no. 3 (1946): 195–219.

13. Giuliana Chamedes, "Pius XII, Rights Talk, and the Dawn of the Religious Cold War," in *Religion and Human Rights,* ed. Devin Pendas (Oxford: Oxford University Press, forthcoming); David Hollenbach, *Claims in Conflict: Retrieving and Reviewing the Catholic Human Rights Tradition* (Toronto: Paulist Press, 1979), 59; J. Bryan Hehir, "Religious Activism for Human Rights: A Christian Case Study," in *Religious Human Rights in Global Perspective: Religious Perspectives,* ed. John Witte Jr. and Johan D. van der Vyver (The Hague: Martinus Nijhoff, 1996), 97–120, at 102; Daniele Menozzi, *La Chiesa e i diritti umani: Legge naturale e moralità politica dalla Rivoluzione francese ai nostri giorni* (Bologna: Il Mulino, 2015); Moyn, *Christian Human Rights.*

14. Piotr H. Kosicki, "Masters in Their Own Home or Defenders of the Human Person? Wojciech Korfanty, Anti-Semitism, and Polish Christian Democracy's Illiberal Rights-Talk," *Modern Intellectual History* 14, no. 1 (April 2017): 99–130.

15. For the text of the treaty, see Emmanuel Mounier, *Oeuvres complètes* (Paris: Éditions du Seuil, 1961–1962), 3:99–104.

16. See, e.g., the "Codice di Camaldoli," penned in 1943 by future leaders of the Italian Christian Democratic party, as reprinted in *Pensiero sociale della Chiesa e impegno politico dei Cattolici democratici: I testi della* Rerum novarum, *del* Codice di Camaldoli, *e della* Centesimus annus, ed. Angelo Gatti and Giovanni Allara (Rome: Cinque Lune, 1991), 88ff. From his earliest speeches, the German Christian Democrat Konrad Adenauer also stressed the importance of rights. See Adenauer, *Reden, 1917–1967,* ed. Hans-Peter Schwarz (Stuttgart: Deutsche Verlags-Anstalt, 1975), esp. 82–106. Gilibert Dru, who, had he survived, would have certainly played an active role in France's MRP, sought to fuse Christian mysticism with "la mystique des droits de l'homme" (Pierre Letamendía, *Le mouvement républicain populaire: Le MRP, l'histoire d'un grand parti français* [Paris: Beauchesne Editeur, 1995], 58). The French-Catholic politician Pierre-Henri Teitgen similarly stressed the role of human rights in postwar reconstruction. Teitgen, "Le cours de justice," April 5, 1946, speech, Paris, as cited in

Laurence Bertrand Dorléac, *L'art de la défaite, 1940–1944* (Paris: Éditions du Seuil, 1993), 386.

17. Both quotations, the first from Christian Democracy's *Il Popolo,* and the second, attributed to Isocrates following the Peloponnesian Wars, are found in Judt, *Postwar,* 61.

18. See, e.g., Michele Battini, *The Missing Italian Nuremberg: Cultural Amnesia and Postwar Politics* (New York: Palgrave Macmillan, 2007); Richard Ned Lebow, Wulf Kansteiner, and Claudio Fogu, eds., *The Politics of Memory in Postwar Europe* (Durham, NC: Duke University Press, 2006); Peter Novick, *The Holocaust in American Life* (Boston: Houghton Mifflin, 2007); and Henry Rousso, *The Vichy Syndrome: History and Memory in France since 1944,* trans. Arthur Goldhammer (Cambridge, MA: Harvard University Press, 1994).

19. Preamble, The Charter of the United Nations, June 26, 1945. Available online at http://www.un.org/en/charter-united-nations/index.html.

20. See the letter from Acting Secretary-General of the UN, Arkady Sobolev, to Fifty-One Member Governments, New York, July 12, 1946, Commission on Human Rights, S-0472-0070-03, United Nations Archives, New York City.

21. See Dina Gusejnova, *European Elites and the Ideas of Empire, 1917–1957* (Cambridge: Cambridge University Press, 2016); and Martin Thomas, "The Colonial Policies of the *Mouvement Républicain Populaire,* 1944–1954: From Reform to Reaction," *English Historical Review* 118, no. 476 (April 2003): 380–411.

22. Elizabeth Borgwardt, *A New Deal for the World: America's Vision for Human Rights* (Cambridge, MA: Harvard University Press, 2005); Ilya Gaiduk, *Divided Together: The United States and the Soviet Union in the United Nations, 1945–1965* (Stanford, CA: Stanford University Press, 2012); Mark Mazower, "The Strange Triumph of Human Rights," *Historical Journal* 47, no. 2 (2004): 379–398; Mazower, *No Enchanted Place: The End of Empire and the Ideological Origins of the United Nations* (Princeton, NJ: Princeton University Press, 2009); Samuel Moyn, *The Last Utopia: Human Rights in History* (Cambridge, MA: Harvard University Press, 2012); Stefan-Ludwig Hoffmann, ed., *Human Rights in the Twentieth Century* (Cambridge; Cambridge University Press, 2011); and Brian Simpson, *International Human Rights and the End of Empire: Britain and the Genesis of the European Convention* (Oxford: Oxford University Press, 2004).

23. *AAS,* 37 (1945), 19, 166. Edward J. Gratsch, *The Holy See and the United Nations, 1945–1995* (New York: Vantage Press, 1997).

24. Ivan T. Berend, *Central and Eastern Europe, 1944–1993: Detour from the Periphery to the Periphery* (Cambridge: Cambridge University Press, 1996), 16–19; Hugh Seton-Watson, *The East European Revolution* (London: Methuen, 1961), 169–171.

25. Letter, Pope Pius XII to Truman, Castel Gandolfo, August 26, 1947, Rare and Manuscript Collections, Cornell University, Myron Taylor Papers, box 1, folder "Correspondence between President Harry S. Truman, His Holiness Pope Pius XII and Hon. Myron C. Taylor, 1945–1949."

26. Melvyn Leffler, *Cambridge History of the Cold War* (Cambridge: Cambridge University Press, 2012), 1:175.
27. The phrase is Peter Kent's, in his *The Lonely Cold War of Pope Pius XII: The Roman Catholic Church and the Division of Europe* (Montreal: McGill-Queen's University Press, 2014), 82.
28. "Foreign Relations: The Bishop Speaks," *Time Magazine*, November 27, 1944.
29. See John LaFarge, SJ, *Judgment on the Dumbarton Oaks Proposals* (Washington, DC: Catholic Association for International Peace, 1945). For more on the lobbying, see Joseph S. Rossi, *Uncharted Territory: The American Catholic Church at the United Nations, 1946–1972* (Washington, DC: Catholic University of America Press, 2006); Rossi, *American Catholics and the Formation of the United Nations* (Lanham, MD: University Press, of America, 1993).
30. Papal communication of November 1, 1945, as reprinted in *Amtsblatt der Erzdiözese München und Freising*, no.1, January 20, 1946. The German episcopacy is cited in H. W. Schoenberg, *Germans from the East: A Study of Their Migration, Resettlement and Subsequent Group History since 1945* (The Hague: Martinus Nijhoff, 1970), 149.
31. The American bishops are cited in *New York Times*, October 7, 1946. "Oppose Russian imperialism" is from Mons. Roncalli notes, September 4, 1946, ACC, Fondo Martegani, as cited in Giovanni Sale, *De Gasperi, gli USA e il Vaticano all'inizio della guerra fredda* (Milan: Jaca Books, 2005), 32. For similar views, see Antonio Messineo, "I trattati di pace: Diktat o contratto?," *Civiltà Cattolica* 97 (1946): 401–410. For the pope on the need for a "universalist" praxis, see Pius XII, speech at the February 1946 Consistory; on the "heroic death," see January 18, 1947, audience with American journalists, as reprinted in *Discorsi e radiomessaggi di Sua Santità*, 8: 381.
32. *New York Times*, February 10, 1947.
33. For a contemporary account of the Vatican's reaction to these cases, see, e.g., Gaetano Salvemini, "The Vatican and Mindszenty," *The Nation*, August 6, 1949. On how these cases played out at the United Nations, see Moyn, *The Last Utopia*, 71–72.
34. Pedro Ramet, "The Interplay of Religious Policy and Nationalities Policy in the Soviet Union and Eastern Europe," in *Religion and Nationalism in Soviet and Eastern European Politics*, ed. Pedro Ramet (Durham, NC: Duke University Press, 1989), 19–21; Norman Davies, *God's Playground: A History of Poland*, 2 vols. (New York: Columbia University Press, 1987); Vincent C. Chrypinski, "Church and Nationality in Postwar Poland," in *Religion and Nationalism in Soviet and East European Politics*, 131–132.
35. The literature on postwar Americanization and the European reaction to it is vast. For a start, see Alessandro Brogi, *Confronting America: The Cold War between the United States and the Communists in France and Italy* (Chapel Hill: University of North Carolina Press, 2014); Victoria De Grazia, *Irresistible Empire: America's Advance through Twentieth-Century Europe* (Cambridge, MA: Harvard University Press, 2006); and Richard F. Kuisel, *Seducing the French: The Dilemma of Americanization* (Berkeley: University of California Press, 1993).

36. Thomas H. Greene, "The Communist Parties of Italy and France: A Study in Comparative Communism," *World Politics* 21, no. 1 (October 1968): 1–38, at 8–9.

37. Donald Sassoon, *One Hundred Years of Socialism: The West European Left in the Twentieth Century* (London: Tauris, 2014), 118.

38. Martin Conway, *Catholic Politics in Europe, 1918–1945* (London: Routledge, 2017); Conway, "The Rise and Fall of Europe's Democratic Age, 1945–1973," *Contemporary European History* 13, no. 1 (2004): 67–88; Anne Deighton, *The Impossible Peace: Britain, the Division of Germany and the Origins of the Cold War* (Oxford: Oxford University Press, 1990); William Hitchcock, *France Restored: Cold War Diplomacy and the Quest for Leadership in Europe, 1944–1954* (Chapel Hill: University of North Carolina Press, 1998); Wolfram Kaiser, *Christian Democracy and the Origins of the European Union* (Cambridge: Cambridge University Press, 2007); and Peter Van Kemseke, *Towards an Era of Development: The Globalization of Socialism and Christian Democracy, 1945–1965* (Leuven: Leuven University Press, 2006).

39. See cables from J. G. Parsons to the Secretary of State, December 19, 1947, cable 4378; and Gowen to the Secretary of State, November 19, 1948, cable 4379; both National Archives and Records Administration, Archive II, College Park, MD (hereafter cited as NARA), RG 59: General Records of the Department of State, Entry 1071: Records of the Personal Representative of the President to Pope Pius XII, box 30, folders, "Airgrams (Outgoing) 1946" and "Airgrams (Outgoing) 1947."

40. Promemoria from *Civiltà Italica*, as cited in Riccardi, *Il partito romano nel secondo dopoguerra, 1945–1954* (Brescia: Morcelliana, 1983), 190.

41. Pius XII Christmas message, December 1948.

42. Marco Formigoni, *Storia d'Italia nella guerra fredda* (Bologna: Il Mulino, 2016), 142.

43. De Gasperi's request is mentioned in Dunn to Marshall, December 5, 1947, in *FRUS* (1948), 3:736–737, as cited in Formigoni, *Storia d'Italia*, 126, 128–129.

44. Marc Trachtenberg, *A Constructed Peace: The Making of the European Settlement, 1945–1963* (Princeton, NJ: Princeton University Press, 1993).

45. "Logical and well-timed," in Gowen to Marshall, March 20, 1947, as reprinted in Ennio Di Nolfo, *Vaticano e Stati Uniti, 1939–1952* (Milan: Angeli, 1978), 578; Byrnes in notes by Monsignor Howard Carroll, national secretary for the National Catholic Welfare Conference (hereafter cited as NCWC), on his conversation with Byrnes in Paris, following the Paris Peace Conference, October 11, 1946, NCWC Archives, Catholic University of America, Washington, DC, box 8, Communism: General 1946, as cited in Kent, *The Lonely Cold War*, 178–179. On the papal nuncio's and Father Martegani's views, see documents from February 12, 1947, and April 25, 1947, ACC, Fondo non ordinato, as cited in Sale, *De Gasperi, gli USA*, 93.

46. Philip E. Muehlenbeck, *Religion and the Cold War: A Global Perspective* (Nashville, TN: Vanderbilt University Press, 2012), introduction; Andrew Preston, *Sword of the Spirit, Shield of Faith: Religion in American War and Diplomacy* (New York: Alfred Knopf, 2012).

47. Radio message of September 1, 1944, as reprinted in *Discorsi e radiomessaggi di Sua Santità*, 6:124. See also *Orientalis Ecclesiae* of April 9, 1944, esp. chap. 26.

48. Joseph Prunskis, J.C.L., *Comparative Law, Ecclesiastical Law and Civil, in [sic] Lithuanian Concordat* (Washington, DC: Catholic University of America Press, 1945), 1.

49. Pius XII's audience with Roman nobility, January 14, 1945, as reprinted in *Discorsi e radiomessaggi di Sua Santità*, 6:273.

50. Conversation between Borgongini Duca and De Gasperi, June 28, 1946, as cited in Sale, *De Gasperi, gli USA*, 41.

51. Pius XII's speech of April 20, 1946, at a Catholic Action conference. As reprinted in *Discorsi e radiomessaggi di Sua Santità*, 8:56.

52. Andrea Oddone, "Funzione sociale della religione," *Civiltà Cattolica*, May 18, 1946.

53. See Silvio Tramontin, "La Democrazia Cristiana: Dalla resistenza alla Repubblica, 1943–1948," in *Storia della Democrazia Cristiana*, ed. Francesco Malgeri (Rome: Cinque Lune, 1989), 1:114; and Celso Ghini, *L'Italia che cambia: Il voto degli italiani, 1946–1974* (Rome: L'Unità, 1977), 21–54.

54. Martin Conway, "Christian Democracy: One Word or Two?," *Historia y Religión*, September 1, 2012.

55. Elisa A. Carrillo, *Alcide De Gasperi: The Long Apprenticeship* (Notre Dame, IN: University of Notre Dame Press, 1965), 7; Alan Paul Fimister, *Robert Schuman: Neo-Scholastic Humanism and the Reunification of Europe* (Brussels: PIE-Peter Lang, 2008), 197; Brent Nelsen and James Guth, *Religion and the Struggle for European Union: Confessional Culture and the Limits of Integration* (Washington, DC: Georgetown University Press, 2015), 192; Giulia Prati, *Italian Foreign Policy, 1947–1951: Alcide De Gasperi and Carlo Sforza between Atlanticism and Europeanism* (Göttingen: V&R Unipress, 2006), 135–136; Robert Keyserlingk, *Fathers of Europe: Patriots of Peace* (Montreal: Palm, 1972), 143.

56. As cited in R. C. Mowat, *Creating the European Community* (New York: Barnes and Noble, 1973), 52.

57. See Keyserlingk, *Fathers of Europe*, 24, 55; Charles Williams, *Adenauer: The Father of the New Germany* (New York: Wiley, 2000), 221; Nelsen and Guth, *Religion and the Struggle*, 193.

58. Guido Gonella, "Il programma della Democrazia Cristiana per la nuova costituzione," in *I cattolici democratici e la costituzione*, ed. Nicola Antonetti, Ugo De Siervo, and Francesco Malgeri (Bologna: Il Mulino, 1998), 2:729.

59. See F. P. Casavola, introduction to *I valori della Costituzione*, ed. Giuseppe Dossetti and Franco Monaco (Reggio Emilia: Edizioni San Lorenzo, 1995), 14; François Bazin, "Les deputes MRP élus en 1945 et 1946: Itinéraire politique d'une génération politique" (PhD diss., Institut d'études politiques, Paris, 1981); and Renato Moro, "I movimenti intellettuali cattolici," in *Cultura politica e partiti nell'età della Costituente*, vol. 1, *L'area liberal-democratica: Il mondo cattolico e la Democrazi Cristiana*, ed. Roberto Ruffilli (Bologna: Il Mulino, 1979), 238ff.

60. The *Osservatore Romano* article is reported in the *Washington Star*, July 23, 1944. As cited in Kent, *The Lonely Cold War*, 29–30.
61. For more on this, see Jean-Louis Jadoulle, "The Milieu of Left Catholics in Belgium (1940s–1950s)," in *Left Catholicism: Catholics and Society in Western Europe at the Point of Liberation, 1943/1955*, ed. Gerd-Rainer Horn and Emmanuel Gerard (Leuven: Leuven University Press, 2001), 102–117; Menozzi, *La Chiesa e i diritti umani*, 154–155.
62. Dossetti and Monaco, *I valori della Costituzione*, 13.
63. Assemblea Costituente, Commissione per la Costituzione, Prima Sottocommissione, 21, as cited in Sale, *De Gasperi, gli USA*, 19.
64. Pius XII speech to the Sacred College of Cardinals, June 1, 1946, as reprinted in *Discorsi e radiomessaggi di Sua Santità*, 8:105.
65. October 16, 1946, Secretariat of State note, ACC, Fondo p. Martegani, as cited in Giovanni Sale, *Il Vaticano e la Costituzione* (Milan: Jaca Book, 2008), 31.
66. Borgongini Duca to De Gasperi, June 28, 1946, ACC, Fondo non ordinato, as cited in Sale, *De Gasperi, gli USA*, 40.
67. "Gli Stati Uniti e l'Italia," February 1946 report, as cited in Miss Quinn, "The Neofascist Movement," April 10, 1946, intelligence files stored at NARA, RG 226, s. 108A, b. 272, f. jzx-7740. As reprinted in Nicola Tranfaglia, *Come nasce la repubblica: La mafia, il Vaticano e il neofascismo nei documenti americani e italiani, 1943–1947* (Milan: Bompiani, 2004), 80–87, at 87.
68. Secretariat of State notes from October 16 and November 18, 1946, ACC, Fondo p. Martegani; and Borgongini Duca to De Gasperi, June 28, 1946, ACC, Fondo non ordinato, as cited in Sale, *Il Vaticano*, 23, 31; and Sale, *De Gasperi, gli USA*, 40.
69. The document was presented on October 16, 1946. See Mario Casella, *Cattolici e Costituente: Orientamenti e iniziative del cattolicesimo organizzato (1945–1947)* (Naples: Edizioni Scientifiche Italiane, 1987), 287ff; Agostino Giovagnoli, "Le organizzazioni di massa d'Azione Cattolica," in *Cultura politica e partiti nell'età della Costituente*, ed. Robert Ruffilli (Bologna: Il Mulino, 1979), 1:435–492.
70. See Secretariat of State notes from October 16, October 19, and November 18, 1946, ACC, Fondo p. Martegani, as cited in Sale, *Il Vaticano*, 13, 23, 33–34.
71. See Dossetti, undated files (likely mid-November 1946), ACC, Fondo p. Martegani, as cited in Sale, *Il Vaticano*, 36–37.
72. Note of the Vatican Secretary of State, December 13, 1946, ACC, Fondo p. Martegani; Pietro Nenni, Assemblea Costituente, March 25, 1947, session, 2.458; Bruni in Assemblea Costituente, March 14, 1947, session, 2.094; Assemblea Costituente, March 11, 1947, session, 2.008. As cited in Sale, *Vaticano e Costituzione*, 39, 61, 75, 109.
73. Luigi Paganelli, *I Cattolici e l'Azione Cattolica a Modena durante il fascismo, dal 1926 al 1945* (Modena: Mucchi e Sias Editori, 2005), 458; Frank Coppa, "Pius XII and the Cold War," in *Religion and the Cold War*, ed. Dianne Kirby (New York: Palgrave Macmillan, 2003), 59.
74. On U.S. intervention in the 1948 elections, see, *inter alia*, Kaeten Mistry, "The Case for Political Warfare: Strategy, Organization and U.S. Involvement in the 1948 Italian Election," *Cold War History* 6, no. 3 (August 2006): 301–329;

James Miller, "Taking Off the Gloves: The United States and the Italian Elections of 1948," *Diplomatic History* 7 (1983): 35–55; Miller, "Roughhouse Diplomacy: The United States Confronts Italian Communism, 1945–1958," *Storia delle Relazioni internazionali* 5, no. 2 (1989): 279–311; Morris Janowitz and Elizabeth Marvick, "U.S. Propaganda and the 1948 Italian Elections," in *A Psychological Warfare Casebook: Part 1*, ed. William Daugherty and Morris Janowitz (Baltimore: John Hopkins University Press, 1958); David Ellwood, "The 1948 Elections in Italy: A Cold War Propaganda Battle," in *Ripensare il 1948: Politica, economia, società, cultura*, ed. Giovanni Tocci (Ancona: Il lavoro editorial, 2000); and Mario Del Pero, "The United States and 'Psychological Warfare' in Italy, 1948–1955," *Journal of American History* 87, no. 4 (March 2001): 1304–1324.

75. Casella, *Cattolici e Costituente*; Ernesto Preziosi, *Obbedienti in piedi: La vicenda dell'Azione Cattolica in Italia* (Turin: Società Editrice Internazionale, 1996).

76. Formigoni, *Storia d'Italia nella guerra fredda*, 127.

77. See Wendy Wall, "America's 'Best Propagandists': Italian Americans and the 1948 'Letters to Italy' Campaign," in *Cold War Constructions: The Political Culture of United States Imperialism, 1945–1966* (Amherst: University of Massachusetts Press, 2000), 99–109; and Stefano Luconi, "Anticommunism, Americanization and Ethnic Identity: Italian Americans and the 1948 Parliamentary Elections in Italy," *Historian* 62 (2000): 295–302.

78. See Thomas M. Gauly, "Katholiken: Machtanspruch und Machtverlust" (PhD diss., University of Bonn, 1992); Johannes Zachhuber, "Churches as 'Value Mediators': Religion and Collective Identity in Germany," in *Religion and Politics in the United States and Germany: Old Divisions and New Frontiers*, ed. Dagmar Pruin, Rolf Schieder, and Johannes Zachhuber (Berlin: Lit-Verlag, 2007), 187–200; Franz Walter, "Katholizismus in der Bundesrepublik," *Blätter für deutsche und internationale Politik* 41, no. 9 (1996): 1102–1110; Wolfgang Schroeder, *Katholizismus und Einheitsgewerkschaft* (Bonn: Dietz, 1992); Klaus Gotto, "Die deutschen Katholiken und die Wahlen in der Adenauer-Ära," in *Katholizismus im politischen System der Bundesrepublik*, ed. Albrecht Langner (Paderborn: Schöningh, 1978).

79. Walter, "Katholizismus in der Bundesrepublik," 1103.

80. Maria Mitchell, "Catholicism and Interconfessional Politics: The Catholic Church and the Christian Democratic Union," *Kirchliche Zeitgeschichte* 19, no. 2 (2006): 347–358, at 351–352; and *Katholizismus, Wirtschaftsordnung und Sozialpolitik, 1945–1963*, ed. Albrecht Langner (Paderborn: Schöningh, 1980).

81. Pastoral Letter, "A World of Love," cited by the U.S. Civil Censorship Division report of June 9, 1947, NARA, RG 260, box 15, folder 24 (equivalent of—folder is untitled).

82. Karl-Egon Lönne, "Germany," in *Political Catholicism in Europe, 1918–1965*, ed. Tom Buchanan and Martin Conway (Oxford: Clarendon Press, 1996), 156–186, at 180–183; Andreas Lienkamp, "Socialism out of Christian Responsibility: The German Experiment of Left Catholicism (1945–1949),"

in *Left Catholicism: Catholics and Society in Western Europe at the Point of Liberation, 1943–1955*, ed. Gerd-Rainer Horn and Emmanuel Gerard (Louvain: KADOC, 2001), 196–227.

83. Aline-Florence Manent, "Democracy and Religion in the Political and Legal Thought of Ernst-Wolfgang Böckenförde," *Oxford Journal of Law and Religion* 7, no. 1 (February 1, 2018): 74–96. For secondary literary substantiating this interpretation of the CDU's revisionist history, see Jeffrey Herf, "Multiple Restorations: German Political Traditions and the Interpretation of Nazism, 1945–1946," *Central European History* 26 (1993), 21–55; Maria Mitchell, "Materialism and Secularism, CDU Politicians and National Socialism, 1945–1949," *Journal of Modern History* 67 (1995): 278–308; and Maria Mitchell, "'Antimaterialism' in Early German Christian Democracy," in *European Christian Democracy: Historical Legacies and Comparative Perspectives*, ed. Thomas A. Kselman and Joseph A. Buttigieg (Notre Dame, IN: University of Notre Dame Press, 2003).

84. Letter from Robert A. McClure, Director of Information Control, to Ambassador Murphy, U.S. Political Advisor, November 14, 1946, NARA, RG 260, box 181, folder "Muench, Bishop." Emphasis in the original.

85. Suzanne Brown-Fleming, "'The Worst Enemies of a Better Germany': Postwar Antisemitism among Catholic Clergy and U.S. Occupation Forces," *Holocaust and Genocide Studies* 18, no. 3 (December 1, 2004): 379–401, at 388; Joseph W. Bendersky, *The "Jewish Threat": Antisemitic Politics of the U.S. Army* (New York: Basic Books, 2000); Frank Stern, *The Whitewashing of the Yellow Badge: Antisemitism and Philosemitism in Postwar Germany* (Oxford: Pergamon Press, 1992).

86. On the relationship between the United States and the CDU, see Ronald J. Granieri, "Political Parties and German-American Relations, 1945–1968: Politics beyond the Water's Edge," in *Germany and the United States in the Era of the Cold War, 1945–1990: A Handbook*, 2 vols., ed. Detlef Junker (Cambridge: Cambridge University Press, 2004), 1:141–149.

87. The citations are drawn from a Top Secret note from Anthony B. Kenkel to Brig. Gen. William J. Donovan, received December 12, 1944, NARA, RG 226, box 328, folder 13525. Also see undated handwritten note, attached to Top Secret note from Anthony B. Kenkel to Brig. Gen. William J. Donovan, received December 12, 1944, NARA, RG 226, box 328, folder 13525. Schäfer would later be removed from his post on account of his rabid anti-Semitic views. Paul W. Freedman, Editorial Unit, Office of Military Government for Germany (hereafter cited as OMGUS), "The Catholic Church in Bavaria," pp. 1–28, undated report prepared by OMGUS, most likely in August 1946, NARA, RG 260, box 15, folder 23A, "Catholic Church"; "Religious Affairs Branch: Summary Report, 1949," NARA, RG 260, box 204, folder "Summary of the Fiscal Year—1949 Program of the Religious Affairs Branch, E+CR Div."

88. See James Byrnes, U.S. Secretary of State, "Restatement of Policy on Germany," September 6, 1946, Stuttgart, NARA, RG 260, box 204, folder "Summary of the Fiscal Year—1949 Program of the Religious Affairs Branch, E+CR Div."

89. Peter Löffler, ed., *Bischof Clemens August Graf von Galen: Akten, Briefe und Predigten, 1933–1946*, vol. 2, *1939–1946* (Mainz: Grünewald, 1996), 2:1238 (October 22, 1945).

90. Konrad Adenauer, "Grundsatzrede des 1. Vorsitzenden der Christlich-Demokratischen Union für die Britische Zone in der Aula der Kölner Universität," March 24, 1946, as reprinted in *Die Demokratie ist für uns eine Weltanschauung: Reden und Gespräche 1946–1967*, ed. Felix Becker (Köln: Böhlau, 1998). On Adenauer's tendency to underemphasize German guilt, see Jeffrey Herf, *Divided Memory: The Nazi Past in the Two Germanies* (Cambridge, MA: Harvard University Press 1997), 226.

91. Brown-Fleming, "'The Worst Enemies,'" 383; Mitchell, "Materialism and Secularism"; Noah Benezra Strote, *Lions and Lambs: Conflict in Weimar and the Creation of Post-Nazi Germany* (New Haven, CT: Yale University Press, 2017); and Mark Edward Ruff, *The Battle for the Catholic Past in Germany, 1945–1980* (Cambridge: Cambridge University Press, 2017).

92. Dieter A. Binder, "'Rescuing the Christian Occident' and 'Europe in Us': The People's Party in Austria," in *Christian Democracy in Europe since 1945*, ed. Michael Gehler and Wolfram Kaiser (London: Routledge, 2004), 2:139–154, at 142–143.

93. Konrad Repgen, "Der Konkordatsstreit der fünfziger Jahren: Von Bonn nach Karlsruhe (1949–1955 / 57)," *Kirchliche Zeitgeschichte* 3 (1990): 201–245, at 212; Ulrike Marga Dahl-Keller, *Der Treueid der Bischöfe gegenüber dem Staat: Geschichtliche Entwicklung und gegenwärtige staatskirchenrechtliche Bedeutung* (Berlin: Duncker und Humblot, 1994), 157ff.

94. Freedman, "The Catholic Church in Bavaria," NARA, RG 260, box 15, folder 23A, "Catholic Church."

95. Religious Affairs Section, "Statement of Principle Differences Encountered with Soviet Representatives on Official Matters," 1946, NARA, RG 260, box 202, folder "Intelligence Reports—Mitropa—1946"; letter from Ambassador Murphy to Captain Richey, Berlin, August 5, 1945, NARA, RG 260, box 203, folder "Religious Affairs—Misc."; Memorandum of conversations between John O. Riedl, Father Zeiger, Assistant to Bishop Muench, Monsignor Tardini, and Father Leiber, December 30, 1947, NARA, RG 59: General Records of the Department of State, Entry 1068: Office of the Personal Representative of the President to Pope Pius XII, box 15, folder "Memoranda of Conversations."

96. "Religious Affairs Branch: Summary Report, 1949."

97. Historisches Archiv des Erzbistums Köln (HAEK), Kath. Büro I, 81, Education and Religious Affairs, Regulations of Allied Control Council, Title 8. Clemens Vollnhalls, "Das Reichskonkordat von 1933 als Konfliktfall im Alliierten Kontrollrat," *Vierteljahrshefte für Zeitgeschichte* 35 (1987): 677–706, as cited in Mark Ruff "Clarifying Present and Past: The Reichskonkordat and Drawing Lines between Church and State in the Adenauer Era," *Schweizerische Zeitschrift für Religions und Kulturgeschichte* 106 (2012): 257–279, at 260.

98. Anne Martin, *Die Entstehung der CDU in Rheinland-Pfalz* (Mainz: V. Hase und Koehler, 1995), 222ff.

99. Pius XII speech to the Sacred College of Cardinals, June 2, 1945, as reprinted in *Discorsi e radiomessaggi di Sua Santità*, 7:68–73.

100. Pius XII audience with American senators and diplomats, November 2, 1945, as reprinted in *Discorsi e radiomessaggi di Sua Santità*, 7:259.

101. Hermann Höpker-Aschoff, "Bonn und die christlischen Kirchen," *Die Zeit*, January 6, 1949.

102. As cited in Mark Edward Ruff, *The Wayward Flock: Catholic Youth in Postwar Germany, 1945–1965* (Chapel Hill: University of North Carolina Press, 2005), 33.

103. Martin, *Die Entstehung der CDU*, 224.

104. Letter from Cardinal Faulhaber to Bishop Aloysius Muench, Munich, January 7, 1948, NARA, RG 260, box 195, folder "School Reform."

105. Letter from Ambassador Robert Murphy, U.S. Political Advisor, to Dr. J. W. Taylor, Education Section, IA & C Division, OMGUS, November 4, 1946, citing a recent memorandum from Bishop Muench, NARA, RG 260, box 181, folder "Muench, Bishop."

106. "General Goals and Tasks of Bavarian School Reform," April 1, 1947, NARA, RG 260, box 195, folder "School Reform."

107. Letter from the Bishop of Mainz to His Excellency, Ambassador Murphy, Control Council, Berlin, Mainz, October 29, 1946, NARA, RG 260, folder "000.3—Religion: Clergymen—Bishop Stohr (Bishop of Mainz)." Also see "General Goals and Tasks of Bavarian School Reform," April 1, 1947, NARA, RG 260, folder "School Reform"; "Functional Program for Religious Affairs, 1 July to 31 December 1947," NARA, RG 260, box 202, folder "Functional Program, R A Branch—1947."

108. See Ruff, "Clarifying Present and Past," 261–262; Carolyn Warner, *Confessions of an Interest Group: The Catholic Church and Political Parties in Europe* (Princeton, NJ: Princeton University Press, 2000); Annie Lacroix-Riz, *Le Vatican, l'Europe et le Reich: De la première guerre mondiale à la guerre froide* (Paris: Armand Colin, 2010). The complaints immediately earned the ire of Catholic integralists, who noted that the CDU was not behaving as it should—that is, as a "purely Catholic party." Letter from Father Ivo Zeiger, SJ, to Father Leiber, April 27, 1948, as cited in Ludwig Volk, "Der heilige Stuhl und Deutschland, 1945–1949," in *Katholische Kirche und Nationalsozialismus. Ausgewählte Aufsätze*, ed. Ludwig Volk (Mainz: Matthias-Grünewald, 1987), 144–174, at 174.

109. This ultimately became article 123. See Repgen, "Der Konkordatsstreit der fünfziger Jahren."

110. Dépêche of October 15, 1948, Archives du Ministère des Relations Extérieures, Paris, Europe, Saint-Siège (1944–1949), vol. 10, as cited in Philippe Chenaux, "Le Vatican et l'Europe, 1947–1957," *Storia delle relazioni internazionali* (1988): 47–81, at 52.

111. In 1930 Hundhammer published a book entitled *Staatsbürgerlichen Vorträgen* (Civic lectures) in which he defended the idea of a state based in Catholic teachings and moral principles, and strongly criticized both socialist and liberal concepts of state and society. He suggested that the 1918 revolutions in Germany delegitimized both democracy and republicanism

in Germany, and argued that the principle of popular sovereignty (as enshrined in the democratic constitution of the Reich of 1919) was in contradiction with the Catholic view of the divine legitimacy of the state. For more on the CSU, see Alf Mintzel, "Die Christlich-soziale Union in Bayern," in *Parteien-Handbuch*, ed. Richard Stoss (Opladen: Westdeutscher Verlag, 1986), 661–718.

112. In Bavaria, the SPD agreed to the CSU's proposals—as the Social Democratic Party leader, Wilhelm Hoegner, put it, he and his party did not want to be responsible for starting a "religious war" in Bavaria right after the conclusion of hostilities. See Oliver Braun, *Existenz in der Moderne: Das politische Weltbild Alois Hundhammers* (Munich: Hans-Seidel-Stiftung, 2006).

113. Jaimey Fisher, *Disciplining Germany: Youth, Re-Education and Reconstruction after the Second World War* (Detroit: Wayne State University Press, 2007), 72–77.

114. Pius XII's radio message to the people of Spain, November 18, 1945, as reprinted in *Discorsi e Radiomessaggi di Sua Santità*, 7:284.

115. Cardinal Alfredo Ottaviani, *Doveri dello stato cattolico verso la religione* (Rome: Libreria del Pont. Ateneo Lateranense, 1953), 8–9.

116. In response to these attacks, Spain would reform article 6; the new article protected freedom of religion in Spain, and implied that Spain would work to protect that freedom under law—something further reaffirmed by a law of June 28, 1967, according to which Spain definitively committed itself to protecting freedom of religion. José Toméas Martín de Agar y Valverde, *El matrimonio canónico en el derecho civil español* (Pamplona: Eunsa, 1985), 85. For a defense of the original Fuero text and its restrictions on non-Catholic activity, see Eustaquio Guerrero and Joaquín María Alonso, *Libertad religiosa en España* (Madrid: Fe catolica, 1962).

117. *XIX Congreso Mundial de Pax Romana* (Madrid: Pax Romana, 1946), 77, 78, 85; "Discurso del Presidente," *Boletín de la Asociación Católica Nacional de Propagandista*, April 1, 1937, p. 4, as cited in Michael Richards, "'Opening the Door Again to the Marxist Enemy: Catholicism, Transnational Anti-communism and Legitimation in Franco's Spain, 1936–59," unpublished article, 2015.

118. Edmund Walsh's pamphlet "Facts about Spain" was published in Spain and in the United States in *The Tablet*, February 23, 1946.

119. "A Mistaken Scruple," *Catholic Times*, April 29, 1949; "Position of Spain," *Catholic Times*, April 29, 1949; "Sciocchezzaio Realista," *Europa Federata: Periodico del Movimento Federalista Europeo*, June 13, 1949, as cited in Duranti, *Conservative Human Rights Revolution*, 175.

120. Luigi Sturzo, *La comunità internazionale e il diritto di guerra* (Bologna: Zanichelli, 1954), 28.

121. Murray, "The Crisis in Church-State Relationships in the U.S.A.," Clare Booth Luce papers, box 703, folder 14, Library of Congress, Washington, DC, as cited in Agnes de Dreuzy, "*Dignitatis Humanae* as an Encounter between Two 'Towering Theologians,' John Courtney Murray, SJ, and Yves Congar, O.P.," *U.S. Catholic Historian* 24 (Winter 2006): 33–43, at 37.

122. Eloy Montero y Gutiérrez, *El nuevo concordato español* (Madrid: Impr. Viuda de Galo Sáez, 1954).

123. Giuseppe Pizzardo "Preface," in *Intellectuels dans la chrétienté*, ed. Adriano Bernareggi (Rome: Pax Romana, 1948), 7.

124. *The Tablet*, July 13, 1946; *XIX Congreso Mundial de Pax Romana* (Madrid: Pax Romana, 1946), 145, as cited in Richards, "Opening the Door Again."

125. *XIX Congreso Mundial*, 62.

126. See Pius XII allocution of December 6, 1953, as reprinted in *Documents Pontificaux (1953)*, 619; and his speech to the Tenth International Congress of Historical Sciences, September 7, 1955, as reprinted in *Documents Pontificaux* (1955), 291–292.

127. José Sánchez Jiménez, *El Cardenal Herrera Oria: Pensiamento y acción social* (Madrid: Encuentro, 1986), 10–1, as cited in Richards, "Opening the Door Again."

128. Radio message to Spanish workers, March 11, 1951, as reprinted in *Documents Pontificaux de sa Sainteté Pie XII (1951)*, ed. Robert Kothen (Paris: Éditions Labergerie, 1954), 86–90.

129. Pius XII radio message to the young women of Spanish Catholic Action, November 27, 1955, as reprinted in *Documents Pontificaux de sa Sainteté Pie XII (1955)*, 457.

130. Arnaldo Cortesi, "Spain and Vatican Sign a Concordat," *New York Times*, August 28, 1953.

131. Francisca Montilla, "La escuela primaria en el concordato español de 1953," *Revista Española de Pedagogía* (January–March 1957): 43–48.

132. "Pact with Vatican Ratified by Spain," *New York Times*, October 27, 1953.

133. E. J. Heubel, "Church and State in Spain: Transition toward Independence and Liberty," *Western Political Quarterly* 30, no. 1 (March 1977): 125–139, at 129.

134. Pius XII's speech to the Ambassador of Ecuador, César Coloma Silva, June 18, 1951, as reprinted in *Documents Pontificaux de sa Sainteté Pie XII (1951)*, 254.

135. As cited in Heubel, "Church and State in Spain," 130.

136. Salvador Madariaga, *Spain: A Modern History* (New York: Praeger, 1958), 609.

CHAPTER 9 ▪ HISTORY HAUNTS THE CHURCH

Epigraph: Ernst-Wolfgang Böckenförde, "Formen christlichen Weltverhaltens während der NS-Herrschaft" (1965), as reprinted in Böckenförde, *Kirche und christlicher Glaube in den Herausforderungen der Zeit: Beiträge politisch-theologischen Verfassungsgeschichte, 1957–2002* (Münster: LIT Verlag, 2004), 181–190, at 190.

1. The study of Christian Democratic internationalism is in its infancy. For an introduction see Tom Buchanan and Martin Conway, eds., *Political Catholicism in Europe, 1918–1965* (Oxford: Clarendon Press, 1996); Michael Gehler, Wolfram Kaiser, and Helmut Wohnout, eds., *Christdemokratie in Europa im 20. Jahrhundert / Christian Democracy in the 20th Century* (Vienna:

Bohlau, 2001); Michael Gehler and Wolfram Kaiser, eds., *Christian Democracy in Europe since 1945*, vol. 2 (London: Routledge, 2004); Wolfram Kaiser, *Christian Democracy and the Origins of the European Union* (Cambridge: Cambridge University Press, 2007); Piotr Kosicki and Sławomir Łukasiewicz, eds., *Christian Democracy Across the Iron Curtain: Europe Redefined* (Basingstoke: Palgrave Macmillan, 2018); Thomas Kselman and Joseph A. Buttigieg, eds., *European Christian Democracy: Historical Legacies and Comparative Perspectives* (South Bend, IN: University of Notre Dame Press, 2003); Emiel Lamberts, ed., *Christian Democracy in the European Union, 1945–1995* (Leuven: Leuven University Press, 1997); and Roberto Papini, *The Christian Democrat International*, trans. Robert Royal (London: Rowman and Littlefield, 1997).

2. Martin Rosenberg to Josef Meier, October 11, 1946, and Meier to Rosenberg, October 29, 1946, Bundesarchiv, Bern, Switzerland, Belgian Christian Democracy Archive, JII.181, 2659, as cited in Kaiser, *Christian Democracy*, 180. For context, see Laurent Gothelf, "Jacques Maritain, Monseigneur Montini et l'internationalisation du Saint-Siège, 1945–1948," *Revue d'histoire diplomatique* 1–2 (1985): 149–155; and Philippe Chenaux, "Le Vatican et l'Europe, 1947–1957," *Storia delle relazioni internazionali* 1 (1988): 47–83.

3. "Une communication du Louis Joseph Lebret, Directeur d'Economie et Humanisme" to the NEI congress at Liège, May 1946; speech by Luigi Sturzo, "Objectifs de la Démocratie chrétienne dans l'Europe actuelle," given at the NEI congress in Sorrento, April 12–14, 1950; speech by André Colin to the NEI's Geneva congress, January 14, 1952; and speech by Robert Houven at the NEI's Geneva congress of February 13. 1950; all stored in Centre Historique des Archives Nationales, Paris, Fonds Robert Bichet, c. 9 and c. 10, Archive Privée 519. As cited in Paolo Acanfora, "Christian Democratic Internationalism: The *Nouvelles Equipes Internationales* and the Geneva Circles between European Unification and Religious Identity, 1947–1954," *Contemporary European History* 24, no. 3 (2015): 375–391, at 379, 381, 385.

4. Guido Formigoni, "La sinistra cattolica e il Patto atlantico (1948–1949), *Il Politico* 4 (1985): 631–668.

5. Pope Pius XII, *Summi Maeroris* (July 19, 1950), available online at http://w2.vatican.va/content/pius-xii/en/encyclicals/documents/hf_p-xii_enc _19071950_summi-maeroris.html.

6. Pius XII, homily delivered at Saint-Paul-Hors-le-Murs, September 18, 1947, as reprinted in *Documents Pontificaux de Sa Sainteté Pie XII* (Saint-Maurice, Switzerland: Éditions Saint-Augustin, 1950–1984), 9:282.

7. Piotr H. Kosicki, "The Soviet Bloc's Answer to European Integration: Catholic Anti-Germanism and the Polish Project of a 'Catholic-Socialist' International," *Contemporary European History* 24, no. 1 (2015): 1–36, at 4.

8. Andrea Riccardi, *Il partito romano nel secondo dopoguerra* (Brescia: Morcelliana, 1983), 133.

9. Palmiro Togliatti, "Comrade Togliatti's Report: Working-Class Unity and the Tasks of the Communist and Workers' Parties," November 17, 1949, in *The Cominform*, ed. Giuliano Procacci (Milan: Feltrinelli, 1994), 783–803, at 797.

10. *New York Times*, April 11, 1951, as cited in Lawrence S. Wittner, *One World or None: A History of the World Nuclear Disarmament Movement through 1953* (Stanford, CA.: Stanford University Press, 1993), 189.

11. *Osservatore Romano*, July 2, 1949.

12. Assembly of Archbishops and Bishops, January 8–10, 1952. From the private archive of Andrea Riccardi, as cited in Riccardi, *Il partito romano*, 178.

13. Cingolani to De Gasperi, October 17, 1951, Historical Archives of the European Union, Villa Salviati, Florence, Carte De Gasperi, "Corrispondenza," b.7, f. 15, as cited in Augusto D'Angelo, *De Gasperi, le destre e l'Operazione Sturzo: Voto amministrativo del 1952 e progetti di riforma elettorale* (Rome: Studium, 2002), 20–21.

14. Danilo Veneruso, "Pio XII e Truman: Dietro le Quinte della Grande Intesa Politico-Diplomatica tra Vaticano e USA," *Enne Effe* (2004): 131–140, at 138.

15. Assembly of Archbishops and Bishops, January 8–10, 1952. From the private archive of Andrea Riccardi, as cited in Riccardi, *Il partito romano*, 178.

16. *Vie Nuove*, February 12, 1949, as cited in Philippe Chenaux, *L'Église catholique et le communisme en Europe (1917–1989): De Lénine à Jean-Paul II* (Paris: Les Éditions du Cerf, 2010), 156–157.

17. Togliatti, "Comrade Togliatti's Report," 797.

18. "Secret Memorandum" on the conversation between Myron Taylor and Roncalli, Paris, July 19, 1949, Supreme Sacred Congregation of the Holy Office: Decree, 1 July 1949. As translated and reprinted in Rare and Manuscript Collections, Cornell University, Myron Taylor papers, #3308, box 3, "Summary of Contacts by Mr. Myron C. Taylor with Leaders in Religion, 1940–1953."

19. M.G.S.I., "Le dichiarazioni del S. Ufficio e il comunismo," *La Civiltà Cattolica*, July 30, 1949.

20. Riccardi, *Il partito romano*, 133; Sandro Magister, *La politica vaticana e l'Italia (1943–1978)* (Rome: Ed. Riuniti, 1979), 134.

21. Father Lombardi, "Brevi rilievi sulle forze cattoliche in Italia (Per una mobilitazione generale)," *Civiltà Cattolica*, May 28, 1947.

22. As cited in John Cooney, *The American Pope: The Life and Times of Francis Cardinal Spellman* (New York: Times Books, 1984), 167–168.

23. Jaime M. Pensado, "A 'Third Way' in Christ: The Project of the Corporation of Mexican Students (CEM) in Cold War Mexico," in *Local Church, Global Church: Catholic Activism in Latin America from Rerum Novarum to Vatican II*, ed. Stephen J. C. Andes and Julia G. Young (Washington, DC: Catholic University of America Press, 2016), 165–184, at 177.

24. Sergio Lariccia, *Stato e Chiesa in Italia, 1948–1980* (Brescia: Queriniana, 1981), 15.

25. The point was made by the Communist Party member and historian of Christianity, Ambrogio Donini, in the Communist Party's *Rinascita*, in 1950. The *Osservatore Romano* also grumbled about the news, noting that it was exclusively the task of the Secretariat of State to conclude concordats. As cited in Franco Bertone, *L'anomalia polacca. I rapporti tra Stato e Chiesa cattolica* (Rome: Ed. Riuniti, 1981), 166–175.

26. Peter Van Kemseke, "From Permission to Prohibition: The Impact of the Changing International Context on Left Catholicism in Europe," in *Left*

Catholicism: Catholics and Society in Western Europe at the Point of Liberation, ed. Emmanuel Gerard and Gerd-Rainer Horn (Leuven: Leuven University, 2001), 266.

27. See Robert John Petrie Hewison, *The Worker Priests, a Collective Documentation* (New York: Macmillan, 1956); François Leprieur, *Quand Rome condamne: Dominicains et prêtes-ouvriers* (Paris: Cerf, 1989), 340–347; and Jean Vinatier, *Les prêtres ouvriers, le cardinal Lienart et Rome: Histoire d'une crise, 1944–1967* (Paris: Témoignage chrétien, 1985), 69–104.

28. Giovanni Battista Montini was sent to an arch-episcopal post in Milan following a crossing of swords with Pius XII on this very issue.

29. Cardinal Elia Dalla Costa, as cited in Giulio Villani, *Il vescovo Elia Dalla Costa* (Florence: Vallecchi, 1974), 223–226.

30. Salvatore Lener, "Libertà di voto, democrazia, religione," *La Civiltà Cattolica*, May 26, 1951.

31. See Antonio Messineo, "Dopo le elezioni politiche del 7 giugno," *La Civiltà Cattolica*, June 27, 1953.

32. Nicola Adelfi, "Sei giorni di congiura," *L'Europeo*, May 10, 1952, 7. Luigi Sturzo supported the idea of a right-wing coalition. See Sturzo, "Il pericolo dell'*Operazione Sturzo*," *Il Giornale d'Italia*, February 21, 1959.

33. As cited in Riccardi, *Il partito romano*, 181.

34. Luigi Sturzo, *Politica di questi anni: Consensi e critiche (dal luglio 1951 al dicembre 1953)* (Bologna: Zanichelli,1966), 208ff.

35. As cited in Gianni Baget Bozzo, *Il partito Cristiano al potere* (Florence; Vallecchi, 1978), 2:399–402.

36. Antonio Messineo, "I cattolici e la vita politica," *La Civiltà Cattolica*, March 27, 1954. On Pius XII's role in getting *Civiltà Cattolica* to issue an immediate response to De Gasperi, see Giacomo Martina, *La Chiesa in Italia negli ultimi trent'anni* (Rome: Edizioni Studium, 1977), 35–36. For more on the contrast between Pius XII and De Gasperi, which lasted until De Gasperi's death in 1954, see Riccardi, *Il partito Romano*, 143–149; Jonathan Luxmoore and Jolanta Babuich, *The Vatican and the Red Flag: The Struggle for the Soul of Eastern Europe* (New York: G. Chapman, 1999), 98–99; Peter Hebblewaite, *Paul VI: The First Modern Pope* (New York: Paulist Press, 1993), 230.

37. For a discussion, see Florian Michel, *Étienne Gilson: Une biographie intellectuelle et politique* (Paris: VRIN, 2018).

38. Arnaldo Cortesi, "Pope Hints Belief Ban Is Effective," *New York Times*, August 18, 1949. For context, see John M. Kramer, "The Vatican's 'Ostpolitik,'" *Review of Politics* 42, no. 3 (July 1980): 283–308, at 285.

39. See Vincent Auriol, *Journal du septennat* (Paris: Colin, 2004), 5:463; and Joseph Hours, "L'idée européenne et l'idéal du St. Empire," *L'année politique et économique* (January–March 1953): 1–15. For context, see Jean-Marie Mayeur, "Pio XII e i movimenti cattolici," in *Pio XII*, ed. Andrea Riccardi (Rome: Laterza, 1984), 277–293, at 290.

40. Pius XII's letter was presented at the 40th Semaine sociale, held in Paris in July 1953. *Documents Pontificaux de sa Sainteté Pie XII*, 15:290–291.

41. Andrea Riccardi, "Ambienti cattolici romani e politica italiana negli anni del dopoguerra," in *Democrazia Cristiana e Costituente*, ed. Giuseppe Rossini (Rome: Cinque Lune, 1980), 1:263–320.

42. Letter from Monsigor Acqua, substitute to the Secretary of State, to M. Bernard Jousset, president of the International Catholic Organizations, March 11, 1955, as reprinted in *Documents Pontificaux de sa Sainteté Pie XII* (1955), ed. Simon Delacroix (Saint-Maurice: Éditions Saint-Augustin, 1957), 55.

43. Speech, May 31, 1954, as reprinted in *AAS* 46 (1954), 316.

44. Pius XII, *Atti e discorsi di Sua Santità Pio XII* (Rome: Edizioni Paoline, 1939–1959), 15:545–555.

45. In 1966 Charles De Gaulle would take France out of the military alliance.

46. Pius XII, Christmas message, 1954, as reprinted in *Discorsi e Radiomessaggi di Sua Santità Pio XII*, 16:329–345.

47. Father Messineo, "L'Europa alla deriva?," *Civiltà Cattolica*, October 2, 1954.

48. On La Pira's 1959 trip, see *Giorgio La Pira e la Russia*, ed. Marcello Garzantini and Maria Lucia Tonni (Florence: Giunti, 2005).

49. Letter from Monsignor Dell'Acqua to Monsignor Montini, April 4, 1957, Giorgio La Pira papers, as cited in Philippe Chenaux, *Une Europe Vaticane? Entre le Plan Marshall et les traités de Rome* (Bruxelles: Ciaco, 1990), 242.

50. *Frankfurter Allgemeine Zeitung*, November 12, 1955; December 12, 1955; March 13, 1956; and April 12, 1956.

51. Andrea Riccardi, "Governo e 'profezia' nel pontificato di Pio XII," in Riccardi, *Pio XII*, 59.

52. Pius XII, radio message for the beatification of Innocent XI, October 7, 1956, as reprinted in *Discorsi e Radiomessaggi di Sua Santità Pio XII*, 18:531–549.

53. Pius XII, radio message on Christmas eve, 1956. The only exception to this rule was for members of the upper clergy, who could dialogue with communist powers for one exclusive reason: "to obtain the recognition of the rights and freedom of the Church."

54. *L'Osservatore Romano*, March 13, 23, and 27, 1956.

55. See *Everson v. Board of Education of Ewing TP* (1947).

56. See William Inboden, *Religion and American Foreign Policy, 1945–1960: The Soul of Containment* (Cambridge: Cambridge University Press, 2008), 140–158.

57. D'Ormesson (Holy See) to Schuman, January 20 and 25, 1950, Quai d'Orsay, EU—Europe 1949–1955, Saint Siège 4; Perowne (Holy See) to Hoyer Millar (Washington), March 20, 1950, Foreign Office, WVI901/13, as cited in Peter Kent, *The Lonely Cold War of Pope Pius XII: The Roman Catholic Church and the Division of Europe* (Montreal: McGill-Queen's University Press, 2014), 254.

58. For similar sentiments, see Pius XII's Christmas messages for 1956 and 1954, as reprinted in *Discorsi e Radiomessaggi di Sua Santità Pio XII* (Milan: Vita e pensiero, 1941–1960), 18:740, 16:342.

59. Exhortation to the priests and preachers of Carême de Rome, March 10, 1955, as reprinted in *Discorsi e Radiomessaggi*, 17:5–9.

60. Pius XII, "Radio Message to the World," December 24, 1951, as reprinted in *Discorsi e Radiomessaggi*, 13:421–433.

61. Pius XII, allocution to the Congress of the Latin Medical Union, April 7, 1955; also see Pius XII, speech to the directors and employees of the Bank of Naples, May 29, 1955; both as reprinted in *Documents Pontificaux de sa Sainteté Pie XII*, 17:77, 160.

62. Pius XII, exhortation to the world of cinema, October 28, 1955, as reprinted in *Documents Pontificaux de sa Sainteté Pie XII*, 17:400–415, at 408.

63. Pius XII, speech to the Italian Center for International Reconciliation, October 13, 1955, as reprinted in *Documents Pontificaux de sa Sainteté Pie XII*, 17:371–383, at 376.

64. Pensado, "A 'Third Way' in Christ," 174.

65. Joseph A. Komonchak, "Religious Freedom and the Confessional State: The Twentieth-Century Discussion," *Revue d'Histoire Ecclésiastique* (2000): 634–650, at 646.

66. Pius XII, in an audience with American journalists, July 11, 1946, as reprinted in *Discorsi e radiomessaggi di Sua Santità*, 8:171.

67. See Fiorello Ignazio Cavalli, "La condizione dei Protestanti in Spagna," in *La Civiltà Cattolica* 99, no. 2 (1948): 29–47.

68. Antonio Messineo, "La tolleranza e il suo fondamento morale," *La Civiltà Cattolica* (November 4, 1950): 314–325, at 324.

69. Holy Office, December 20, 1949, instruction, as reprinted in *AAS*, 41:42–142.

70. Yves Congar, *Journal d'un Théologien (1946–1956)* (Paris: Le Cerf, 2000); Congar, "Lettre sur la liberté religieuse: À propos de la situation des Protestants en Espagne," *La Revue Nouvelle* 7 (May 15, 1948): 449–466; Edmond Chavaz, "La situation du Protestantisme en Espagne," *La vie intellectuelle* 16 (July 1948): 6–36; Jérôme Hamer, "Dialogue sans polémique sur la condition des Protestants en Espagne," *La Revue Nouvelle* 10 (December 15, 1949): 558–565; and "Protestants Eyeing Statement by Pope," *New York Times*, November 19, 1954. For context, see John A. Komonchak, "The Silencing of John Courtney Murray," *Cristianesimo nella Storia*, ed. A. Melloni (Bologna: Il Mulino, 1996), 657–702; and Donald E. Pelotte, *John Courtney Murray: Theologian in Conflict* (New York: Paulist Press, 1976).

71. Komonchak, "Religious Freedom," 646–647.

72. For more details, see Komonchak, "The Silencing," 657–702. The original talk can be found in the papers of the National Catholic Welfare Council/United States Catholic Conference in the archives of the Catholic University of America.

73. A copy of the Holy Office statement can be found in the 1954 Roman Diary of Fenton and in the papers of Francis Connell, as cited in Komonchak, "Religious Freedom," 648.

74. Antonio Messineo, "L'umanesimo integrale," *Civiltà Cattolica*, August 25, 1956.

75. Jan Eckel, "Human Rights and Decolonization: New Perspectives and Open Questions," *Humanity*, June 10, 2014.

76. Pius XII, speech to the leaders of the pontifical missions, June 24, 1944, *Discorsi e Radiomessagi*, 6:47–52. For similar themes, see Pio XII's encyclical, *Evangelii Praecones*, June 2, 1951.
77. Charles Keith, *Catholic Vietnam: A Church from Empire to Nation* (Berkeley: University of California Press, 2012), 236–238.
78. As referenced in Charles-Édouard Harang, *Quand les jeunes catholiques découvrent le monde: Les mouvements catholiques de jeunesse, de la colonization à la cooperation, 1920–1991* (Paris: Cerf, 2010), 106.
79. See Aline Coutrot, "Les Scouts de France et la guerre d'Algérie," *Les Cahiers de l'IHTP* 9 (October 1988): 121–138; and Frederick Cooper, *Decolonization and African Society: The Labor Question in French and British Africa* (Cambridge: Cambridge University Press, 1996), 291.
80. Charlotte Walker-Said, "Science and Charity: Rival Catholic Visions for Humanitarian Practice at the End of Empire," *French Politics, Culture and Society* 2 (June 2015): 33–54.
81. In 1949 there were 4,000 African students in France; in 1960, there were 8,000. Fabienne Guimont, *Les étudiants africains en France, 1950–1965* (Paris: Éditions de L'Harmattan, 1997), 72.
82. Joseph Ki-Zerbo, "Discours addressé au Cardinal Feltin au nom des étudiants catholiques d'outre-mer," *Tam-Tam*, December 1954, 15; and Joseph Michel, "Le devoir de décolonisation," supplement, *Alizés* (April–May 1954), as cited in Elizabeth Foster, "Entirely Christian and Entirely African: Catholic African Students in France in the Era of Independence," *Journal of African History* 56, no. 2 (2015): 239–259, at 253, 255.
83. Joseph-Vincent Ducatillon, "Théologie de la colonization," *Revue de l'action populaire* 90 (July–August 1955): 769–785, at 780; "Discours de son Eminence Cardinal Feltin aux étudiants d'outre-mer," *Tam-Tam*, December 1954, 18. Ducattilon is cited in Foster, "'Theologies of Colonization': The Catholic Church and the Future of the French Empire in the 1950s," *Journal of Modern History* 87 (June 2015): 281–315; Feltin is cited in Foster, "Entirely Christian," 255–256.
84. *Des prêtres noirs s'interrogent* (Paris: Cerf, 1956); Archives de la Congrégation du Saint-Esprit, Chevilly-Larue, France (ACSSp), SF 272, "Déclaration des étudiants catholiques d'Afrique noire en France"; and Discours de M. Ki-Zerbo au nom des étudiants," *Tam-Tam*, June–July 1957, 8. As cited in Foster, "Entirely Christian," 239–240, 256–257.
85. See Benedict XV's apostolic letter *Maximum illud* (1919) and Pius XI's encyclical *Rerum ecclesiae* (1926). Elizabeth Foster has shown that on the eve of independence, the Catholic hierarchy in French Africa was still almost entirely composed of French prelates and clergy. See Foster, "A Mission in Transition: Monsignor Joseph Faye and the Decolonization of the Catholic Church in Senegal," in *In God's Empire: French Missionaries and the Modern World* (New York, 2012), 257–277.
86. Pius XII, "Christmas Radio Message," December 24, 1955, as reprinted in *Discorsi e Radiomessaggi*, 17:433–449.
87. Pius XII, *Fidei Donum* (April 21, 1957). Available online at http://w2.vatican.va/content/pius-xii/en/encyclicals/documents/hf_p-xii_enc_21041957_fidei-donum.html.

88. Papini, *The Christian Democrat International*, 66.
89. Aldo Moro, October 6, 1971, speech at the United Nations, as reprinted in Aldo Moro, *Per la società italiana e la comunità internazionale* (Rome: Agenzia "Progetto," 1971).
90. On France, see *Théologies de la libération: Documents et débats*, ed. Bruno Chenu and Bernard Lauret (Paris: Cerf-Le Centurion, 1985); Claude Prudhomme, "De l'aide aux missions à l'action pour le tiers monde: Quelle continuité?," *Le Mouvement sociale* 177 (October–December 1996): 9–28; and Sabine Rousseau, "*Frères du Monde* et la guerre du Vietnam (1965–1973): Du tiers-mondisme à l'anti-impérialisme," *Le Mouvement sociale* 177 (October–December 1996): 71–88. On Italy, see Simone Paoli, "Alle origini del terzomondismo cattolico: La visione internazionale del dissenso negli anni della contestazione (1958–1968)," *Ventunesimo secolo* 2 (2014): 95–121. On Germany, see Marc-Dietrich Ohse, *Jugend nach dem Mauerbau: Anpassung, Protest und Eigensinn (DDR 1961–1974)* (Berlin: Christoph Links Verlag, 2003), 221–280; and Peter-Paul Straube, *Katholische Studentengemeinde in der DDR als Ort einer ausseruniversitären Studium generale* (Leipzig: Benno-Verlag, 1996).
91. Piotr Kosicki, "The Catholic 1968: Poland, Social Justice, and the Global Cold War," *Slavic Review* 77, no. 3 (Fall 2018): 638–660, at 653, 655–656.
92. Quinn Slobodian, *Foreign Front: Third World Politics in Sixties West Germany* (Durham, NC: Duke University Press, 2012), 25.
93. On the 1954 Bavarian elections, see Hans-Peter Schwarz, *Die Ära Adenauer, 1949–1957: Gründerjahre der Republik* (Stuttgart: DVA, 1981), 129–132.
94. See Mark Ruff, "Clarifying Present and Past: The *Reichskonkordat* and Drawing Lines between Church and State in the Adenauer Era," *Schweizerische Zeitschrift für Religions-und Kulturgeschichte* 106 (2012): 257–280, at 264.
95. See Noah Strote, *Lions and Lambs: Conflict in Weimar and the Creation of Post-Nazi Germany* (New Haven, CT: Yale University Press, 2017).
96. Ernst-Wolfgang Böckenförde, "Das Ethos der modernen Demokratie und die Kirche," *Hochland* 50 (1957/1958), 4–19. Böckenförde elaborated on these views in *Kirche und christlicher Glaube in den Herausforderungen der Zeit: Beiträge zur politisch-theologischen Verfassungsgeschichte, 1957–2002* (Münster: LIT, 2004), 137.
97. See, e.g., Böckenförde, *Recht, Staat, Freiheit: Studien zur Rechtsphilosophie, Staatstheorie und Verfassungsgeschichte* (Frankfurt am Main: Suhrkamp, 2016), 113.
98. Hans Kelsen, "Foundations of Democracy," *Ethics* 66 (1955): 1–101, at 40–42.
99. See Hermann Joseph Spital, "Noch einmal: Das Ethos der modernen Demokratie und die Kirche," *Hochland* 50 (1958): 409–421.
100. The sources had just been published in Erich Matthias and Rudolph Morsey, eds., *Das Ende der Parteien, 1933: Darstellungen und Dokumente* (Düsseldorf: Droste, 1960). Equally important for Böckenförde's analysis were newly published excerpts from Prelate Ludwig Kaas's diaries and correspondence. See Ludwig Kaas, "Tagebuch 7.–20. April 1933," *Stimmen der*

Zeit 166 (1960): 422–431; and Ludwig Kaas and Franz von Papen, "Briefwechsel zum Reichskonkordat," *Stimmen der Zeit* 167 (1960): 11–30; as referenced in Aline-Florence Manent, "Democracy and Religion in the Political and Legal Thought of Ernst-Wolfgang Böckenförde," *Oxford Journal of Law and Religion* 7, no. 1 (February 1, 2018): 74–96.

101. Böckenförde, "Der deutsche Katholizismus im Jahre 1933: Eine kritische Betrachtung," *Hochland* 53 (1961): 215–239.

102. See Mark Ruff, "Böckenförde und die Auseinandersetzung um den deutschen Katholizismus," in *Religion–Recht–Republik: Studien zu Ernst-Wolfgang Böckenförde*, ed. Klaus Große Kracht and Hermann-Josef Große Kracht (Paderborn : Schöningh, 2014), 33–68.

103. Father Leiber, Pius XII's private secretary, describing the pope's state of mind in the late 1950s. As cited in Hansjakob Stehle, *Eastern Politics of the Vatican, 1917–1979* (Athens, OH: Ohio University Press, 1981), 287.

104. Pius XII, *Discorsi* (1957), 19:91–96. For a discussion of how Pius XII became increasingly apocalyptic and concerned with death toward the end of his life, see Andrea Riccardi, "Governo e 'profezia' nel pontificato di Pio XII," in Riccardi, *Pio XII*, 31–92.

105. Robert Leonardi, *Italian Christian Democracy: The Politics of Dominance* (London: Palgrave Macmillan, 2014), 199.

106. The phrase "rude debate" is drawn from Alberto Melloni, "Review: *What Happened at Vatican II*, by John O'Malley," *Catholic Historical Review* 95, no. 2 (April 2009): 414–415.

CHAPTER 10 ▪ THE UPENDING OF CATHOLIC INTERNATIONALISM

Epigraph: Jean Guitton, in *Le Figaro*, August 28, 1976.

1. John O'Malley, *What Happened at Vatican II* (Cambridge, MA: Harvard University Press, 2010), 25.

2. Thomas T. McAvoy, "American Catholicism and the Aggiornamento," *Review of Politics* 30, no. 3 (July 1968): 275–291, at 284.

3. For an account from the inside of how this played out, see the diary of a rather lonely Spanish progressive priest, José L. Martín Descalzo, *Un Periodista en el Concilio*, 4 vols. (Madrid: Propaganda Popular Católica, 1963–1966).

4. Melissa Wilde, *Vatican II: A Sociological Analysis of Religious Change* (Princeton, NJ: Princeton University Press, 2007), 32–42.

5. Michael G. Lawler, Todd A. Salzman, and Eileen Burke-Sullivan, *The Church in the Modern World: "Gaudium et Spes" Then and Now* (Collegeville, MN: Liturgical Press, 2014), 4.

6. For more on the theological dimensions of the unresolved disputes, see Joseph A. Komonchak, "Augustine, Aquinas, or the Gospel *sine glossa*?," in *Unfinished Journey: The Church 40 Years after Vatican II: Essays for John Wilkins*, ed. Austin Ivereigh (New York: Continuum, 2005), 102–118. Also see Sydney E. Ahlstrom, "The Radical Turn in Theology and Ethics:

Why It Occurred in the 1960s," *Annals of the American Academy of Political and Social Science* 387, no. 1 (January 1970): 1–13.

7. Charles Cohen, "Introduction: Some Declarations on the Relation of the Non-Christian Religions to the Church," in *The Future of Interreligious Dialogue: A Multi-Religious Conversation on* Nostra Aetate, ed. Charles L. Cohen, Paul F. Kniter, and Ulrich Rosenhagen (New York: Orbis Books, 2017), 1–22.

8. This was asserted again in a second text from Vatican II entitled *Evangelii nuntiandi*, which specified that all Catholics (not just ordained priests) have a duty to spread the Catholic religion and grow the community of the faith. Accompanying texts changed the language of Church services from Latin to the vernacular, and specified that the officiant must turn 180 degrees, to face the congregation. See Pope Paul VI, *Sacrosanctum Concilium* (December 4, 1963), §14. Available online at http://www.vatican.va/archive/hist_councils/ii_vatican_council/documents/vat-ii_const_19631204_sacrosanctum-concilium_en.html.

9. Pope Paul VI, *Lumen Gentium* (November 21, 1964), chap. 2. Available online at http://www.vatican.va/archive/hist_councils/ii_vatican_council/documents/vat-ii_const_19641121_lumen-gentium_en.html.

10. Hubert Jedin and Konrad Repgen, *History of the Church: The Church in the Modern Age*, vol. 10 (New York: Crossroads, 1980), 131; Joseph H. Fichter, "Catholic Church Professionals," *Annals of the American Academy of Political and Social Science* 387 (January 1970): 77–85, at 80.

11. *Lumen Gentium*, chap. 1, §14.

12. A copy of the draft, *Ecclesia et Status: De officiis Status catholici erga religionem*, authored by Father Gagnebet, is stored in the Gagnebet papers (III, 1, 18) at the Istituto per le Scienze Religiose in Bologna (Holy Office stationery, Prot. N. 551/53/1). As cited in Joseph A. Komonchak, "Religious Freedom and the Confessional State: The Twentieth-Century Discussion," *Revue d'Histoire Ecclésiastique* (2000): 634–650, at 648–649.

13. Pope Paul VI, *Dignitatis Humanae* (December 7, 1965), §3. Available online at http://www.vatican.va/archive/hist_councils/ii_vatican_council/documents/vat-ii_decl_19651207_dignitatis-humanae_en.html.

14. For how Catholics at the United Nations, such as Charles Malik and the Commission of the Churches on International Affairs, influenced this definition of religious liberty at the UN, see Linde Lindkvist, "The Politics of Article 18: Religious Liberty in the Universal Declaration of Human Rights," *Humanity: An International Journal of Human Rights, Humanitarianism, and Development* 4, no. 3 (Winter 2013): 429–447.

15. *Dignitatis Humanae*, §§1, 2.

16. In 1965 the *Actes et documents du Saint-Siège relatifs à la seconde guerre mondiale* started being released to the public. The Good Friday prayer was revised in 1959, 1965, and 1970.

17. Pope Paul VI, *Nostra Aetate* (October 28, 1965), §§2, 4, 5. Available online at http://www.vatican.va/archive/hist_councils/ii_vatican_council/documents/vat-ii_decl_19651028_nostra-aetate_en.html.

18. As cited in John Connelly, *From Enemy to Brother: The Revolution in Catholic Teaching on the Jews* (Cambridge, MA: Harvard University Press, 2012), 263.

19. See Jerusha Lamptey, "Beyond the Rays of Truth? *Nostra Aetate*, Islam, and the Value of Difference," and John J. Thatamanil, "Learning From (and Not Just About) Our Religious Neighbors: Comparative Theology and the Future of Nostra Aetate," both in Cohen, Kniter, and Rosenhagen, *Future of Interreligious Dialogue*, 203–218, 289–302.

20. Paul F. Knitter, "*Nostra Aetate*: A Milestone in the History of Religions? From Competition to Cooperation," in Cohen, Kniter, and Rosenhagen, *Future of Interreligious Dialogue*, 45–60.

21. Pope Paul VI, *Gaudium et Spes* (December 7, 1965), §§63–64. Available online at http://www.vatican.va/archive/hist_councils/ii_vatican_council/documents /vat-ii_const_19651207_gaudium-et-spes_en.html.

22. Ibid., §§63, 65, 86.

23. Ibid., §§83, 92.

24. Ibid., §§29, 74, 76, 77, 78, 81.

25. On Lebret, see Denis Pelletier, "*Économie et Humanisme*": de l'utopie communautaire au combat pour le tiers-monde, 1941–1966 (Paris: Cerf, 1996); and Giuliana Chamedes, "The Catholic Origins of Economic Development after World War II," *French Politics, Culture and Society* (June 2015): 55–75.

26. Archives nationales, Pierrefitte (hereafter cited as AN-P), fonds Lebret, 19860461, art. 34, f. "Notations après voyage au tour de monde, 1955," p. 16.

27. Lebret, *Suicide ou survie de l'Occident?* (Paris: Économie et humanisme, éditions ouvrières, 1958), 178, 179, 340.

28. Ibid.,159–160.

29. Lebret's commissioned report for the Holy See, 1957, AN-P, fonds Lebret, 19860461, art. 34, f. 'Rapport Mgr del Aqua, 1957."

30. *National Review*, July 1961, as cited in John B. Judis Jr., *William F. Buckley, Jr.: Patron Saint of Conservatives* (New York: Simon and Schuster, 1988), 186.

31. Petition of September 29, 1965, as reprinted in Giovanni Caprile, *Il Concilio Vaticano II* (Rome: Civiltà Cattolica, 1969), 5:119.

32. *Documentation Catholique*, 1966, cols. 361–363.

33. Xavier Rynne, *Vatican Council II* (Maryknoll, NY: Orbis Books, 1999), 417.

34. For more on the place of communism at Vatican II, see Jean-Yves Calvez, "Le marxisme au Concile," in *Le Deuxième Concile du Vatican (1959–1965)* (Rome: École française de Rome, 1989), 689–701; Vincenzo Carbone, "Schemi e discussion sull'ateismo e sul marxismo nel Concilio Vaticano II: Documentazione," *Rivista di Storia della Chiesa in Italia* 44 (1990): 10–68; Paul Ladrière, "L'athéisme à Vatican II: De la condemnation du communisme à la négociation avec l'humanisme athée," *Social Compass* 24 (1977): 374–391; Giovanni Turbanti, "Il problema del comunismo al Concilio Vaticano II," in *Vatican II in Moscow (1959–1965)*, ed. Alberto Melloni (Louvain: Bibliotheek van de Faculteit Godgeleerdheid, 1997), 147–187; and Melloni, "Le riflessioni sul comunismo nel concilio Vaticano II," in *La chiesa cattolica e il totalitarismo*, ed. Vincenzo Ferrone (Florence: L. S. Olschki, 2004), 153–183.

35. *Documentation Catholique,* 1966, col. 365.

36. The conference proceedings were later published as *Marxistes et Chrétiens: Entretiens de Salzbourg,* ed. Rich Kellner (Paris: Mame, 1968).

37. Consider the work of Pierre Bigo, *Marxisme et humanisme* (Paris: Presses Universitaires de France, 1961); Jean-Yves Calvez, *The Church and Social Justice: The Social Teaching of the Popes from Leo XIII to Pius XII, 1878–1958* (London: Burns and Oates, 1961); and Henri Chambre, *Christianity and Communism* (New York: Hawthorn Books, 1961).

38. Father Jean-Baptiste Janssens, *Instruction on the Social Apostolate* (Woodstock, MD: Woodstock College Press, 1950).

39. Father Chenu, interview with *Informations catholiques internationals* (January 1, 1960), as cited in Philippe Chenaux, *L'Église catholique et le communisme en Europe, 1917—1989: De Lénine à Jean-Paul II* (Paris: Cerf, 2009), 239.

40. Louis Althusser, *L'Avenir dure longtemps: Les Suivi de faits* (Paris: Flammarion, 2013), 230.

41. Hansjakob Stehle, *The Eastern Politics of the Vatican, 1917–1979* (Athens, OH: Ohio University Press, 1981), 314.

42. Paul R. Waibel, "Politics of Accommodation: The SPD Visit to the Vatican, March 5, 1964," *Catholic Historical Review* 65, no. 2 (April 1979): 238–252.

43. As cited in Ronald J. Granieri, "Politics in C Minor: The CDU/CSU between Germany and Europe since the Secular Sixties," *Central European History* 42, no, 1 (March 2009): 1–32, at 17.

44. Horst Osterheld, *"Ich gehe nicht leichten Herzens . . .": Adenauers letzte Kanzlerjahre—Ein dokumentarischer Bericht* (Mainz: Matthias-Grünewald-Verlag, 1987), 138, 218.

45. Communist Congress of March 20, 1963, Bergamo, as cited in *Comunisti e mondo cattolico oggi,* ed. Antonio Tatò (Rome: Editori Riuniti, 1977), 102. Also see Francesco Skoda, *Il concilio Vaticano II nella critica sovietica* (Turin: Elle Di Ci, 1970).

46. Pope Paul VI, *Octogesima Adveniens* (May 14, 1971). Available online at http://w2.vatican.va/content/paul-vi/en/apost_letters/documents/hf_p-vi _apl_19710514_octogesima-adveniens.html.

47. Paul Hofmann, "Papal Letter Seen as Pragmatic on Social and Political Issues," *New York Times,* May 15, 1971.

48. Reinhard Schmoeckel and Bruno Kaiser, *Die Vergessene Regierung: Die grosse Koalition 1966–1969 und ihre langfristigen Wirkungen* (Bonn: Bouvier Verlag, 1991).

EPILOGUE: ONE AMONG MANY

1. Hilaire Belloc, *Europe and the Faith* (London: Constable, 1921), introduction.

2. On the mutual fortification of internationalism and nationalism, see, e.g., James Belich, *Replenishing the Earth: The Settler Revolution and the Rise of the Angloworld, 1783–1939* (Oxford: Oxford University Press, 2009); Sebastian Conrad, *Globalisation and the Nation in Imperial Germany*

(Cambridge: Cambridge University Press, 2010); Rebecca Karl, *Staging the World: Chinese Nationalism at the Turn of the Twentieth Century* (Durham, NC: Duke University Press, 2002); and Glenda Sluga, *Internationalism in the Age of Nationalism* (Philadelphia: University of Pennsylvania Press, 2013).

3. See Leo Kenis, Jaak Billiet, and Patrick Pasture, eds., *The Transformation of the Christian Churches in Western Europe, 1945–2000* (Leuven: Leuven University Press, 2010); Mark Ruff, *The Wayward Flock: Catholic Youth in Postwar West Germany, 1945–1965* (Chapel Hill: University of North Carolina Press, 2005), 156; Robert Leonardi and Douglas Wertman, *Italian Christian Democracy: The Politics of Dominance* (London: Macmillan, 1989), 212; Axel Schildt and Detlef Siegfried, eds., *Between Marx and Coca-Cola: Youth Cultures in Changing European Societies* (New York: Berghahn Books, 2006); and Axel Schildt, Detlef Siegfried, and Karl Christian Lammers, eds., *Dynamische Zeiten: Die 6oer Jahren in den beiden deutschen Gesellschaften* (Hamburg: Christians, 2000).

4. On the disagreements among Catholics regarding the encyclical, see Piotr Kosicki, "The Catholic 1968: Poland, Social Justice, and the Global Cold War," *Slavic Review* 77, no.3 (October 2018): 638–660.

5. "Infratest-Befragung," from March / April 1971, in Harald Pawlowski, *Krieg gegen die Kinder? Für und wider die Abtreibung, mit einer Dokumentation* (Limburg: Lahn-Verlag, 1971), 146–150, as cited in Kimba Allie Tichenor, "Protecting Unborn Life in the Secular Age: The Catholic Church and the West German Abortion Debate, 1969–1989," *Central European History* 47, no. 3 (September 2014): 612–645.

6. *Osservatore Romano*, February 12, 1972. The sentence was actually originally Paul VI's (of January 13, 1972). As cited in Tichenor, "Protecting Unborn Life," 619.

7. Karl Rahner, *Strukturwandel der Kirche als Aufgabe und Chance* (Freiburg: Herderbücherei, 1971), 69.

8. The Christian parliamentary faction was successful in overturning a Social Democratic attempt to get abortion legalized in the first trimester, however. See Atina Grossman, *Reforming Sex: The German Movement for Birth Control and Abortion Reform* (Oxford: Oxford University Press, 1997), 214.

9. Notes on the audience between Paul VI and Bartoletti, August 18, 1973, in Archivio Bartoletti, IV.11, as cited in Massimo Faggioli, "Il modello Bartoletti nell'Italia mancata," in *Cristiani d'Italia: Chiese, società, Stato, 1861–2001* (Rome: Istituto della Enciclopedia Italiana, 2001): 1:316–329.

10. As cited in G. C. Zizola, "I vescovi e il referendum," *Testimonianze* 164–165 (1974): 295.

11. See Archivio Bartoletti, IV.74, and *Civiltà Cattolica*, June 15, 1974, 622, as cited in Faggioli, "Il modello Bartoletti."

12. On the relation between the Prefect's action and the launching of the concordat commission, see Francesco Margiotta Broglio, "Dalla Conciliazione al giubileo 2000," in *Roma, la città del papa: Vita civile e religiosa dal*

giubileo di Bonifacio VIII al giubileo di papa Woityla, ed. Luigi Fiorani and Adriano Prosperi (Turin: Einaudi, 2000): 1153–1209.

13. In 1977 the Radical Party promoted a popular referendum to abrogate the Lateran Agreements. However, the Constitutional Court declared the referendum inadmissible because the Pact was valid before international (not just Italian) law. Jasmine Ceremigna, "Il Rapporto Stato-Chiesa all Luce del Concordato del 1984" (PhD diss., Libera Università Internazionale degli Studi Sociali, 2014 / 2015), 29.

14. Bettino Craxi, "Discorso a conclusione del dibatitto per la ratifica degli Accordi di Villa Madama," Italian Senate, August 3, 1984.

15. "Accordo tra la Santa Sede e la Repubblica Italiana che apporta modificazioni al concordato Lateranense," November 15, 1984, arts. 2.1, 2.4, 7.1, 8.1–8.3, 9.1, 9.2. "Protocollo Addizionale," 1, *In relazione all'Art. 1,* available online at http://www.vatican.va/roman_curia/secretariat_state/archivio/documents /rc_seg-st_19850603_santa-sede-italia_it.html.

16. As cited in Piero Fornara, "Parolin: 'Il Concordato del 1984 è ancora attuale, perché nasce dalla Costituzione e dal Concilio," *Il Sole 24 Ore,* February 12, 2014.

17. E. J. Heubel, "Church and State in Spain: Transition toward Independence and Liberty," *Western Political Quarterly* 30, no. 1 (March 1977): 125–139, at 134.

18. *Asamblea Conjunta Obispos-Sacerdotes, Historia de la Asamblea,* ed. Secretariado Nacional del clero (Madrid: BAC, 1971), 109–110, as cited in Heubel, "Church and State in Spain," 135–136. For more on the tensions between older clergy (alive during the Spanish Civil War) and younger clergy, see Audrey Brassloff, *Religion and Politics in Spain: The Spanish Church in Transition, 1962–1996* (New York: St. Martin's Press, 1998).

19. Vida Nueva, *Todo sobre el Concordato* (Madrid: PPC, 1971), 7, as cited in Heubel, "Church and State in Spain," 133.

20. "Acuerdo entre la Santa Sede y el Estado Español de 28 de julio de 1976," in *Los acuerdos entre la Iglesia y España: comentario,* ed. Carlos Manuel Corral Salvador, Lamberto de Echeverría, and León del Amo (Madrid: Editorial Católica, 1980), 778–781.

21. Juan María Laboa, *Iglesia y religion en las constituciones españolas* (Madrid: Encuentro, 1981), 100.

22. See José Toméas Martín de Agar y Valverde, *El matrimonio canónico en el derecho civil español* (Pamplona: Eunsa, 1985).

23. U.S. Department of State, *International Religious Freedom 2000: Annual Report* (Washington, DC: U.S. Govt. Printing Office, 2000), 326.

24. Sabrina P. Ramet, "Controversies in the Social and Political Engagement of the Catholic Church in Poland since 1988," in *Religion, Politics, and Values in Poland: Continuity and Change since 1989,* ed. Sabrina P. Ramet and Irena Borowik (London: Palgrave Macmillan, 2017), 19–40, at 22–23.

25. John Hooper, "Vatican Backs Down and Gives Mild Rebuke to American Nuns," *The Guardian,* December 16, 2014.

26. "Pope Denounces Holocaust 'Indifference' amidst Polish Uproar," *Associated Press*, January 29, 2018.

27. Steve Skojec, "Vatican Organization Still Involved in Communist Group," *One Peter Five*, May 29, 2015.

28. Thank you to Rachel Cohen for reading this epilogue at the eleventh hour, offering insightful feedback throughout, and suggesting this final formulation.

Acknowledgments

THE IDEAS IN THIS book first started germinating more than a decade ago, shortly after the attack on the Twin Towers in New York City, the invasions of Afghanistan and Iraq, and the rise of Islamophobia in Europe and the United States. As news outlets condemned Muslim extremism and the purported dangers of political Islam, they suggested that in the Western world, religious extremism and religious politics belonged to a distant past.

Something did not smell right. At the time, I was a graduate student studying modern European history at Columbia University. So I did what graduate students do when they sense that something is fishy: I headed to the library. I devoured Wolfram Kaiser's *Christian Democracy and the Origins of the European Union*; William Inboden's *Religion and American Foreign Policy*; Fabrice Bouthillon's *La naissance de la mardité*; and Renato Moro's *La formazione della classe dirigente cattolica*. These books—and many more—convinced me that a crucial story about the role of religion in shaping European (and transatlantic) politics had been occluded by recent events. I decided that I wanted to revisit this history, focusing on the central government of the Roman Catholic Church. When I informed my adviser, Victoria De Grazia, of the idea, she was both curious and skeptical (initially, mainly the latter). Much more secondary source reading, and a long series of phone calls and face-to-face meetings, followed. Finally,

413

Vicky agreed to support my application for summer funding to travel to Rome. I planned to visit the Secret Vatican Archives, where the papers of Pope Pius XI had recently been opened to the public.

Historians are typically discouraged from engaging in counterfactual reasoning, but my sense is that this book would not have been had I not had the joy and privilege of working so closely with Vicky De Grazia. I owe Vicky an enormous debt of gratitude. Throughout my time at Columbia (and since), Vicky has been an extraordinary friend and mentor, of the sort who challenges you at every step of the way, nudging you along less safe, but more rewarding, paths. In her sharp-witted, warm, and wonderfully direct fashion, Vicky has saved me from some real missteps and introduced me to innumerable key works of Italian and European history, including the scholarship of an old mentor of hers: Arno Mayer. My understanding of the papacy's work in the twentieth century—its quest for hegemony, its interest in civil society, and its struggle for influence against Wilson and Lenin—would have been quite diminished without Vicky De Grazia's tireless assistance.

My second giant intellectual debt is to Samuel Moyn. From our first meeting in a tiny office stacked high with boxes and papers, Sam has been an incredible resource, not just for great reads (though he has handed me plenty of those), but also for provocative new ways of thinking about the past. A nonconformist of the finest sort, Sam has been a source of inspiration for his careful and far-ranging genealogical work and for his willingness to constantly step out of his comfort zone. His support for this project from its murky early days was both surprising and extremely validating. And his willingness to read draft after draft after draft—balancing positive feedback with insightful criticism—has made the book stronger than what it would have been otherwise.

As a graduate student at Columbia, I also benefited from extensive conversations with Mark Mazower, whose work on internationalism, international orders, and neo-imperialism transformed my understanding of the twentieth century. Other New York–based scholars who helped sharpen the rough edges of the project include Volker Berghahn, Matthew Connelly, Paul Hanebrink, Ira Katznelson, Jan-

Werner Müller, Susan Pedersen, Anders Stephanson, and Lisa Tiersten. Talal Asad, Herrick Chapman, Partha Chatterjee, Carol Gluck, Rashid Khalidi, Mahmood Mamdani, Greg Mann, and Rosalind Morris also broadened my vistas and encouraged me to rethink the role of religion and patterns of enemy-making in history. I also was lucky to spend a few years grazing in the green pastures of Harvard University. There, I benefited enormously from exchanges with Peter Gordon, James Kloppenberg, Mary Lewis, Erez Manela, and Charles Maier. In the same years, Elizabeth Foster (at Tufts) became a friend and regular interlocutor. Since then, a series of talks, invited lectures, and workshops—delivered at Princeton, New York University, Stanford, Brown, the University of Chicago, Northwestern, Harvard, Wesleyan, Notre Dame, the University of British Columbia–Vancouver, the University of Maryland at College Park, Duke University, Occidental College, the U.S. Holocaust Museum, and the Istituto Paolo VI in Rome—have proved intellectually stimulating and generative of new ideas. Thanks in particular to Victoria Barnett, Warren Breckman, Suzanne Brown-Fleming, Jeffrey Byrne, Simona Ferrantin, Stefanos Geroulanos, Malachi Hacohen, Jeffrey Herf, David Kertzer, John McGreevy, Alberto Melloni, Jan-Werner Müller, Benjamin Nathans, Philip Nord, John O'Malley, Terence Renaud, Camille Robcis, Victoria Smolkin, Kevin Spicer, and Marla Stone—and many others—for making these opportunities available to me.

Since 2014, I have made the Department of History at the University of Wisconsin at Madison my home. My mentors here, Mary Lou Roberts and Jennifer Ratner-Rosenhagen, have been both generous and great fun to get to know. They have helped make Madison a wonderful landing spot, as have many other faculty members, including Laird Boswell, Emily Callaci, Charles Cohen, Finn Enke, Nan Enstad, Suzanne Desan, Francine Hirsch, Elizabeth Lapina, David McDonald, Tony Michels, Viren Murthy, Jim Sweet, Claire Taylor, Sarah Thal, and Daniel Ussishkin. For reading the entire manuscript carefully and offering insightful comments, I would like to thank Jennifer Ratner-Rosenhagen, Lou Roberts, Laird Boswell, Francine Hirsch, Tony Michels, and Nils Ringe. I am deeply grateful to Renato Moro, John Connelly, and Martin Conway as well; all three read a full draft of the book and helped solve a series of problems I was having trouble solving on my own. Mark Bradley, Holly Case, James Chappel, Charles Gallagher, Udi Greenberg, Piotr Kosicki, Mark Mazower, Andrew Preston, Sarah Shortall, and Victoria Smolkin all provided valuable feedback on my earlier writings, book chapters, and/or the manuscript in its entirety and saved me from some embarrassing mistakes. Marco Duranti, Maria Mitchell, and Noah Strote kindly shared unpublished work. Victoria Baena, Christian Blank, Indra Ekmanis, Piotr Puchalski, and Alissa Valeri helped wade through the soures. Finally, material support made this book possible and enabled many trips to archives on both sides of the Atlantic. For their funding assistance, I would like to thank the American Council of Learned Societies, the Mellon Foundation, the Society for Historians of American Foreign Relations, the Office of the Vice Chancellor for Research and Graduate Education, and the Department of History at the University of Wisconsin at Madison.

I am grateful to the editing team at Harvard University Press for all they have done and for their patience along the way. For her sharp humor and enthusiasm, I would like to give a special thank you to my editor, Joyce Seltzer. I feel so lucky to have caught her just in time, before she wrapped up her time at the Press. It has been a real delight to work with her and eat sandwiches in her kitchen. Thank you also to Kathleen McDermott, production editor Mary Ribesky, and copy editor Wendy Nelson.

This work would never have been possible had it not been for the extraordinary support of my friends and family. Thank you to my father for his clever titling ideas, and to my mother, who shared her passion for languages and history, and fielded my translation doubts. Among my friends, Beatrice Kitzinger, Anaar Desai-Stephens, Lynn Glueck, Valeska Huber, Joseph Lynch, Martha Oatis, Sagi Schaefer, and Owen Miller kept me sane along the way. Farzan Masrour supplied Tum Yum soup. Rachel Cohen held my hand and helped bring the manuscript to completion at the eleventh hour.

Finally, I would like to express my loving gratitude to my husband, Farid Masrour; to our son, Elia, who brims with *joie de vivre*; and to our newborn daughter, Matilde, who has just started breaking into giant toothless smiles. This project began when Farid and I first met, and it really deserves his name in a byline—for his support throughout the research and writing phase, for the incisive (and extremely difficult) questions he has asked along the way, and for the intellectual rigor he inspired me to uphold throughout. With patience, wisdom, and grace, he has helped me get this project off my desk and into the world. To him, with love, I dedicate this book.

Index

Abortion, 313–314, 318

Abyssinia. *See* Ethiopia

Académie française, 152–153

Action Française. *See* French Action

Ad Apostolorum Principis encyclical (1958), 287

Adenauer, Konrad, 18, 261, 282, 306

Africa: Catholic missionaries in, 111, 287, 289–290; decolonization of, 286–290, 301–303, 312–313. *See also* Algeria; Cameroon; Ethiopia

Algeria, 224, 287, 289

Algerian War. *See* Algeria

Althusser, Louis, 306

America magazine. *See* United States

American Catholics. *See* Anti-Americanism; Spanish Civil War; United States

Anarchism, 6, 71, 101, 181

Anschluss. *See* Austria; Nazi Germany; World War II

Anti-Americanism: and Kellog-Briand, 109; and Leo XIII, 21–22; and the Paris peace settlement, 52–56, 77–78, 80, 94; and Pius XI, 98–99, 122, 127–128; and Pius XII, 283–285; and postwar Communist Parties, 245–246; and World War I, 21–26

Anti-capitalism: and Fascism, 103; and Judeo-Bolshevik myth, 85, 206; and Marxism, 82, 88, 307; and papacy, 130, 175, 206, 233, 307, 320

Anticlericalism: and Czechoslovakia, 63–64; and Fascism, 95–96, 99, 101, 117–118; and France, 73, 108–109; and Germany, 70, 138, 139–140; and Mexico, 184, 189–190; and papacy, 2, 18–19, 21, 26, 34, 70; and the Soviet Union, 88, 106; and Spain, 179–180, 183, 194

Anticolonialism: and decolonization, 286–290, 301–303, 312–313; and internationalism, 6–7; and League of Nations, 54, 111, 286–291; and Pius XI, 111; and Pius XII, 286–287; and Woodrow Wilson, 39. *See also* Africa: decolonization of; Internationalism; League of Nations; Wilson, Woodrow

Anticommunism: Austrian Catholicism and, 123–124; *Divini Redemptoris* encyclical and, 186–189; Eugenio Pacelli (as diplomat) and propagation of, 72, 84, 89, 125; *Firmissimam Constantiam* encyclical and, 189–193; Germany and, 123–124, 139–141, 217–218; Italian Fascism and, 103; papal

419